THE
Adams-Jefferson
LETTERS

The Institute of Early American History and Culture is sponsored jointly by the College of William and Mary and Colonial Williamsburg, Incorporated. Publication of this book has been assisted by a grant from the Lilly Endowment, Inc.

JOHN ADAMS

Portrait by Mather Brown, painted in London, 1788
(See p. xxiii)

THE
Adams-Jefferson
LETTERS

*The Complete Correspondence
Between Thomas Jefferson
and Abigail and John Adams*

*

EDITED BY

LESTER J. CAPPON

IN TWO VOLUMES

Vol. I, 1777-1804

PUBLISHED FOR
*The Institute of Early American History and Culture
at Williamsburg, Virginia*
by The University of North Carolina Press · Chapel Hill

For
DOROTHY BERNET CAPPON
"with every sentiment of tenderness,
esteem, and admiration"

CONTENTS

* * *

VOLUME I

3. *"As We are poor We ought to be Œconomists"* . . . 72

September 1785–February 1786

✳ 1785 ✳

✳ 1786 ✳

✳ 1787 ✳

5. "The first principle of a good government" 163

January–October 1787

✳ 1787 ✳

6. *"On . . . Guard against the immeasurable avarice of
   Amsterdam"* . . . .
   November 1787–May 1789

✳ 1787 ✳

✳ 1788 ✳

7. *"The Age of Experiments in Government"* 239

April 1790–March 1801

❋ 1795 ❋

❋ 1796 ❋

❋ 1801 ❋

❋ 1804 ❋

VOLUME II

✳ 1819 ✳

13. *"Calms succeeding the storm which our Argosy . . .
so stoutly weathered"* 552

January 1820–April 1826

✳ 1820 ✳

✳ 1824 ✳

✳ 1825 ✳

✳ 1826 ✳

ILLUSTRATIONS

Volume One

JOHN ADAMS   *frontispiece*

Mather Brown painted Jefferson's portrait in London in 1786 and this portrait of Adams in 1788. Jefferson had tried to prevail on Adams, through Adams's son-in-law, William Stephens Smith, to sit for his portrait. Jefferson was collecting pictures of "principal American characters" and "must not be disappointed of Mr. Adams's." Although Adams could spare little time, by early March of 1788 Brown was at last "busy about the pictures"—the portrait of Adams and a copy of the Jefferson. They were completed during that summer and delivered to Jefferson in August or September through the good offices of Trumbull. TJ to William Stephens Smith, Oct. 23, 1786, Boyd, X, 479; TJ to Smith, Feb. 2, 1788, *ibid.*, XII, 558; John Trumbull to TJ, March 6, 1788, *ibid.*, 647; John Trumbull to TJ, Aug. 15, 1788, *ibid.*, XIII, 519; TJ to John Trumbull, Sept. 10, 1788, *ibid.*, 597. (Courtesy of the Boston Athenaeum)

ABIGAIL ADAMS   *facing page 138*

This portrait by Ralph Earl was painted in England about 1785. A native of Massachusetts, Earl lived in England from 1778 until the summer or fall of 1785. Mrs. Adams may have sat for him not long after her arrival in London in May 1785. (Courtesy of the New York State Historical Association, Cooperstown, New York)

ADAMS HOUSE   *facing page 139*

The house in Quincy, Massachusetts, was drawn by Sarah Apthorp in 1822. On the back of the drawing are the following two inscriptions: "S. Hull Adams says Drawn in 1822 by Sarah Apthorp, Quincy" and "Mrs. Anger from her friend Sarah Apthorp, Medford, August 9th, 1838." (Courtesy of the Adams National Historic Site, Quincy, Massachusetts, National Park Service, Department of the Interior)

PREFACE

No CORRESPONDENCE in American history is more quotable or more readily recognized for its historical significance than that of John Adams and Thomas Jefferson. Yet, only now, a century and a third after their deaths in 1826, is their exchange of letters presented in full. Publication was first anticipated in their lifetime but never encouraged by them. During the political controversies which cast a long shadow over their public careers, they suffered embarrassment from the unauthorized printing of occasional letters written in confidence. The years of retirement, they hoped, would provide a partial escape from the virulence of party strife and the publicity of high office. But statesmen, even in retirement, still belong to the public, as Jefferson learned from personal experience. He concluded in 1815 that his correspondence with Adams had been observed in the post offices, because a printer "has had the effrontery to propose to me the letting him publish it. These people think they have a right to everything however secret or sacred." [1]

If idle curiosity or selfish motives often aroused the momentary interest of the public, the intelligent citizen had some appreciation, however limited, of the writings of these statesmen as records of historical events. Adams and Jefferson, who lived long enough to acquire perspective on their own times, had become historical figures to the younger generation. As actors on the Revolutionary stage, they were asked innumerable questions about that heroic period, scarcely a half-century removed, which had already acquired the aura of history

1. TJ to JA, Aug. 10, 1815, June 1, 1822, below, 453, 578.

in the minds of the American people. The two venerable patriots themselves were well aware of their role as "Argonauts" [2] to be remembered by posterity. Adams best expressed the point when he hoped for publication of all of Jefferson's letters "in volumes." Even though some letters might "not always appear Orthodox," he wrote, "they will exhibit a Mass of Taste, Sense, Literature and Science, presented in a sweet simplicity and a neat elegance of Stile, which will be read with delight in future ages." [3] This is explanation enough for Adams's saving all he had received. Jefferson too preserved his great accumulation of correspondence, although he agreed that "an hour of conversation would be worth a volume of letters." [4] It is the recipients' copies, originally filed at Quincy and Monticello, that provide the basis for the present edition.

"Posterity," asserted Adams, who seemed more willing than Jefferson to designate their papers public property, "would ... know on what kind terms they lived"; [5] but during the course of a century this information was derived only piecemeal from successive editions of their letters, from Henry Randall's discursive account of Jefferson's life and times and friendship with Adams,[6] and, as a centennial commemoration, from Paul Wilstach's selection from their correspondence of 1812-26.[7] Actually, many of the letters exchanged by Adams and Jefferson have been in the public domain a long time, although they are scattered throughout their published writings rather than assembled as the integrated correspondence of both. During the nineteenth century a small percentage of Jefferson's letters appeared in the writings edited soon after his death by his grandson Thomas Jefferson Randolph, by Henry A. Washington in the 1850's, and by Paul Leicester Ford in the 1890's, the last being the most reliable in respect to texts. The sole edition of Adams's *Works*, carefully prepared by his grandson Charles Francis Adams from the manuscripts in the family's custody, was published in the early 1850's. Soon after the turn of the century came the Lipscomb and Bergh edition of Jef-

2. TJ to JA, March 25, 1826, below, 613.

3. JA to TJ, July 12, 1822, below, 582.

4. TJ to JA, April 8, 1816, below, 467.

5. H. A. S. Dearborn to TJ, Nov. 24, 1823, Jefferson Papers, Library of Congress, quoting JA.

6. Henry S. Randall, *The Life of Thomas Jefferson* (N. Y., 1858), III, Chaps. IX-XIII.

7. Paul Wilstach, ed., *Correspondence of John Adams and Thomas Jefferson 1812-1826* (Indianapolis, [1925]). This selection is only a representative sampling.

ferson's *Writings*, more extensive but less authoritative than Ford. All of these were based largely, if not exclusively, upon retained copies (loose or in letter-books, in polygraph or letter-press) rather than upon the recipients' copies which have prime value for research. Until the planning in the mid-1940's of the Princeton edition of *The Papers of Thomas Jefferson* by Julian P. Boyd, no one had dealt with the problem of evaluating for publication the total *correspondence*— what Jefferson read in his mail as well as what he wrote in his own letters.

The richness of the Adams-Jefferson correspondence can be most fully appreciated by following the letters in chronological sequence. Only then can the reader sense the mental vigor of the two men and exclaim with Adams, "So many Subjects crowd upon me that I know not, with which to begin." [8] During their years in public office they gave close attention to the daily problems that pressed upon them, with occasional reflections revealing the statesmanship behind their decisions. Later, as elder statesmen in retirement, they sat in judgment on the world which had passed through two revolutions, on their country which had won independence and confirmed it, and on themselves; and they did so with an open-mindedness and a feeling of conviction that subsequent generations cannot fail to admire.

The present edition began as one of the early projects of the Institute of Early American History and Culture. The plan for complete coverage of the correspondence, first developed in 1948 by Carl Bridenbaugh, then director of the Institute, received cordial support from the editors of the Jefferson Papers at Princeton. They had already established in their offices a photo-print file of the Jefferson Papers in the Library of Congress. They had also secured permission from the Adams Manuscript Trust to make similar copies of its Adams-Jefferson manuscripts and to transmit the microfilm to the Library of Congress.[9] In October 1948 the Trust granted the Institute permission to publish the pertinent letters from the Adams Family Papers.

The following January, Donald H. Mugridge, on leave from the Library of Congress, undertook the editorship, supported by a grant

8. JA to TJ, July 9, 1813, below, 350.
9. Lyman H. Butterfield, "The Jefferson-Adams Correspondence in the Adams Manuscript Trust," Lib. Cong. *Quarterly Journal of Current Acquisitions*, 5, no. 2 (Feb. 1948), 3-6.

from the Rockefeller Foundation to the Institute. Mr. Mugridge assembled the texts and proofread them, wrote headnotes for individual documents or groups of documents, and supplied detailed annotation. By mid-1950 he had completed the editorial work for the first period, 1777-1801, but the funds were exhausted.

In 1951 Lyman H. Butterfield, second director of the Institute and formerly on the staff of *The Papers of Thomas Jefferson*, took over the work and revised the plan of operation to produce an edition for the general reader. Assisted by Mrs. Stella D. Neiman, he proceeded with the editing of the letters in the second period, 1812-26, but administrative duties diverted him and the task remained unfinished when he left the Institute in 1954 to become editor of the Adams Papers.[10]

When I assumed the editorial responsibility in 1956, at the urging of my colleagues, James Morton Smith and Lawrence W. Towner, I reviewed the existing plan in relation to content and presentation. Without doubt the edition ought to be as complete as possible. The prospect of attaining that objective was better than ever before because of the intensive search by Mr. Boyd and his associates for Jefferson material and because of similar work by Mr. Butterfield and his editorial staff on the Adams Papers. Since the letters between Abigail Adams and Jefferson complement perfectly the correspondence of the two statesmen, it seemed to me that they should be included for their personal charm and tang as well as for their subject matter. Moreover, Mrs. Adams played an influential part in the delayed reconciliation between her husband and Jefferson during 1801-12.

It seemed desirable also to simplify the editorial process by eliminating headnotes for individual documents, by reducing the annotation, by presenting the letters chronologically in a series of chapters, each with an introductory essay, and by providing a general introduction on the historical background of the correspondence. To streamline the scholarly trappings of an edition designed primarily for the general reader is more compelling now than it was in 1948.

10. A comprehensive edition of the Adams Papers sponsored by the Massachusetts Historical Society, with editorial funds provided by Time, Inc., on behalf of *Life*, is in course of publication under Mr. Butterfield's editorship by The Belknap Press of Harvard University Press. Though a microfilm edition of the corpus of the papers is available for research purposes, the manuscripts themselves are closed to inspection during the course of editorial work.

The first volume of the monumental *Papers of Thomas Jefferson* was published in 1950; fifteen more volumes have appeared, and the scholar will turn increasingly to this series, rich in annotation and historical criticism. Readers of the present edition will observe that it leans heavily on the *Papers* for basic documentation to 1789. The meticulous scholarship of Mr. Boyd and his associates can only be fully appreciated by working closely with these superb volumes. Furthermore, the accuracy of the texts in the Boyd edition made it possible to use photocopies of them for printer's copy, which were proofread against the original manuscripts (in microfilm or microprint). Grateful acknowledgment is expressed here to the Princeton University Press for permission to make those photocopies.

Publication of *The Papers of Thomas Jefferson* has affected my editorial procedure in other ways. The descriptive data on each document in the *Papers* provide sufficient reason for omitting addresses and endorsements (with a few exceptions) and the location of each manuscript. Decoded passages have been copied as rendered in the *Papers* and printed in italics. The ampersand is changed to *and* (or to the Latin *et* in the abbreviation, *etc.*), except in the names of firms. Obvious slips of the pen are corrected silently. During the last eight years of his life Adams's palsied hands forced him to dictate his letters to amanuenses in his household. He could not see well enough to correct their errors, many of them the result of ignorance, and it would be misleading to retain them. Capitalization in the original manuscripts has been followed, but the first word of the sentence is capitalized despite Jefferson's customary use of lower case. Punctuation likewise follows the original manuscript unless it obscures the meaning; and excessive punctuation, characteristic of Adams, is usually retained in order to convey the style of the original as much as possible. Abbreviated words are not expanded, the full word being supplied only to avoid ambiguity or misunderstanding. So, too, with erratic spelling, common in the eighteenth century, except when clarification demands the modern equivalent; but the Latin word, that favourite [*sic*] of the pedant, is shunned almost to exclusion. The orthography and other devices of communication of the eighteenth century are not so different from our own that we are justified in sacrificing something of the spirit of that era for the sake of modernization as the comfortable road to learning.

Personal names are identified in the index, thus reducing the number of footnotes very considerably. The correspondents are referred to as AA, JA, and TJ. After the first citation of a source or secondary work, subsequent references are by the author's or editor's name and short title. Since numerous citations are made to the collected writings of Adams and Jefferson, the several editions are listed here in chronological order of publication for the reader's convenience:

Thomas Jefferson Randolph, ed., *Memoir, Correspondence, and Miscellanies, from the Papers of Thomas Jefferson.* 4 vols. Charlottesville, Va., 1829.

Charles Francis Adams, ed., *The Works of John Adams ... with a Life of the Author, Notes and Illustrations.* 10 vols. Boston, 1850-56.

H[enry] A. Washington, ed., *The Writings of Thomas Jefferson ... from the Original Manuscripts, deposited in the Department of State....* 9 vols. Washington, D.C., 1853-54.

Paul Leicester Ford, ed., *The Writings of Thomas Jefferson.* 10 vols. New York and London, 1892-99.

Andrew A. Lipscomb and Albert Ellery Bergh, eds., *The Writings of Thomas Jefferson.* Library Edition ... Issued under the Auspices of the Thomas Jefferson Memorial Association. 20 vols. Washington, D.C., 1903-4.

Julian P. Boyd, and others, eds., *The Papers of Thomas Jefferson.* Princeton, 1950– (in progress).

The present edition of the Adams-Jefferson correspondence would have been impossible without the generous co-operation of the two research libraries containing the vast majority of the original manuscripts: the Library of Congress and the Massachusetts Historical Society. A decade ago the Adams Family Papers, deposited in the Society in 1905, were still the property of the Adams Manuscript Trust, whose officers kindly granted permission to the Institute to publish the Adams-Jefferson material. The late Stewart Mitchell, then director of the Society, played an important role in this negotiation. In 1956 the Trust deeded the Adams Papers to the Society. While the Jefferson Papers in the Library of Congress have long been open to investigators, its microfilm copy of that vast collection, originally made for use by the editors of *The Papers of Thomas Jefferson,* accrued to the benefit of the Institute as well. But it was the "control file" of the Jefferson office at Princeton that provided the best checklist of extant manuscripts.

The following analysis of the total correspondence is of considerable interest:

NUMBER OF LETTERS

1777-1801		*1785-1804*	
JA to TJ	80	AA to TJ	24
TJ to JA	91	TJ to AA	21
	171		45

1812-1826		*1813-1817*	
JA to TJ	109	AA to TJ	3
TJ to JA	49	TJ to AA	3
	158		6

Grand Total: 380

The Institute is indebted to the Rockefeller Foundation for the grant which made possible the editorial work of Donald H. Mugridge. His careful research spared me countless hours in a schedule allowing too little time for collateral research. Although the headnotes prepared by Mr. Mugridge were discarded in the final plan for this edition, some of the information has been used profitably in the condensed annotations to the text. During the period in which Mr. Butterfield worked on the correspondence, he as director of the Institute and I as its editor of publications conferred from time to time on editorial problems. His sound judgment and previous experience as a historical editor bore fruit then and later in many intangible ways that are inherent in any scholarly undertaking, and it was always a pleasure to work with him. His revised plan was revised in turn by me, and I must bear the responsibility for the final organization and presentation of the material. That includes also the final proofreading of all texts against the manuscripts.

I express my thanks to Francis L. Berkeley, Jr., and Robert E. Stocking of the University of Virginia Library's Manuscript Division for their never-failing co-operation in making its rich resources readily accessible. I am also grateful to Mrs. Stella D. Neiman for her reference work on the later part of the correspondence and to Professor Talbot R. Selby of the College of William and Mary for supplying the translation of Greek and Latin quotations in the text. To Frederick

A. Hetzel, Diane Smith Leland, and Elizabeth Duncan Brown of the Institute staff, who relieved me of pressing duties at critical moments, I express my gratitude. I have indicated my indebtedness to my wife in the dedication, which quotes a letter from John Adams to Abigail Adams.[11]

The role of the administrator, even on a small scale, seems ever at odds with time for research and productive scholarship. I can conclude these acknowledgments only by paying tribute to the Institute's editor of books, James Morton Smith, and to the editor of the *William and Mary Quarterly*, Lawrence W. Towner. It was they who urged me to appropriate the time necessary to edit and publish the Adams-Jefferson correspondence, a task I was longing to undertake. I am deeply appreciative of their continuous concern with the Institute program and its long-range objectives. As editor Mr. Smith has been closely involved in this documentary project, keeping a watchful eye on the ever-pressing time schedule, reviewing the annotation, and criticizing essays and notes with a light voice and a sharp pencil. He has been indispensable in making this edition a reality. That is not a minor consideration when our greatest editor of Jefferson's works points out (Boyd, II, 19*n.*) that the Adams-Jefferson correspondence "remains unrivaled, in the United States at least, for its revelation of the writers' minds and characters, its literary distinction, and its historical importance."

L. J. C.

11. May 17, 1776, Charles Francis Adams, ed., *Familiar Letters of John Adams and His Wife Abigail Adams, During the Revolution* (N. Y., 1876), 175.

INTRODUCTION

"Prospect of an immortality in the memories of all the worthy"

FANEUIL HALL, the "Cradle of Liberty," attracted a large crowd of Bostonians on August 2, 1826. The City Council had invited Daniel Webster, well known for his oratory, to deliver the address. It was a day of commemoration rather than of mourning, in recognition of the recent deaths of John Adams and Thomas Jefferson on July 4. The fiftieth anniversary of American independence had been celebrated in this same hall, as it was in countless others throughout the nation. In near-by Quincy, the venerable Adams had been unable to accept the invitation of his fellow citizens to be the guest of honor, and they learned of his death as they were leaving the Quincy town hall.[1]

The speaker was well chosen for the occasion in Boston a month later. A child of the Confederation period, Webster had familiarized himself with the history of the American Revolution in the course of his wide reading; and he could speak on notable events of the past quarter-century from first-hand knowledge. An Adams Federalist, he had held both Jefferson and Adams in great respect; indeed he had been Jefferson's guest at Monticello only a year and a half earlier.[2] His discourse in Faneuil Hall had substance as well as the

1. Daniel Webster, *A Discourse in Commemoration of the Lives and Services of John Adams and Thomas Jefferson, delivered in Faneuil Hall, Boston, August 2, 1826* (Boston, 1826), [3]; JA to John Whitney, Chairman of the Committee of Arrangements for celebrating the approaching anniversary of the fourth of July, in the Town of Quincy, June 7, 1826, Charles Francis Adams, ed., *The Works of John Adams*, 10 vols. (Boston, 1850-56), X, 416-17. Hereafter cited as *Works*.

2. Fletcher Webster, ed., *The Private Correspondence of Daniel Webster* (Boston, 1857), I, 361.

characteristic flowing periods that must have captivated his audience, and it struck a significant historical note in evaluating the lives of Adams and Jefferson.

No two men now live, fellow-citizens, perhaps it may be doubted, whether any two men have ever lived, in one age, who, more than those we now commemorate, have impressed their own sentiments, in regard to politics and government, on mankind, infused their own opinions more deeply into the opinions of others, or given a more lasting direction to the current of human thought. Their work doth not perish with them. . . . No age will come, in which the American Revolution will appear less than it is, one of the greatest events in human history. No age will come, in which it will cease to be seen and felt, on either continent, that a mighty step, a great advance, not only in American affairs, but in human affairs, was made on the 4th of July 1776.[3]

In citing the Revolution as an episode of world-wide significance, Webster inevitably found cause for reflection in the aged patriots' passing from the earthly scene on this fiftieth anniversary. "May not such events," he asked, "raise the suggestion that they are not undesigned, and that Heaven does so order things, as sometimes to attract strongly the attention, and excite the thoughts of men?" [4] Webster reflected, of course, the romanticism of his own generation and indulged in mysticism that would have been sharply confuted by Adams and Jefferson as reasonable men. In that year of jubilee, 1826, which occasioned a great outburst of patriotism, Webster was also expressing the feeling of nationalism of the American people. Their Revolution had been a noble experiment, a notable success in establishing the new nation and in inspiring an unmistakable air of confidence in the future. They were the heirs of an age of progress to which their fathers and grandfathers of the eighteenth century had attested. Webster's evaluation of the American Revolution, however exaggerated its emotional overtones may seem, reflected their outlook and has been confirmed by the judgment of subsequent generations.

If Webster had had access to the correspondence of Adams and Jefferson, he could have found no more conclusive contemporary support of his judgment concerning the Revolution. As political

3. Webster, *Discourse*, 9-10.
4. *Ibid.*, 13.

philosophers the two statesmen had a keen sense of perspective and a consciousness of great events in the making. From their reading of English and Continental philosophers, whose works were common property of eighteenth-century intellectuals, they put theory into practice in government and then reassessed theory in the light of their own experiments. What would make the rebellion of 1775-76 (as the British referred to it) a successful revolution beyond confirmation of independence by the victory at Yorktown? To what degree were the basic principles of republican government workable under American conditions, in the several states and in a federal government? Questions such as these were asked and partially answered as Adams and Jefferson corresponded year after year, never casting doubt on the momentous decision of 1776 but never believing that achievements could be assured without eternal vigilance. Long before they had retired from public life, they fully understood the significance of their own contributions to the Revolution, and on several occasions one or the other displayed some jealousy of his claims in very human fashion. It is obvious that the history of the Revolution and the early federal period of the Republic could not be written adequately without attention to the work of Jefferson and Adams. They were aware of this fact, perhaps a bit egotistically, but with a profound sense of history.

If the correspondence of Adams and Jefferson embodied no other theme than the vicissitudes of their friendship, it would meet the test as an appealing record of human nature. The contribution each made to this relationship becomes clearer by a study of their characters and personalities. Jefferson is the more difficult to approach. His contemporaries, it seems clear, did break through his reserve into easy-flowing conversation. Although he did not lack a sense of humor, he displayed it sparingly in his letters, and he kept no diary which might reveal his character on more intimate terms. Thus history is afforded a half-satisfying record that thwarts our better understanding of a statesman who wrote almost incessantly, but seldom in a personal vein. Perhaps Jefferson was as congenial with John Adams as anyone outside his family; yet even to Adams, Jefferson's expressions of devotion were infrequent. He never wrote with less restraint than when he offered congratulations on Adams's election to the vice-presidency:

"No man on earth pays more cordial homage to your worth nor wishes more fervently your happiness. Tho' I detest the appearance even of flattery, I cannot always suppress the effusions of my heart." [5]

While Jefferson did not shun controversy when a basic principle was involved, he had no ambition and no heart for personal diatribe. In his desire to live in harmony with his associates and friends he preferred to avoid argument and spare their feelings even when self-defense was justified. He put a high premium on privacy of thought and action. In the classical tradition the hearth of Monticello was his sanctum and no outsider penetrated the inner circle of the family; yet in the same tradition, hospitality was a natural art practiced on Jefferson's mountain top and enjoyed by countless visitors as well as invited guests. The private rights of the individual citizen and his valuation of privacy are complementary factors in Jefferson's desire to perpetuate his republican agrarian society. He was too modest to think of himself as the "squire of Monticello," but that title indicates his social position in the society of Albemarle County along with his feeling of responsibility for the public welfare. It also suggests something of the essence of Jeffersonian republicanism.

The contrast between the tall, angular Jefferson and the chubby, rotund Adams must have been striking whenever they were seen together. Even to a casual acquaintance the reserve of the Virginian undoubtedly accentuated the air of cordiality of the New Englander. "Adams has a heart formed for friendship, and susceptible of its finest feelings," declared the loyalist Jonathan Sewall, who was highly gratified by the hearty greeting which Adams gave him in London after the Revolutionary War.[6] Under the circumstances Adams, "humane, generous, and open," could hardly have received a finer compliment. With his good nature went a keen sense of humor, an eye for the ridiculous and the incongruous, and a willingness to poke fun at himself. When discussing religion with Jefferson he recalled that while at Harvard he had been "a mighty Metaphis[ic]ian"; and how, a few years later, when he thought he was in ill health, Dr. Hersey of Hingham looked him over and prescribed as follows: "Persevere, and as

5. TJ to JA, May 10, 1789, below, 238. TJ referred to the office as "the Presidency of the Senate."
6. C. F. Adams, "Life of John Adams," *Works*, I, 57n.

sure as there is a God in Heaven you will recover." [7] Adams found ceremonious interviews with the Tripolitan ambassador in London highly amusing and his vanity was touched by the ambassador's secretary who so admired the American's ability to match the Tripolitan's coffee-sipping and tobacco-whiffing that he exclaimed in ecstasy, "Monsieur votes etes un Turk." [8]

Adams's warm nature did not always make for cordial feelings; it often led to surges of sudden anger, for he felt deeply toward those he loved and those he despised. His outbursts of temper, antagonizing his opponents and inflicting injury often out of proportion to the offense, have unfortunately distorted the historical record concerning his character; his irascibility has overshadowed his kindliness. In retaliation Adams's political enemies sought to damage his reputation and succeeded in large measure. He never forgave Alexander Hamilton and Timothy Pickering for their personal and political offenses. Yet he was no less unselfish than Jefferson concerning the great issues for which they contended. The self-discipline in his Puritan training came to his aid on many an occasion in choosing between duty and his own pleasure, and he was willing to endure long periods of separation from his family in the service of his country. At the age of twenty-three, when Adams was considering the practice of law, Jeremiah Gridley, father of the Boston bar, gave him a piece of advice: "pursue the study of the law, rather than the gain of it." In taking account of seventeen years' practice, Adams concluded that "no lawyer in America ever did so much business as I did afterwards, ... for so little profit." [9] Unconsciously, perhaps, he applied the principle behind this advice to other phases of his career. If virtue was indispensable to good government, as he maintained, so it must be to the best citizenship which Adams exemplified in public service and private life.

The early political and diplomatic careers of Adams and Jefferson are sketched in Chapter 1. As men of principle they doubtless found satisfaction in a friendship that responded to their dissimilar temperaments. In the Continental Congress of 1775 they discovered they could work effectively together, a conclusion borne out during their diplomatic service. When Jefferson expected to join the American peace commissioners, Adams, Jay, and Franklin, in Paris in 1783, he recalled

7. JA to TJ, Sept. 14, 1813, below, 374.
8. JA to TJ, Feb. 17, 1786, below, 121.
9. JA, "Diary" and "Autobiography," *Works,* II, 45-56.

Adams's strong prejudices—his dislike of both Jay and Franklin, of both the French and the English—but he recognized his honesty and integrity.[10] Since Adams's dislike of all parties and all men might balance his prejudices, Jefferson anticipated constructive results, and certainly this prediction proved true during the five years of their joint efforts. Before Jefferson's arrival in Paris, Adams referred to him as "an old Friend . . . with whom I have often had occasion to labour at many a knotty Problem." Other letters contain the implication that he would be a great improvement over Franklin, who as elder diplomat always dominated the scene [11] and was too much of a Francophile in thought and action to please Adams. Since he expected Jefferson to succeed Franklin at the Court of Versailles, Adams, who was going to the Court of St. James, would be "happy in a Correspondence of Friendship, Confidence, and Affection." [12]

In their collaboration abroad, Adams was the senior diplomat in both age and experience, a factor of some weight in their relationship. Although Jefferson often deferred to the judgment of his colleague, he did so without suppressing his own opinions. If the elder man bespoke a paternal attitude at times, the younger did not record it.[13] He was conscious of Adams's vanity and occasional irritableness, but those shortcomings could be overlooked amid the larger issues at stake. After working personally with Adams seven months in France and seven weeks in England and corresponding regularly, Jefferson developed the highest respect for him as a seasoned diplomat: profound in his views, accurate in his judgments, and disinterested in personal gain. He could hardly have spoken more from the heart when he wrote Madison that Adams "is so amiable, . . . I pronounce you will love him if ever you become acquainted with him." [14]

In the Adams-Jefferson friendship Abigail Adams played both a happy and an unhappy role, and her correspondence with Jefferson is

10. TJ to Madison, Feb. 14, 1783, Julian P. Boyd, and others, eds., *The Papers of Thomas Jefferson* (Princeton, 1950–), VI, 241. Hereafter cited as Boyd.

11. JA to James Warren, Aug. 27, 1784, and JA to Elbridge Gerry, Dec. 12, 1784, Boyd, VII, 382n.

12. JA to Richard Cranch, April 27, 1785, *ibid.*, 652n.

13. A quarter-century later Adams remarked that "Jefferson was but a boy to me." JA to Benjamin Rush, 1809, quoted in Saul K. Padover, ed., *The Complete Jefferson . . .* (N. Y., [1943]), 890n.

14. TJ to Madison, Jan. 30, 1787, Boyd, XI, 94-95.

an integral part of the record. Arriving in France about the same time in August 1784, she and Jefferson seem to have discovered almost at once that they were kindred spirits. For, whatever Mr. Adams may have told his wife in advance about the forty-year-old Virginian, her womanly thoughtfulness strengthened the bond between him and the Adams household. Knowing of his wife's death two years earlier, Mrs. Adams could appreciate his need for solicitation rather than sympathy. She was much concerned about his prolonged illness in the fall of 1784.[15] Although he lived in Paris, he was apparently a frequent and welcome visitor at the Adams residence in Auteuil, the pleasant suburb near the Bois de Boulogne, and he became strongly attached to young John Quincy, then in his late teens.[16]

The removal of Adams and his family to London in the spring of 1785, on his appointment as first American minister to Britain, ended this pleasant interlude. It also initiated the frequent exchange of letters between Mrs. Adams and the American minister to France which reveal best their high regard and admiration for each other. The Adamses left with great reluctance to take up their residence in the English metropolis. Disliking city life, they felt certain they would dislike the English too, and their anticipation was confirmed on both points.[17] They found the former enemies of America still hostile and unwilling to negotiate constructively on behalf of Anglo-American relations. Mrs. Adams, who could speak as sharply and critically as her husband and sometimes more pungently, gave vent to her ire against a certain newspaper account which she branded as "false—if it was not too rough a term for a Lady to use, I would say false as Hell, but I will substitute, one not less expressive and say, false as the English."[18] Again, in 1787 her mercurial emotions responded to the defiance of government in Massachusetts during Shays's Rebellion. She said some harsh words concerning conditions and events of which she was only partially informed, and Jefferson frankly expressed his disagreement.[19]

15. AA to Mrs. Cranch, Dec. 9, 1784, Charles Francis Adams, ed., *Letters of Mrs. Adams, the Wife of John Adams* (Boston, 1841) II, 62.

16. Samuel F. Bemis, *John Quincy Adams and the Foundations of American Foreign Policy* (N. Y., 1950), 14.

17. AA to Mrs. Cranch, June 24, 1785, *ibid.*, 96-99.

18. AA to TJ, Oct. 19, 1785, below, 84.

19. See Chap. 5, below, *passim.*

His respect for Mrs. Adams as a woman of taste and versatility heightened the pleasure of his correspondence with her. She was keenly interested in the world about her, as he always was, and she was essentially an intellectual, having surmounted most of the barriers confronting those women of the eighteenth century who had the talent and the ambition to become more than ornaments of fashion.[20] Mentally and emotionally she complemented her husband's capacities for accomplishment; her portraits suggest a firmness of decision that he could only have admired as a decisive person himself. Both were positive personalities, sometimes too incontestably right to be pleasing to others who under more congenial circumstances would have conceded the point at issue.

But much of Jefferson's enjoyment of Mrs. Adams came about through her feminine sensitiveness and intuition, her thoughtfulness and insight. Soon after her arrival in London she wrote him about the journey. How characteristic of Mrs. Adams, he must have thought, to find herself in a situation on board the Dover pacquet in which she was given two songbirds "by a young Gentleman whom we had received on Board with us, and who being excessively sick I admitted into the cabin, in gratitude for which he insisted upon my accepting a pair of his Birds." Her own little bird was too frightened to take along from Paris, but as these "had been used to travelling I brought them here [to London] in safety, for which they hourly repay me by their melodious notes." [21] Without hesitation Jefferson turned to Mrs. Adams for little favors, and she to him, as their correspondence flourished between Paris and London. When he made arrangements for his younger daughter Polly to join him in France and learned that she must go via England, he relied on Mrs. Adams to take care of her and send her on to Paris. Polly's visit provided a delightful exchange of letters between Jefferson and Mrs. Adams, and Mr. Adams inserted his own expression of pleasure in a business letter to Jefferson. When the Adamses were making plans for returning to the United States, Jefferson in Paris was especially regretful because "I have considered you while in London as my neighbor." [22]

20. William Cranch, *Memoir of the Life, Character, and Writings of John Adams* (Washington, 1827), 16.

21. AA to TJ, June 6, 1785, below, 28.

22. TJ to AA, Feb. 2, 1788, below, 222.

To what degree Jefferson and the Adamses were neighbors in Philadelphia and Washington during the years 1790-1800 cannot be stated with certainty. Mrs. Adams wrote her sister in April 1790 that "Mr. Jefferson is here [in New York], and adds much to the social circle." [23] He had just arrived to take up his duties as secretary of state. The federal government soon moved to Philadelphia, and, when Congress was not in session, both Jefferson and Adams spent as much time as possible at home. Then for three years, 1794-96, after resigning his secretaryship, Jefferson was out of office. By the time he became vice-president in 1797 animosity was mounting between Federalists and Republicans.

Jeffersonian Republicanism developed in opposition to the centralizing tendencies in President Washington's administration—against Alexander Hamilton and the High Federalists—not against Adams, the Vice President. Nevertheless, as Washington's successor, Adams inherited the Jeffersonian opposition to encroachment on state powers and on individual rights, and by the late 1790's the Republican party was an effective organization marshalling strength for the contest of 1800. As head of the Republican party, Jefferson was leading the opposition. Again he was upholding the rights of the individual, now threatened by the Alien and Sedition Acts, and he resorted to protest by state action in the Kentucky and Virginia Resolutions of 1798. Mrs. Adams lent weight to the rumor that the Republicans were plotting to force the resignation of President Adams by defamation, "and then they will Reign triumphant, *headed by the Man of the People*." [24] There could be little, if any, neighborliness in this state of affairs. In the election of 1800 the Federalist party suffered a greater defeat than President Adams. It was their first defeat as well as his, but the party never recovered from the disaster. He, however, went home to Quincy, relieved to be dissociated from extremists among the Federalists, although he was bitter over his defeat by the Democratic-Republicans. Jefferson could not resist calling this first turnover in American politics a "revolution." To whatever extent Adams attributed his political defeat to Jefferson, Mrs. Adams apparently agreed, confirming her husband's bitterness and resentment and offering nothing to

23. AA to Mrs. Mary Smith Cranch, April 3, 1790, Stewart Mitchell, ed., *New Letters of Abigail Adams, 1788-1801* (Boston, 1947), 44.
24. AA to Mrs. Cranch, March 20, 1798, *ibid.*, 147.

alleviate the tension straining their friendship. Indeed, her feeling became more deep-seated, more irreconcilable, than his, to judge from her subsequent brief correspondence with Jefferson.[25]

If, in contrast to the philosophical letters between 1812 and 1826, the Adams-Jefferson correspondence before 1801 sometimes seems overburdened with the prosaic details of whale-oil and tobacco contracts and sparse in reflective comment, one must not overlook the fact that the earlier record portrays men of affairs engaged in the routine daily tasks of diplomacy and politics. Policy and decision are usually obscured by detail. One must allow also for the separation of their letters from those of numerous other correspondents whose ideas and reactions had a bearing on what Adams and Jefferson thought and did. But we have the satisfaction of reading almost all the letters exchanged (and a few not delivered) and thus of following what they learned and acted upon day by day. Their years at foreign courts are most revealing of the bonds of friendship and common purpose.

In the game of diplomacy the diplomat must always consider first the interests of his own country, but he must be well informed on those of the nation to which he is accredited and understand the temperament of its people. In these terms, Jefferson may be called the perfect diplomat in the ideal post. He felt a fine rapport with the French people and they with him. It was not an easy post to fill as successor to Dr. Franklin, the philosopher *par excellence*, a great figure at court, frequenter of the fashionable *salons*, and adored by the populace. Jefferson was too young to succeed Franklin as sage, but he admired French culture, and in philosophical and artistic circles he was recognized as a charming intellectual. Although the Marquis de Lafayette was inclined to exaggeration concerning Americans, his countrymen doubtless agreed with him that "nothing can excell M. Jefferson's abilities, virtues, pleasing temper ... [as a] great statesman [and] zealous citizen." [26] He was always informing himself about the French people, how they lived, what they bought and sold, how notoriously they were governed. He was circumspect in dealing with royal favorites and politicians, in order to keep within the bounds of

25. See Chaps. 8, 12, below.
26. Louis Gottschalk, ed., *The Letters of Lafayette to Washington, 1777-1799* (N. Y., 1944), 344.

diplomatic propriety. He cultivated Vergennes, the foreign minister, for obvious reasons, and no other acquaintance of influence at court; "on the contrary," he stated, I "have studiously avoided it." [27]

Adams had developed no sympathetic understanding of the French during his diplomatic career before 1785. Their ways were not his ways and, if Dr. Franklin was a thorn in his flesh, his trucking with the French was no incentive to Adams to turn Francophile. Wisely Congress had not appointed him minister to Versailles, but it gave him a more difficult assignment: to fight for position in London on behalf of the young Republic. To be American minister to Great Britain in the 1780's was an unenviable appointment. The former colonists were now outside the British Empire and Mother England was in no mood to make concessions—not even to her own advantage, said Adams. "John Bull dont see it, and if he dont see a Thing at first, you know it is a rule with him ever after wards to swear that it dont exist, even when he does both see it and feel it." [28] Or as Jefferson stated the case, with reference to the advantage of American neutrality to the English: "I never yet found any other general rule for fore-telling what they will do, but that of examining what they ought not to do." [29] Adams's job was to negotiate and continue to negotiate, no matter how hopeless and distasteful the task, for a weak nation must grasp at small concessions, though always with due caution. It was an irritating, often a humiliating, experience. He compensated for it somewhat by being aggressively patriotic, encouraged by Mrs. Adams who took "a pride in acknowledging my Country." [30] But Adams's responsibility, like Jefferson's, was to keep the peace and always to avoid foreign entanglements.

Jefferson has been characterized as the practical idealist, whose idealism "was durable enough to survive his introduction to European politics" and whose "sense of practicality remained acute enough to restrain him from attempting the impossible." [31] Adams, his worthy colleague across the Channel, may be characterized as the skeptical

27. TJ to Mme Townsend, Nov. 6, 1787, Boyd, XII, 329.
28. JA to TJ, March 1, 1787, below, 175-76.
29. TJ to JA, Sept. 28, 1787, below, 200.
30. AA to Mrs. Elizabeth Smith Shaw, Sept. 15, 1785, quoted in Dorothy S. Eaton, "Some Letters of Abigail Adams," Lib. Cong. *Quart. Jour. of Acquisitions*, 4, no. 4 (Aug. 1947), 4.
31. Boyd, VII, 466.

realist, whose notable success in securing loans from the hard-headed Dutch merchant-diplomats confirmed his basic point of view.[32] Although Adams did not achieve comparable results in England, he laid the groundwork for his successors. Both he and Jefferson had observed European international politics at close range, which spared them a provincial outlook on world affairs later when, in high office at home, the responsibility for foreign policy was theirs. From his experience in Europe and his knowledge of inter-state rivalry in America, Adams drew the following conclusion:

I have long been settled in my own opinion, that neither Philosophy, nor Religion, nor Morality, nor Wisdom, nor Interest, will ever govern nations or Parties, against their Vanity, their Pride, their Resentment or Revenge, or their Avarice or Ambition. Nothing but Force and Power and Strength can restrain them.[33]

The reward for the distinguished diplomatic service of Adams and Jefferson was high office in the new government of the United States —the vice-presidency and the secretaryship of state respectively. They had no part in drafting the Constitution, but they hoped for the perpetuation of republican virtues and the maintenance of balanced government under its provisions. The Adamses had not found an inherent love of liberty in Europe. It seemed to be indigenous to America, where, as Mrs. Adams put it, "diligence integrity Genius and Spirit are the true sources of Superiority . . . instead of titles stars and garters." [34] But Adams warned Jefferson that "you and I have been indefatigable Labourers through our Whole Lives for a Cause which will be thrown away in the next generation, upon the Vanity and Foppery of Persons of whom we do not now know the Names perhaps." [35] Adams, who had just written his *Defence of the Constitutions of the United States*, pointed out to his brother-in-law that only the virtue and moderation of the people could assure good government. "I am no enemy to elegance, but I say no man has a right to think of elegance till he has secured substance; nor then, to seek more

32. See Chap. 6, below, 205-7.
33. JA to TJ, Oct. 9, 1787, Boyd, XII, 221.
34. AA to Mrs. Elizabeth Smith Shaw, Oct. 15, 1786, Lib. Cong. *Quart. Jour. of Acquisitions*, 4, no. 4 (Aug. 1947), 4.
35. JA to TJ, Oct. 8, 1787, Boyd, XII, 221.

of it than he can afford." [36] Adams was referring, of course, to conditions in the states.

No one in 1787-88 could conjure up a conception of the virulent ebb and flow of party politics during the next decade at the national level, where virtue seemed no longer virtuous and a government of men threatened to replace a government of laws. The outlines of this struggle have already been traced to indicate the political vicissitudes of Adams and Jefferson. Adams emerged in 1801 a disillusioned and rejected statesman, who could never quite forget the injustice and abuse he had suffered; a decade later he recalled that "I have been disgraced and degraded and I have a right to complain." [37] Jefferson developed from a disinterested public servant into a party leader, enunciating his political philosophy in workable form and demonstrating by the critical events of 1800-1801 and the orderly establishment of the Jeffersonian regime that republican government could survive a change of party rule.

During Jefferson's presidency his correspondence with Adams lapsed, thus causing a significant hiatus in the documentary record. In 1804 a limited attempt at renewal through Mrs. Adams failed.[38] In spite of a series of international incidents and crises during the Napoleonic Wars, involving the maintenance of a precarious American neutrality, Jefferson's party was more firmly entrenched by the end of his second administration in 1809. He had weathered political opposition both within and outside his party, and he had kept the nation at peace. Adams, however, who had observed the course of events from his seclusion in Quincy, saw little difference between his own republicanism, on which he was something of an authority, and Jefferson's as president. To his friend Dr. Benjamin Rush, who was trying to effect a reconciliation between the two former Presidents, Adams wrote with a drop of vitriol on his pen:

1. In the difference between speeches and messages. I was a monarchist because I thought a speech more manly, more respectful to Congress and the nation. Jefferson and Rush preferred messages.

2. I held levees once a week, that all my time might not be wasted by idle visits. Jefferson's whole eight years was a levee.

36. JA to Richard Cranch, Jan. 15, 1787, *Works*, I, 433.
37. JA to TJ, June 30, 1813, below, 348.
38. See Chap. 8, below, 265-68.

3. I dined a large company once or twice a week. Jefferson dined a dozen every day.

4. Jefferson and Rush were for liberty and straight hair. I thought curled hair was as republican as straight.[39]

Now, in 1811, the ex-Presidents were elder statesmen of republicanism.

The reconciliation of Adams and Jefferson in 1812, as related in Chapter 9,[40] brought about a rich and voluminous correspondence that has no counterpart in any other period of American intellectual history. These letters are almost completely divorced in subject matter from those of the earlier period. In retirement the former Presidents, though very much interested in world affairs, gave chief consideration to philosophical questions and let the events of the day pass without their participation. They delved into history and literature for examples to illustrate and reinforce their philosophical commentary. They recalled the more recent past of their own experience and reviewed themselves in company with others of the *dramatis personae* who had appeared on the Revolutionary stage.

It is not surprising that events before 1800 rather than afterward occupied the greater share of their reminiscence and that the critical occurrences of 1776 loomed largest. Adams had the more retentive memory for specific incidents. His manner of recording them in writing suggests the loquaciousness of an entertaining conversationalist. Both he and Jefferson had reason to be proud of their early support of independence, but Adams was more inclined to talk about it. Some of his friends in 1775, he told Jefferson, wondered "that a Man of Forty Years of Age, and of considerable Experience in business, and in life should have been guilty of such an Indiscretion." He could boast that by June 1776 his stand had been vindicated. Justification and vindication were essential to Adams, who felt that history had misused and abused him. "How many Gauntletts am I destined to run?" he complained. "How many Martyrdoms must I suffer?"[41]

The two intellectuals were well matched in mental baggage and in the quality of their formal training. Practice of the law had sharpened their agility of thought and powers of reasoning. More especially they

39. JA to Rush, Dec. 25, 1811, *Works*, X, 11.
40. Below, 283-89.
41. JA to TJ, July 12, 1813, below, 354.

expanded their reading early, beginning with the classics which they could hardly escape in the education of their day and finding stimulus in many subjects of inquiry and speculation. Jefferson, in the universality of his interests and his insatiable curiosity about the world of nature, was the more typical eighteenth-century man of learning. The twentieth-century specialist never ceases to wonder at this Virginian's ceaseless compilation of data which made significant contributions toward a more accurate understanding of man and nature.

Adams's mind ran to moral philosophy rather than natural philosophy—the social sciences and ideology rather than to the natural sciences. This preference is borne out in the subject matter of his correspondence with Jefferson during their years of reflection. While it was broad in range and sharpened with provocative ideas, the absence of certain subjects is significant: the fine arts and architecture, gardening and agriculture, medicine and other "practical sciences," and the physical sciences except in relation to cosmology. In most of these fields Jefferson corresponded at length with other friends and acquaintances, but not with Adams, whose interests lay in law and government, theology and religion, philosophy and the classics.

When Jefferson asked for suggestions concerning the academic program for his proposed university, Adams was not especially helpful when he remarked that education "has so long laboured with a Dropsy, that it is a wonder the Patient has not long since expired. Sciences of all kinds have need of Reform, as much as Religion and Government." [42] He felt no urge to wrestle with the problems of formal education. But Adams was a more profound thinker than Jefferson, more intrigued by the abstract proposition, though not as an end in itself. The Age of Enlightenment demanded scientific proof. Jefferson, the practical philosopher, strove always to put things to work; having grasped the principle, he tried to make the best use of the knowledge acquired and the material objects brought under control. "When I meet with a proposition beyond finite comprehension," he confessed, "I abandon it." [43]

Neither Adams nor Jefferson thought of himself as a literary man, although each devoted a large proportion of his time to reading and writing. "I cannot live without books," declared Jefferson, when he began to acquire another library to replace the one he sold to the

42. JA to TJ, June 19, 1815, below, 444.
43. TJ to JA, March 14, 1820, below, 562.

United States in 1815. The collection he had just disposed of numbered some seven thousand volumes, accumulated during a period of over forty years.[44] During the last decade of his life he assembled approximately nine hundred items (many in sets of several volumes each), which were sold at auction in 1829 to help settle his heavily indebted estate.[45] Books were likewise essential to Adams, who as a young man "procured the best library of law in the State."[46] During his later years he read much more than Jefferson, whose responsibilities in administering his plantations commanded a daily portion of his time. "I wish I owned this Book and 100,000 more that I want every day," remarked the acquisitive Adams in 1817. It pleased him that friends "overwhelm me with Books from all quarters."[47] He kept his old friend in Virginia informed on what he was reading, with a tinge of pride in the quantity of matter he covered. Jefferson was duly impressed but would make no attempt to compete. He was frank in admitting that he was "not fond of reading what is merely abstract, and unapplied immediately to some useful science."[48]

Aside from letter writing, which was almost a daily occupation throughout their lives, leaving a priceless heritage that only today is becoming easily available as a whole, Adams and Jefferson engaged frequently in occasional writings, in response to a specific urge or public need. They were designed for practical purposes and in numerous instances took the form of letters to the newspaper press, often reprinted in pamphlet form. All these comprise a large body of material, including "state papers," composed by Adams and Jefferson in their capacity as public officials. Although Jefferson produced nothing so comprehensive and formidable as Adams's *Defence of the Constitutions of the United States of America*, his *Notes on the State of Virginia* is a classic compendium spiced with the author's philosophical commentary on the practical problems of his native "country." He was a more prolific writer than Adams on a much greater variety of subjects, in keeping with the universality of his interests. In fact, Jefferson was an early exponent of "do it yourself" with the pen. When

44. TJ to JA, June 10, 1815, below, 443; G. S. Hillard, ed., *Life, Letters, and Journals of George Ticknor* (Boston, 1877), I, 35.

45. *Catalogue. President Jefferson's Library ... to be sold at auction ... 1829* (Washington, 1829), 3-14; Randolph G. Adams, *Three Americanists ...* (Philadelphia, 1939), 84-89.

46. JA, "Diary," *Works*, III, 50n.

47. JA to TJ, Dec. 25, 1813, April 19, May 18, 1817, below, 411, 508, 515.

48. TJ to JA, Oct. 14, 1816, below, 491.

a *Manual of Parliamentary Practice* was needed in the United States Senate, he prepared it; when he saw the need for a more convenient system of currency, he wrote *Notes on ... a Money Unit;* and when he felt that Christians ought to dispense with theological verbiage and inform themselves on the basic principles of their religion, he compiled The Life and Morals of Jesus of Nazareth. These are only a few examples of the versatility and expediency of Jefferson's writing, some for public consumption, others for his personal satisfaction, whether published or unpublished at the time. Those of a confidential nature often provoked vigorous expressions of opinion in their private correspondence.

Religious issues occupied Adams's thoughts much more than Jefferson's, but both men were especially outspoken on the subject. Deploring the lack of free inquiry which still prevailed, Adams condemned the Christian world for conveying the impression that Christianity would not bear examination and criticism.[49] The impact of scientific thought on religious belief was not a novelty in the eighteenth century, nor had the achievement of religious freedom in many places subdued the antagonism between the rationalists and the revelationists. The persistent threat of religious bigotry and the upsurge of the evangelistic spirit in the early nineteenth century were matters of serious concern to Adams and Jefferson, who felt that freedom of the mind must be maintained at all cost.[50] Both regarded religious belief as a very personal and private affair, "known to my god and myself alone," insisted Jefferson. Adams, however, would not be secretive about his religion. He summed it up in the Ten Commandments and the Sermon on the Mount.[51]

In the course of their philosophical correspondence Adams and Jefferson indulged in a good deal of reflection about the revolutionary age through which they had lived so long, of the men and times they had known, and of hopes realized and unfulfilled. They sensed and saw a rapidly changing American nation during and after the War of 1812. Adams's comment on the arrival of a letter from Jefferson within a week's time indicated his consciousness of material improvements altering the lives of the people.[52] New economic issues were

49. JA to TJ, Jan. 23, 1825, below, 607.
50. See introduction to Chap. 10, below, 345.
51. JA to TJ, Nov. 4, 1816, below, 494.
52. JA to TJ, Feb. 3, 1812, below, 293-94.

coming to the fore and westward expansion of population beyond the Mississippi had raised the "black cloud" of slavery, giving serious pause to both elder statesmen.[53]

One might presume to say that they had lived almost too long. They were among the last of their generation, only a few of whom still wore the wig and the cocked hat. "Yours as ever" had replaced "Your most humble and obedient servant" and "Esquire" was becoming a badge of courtesy rather than of gentility. New political parties would soon appear to contend for control in a new age. But in the twilight of the Revolutionary era Adams was still occupied with his books and correspondence and Jefferson was building his university on a new plan. They had contributed stature to the government of the United States and to its position in international affairs. In old age they provided a historical tie between the republicanism of the eighteenth century and the democracy of the nineteenth.

At the age of twenty-five Adams said he had few hopes of fame, but added, "I am not ashamed to own that a prospect of an immortality in the memories of all the worthy, to the end of time, would be a high gratification to my wishes." [54] This achievement by both Adams and "the Sage of Monticello," as he first called Jefferson,[55] was realized in their lifetime and confirmed by the judgment of successive generations. To the audience in Faneuil Hall in 1826, Webster observed that "their fame, indeed, is secure. That is now treasured up beyond the reach of accident . . . for with American liberty it rose, and with American liberty only can it perish."

Although the two statesmen would have been too modest to acknowledge this personal praise, they would have agreed with the substance of Webster's peroration.

It cannot be denied, [Webster declared], but by those who would dispute against the sun, that with America, and in America, a new era commences in human affairs. This era is distinguished by Free Representative Governments, by entire religious liberty, by improved systems of national intercourse, by a newly awakened, and an unconquerable spirit of free inquiry, and by a diffusion of knowledge

53. JA to TJ, Feb. 3, 1821, and TJ to JA, Feb. 21, 1820, Jan. 22, 1821, below, 571, 560, 569.
54. JA to Jonathan Sewall, Feb. 1760, Works, I, 52.
55. JA to TJ, Feb. 2, 1817, below, 507.

through the community, such as has been before altogether unknown and unheard of. America, America, our country, fellow-citizens, our own dear and native land, is inseparably connected, fast bound up, in fortune and by fate, with these great interests. If they fall, we fall with them; if they stand, it will be because we have upholden them.[56]

56. Webster, *Discourse,* 58, 61-62.

THE
Adams-Jefferson
LETTERS

1

"The great Work of Confederation, draggs heavily on"

✳ MAY 1777 – OCTOBER 1781 ✳

JOHN ADAMS and Thomas Jefferson first met in Philadelphia during the summer of 1775 as delegates to the Continental Congress. Adams was thirty-nine, Jefferson thirty-two. Both were lawyers and each had to his credit several years' experience in the lower house of his provincial legislature. The elder, who had represented Massachusetts in the Congress of 1774, quickly became identified as a radical in the conflicting loyalties and emotions of the times. His authorship of the anonymous *Novanglus* letters, printed in January 1775, was not long in doubt, so vigorously did they uphold the rights of the Bay Colony against the oppression of the British government. The younger delegate had exposed himself even earlier to the charge of radicalism in his *Summary View of the Rights of British America*, resolutions which he sent to friends in advance of his attending the Virginia House of Burgesses in 1774. Without asking his permission, they supplied the title, "By a Native, and Member of the House of Burgesses," and had it printed at Williamsburg in August of that year. Within a few months it was reprinted in Philadelphia, again anonymously, thus branding the author, who was easily identified, as one of the revolutionary vanguard even before he took his seat in Congress.[1]

During 1775-76 Jefferson and Adams found themselves on the same side of the debates, impatient with the moderates whose hope for conciliation was stronger than their love of liberty, and they readily took each other's measure. The fledgling from Virginia was impressed by Adams's clarity of argument and forcefulness of phrase, and by his

1. John R. Alden, *The American Revolution* (N. Y., 1954), Chap. III.

"sound head on substantial points"; [2] the latter probed the depth of the reticent Jefferson, whose "reputation of a masterly pen" had won considerable recognition. [3]

During May 1776 the movement in Congress on behalf of independence was accelerated in response to the more advanced developments in some of the colonies; and after Richard Henry Lee's resolution of June 7 that "the Congress should declare that these United Colonies are and of right ought to be free and independent states," Adams and Jefferson were appointed to the committee of five, with Benjamin Franklin, Roger Sherman, and Robert R. Livingston, to draft a declaration of independence. To Adams it seemed a foregone conclusion that Jefferson the Virginian, rather than an "obnoxious" New Englander, should write the declaration. [4] There is no uncertainty as to authorship, however much some critics may question its originality. Although Adams hailed Congress's adoption of Lee's resolution for independence on July 2 as "the most memorable epocha in the history of America," [5] Jefferson's Declaration, designed to convince a "candid world" that separation from Great Britain was both just and justifiable, has forever fixed the Fourth of July as the anniversary of American independence.

The association of Adams and Jefferson in the Continental Congress continued until September 2, 1776, when Jefferson left Philadelphia to return to Monticello. During the next five years, however, he spent only intermittent periods of a few weeks or months at home, for he was a conscientious member of the Virginia House of Delegates and served on innumerable committees. His attendance in Congress had deprived him of the opportunity to participate in the revolutionary Convention which established the Commonwealth of Virginia, but he now played an important part in assuring the reality of the Revolution to his own people through the orderly operation of government. Two of those years, 1779-81, were spent as governor, when military necessity often threatened civil rights. [6] Adams's services continued

2. TJ to James Madison, Feb. 14, 1783, Julian P. Boyd, and others, eds., *The Papers of Thomas Jefferson* (Princeton, 1950–), VI, 241. Hereafter cited as Boyd.
3. JA, "Autobiography," Charles Francis Adams, ed., *The Works of John Adams . . .* (Boston, 1850-56), II, 511. Hereafter cited as *Works*.
4. *Ibid.*, 514-15.
5. JA to AA, July 3, 1776, *ibid.*, IX, 420.
6. "Itinerary and Chronology of Thomas Jefferson, 1776-1781," Paul Leicester Ford, ed., *The Writings of Thomas Jefferson* (N. Y. and London, 1892-99), II, xxii-xxvii. Hereafter cited as Ford.

on the national stage which, for him, merged with the international early in 1778. He had been a member of the American delegation that met Lord Howe on Staten Island in June 1776 to consider impossible terms of reconciliation with Great Britain. Among his many committee assignments, Adams drafted the credentials of the commissioners to France (originally Franklin, Arthur Lee, and Silas Deane), and in February 1778 he was aboard the frigate *Boston* en route to France to replace Deane. Ten years of diplomatic service were to be interrupted only by his brief stay in Massachusetts in 1779 as a member of its Constitutional Convention.[7]

Though Jefferson and Adams thus viewed the issues of the war years from different vantage points, one as a local legislator and executive, the other as a national legislator and diplomat, they still found themselves in fundamental agreement harking back to their collaboration in Congress. From this background and set of circumstances began their correspondence, on a limited scale: six letters in seven years of war and revolution.[8]

In the opening letters of May 1777 they discussed a crucial need of their time—strength and unity of purpose at home in order to win sympathy and support abroad. It was questionable how long the resolute "join or die" spirit that initiated the conflict could survive the attrition of localism and provincial prejudice. In the protracted winning of the war the Americans left an abundant record of defeatism, promoted by successive armies of occupation and the disintegration of civilian life and loyalties. Despite the untiring efforts of Adams and Jefferson on behalf of independence, it was a distant goal when they began their correspondence in 1777. An undercurrent of discouragement runs through it, in their discussion of requisitioning troops for the Continental Army, financing the war—"Financiers," declared Adams, "we want more than Soldiers" [9]—and regulating trade.

Both men were convinced that confederation was "a great and necessary work," but Jefferson doubted that any implied power should be left open to Congress. He was also concerned about the voting power of the states under the Articles and his proposal for reconciling the differences between the large and the small states anticipated one

7. Worthington C. Ford, "Adams, John," *Dictionary of American Biography*, I, 72-82. Hereafter cited as *DAB*.
8. JA's letter to TJ, Paris, June 23, 1783, delivered by Philip Mazzei in 1784, has not been found. Boyd, VI, 318.
9. JA to TJ, May 26, 1777, below, 6.

of the fundamental issues in the Federal Convention of 1787. Although Adams conceded that the "Work of Confederation, draggs heavily on," he was the more optimistic: "I don't despair of it." [10] But it was four years before the Articles of Confederation were ratified by nine states and went into effect in 1781; and it was three more years before the careers of Jefferson and Adams converged on the diplomatic scene in Europe.

Jefferson to Adams

Williamsburgh May 16. 1777.

DEAR SIR

Matters in our part of the continent are too much in quiet to send you news from hence. Our battalions for the Continental service were some time ago so far filled as rendered the recommendation of a draught from the militia hardly requisite, and the more so as in this country it ever was the most unpopular and impracticable thing that could be attempted. Our people even under the monarchical government had learnt to consider it as the last of all oppressions. I learn from our delegates that the Confederation is again on the carpet. A great and a necessary work, but I fear almost desperate. The point of representation is what most alarms me, as I fear the great and small colonies are bitterly determined not to cede. Will you be so good as to recollect the proposition I formerly made you in private and try if you can work it into some good to save our union? It was that any proposition might be negatived by the representatives of a majority of the people of America, or of a majority of the colonies of America. The former secures the larger the latter the smaller colonies. I have mentioned it to many here. The good whigs I think will so far cede their opinions for the sake of the Union, and others we care little for. The journals of congress not being printed earlier gives more uneasiness than I would ever wish to see produced by any act of that body, from whom alone I know our salvation can proceed. In our assembly even the best affected think it an indignity to freemen to be voted away life and fortune in the dark. Our house have lately written for a M.S. copy of your journals, not meaning to desire a communication of any thing ordered to be kept secret. I wish the regulation of the post office adopted by Congress last September could be put in practice. It was for the riders to

10. JA to TJ, May 26, 1777, below, 5.

travel night and day, and to go their several stages three times a week. The speedy and frequent communication of intelligence is really of great consequence. So many falshoods have been propagated that nothing now is beleived unless coming from Congress or camp. Our people merely for want of intelligence which they may rely on are become lethargick and insensible of the state they are in. Had you ever a leisure moment I should ask a letter from you sometime directed to the care of Mr. Dick, Fredericksburgh: but having nothing to give in return it would be a tax on your charity as well as your time. The esteem I have for you privately, as well as for your public importance will always render assurances of your health and happiness agreeable. I am Dear Sir Your friend and servt:

TH: JEFFERSON

Adams to Jefferson

Philadelphia May 26. 1777

MY DEAR SIR

I had this Morning, the Pleasure of your Favour of the Sixteenth inst, by the Post; and rejoice to learn that your Battallions, were so far fill'd, as to render a Draught from the Militia, unnecessary. It is a dangerous Measure, and only to be adopted in great Extremities, even by popular Governments. Perhaps, in Such Governments Draughts will never be made, but in Cases, when the People themselves see the Necessity of them. Such Draughts are widely different from those made by Monarchs, to carry on Wars, in which the People can see, no Interest of their own nor any other object in View, than the Gratification of the Avarice, Ambition, Caprice, Envy, Revenge, or Vanity of a Single Tyrant. Draughts in the Massachusetts, as they have been there managed, have not been very unpopular, for the Persons draughted are commonly the wealthiest, who become obliged to give large Premiums, to their poorer Neighbours, to take their Places.

The great Work of Confederation, draggs heavily on, but I dont despair of it. The great and Small States must be brought as near together as possible: and I am not without Hopes, that this may be done, to the tolerable Satisfaction of both. Your Suggestion, Sir, that any Proposition may be negatived, by the Representatives of a Majority of the People, or of a Majority of States, shall be attended to, and I will endeavour to get it introduced, if We cannot Succeed in our Wishes for a Representation and a Rule of voting, perfectly equitable, which has no equal, in my Mind.

Nothing gives me, more constant Anxiety, than the Delays, in publishing the Journals. Yet I hope, Gentlemen will have a little Patience with Us.[11] We have had a Committee constantly attending to this very Thing, for a long Time. But we have too many Irons in the Fire, you know for Twenty Hands, which is nearly the whole Number We have had upon an Average Since, last fall. The Committee are now busy, every day in correcting Proof Sheets, So that I hope We Shall Soon do better.

A Committee on the Post office, too, have found, a thousand difficulties. The Post is now very regular, from the North and South, altho it comes but once a Week. It is not easy to get faithfull Riders, to go oftener. The Expence is very high, and the Profits, (so dear is every Thing, and so little Correspondence is carried on, except in franked Letters), will not Support the office. Mr. Hazard is now gone Southward, in the Character of Surveyor of the Post office, and I hope will have as good Success, as he lately had eastward, where he has put the office into good order.

We have no News from Camp, but that the General and Army are in good Spirits, and begin to feel themselves powerfull. We are anxiously waiting for News from abroad, and for my own Part I am apprehensive of some insidious Maneuvre from Great Britain, to deceive Us into Disunion and then to destroy.

We want your Industry and Abilities here extreamly. Financiers, We want more than Soldiers. The worst Enemy, We have now is Poverty, real Poverty in the Shape of exuberant Wealth. Pray come and help Us, to raise the Value of our Money, and lower the Prices of Things. Without this, We cannot carry on the War. With it, We can make it a Diversion.

No poor Mortals were ever more perplexed than We have been, with three Misfortunes at once, any one of which would have been, alone, sufficient to have distressed Us. A Redundancy of the Medium of Exchange. A Diminution of the Quantity, at Markett of the Luxuries, the Conveniences and even the Necessaries of Life, and an Increase of the Demand for all these, occasioned by two large Armies in the Country.

I shall, ever esteam it a Happiness to hear of your Welfare, my dear Sir, and a much greater Still to see you, once more in Congress. Your Country is not yet, quite Secure enough, to excuse your Retreat to the Delights of domestic Life. Yet, for the Soul of me, when I attend to my own Feelings, I cannot blame you. I am, Sir your Friend and most obedient Servant,

JOHN ADAMS

11. In his letter-book JA originally wrote: "Yet, for God's sake, have a little Mercy on Us."

Jefferson to Adams

Albemarle in Virginia. Aug. 21. 1777.

DEAR SIR

Your favor of May 26. came safely to hand. I wish it were in my power to suggest any remedy for the evil you complain of. Tho' did any occur, I should propose it to you with great diffidence after knowing you had thought on the subject yourself. There is indeed a *fact* which may not have come to your knolege, out of which perhaps some little good may be drawn. The borrowing money in Europe (or obtaining credit there for necessaries) has already probably been essayed, and it is supposed with some degree of success. But I expect your applications have as yet been only to France, Holland, or such other states as are of principal note. There is however a smaller power, well disposed to our cause, and, as I am informed, possessed of abilities to assist us in this way. I speak of the Grand Duke of Tuscany. The little states of Italy you know have had long peace and shew no disposition to interrupt that peace shortly. The Grand Duke being somewhat avaritious in his nature has availed himself of the opportunity of collecting and hoarding what money he has been able to gather. I am informed from good authority (an officer [Charles Bellini] who was concerned in the business of his treasury) that about three years ago he had ten millions of crowns lying dead in his coffers. Of this it is thought possible as much might be borrowed as would amount to a million of pounds lawful money. At any rate the attempt might be worth making. Perhaps an application from Dr. Franklin who has some acquaintance in that court might be sufficient. Or, as it might be prudent to sound well before the application, in order to prevent the discredit of a rebuff, perhaps Congress would think it worth while to send a special agent there to negotiate the matter. I think we have a gentleman here [Philip Mazzei] who would do it with dexterity and fidelity. He is a native of that dutchy, well connected there, conversant in courts, of great understanding, and equal zeal in our cause. He came over not long since to introduce the cultivation of vines, olives etc. among us. Should you think the matter worth a further thought, either of the Colo. Lees,[12] to whom he is known, can acquaint you more fully of his character. If the money can be obtained in specie, it may be applied to reduce the quantity of circulating paper, and in such a way as to help

---

12. Richard Henry Lee (1732-92) and his brother Francis Lightfoot Lee (1734-97), members of the Virginia delegation in Congress.

the credit of that which will remain in circulation. If credit alone can be obtained for the manufactures of the country, it will still help us to clothe our armies or to encrease at market the necessaries our people want.

What upon earth can Howe mean by the manoeuvre he is now practising? There seems to me no object in this country which can either be of utility or reputation to his cause. I hope it will prove of a peice with all the other follies they have committed. The forming a junction with the Northern army up the Hudson's river, or the taking possession of Philadelphia might have been a feather in his cap and given them a little reputation in Europe. The former as being the design with which they came. The latter as being a place of the first reputation abroad and the residence of Congress. Here he may destroy the little hamlet of Williamsburgh, steal a few slaves, and lose half his army among the fens and marshes of our lower country, or by the heats of our climate. I am Dear Sir with the greatest esteem Your friend and servt.,

TH: JEFFERSON

Jefferson to Adams

Wmsbgh. Dec. 17. 1777.

DEAR SIR

Congress will receive by this post our approbation of the Confederation. It passed the house of Delegates on Monday and the Senate on Tuesday last. Tho' our house of delegates is almost wholly of those who are truly zealous, yet there have ever been a few who have endeavored to throw obstructions in our way. Objections to this important instrument came therefore not unexpectedly. The most difficult articles however were surmounted by the spirit of the house, determined to secure if possible the union of the states. One objection only, stuck with them. It was urged that by the 9th. article reserving to congress a power 'of entering into treaties and alliances' with the proviso immediately following that they should not give to foreigners an exemption from such imposts as should be paiable by natives; the congress would have the whole regulation of our trade, and consequently might grant a monopoly of it: and it was intimated that such a measure had been in contemplation; and might be given away by those states, which have no staple, as the price of commercial privileges to them. Some warm members kindled at this idea, and all seemed to be struck with it. The advocates however for the confederation insisted that Congress would have no such power by the confederation: that a power to treat, did not include ex vi termini ["from the force of the expression"] a power to pass away every thing by treaty which might be the subject of a treaty; and consequently no more gave such power over our commerce than over every thing else; that the inference from the proviso was merely an *implication* and that congress were by that instrument to derive no powers by implication or construction, but such only (art. 2) as were *expressly* delegated to them: that by the 2d proviso in the same 9th. clause allowing each legislature to prohibit the exportation of any article to all places, an inference arose in our favor that we might prohibit it to certain places, and consequently to the very place making title to the monopoly: that it appeared Congress themselves did not suppose these words gave them so very ample a power over trade, because in a subsequent part they reserve in express terms a right of regulating our trade with the Indians. This reasoning removed the difficulty and satisfied the house that the instrument would give to congress no such powers. Yet there remains a great anxiety that an article so important should not be laid down in more express terms, and so as to exclude all possible doubt; and a fear that at some future day such a power should be assumed. As I am myself of opinion the instrument gives no such powers, I naturally conclude congress had them not in contemplation, and consequently that they would have no objections to pass an explanatory vote declaring that the Confederation will give them no such powers. If the confirming in their affections an assembly which have ever witnessed the highest respect for congress, would be an object with them, I know nothing which would produce that effect more powerfully than such vote passed before the final ratification of the instrument. Knowing your candour I have taken the liberty of mentioning this subject to you, that if you should think it worthy your attention you may favor it with the assistance of your abilities.

I greatly fear your requisition of money by quarterly paiments will be impracticable here. Our counties are so large that an annual collection is as much as we ever attempted to complete. Our people too are quite unaccustomed to be called on oftener than once a year. We are proceeding to make good our numbers in the feild by a draught. I am Dr. Sir with every sentiment of esteem Your friend and servt.,

TH: JEFFERSON

Adams to Jefferson

Paris June 29. 1778. [i.e., 1780]

MY DEAR SIR

Mr. Mazzei, called on me, last Evening, to let me know that he was this morning at three to Sett off, on his Journey, for Italy. He desired me to write you, that he has communicated to me the Nature of his Errand: but that his Papers being lost, he waits for a Commission and Instructions from you. That being limited to five Per Cent, and more than that being given by the Powers of Europe, and indeed having been offered by other States and even by the Ministers of Congress, he has little hopes of succeeding at so low an Interest. That he shall however endeavour to prepare the Way, in Italy for borrowing, and hopes to be usefull to Virginia and the United States.

I know nothing of this Gentleman, but what I have learned of him here. His great affection for you Mr. Wythe, Mr. Mason, and other choice Spirits in Virginia, recommended him to me. I know not in what Light he Stands in your Part: but here, as far as I have had opportunity to See and hear, he has been usefull to Us. He kept good Company and a good deal of it. He talks a great deal, and was a zealous defender of our Affairs. His Variety of Languages, and his Knowledge of American affairs, gave him advantages which he did not neglect.

What his Success will be in borrowing money, I know not. We are impatient to learn whether Virginia and the other States have adopted the Plan of Finances recommended by Congress on the 18 of March. I think We shall do no great Things at borrowing unless that System or some other, calculated to bring Things to some certain and Steady Standard, Succeeds.

Before this reaches you, you will have learned, the Circumstances of the Insurrections in England,[13] which discover So deep and So general a discontent and distress, that no wonder the Nation Stands gazing at one another, in astonishment, and Horror. To what Extremities their Confusions will proceed, no Man can tell. They Seem unable to unite in any Principle and to have no Confidence in one another. Thus it is, when Truth and Virtue are lost: These Surely, are not the People who ought to have absolute authority over Us. In all Cases whatsoever, this is not the nation which is to bring Us to unconditional Submission.

13. The Gordon Riots broke out in London, June 2-8, 1780.

The Loss of Charlestown has given a rude Shock to our Feelings. I am distressed for our worthy Friends in that Quarter. But the Possession of that Town must weaken and perplex the Ennemy more than Us.

By this Time you know more than I do, of the Destination and the operations of French and Spanish armaments. May they have Success, and give Us Ease and Liberty, if the English will not give Us Peace. I have the Honour to be with an affectionate Respect, Sir your Frnd and Servt.

Jefferson to Benjamin Franklin, to John Adams, and to John Jay

Virginia Oct. 5. 1781.

DEAR SIR

The bearer hereof Colo. James Monroe who served some time as an officer in the American army and as such distinguished himself in the affair of Princetown as well as on other occasions, having resumed his studies, comes to Europe to complete them. Being a citizen of this state, of abilities, merit and fortune, and my particular friend, I take the liberty of making him known to you, that should any circumstances render your patronage and protection as necessary as they would be always agreeable to him, you may be assured they are bestowed on one fully worthy of them.

He will be able to give you a particular detail of American affairs and especially of the prospect we have thro' the aid of our father of France, of making captives of Ld. Cornwallis and his army, of the recovery of Georgia and South Carolina, and the possibility that Charlestown itself will be opened to us. I have the honour to be with the most profound respect & esteem, Your Excellency's Most obedient and most humble servt,

TH: JEFFERSON [14]

14. On the same day TJ wrote to Monroe: "I enclose you three letters, the one directed to Dr. Franklin, the other two for Mr. Jay and Mr. Adams...." However, "a series of disappointments," Monroe informed TJ on May 6, 1782, had prevented him from going to Europe and using the letters.

2

"The Subject of a Treaty of Commerce"

✳ JUNE 1784 – SEPTEMBER 1785 ✳

EVEN BEFORE the Declaration of Independence, a major objective of the Continental Congress was the negotiation of treaties of amity and commerce with foreign nations. During the summer of 1776, Congress approved a plan embracing the most-favored-nation principle and the protection of private property from devastation and confiscation in time of war. The "Plan of 1776" became the basis for such negotiation throughout the Confederation period,[1] and Congress promptly dispatched commissioners and agents in quest of commercial conventions. These treaties were among the joint responsibilities of the ministers plenipotentiary, Adams and Jefferson, and therefore occupied a major portion of their deliberations and correspondence.

When Jefferson joined Adams and Franklin in France in 1784, Adams was again the senior member in this partnership of equals (Franklin soon retired because of illness and old age). He had served as commissioner to France in 1777-79 although he arrived too late to participate with Franklin and Arthur Lee in concluding the French alliance and commercial treaty of 1778. In 1780 he returned to France to negotiate with Great Britain as soon as the course of war turned toward peace. In the interim he was appointed minister to the United Dutch Provinces where he signed a treaty of amity and commerce in 1782 and secured the first loan from the Dutch government. These amicable relations, together with his personal acquaintance in

1. Samuel F. Bemis, *The Diplomacy of the American Revolution* (N. Y., 1935), 45-48.

Amsterdam, were to be of great service to the debt-ridden United States six years later.[2] In October 1782 he returned to Paris to serve with Franklin and John Jay in negotiating the formal recognition of American independence by Great Britain. Meanwhile Franklin had negotiated a commercial treaty with Sweden, which was signed in 1783, and conversations for the same purpose were under way in Denmark, Portugal, and Austria.[3]

When Jefferson arrived in France in 1784, therefore, Adams had had nearly seven years' intermittent experience in foreign affairs. As a matter of fact, Jefferson had been appointed commissioner to France almost eight years earlier but had declined to serve; again in June 1781 he declined an appointment as peace commissioner. Following the death of his wife in 1782, however, he accepted when this offer was renewed in November, but Congress suspended the appointment in February 1783 because peace negotiations were nearly complete. Instead, he returned to Congress where he served on the committee which approved the definitive treaty with Great Britain.

In peace as in war, however, the United States needed commercial treaties and on May 7, 1784, Congress named Jefferson as minister plenipotentiary to collaborate with Franklin and Adams. Within a week Jefferson was en route through the northern states, gathering commercial data.[4] Accompanied by his eldest daughter Martha ("Patsy"), he sailed from Boston on July 5 and arrived in Paris on August 6.

Jefferson's appointment, Adams wrote to his old fellow patriot James Warren, "gives me great pleasure. He is an old Friend with whom I have often had occasion to labour at many a knotty Problem, and in whose Abilities and Steadiness I have always found great Cause to confide."[5] Perhaps Jefferson was more circumspect in his anticipation, if we may judge from his observation to Madison a year earlier concerning Adams: "His dislike of all parties, and all men, by balancing his prejudices, may give the same fair play to his reason as would a general benevolence of temper."[6] As they shared the common prob-

2. See below, Chap. 6.
3. Edmund C. Burnett, "Note on American Negotiations for Commercial Treaties," *Amer. Hist. Rev.*, 16 (1910-11), 579-87.
4. "Notes on Commerce of the Northern States," Boyd, VII, 323 ff; Dumas Malone, *Jefferson and His Time* (Boston, 1948-), I, 419-22.
5. Aug. 27, 1784, Boyd, VII, 382*n*.
6. TJ to Madison, Feb. 14, 1783, *ibid.*, VI, 241.

lems of the young Republic under stress of European politics, so their friendship ripened.

Mrs. Adams and young Abigail had sailed for Europe shortly before Jefferson, and Adams met them in London on August 7, after a separation of four years and a half. The next day they set out for Paris.[7] Jefferson had arrived the previous day. Here he renewed his acquaintance with Adams and with Mrs. Adams, whom he had met briefly in Boston, and he often visited them in their commodious house at Auteuil, four miles from the city.[8] During the ensuing nine months the two diplomats developed a heightening respect for each other from the collaboration that was so essential to their country's welfare. When their assignments separated them, Adams's feeling was reflected by his wife, who wrote Jefferson that she was "loth ... to leave behind me the only person with whom my Companion could associate with perfect freedom, and unreserve." [9] Earlier she had characterized Jefferson as "one of the choice ones of the earth." [10] The pleasure of her association with a "respected Friend" was now projected into their correspondence, to the good fortune of posterity.

In March 1784 Adams had gone to the Netherlands to discuss with the Prussian minister, Baron de Thulemeier, a commercial treaty between the United States and Frederick the Great; by June it was drafted. After Jefferson's arrival with new instructions, it was revised and finally signed in 1785. In negotiations with Portugal, Denmark, and Tuscany, the Prussian treaty served as a model. In a modified form it was applied to Morocco, and parts of it were offered to the British, who displayed an attitude of indifference, if not hostility.[11]

In the spring of 1785, however, the diplomatic approach to British trade was facilitated by a major shift of American ministers abroad. In France, Jefferson was to succeed Franklin, ill and anxious to go home, who could retire at last; in Great Britain, Adams became the first American minister. The news of their diplomatic assignments reached the ministers on May 2, 1785. Later that month the Adamses

7. JA, "Diary," Aug. 7, 1784, Works, III, 389.
8. Charles Francis Adams, ed., Letters of Mrs. Adams, the Wife of John Adams (Boston, 1841), II, 45. Hereafter cited as Letters of Mrs. Adams.
9. AA to TJ, June 6, 1785, below, 28.
10. AA to Mrs. Richard Cranch, May 8, 1785, Letters of Mrs. Adams, II, 94.
11. Burnett, "Note on American Negotiations...," Amer. Hist. Rev., 16 (1910-11), 579-87; Dorset to the American Commissioners, March 26, 1785, Boyd, VIII, 55-56, 56-59n.

moved to London, and on June 1 the former subject of George III was presented to His Majesty at the Court of St. James. The King, Adams reported to John Jay, "was indeed much affected, and I confess I was not less so." [12] But the British were in no mood to deal amicably with their former colonists. While Adams was complaining that "the Britons Alliens Duty is a very burthensome Thing," [13] Jefferson was drafting a proposal for a reciprocal-rights treaty between nations, "believing that a free and unfriendly intercourse between them . . . cannot be established on a better footing than that of a mutual adoption by each of the citizens or subjects of the other, insomuch that while those of the one shall be travelling or sojourning with the other, they shall be considered to every intent and purpose as members of the nation where they are, entitled to all the protections, rights and advantages of it's native members. . . ." He suggested to Adams that it be proposed to the courts of London and Versailles, but added, "I know it goes beyond our powers; and beyond the powers of Congress too." [14] Indeed it went beyond the serious comprehension of his generation.

Almost as incomprehensible to the Americans was European acquiescence in the outrageous practices of the Barbary states. Although the nations of western Europe and their West Indian possessions offered the sources of trade most essential to the United States, the Mediterranean countries on ancient trade routes might also do business with America if they were accessible. But it was becoming increasingly difficult to approach the piratical states through the good offices of France or Spain, or by more direct means. Congress allowed its ministers a large measure of leeway as to personnel and procedure,[15] and American diplomats took the initiative without hesitation, but it was slow business at best, and unrewarding. This drama would unfold more relentlessly in 1786.

12. June 2, 1785, *Works*, VIII, 257-58.
13. JA to TJ, July 24, 1785, below, 43.
14. TJ to JA, July 28, 1785, Boyd, VIII, 317-18.
15. John Jay to American Commissioners, March [11], 1785, Boyd, VIII, 19-21.

Jefferson to Adams

Boston June 19. 1784.

DEAR SIR

Supposing that you would receive from Congress a direct communication of the powers given to yourself, Doctr. Franklin and myself, I have deferred from day to day writing to you, in hopes that every day would open to me a certainty of the time and place of my departure for the other side of the Atlantic. Paris being my destination I have thought it best to enquire for a passage to France directly. I have hastened myself on my journey hither in hopes of having the pleasure of attending Mrs. Adams to Paris and of lessening some of the difficulties to which she may be exposed. But after some unexpected delays at Philadelphia and New York I arrived here yesterday and find her engaged for her passage to London and to sail tomorrow. It was therefore too late for her to alter her measures tho' I think she might probably meet with you the sooner could she have taken her passage as I shall on board the French packet from N. York where I had ensured her choice of accomodations, and was promised that the departure of the vessel should be made agreeable to our movements. She goes however in a good ship, well accomodated as merchants' ships generally are and I hope will have soon the pleasure of meeting with you. With respect to our joint agency, our instructions are more special than those formerly sent. These I shall have the pleasure of communicating together with the commissions to yourself and Doctr. Franklin at Paris. My expectation is to sail from New York about the first or second week of the next month. The time of my arrival in Paris will depend on winds and weather: but probably it may be the middle or latter part of August.

We are informed that Congress adjourned on the 3d. of June to meet again at Trenton the 1st. Monday in November, leaving a committee of the states at the helm during their recess. The particulars of affairs here I shall have the pleasure of communicating to you more fully than I can by letter. For the present I will only inform you in general that their aspect is encouraging. I beg you to be assured of the sincere esteem and regard with which I have the honor to be Dear Sir Your most obedient and most humble servt.,

TH: JEFFERSON

Jefferson to Adams

On board the Ceres off Scilly. July 24. 1784.

Dr. Sir

When I did myself the honor of writing you on the 19th. Ult. it was my expectation that I should take my passage in the French packet which was to sail the 15th. of this month, and of course that I should not be in Paris till the middle or last of August. It had not then been suggested to me, and being no seaman it did not occur to myself, that even from a London-bound vessel I might get ashore off Ushant or elsewhere on the coast of France. On receiving this information I took my passage with Mr. Tracy in this vessel, leaving Boston the 5th. instant and having had a most favourable run am now as you will see above, and on the lookout for a vessel to take me off. My wish is to land at Brest, Morlaix or elsewhere on that part of the coast, in which, if I succeed, I shall go by the way of L'Orient and Nantes to Paris where I shall probably be a fortnight after the date of this letter. Colo. Humphries, Secretary to the legation, having failed getting to Boston in time, I suppose he will pass in the French packet. However our business need not await him as I am possessed of the papers relative to that. In a situation which hardly admits writing at all, and in hopes of seeing you in Paris as soon as your convenience and that of Mrs. Adams will admit, who I hope is now safe with you, I have the honor to be with the most perfect esteem Dr. Sir Your most obedt and most humble servt,

Th: Jefferson

Jefferson to Adams and Franklin

Cul-de-sac Tetebout. Oct. 17. 1784.

Mr. Jefferson's compliments to Mr. Adams and Dr. Franklin, and incloses to them the letter to the D. of Dorset on the separate articles. He also sends one on the general subject and in the general form as had been agreed when they parted last: but thinking that it might be better, by reciting what had been done with Mr. Hartley [16] to keep the ground we

16. Hartley, advocate of conciliation with America, met only once with the American commissioners for commercial treaties before being recalled.

have gained, and not to admit that we misplaced our overtures, by taking no notice of them, he submits to the gentlemen a second draught, copied from the first as to the recital of the powers but varied in the latter paragraph. They will be so good as to take their choice of the two forms and having signed the one they prefer Mr. J. will add his signature to the same. P.S. He is ready at any moment to concur in a letter or letters on the subject of the man in the inquisition.[17]

Jefferson to Adams and Franklin

Mar. 1. 1785

Mr. Jefferson's compliments to Mr. Adams and Doctr. Franklin and sends them his notes on the treaty with Prussia. He prays Mr. Adams, when he shall have perused them to send them to Dr. Franklin and proposes to meet them on the subject at Passy on Thursday [March 3] at 12. o'clock. He sends the Prussian propositions, Mr. Adams's and Dr. Franklin's notes, and the former project and observations which were in the hands of Colo. Humphreys.[18]

Adams to Franklin and Jefferson

Auteuil March 20. 1785

GENTLEMEN

According to your desire I went early this morning to Versailles and finding the Ct. de Vergennes unembarrassed with company, and only attended by his private Secretaries, I soon obtained the honor of a conference, in which I told him that my colleagues were very sorry that

17. Blair McClenachan of Philadelphia, arrested in London on a charge of debt. Boyd, VII, 444*n*.
18. Negotiations for a commercial treaty with Prussia were begun at The Hague in February 1784 between Adams and Friedrich Wilhelm von Thulemeier, Frederick the Great's perennial ambassador to the Netherlands. Modifications in the model Swedish-American treaty of 1783, proposed by Franklin and John Jay, constituted the "former project" of the present note. On November 10, 1784, JA, TJ, and Franklin had sent Thulemeier a "counter project," which as amended was ready for signature on March 14, 1785. *Diplomatic Correspondence of the United States, 1783-1789* (Washington, 1837), I, 520-29, 554-60; Boyd, VIII, 26-33; and subsequent letters, below.

indisposition necessarily prevented their paying their respects to him in person, and obliged them to request me alone to wait on him and ask his advice upon a thorny question we had with the Barbary Powers. He asked what it was and I put into his hand all the letters upon the subject in french, spanish, italian and english—all of which he read very attentively and observed that it was obvious what was wanted and what had piqued the Emperor of Morocco, viz, that Congress had not written to him nor sent him a consul with the customary presents, for that he was the most interested man in the world and the most greedy of money. He asked whether we had written to Congress and obtained their instructions. I answered that we had full powers to treat with Morocco, Algiers, Tunis, Tripoli and the rest, but that it was impossible for us to go there and that we had not a power of substitution. He said then we should write to the Emperor. I asked if he would do us the favour to convey a letter for us through the french consul? He said he could not do this himself, because it was not in his department, but if we would make an office of it he would communicate it to the Marquis de Castries and return us his answer.

I told him that in looking over the treaties between the several christian Powers and the Barbary States, we found that the treaty between the crown of France and Algiers of the 25 April 1684 was expired or near expiring, and we were desirous of knowing, if the question was not indiscreet, whether it had been renewed. He smiled upon this and said, it was true their treaty was upon the point of expiring, but he could not tell me whether it were renewed, as it was not in his department, but if we would insert this inquiry in our office he would endeavour to obtain the Marshall de Castries' Answer.

I told him, that in order to lay before Congress all the information we could, and to enable them to judge the better what orders to give us or what other course to take we had obtained authentic information from Mr. Bisdom and Mr. Vanderhope, concerning the presents annually given by their high Mightinesses and that we should be very glad to know (if it was not improper) what was the annual amount of the presents made by his Majesty to each of those States, and in what articles they consisted. He said the King never sent them any naval or military stores, but he sent them glasses and other things of value, but that as it was not in his department he could not give me particular information, but that we might put this into our office with the other things.

I asked if there was not a considerable trade and frequent intercourse between some ports of this Kingdom and the coast of Barbary. He said there was from Marseilles and the other ports upon the Mediterranean: but he thought if we had presents to send it would be more convenient to send them from Cadiz.

I then asked the favour of his advice whether in our letter to the Emperor of Morocco we should leave it to his option to send a Minister here to treat with us, or to wait until we could write to Congress and recommend it to them to send a consul. He said he would by no means advise us to invite the Emperor to send a Minister here to treat with us because we must maintain him here and bear all the expences of his voyages and journeys which would be much more costly than for Congress to send a Consul.

But the Comte concluded the whole conference by observing that every thing relative to this business was out of his department, and that we must state to him in writing all we desired to know or to have done, and he would convey it to the Minister of Marine, and communicate to us his answer, and that we might depend upon it that whenever we thought proper to make any office to him it should be carefully attended to.

He added very particular enquiries concerning the health of Dr. Franklin and Mr. Jefferson which I answered to the best of my knowledge and took my leave. With great respect I have the honor to be Gentlemen Your most obedient and Most humble Servt.,

JOHN ADAMS

Adams to Jefferson

Auteuil May. 19. 1785

DEAR SIR

Messieurs Wilhem and Jan Willink, Nicholas and Jacob Vanstaphorst and De la Lande and Fynje of Amsterdam, have lodged in the Hands of Messrs. Van den Yvers Bankers in Paris one Thousand Pounds Sterling for the Purpose of paying for certain Medals and Swords which Coll. Humphreys has orders to cause to be made for the United States. This is therefore to authorize and to request you to draw upon Messrs. Van den Yvers in favour of Coll. Humphreys, for Cash to pay for those Medals and Swords as they shall be made, not to exceed however the Said Sum of one Thousand Pounds Sterling. With great esteem I have the Honour to be, dear Sir, your affectionate Colleague and most obedient Servant,

JOHN ADAMS

Adams to Jefferson

Montreuil sur mer May 22. 1785

MY DEAR SIR

We left Auteuil the 20th. afternoon and have made easy Journeys. Indeed We could not have done otherwise, because the Posthorses were engaged, by the unusual Number of Travellers, in such Numbers that We have been sometimes obliged to wait. The Country is an heap of Ashes. Grass is scarcely to be seen and all sorts of Grain is short, thin, pale and feeble while the Flax is quite dead. You see indeed more green Things than in some of our sharp Drouths in America, but as the Heat of this Clymate is not sufficient to destroy vegetation so effectually as with Us, it is not enough neither to produce so rapid a Revivication of the Universe, upon the Return of Rains, so that their Prospects are more melancholly than ours upon such Occasions. I pity this People from my soul. There is at this Moment as little appearance of a change of Weather as ever.

Tomorrow We shall reach Calais, but I cannot calculate how long it will take Us to cross the Channel. I allow two days from Dover to London as I am determined to be in a hurry about nothing from the Beginning to the End of this Adventure. It is best to give myself as well as others time to think.

The Ladies [19] join in respects to you and Mr. Humphreys and Mr. Williamos, the Marquis [20] and his Lady and all other Friends. Be so good as to inform me, if you learn any Thing of the sailing of the Packet, and of the Health of my Boy.[21] I thank you kindly for your Book.[22] It is our Meditation all the Day long. I cannot now say much about it, but I think it will do its Author and his Country great Honour. The Passages upon slavery, are worth Diamonds. They will have more effect than Volumes written by mere Philosophers. The Ladies say you should have mentioned West and Copeley at least among your American Genius's, because they think them the greatest Painters of the Age. Madam[e says] I have not expressed her sentiments politely enough. It should run thus: The Ladies desire that in the next Edition you would insert West and Copeley etc.

19. AA and her daughter Abigail, twenty years old.
20. The Marquis de Lafayette.
21. John Quincy Adams, eighteen years old, en route to the United States to study at Harvard College.
22. *Notes on the State of Virginia*, privately printed, 200 copies, Paris, May 1785, for distribution to TJ's friends.

The melancholly Face of Nature, added to the dull political Prospect before us, on the other side of the Channell, coming upon the Back of our natural Regretts at parting with our Son and our fine summer situation at Auteuil, and all our Friends in and about Paris, make the Journey rather triste, but we have passed through scenes bien plus triste encore. Adieu.

J. ADAMS

Adams to Jefferson

Dessin's Calais May 23. 1785. Monday.

DEAR SIR

We are just arrived, covered with Dust, and we have hired our Boat, to go over tomorrow at ten. No green Peas, no Sallad, no Vegetables to be had upon the Road, and the Sky is still as clear dry and cold as ever. The Flocks of Sheep and herds of Cattle, through the Country, Stalk about the Fields like Droves of Walking Skeletons. The Sheep are pastured chiefly I think in the plowed grounds, upon the Fibres as I suppose of the Roots of Grass turn'd up by the Plow.

From a motive of Humanity I wish that our Country may have plenti-full Rains, and our Husbandmen Industry, that they may Supply the Wants of their Suffering Fellow Creatures in Europe. You see I have nothing so mean as a selfish or even a patriotic Wish in all this. But from the same regard to Europe and her worthy Colonists in the West Indies, I hope that these rainless, heatless Heavens will convince them that it is abundantly for their good that We should bring and carry freely, our Flour, Wheat, Corn, Rice, Flesh, and Fish for their Soulagement. Yours affectionately,

J. ADAMS

The Ladies Compliments of course.

Jefferson to Adams

Paris May 25. 1785.

DEAR SIR

Your letter of the 22d. from Montreuil sur mer is put into my hands this moment, and having received information of your son, and two Amer-ican gentlemen being to set out for London tomorrow morning, I seize a moment to inform you that he had arrived well at l'Orient and was well on the 20th. when the packet was still detained by contrary winds. Mr. Barclay, who is arrived, had also seen him. Be so good as to inform the ladies that Mrs. Hayes is arrived. I have not yet seen her, but am this moment going to perform that duty. I fear the ladies have had a more triste journey than we had calculated on. The poverty of the country and distress of the drought would of course produce this effect. I am the more convinced of this as you say they have found amusement in my notes. They presented themselves to their notice under fortunate circumstances. I am happy if you find any thing in them worthy your approbation. But my country will probably estimate them differently. A foreknowlege of this has retarded my communicating them to my friends two years. But enough of them. The departure of your family has left me in the dumps. My afternoons hang heavily on me. I go sometimes to Passy and Mont Parnasse. When they are gone too I shall be ready for the dark and narrow house of Ossian. We attended the Queen's entrance yesterday, but lost the sight of her. You can calculate, and without many figures, the extent of this mortification to me. To render it more complete I had placed myself and my daughter in my carriage very finely before the Palais Bourbon to see the illuminations of the Garde meubles which are to cost the king of Spain two or three thousand guineas. But they sent a parcel of souldiers to drive us all away. We submitted without making battle; I carried my daughter to the Abbaye and came home to bed myself. I have now given you all the news of Paris as far as I know it and after recommending myself to the friendly recollection of the ladies I conclude with assurances of the esteem with which I have the honour to be dear Sir Your affectionate friend and servt.,

TH: JEFFERSON

P.S. Send me your address au plutot.

Adams to Jefferson

London May 27. 1785

DEAR SIR

I arrived yesterday and have made my visit to day, and been very politely received by the Marquis [of Carmarthen], but of this more hereafter. This is devoted to a smaller subject.

Upon Enquiry I find that I cannot be exempted from paying duties upon my Wines, because no foreign Minister is, except for a less quantity than I have of the best qualities in my Cellar at the Hague, so that I must stop all that I have in France if I can. To pay Six or Eight Shillings Sterling a Bottle upon the Small Wines I packed at Auteuil would be folly. I must beg you then if possible to stop it all except one Case of Madeira and Frontenac together. Let me beg you too to write to Mr. Garvey and stop the order for five hundred Bottles of Bourdeaux. All my other Things may be sent on to me, as proposed.

Coll. Smith has Letters for you, but waits a private Hand. He Sends his Respects to you and Coll. Humphreys. If my Things are gone and cannot be stopped I must pay the Impost, heavy as it is. I am sorry to give you this Trouble but I beg you to take the Wine, at any Price you please. Let your own Maitre D'Hotel judge, or accept it as a present or sell it at Vendue, i.e. let Petit dispose of it as he will give you an Account of proceeds and give me credit, and then order me to pay Stockdale or any Body here for you to the amount. My Esteem, and Regards as due. Yours affectionately

JOHN ADAMS

Adams to Jefferson

Bath Hotel London May 27. 1785

DEAR SIR

I found that either the Duke of Dorsetts Letter to the Premier had produced an order at Dover or that his Graces Letter to the Custom House Office had as good an effect, for I was allowed to pass without Molestation, and indeed received Marks of particular Respect.

We arrived yesterday 26. in the afternoon, and as Fortune would have it Coll. Smith arrived the Night before 25. We soon met. I wrote a Card to the Marquis of Carmarthen, at Nine at Night, acquainting his Lordship of my Arrival and desiring an Hour to wait on him. This Morning I had an Answer, that his Lordship would be glad to see me at one at his House, or at four at his office, as I chose. I replyed that I would have the Honour to wait on him at one.

Coll. Smith went with me, we were admitted in an Instant, and politely received. I laid before him my Commission, and left him a Copy. Coll. Smith did the same with his. I consulted his Lordship about the Ettiquette of my Letter of Credence, and he gave me the same Answers as the Comte de Vergennes gave you. His Lordship then said that on Wednesday next after the Levee, I should be presented to his Majesty in his Closett, and

there deliver my Letter of Credence, and that on the next Levee Day
Coll. Smith would be presented. This he said was according to the usage.

I have since seen the Dutch Minister,[23] who enquired of every particular
step by step, and then said that I was received precisely upon the same
Footing with all the other Ministers. I learned from the Dutch Minister
too another Particular which gave me Pleasure, vizt that the usage here is
directly contrary to that in Holland and France. Here the new Minister
receives the first Visit, from all the foreign Ministers, whereas in France
and Holland the new Minister makes the first Visit to all the foreign
Ministers and notifies formally to them his Reception. This saves me from
an Embarrassment, and We shall now see who will and who will not. We
shall see what will be done by Imperial Ministers, etc. With the most
cordial Esteem I have the Honour to be, Sir, your most obedient and most
humble Servant,

JOHN ADAMS

Adams to Franklin and Jefferson

Bath Hotel May 29. 1785. Westminster

GENTLEMEN

Our Secretary of State for foreign affairs, in a Letter of 13. Ap. informs
me, that he wrote Us a Letter by Capt. Lamb dated 11. March, inclosing
a Variety of Papers respecting the Treaties we are directed to negotiate
and conclude with the Barbary Powers.

Inclosed is a Copy of a Resolution of Congress of 14. Feb. 1785,[24] inclosed to me, in the Secretary's Letter. I know nothing of Capt. Lambs
Arrival or of the Dispatches by him.

On the 26. I communicated to Lord Carmarthen my Credentials, and
left him Copies, as we have done upon former occasions in France, and
am to have my Audience of the King in his Closet as the Secretary of State
informs me, next Wednesday. I have the Honour to be, very respectfully,
Gentlemen, your most obedient and most humble Servant,

JOHN ADAMS

23. Baron D. W. van Lynden, like Adams, was a "complete ... cypher" at the Court
of St. James, as JA wrote to John Jay, Dec. 3, 1785, *Works*, VIII, 352.

24. "Resolved that the Ministers of the United States who are directed to form
Treaties with the Emperor of Morocco, and the Regencies of Algiers, Tunis, and
Tripoli, be empowered to apply so much of the money borrowed in Holland, or
any other money in Europe belonging to the United States ... not exceeding Eighty
Thousand Dollars." Full text in Boyd, VIII, 19-20.

Jefferson to Adams

Paris June 2. 1785.

DEAR SIR

Your favours of May 23. and the two of May 27. came safely to hand, the first being open. That of the 22d. from Montreuil sur mer had been received and answered on the 25th.

The day before the receipt of the letters of the 27th. we had had your cases brought to the barrier of Paris in order to get the proper officer to go that far to plumb them. From there they were put on board the boat for Rouen and their portage paid. In the instant of receiving your letter I sent Petit off to try to stop them if not gone. The boat was just departing and they declared it impossible to reland them: and that could it be done, a new passport from the C. d. Vergennes would be necessary for the part not landed. I now forward your letter to Mr. Garvey, countermanding your order of the wine from him, and praying him to retain all the cases of wine now sent except that which has the Madeira and Frontignac, till he shall receive your orders. These therefore you will be so good as to send him as soon as convenient. I was very sorry we could not stop the wine. It would have suited me perfectly to have taken it either at the prices it cost you, if known to Petit, or if not known, then at such prices as he and Marc should have estimated it at: and this would have saved you trouble. I inclose you Petit's note of disbursements which I immediately repaid him. You will know the exchange between London and Paris, which is considerably in favor of the former. Make the allowance for that and either retain the money in your own hands or put it into Stockdale's as most convenient. Can you take the trouble of ordering me the two best of the London papers (that is to say one of each party) and by any channel which will save me postage and the search of government?

The inclosed letter to Miss Adams is from a young gentleman [25] of her acquaintance who has a very sincere and high affection for her. When you transferred to her the commission of Secretary, I well hoped the pleasure of her being the intermediate of our communications: but I did not flatter myself with the further one of becoming the confident between herself and persons of the foregoing description. The following paragraphs are for her eye only. Be so good therefore as to deliver over the letter to her. The cypher I suppose to be in her custody.

25. John Quincy Adams, according to TJ's Summary Journal of Letters.

By a dutch Courier which went yesterday we sent an answer to Baron Thulemyer. It contained what we had agreed on when you were here. That is to say we closed and expressing our doubts that it might not suit him to come here, we propose[d] that every one should sign separately puting the date and place of his Signature. We mean to sign here, send it by some confidential Person to you and that he shall carry it on to the Baron, deliver it to him and receive in exchange the copy signd by him.

Our answer to Tuscany is copying. It is precisly what we had agreed when you were with us.[26] Be so good as to present my highest esteem to the ladies and to be assured of the sincerity with which I am Dear Sir Your friend and servt.,

TH: JEFFERSON

P.S. *My visits have been all returned save by the Portuguese [ambassador] who I imagine has [neglect]ed [others?].*

Adams to Jefferson

Bath Hotel Westminster June 3. 1785

SIR

I have now the Honour to inform you, that having shewn my Commission to the Right Honourable the Marquis of Carmarthen, and left an authenticated Copy together with a Copy of my Letter of Credence to the King according to the usage, I had the Honour on the first of this Month to be introduced by his Lordship to his Majesty, in his Closet with all the Ceremonies and Formalities, practised on such occasions, with other foreign Ministers, where I delivered to his Majesty, my Letter of Credence from the United States of America, as their Minister Plenipotentiary to the Court of Great Britain. The Mission was treated by his Majesty with all the Respect, and the Person with all the Kindness, which could have been expected or reasonably desired, and with much more, I confess, than was in fact expected by me.[27]

Coll. Smith, has also shewn his Commission as Secretary of Legation, to the Secretary of State and left an authenticated Copy, and is to be presented to the King on the next Levee Day. The Time is not yet fixed for my Introduction to the Queen, but having received an Invitation to dine with the Secretary of State, on Saturday the fourth of this Month, being

26. Italicized passages were decoded by young Abigail Adams.
27. JA described his audiences with George III and with Queen Charlotte in greatest detail to John Jay, *Works*, VIII, 255-59, 265-66; also Boyd, VIII, 526.

the Anniversary of his Majestys Birth, I must go to Court again on that Day. With great Respect, I have the Honour to be, Sir your most obedient and most humble servant,

JOHN ADAMS

Abigail Adams to Jefferson, with Enclosure

London Bath Hotel Westminster
June 6. 1785

DEAR SIR

Mr. Adams has already written you that we arrived in London upon the 27 of May.[28] We journey'd slowly and sometimes silently. I think I have somewhere met with the observation that nobody ever leaves paris but with a degree of tristeness. I own I was loth to leave my garden because I did not expect to find its place supplied. I was still more loth on account of the increasing pleasure, and intimacy which a longer acquaintance with a respected Friend promised, to leave behind me the only person with whom my Companion could associate with perfect freedom, and unreserve: and whose place he had no reason to expect supplied in the Land to which he is destined.

At leaving Auteuil our domesticks surrounded our Carriage and in tears took leave of us, which gave us that painfull kind of pleasure, which arises from a consciousness, that the good will of our dependants is not misplaced.

My little Bird I was obliged, after taking it into the Carriage to resign to my parisian chamber maid, or the poor thing would have fluttered itself to Death. I mourned its loss, but its place was happily supplied by a present of two others which were given me on board the Dover pacquet, by a young Gentleman whom we had received on Board with us, and who being excessively sick I admitted into the cabin, in gratitude for which he insisted upon my accepting a pair of his Birds. As they had been used to travelling I brought them here in safety, for which they hourly repay me by their melodious notes. When we arrived we went to our old Lodgings at the Adelphia, but could not be received as it was full, and almost every other hotel in the city. From thence we came to the Bath Hotel where we at present are, and where Mr. Storer had partly engaged Lodgings for us, tho he thought we should have objections upon account of the Noise, and the constant assemblage of carriages round it, but it was no time for choice, as the sitting of parliament, the Birth Day of the King, and the celebration of Handles Musick had drawn together such a Number of people as all-

28. They arrived on May 26, according to JA's letter of May 27.

ready to increase the price of Lodgings near double. We did not however hesitate at keeping them, tho the four rooms which we occupy costs a third more than our House and Garden Stables etc. did at Auteuil. I had lived so quietly in that calm retreat, that the Noise and bustle of this proud city almost turnd my Brain for the first two or three Days. The figure which this city makes in respect to Equipages is vastly superiour to Paris, and gives one the Idea of superiour wealth and grandeur. I have seen few carriages in paris and no horses superiour to what are used here for Hackneys. My time has been much taken up since my arrival in looking out for a House. I could find many which would suit in all respects but the price, but none realy fit to occupy under 240 £. 250. besides the taxes, which are serious matters here. At last I found one in Grovenor Square which we have engaged.

Mr. Adams has written you an account of his reception at Court, which has been as gracious and as agreeable as the reception given to the Ministers of any other foreign powers. Tomorrow he is to be presented to the Queen.

Mr. Smith appears to be a modest worthy man, if I may judge from so short an acquaintance. I think we shall have much pleasure in our connection with him. All the Foreign Ministers and the Secretaries of Embassies have made their visits here, as well as some English Earls and Lords. Nothing as yet has discovered any acrimony. Whilst the Coals are cover'd the blaize will not burst, but the first wind which blows them into action will I expect envelop all in flames. If the actors pass the ordeal without being burnt they may be considerd in future of the Asbestos kind. Whilst I am writing the papers of this day are handed me. From the publick Advertiser I extract the following. "Yesterday morning a messenger was sent from Mr. Pitt to Mr. Adams the American plenipotentiary with notice to suspend for the present their intended interview" (absolutely false). From the same paper:

"An Ambassador from America! Good heavens what a sound! The Gazette surely never announced any thing so extraordinary before, nor once on a day so little expected. This will be such a phœnomenon in the Corps Diplomatique that tis hard to say which can excite indignation most, the insolence of those who appoint the Character, or the meanness of those who receive it. Such a thing could never have happened in any former Administration, not even that of Lord North. It was reserved like some other Humiliating circumstances to take place

> Sub Jove, sed Jove nondum
> Barbato _____." [29]

29. "Under Jove, but Jove not yet barbaric."

From the morning post and daily advertiser it is said that "Mr. Adams the Minister plenipotentiary from America is extremly desirious of visiting Lord North whom he Regards as one of the best Friends the Americans ever had." Thus you see sir the beginning squibs.

I went last week to hear the musick in Westminster Abbey. The Messiah was performd. It was sublime beyond description. I most sincerely wisht for your presence as your favorite passion would have received the highest gratification. I should have sometimes fancied myself amongst a higher order of Beings; if it had not been for a very troublesome female, who was unfortunately seated behind me; and whose volubility not all the powers of Musick could still.

I thank you sir for the information respecting my son from whom we received Letters. He desires to be remembered to you, to Col. Humphries and to Mr. Williamos. My Daughter also joins in the same request. We present our Love to Miss Jefferson and compliments to Mr. Short. I suppose Madam de la Fayette is gone from paris. If she is not, be so good sir as to present my respects to her. I design writing her very soon. I have to apoligize for thus freely scribling to you. I will not deny that there may be a little vanity in the hope of being honourd with a line from you. Having heard you upon some occasions express a desire to hear from your Friends, even the Minutia respecting their Situation, I have ventured to class myself in that number and to subscribe myself, Sir, your Friend and Humble Servant,

A. ADAMS

ENCLOSURE

The publick Advertiser—

"Yesterday Lord George Gordon had the Honour of a long conference with his Excellency John Adams (honest John Adams), the Ambassador of America, at the hotel of Mons. de Lynden Envoye extrordinaire de Leur Hautes puissances."

This is true, and I suppose inserted by his Lordship who is as wild and as enthusiastic as when he headed the mob. His Lordship came here but not finding Mr. Adams at home was determind to see him, and accordingly followed him to the Dutch Ministers. The conversation was curious, and pretty much in the Stile of Mrs. Wright with whom his Lordship has frequent conferences.

An other paragraph from the same paper—"Amongst the various personages who drew the attention of the drawing-room on Saturday last, Mr. Adams, minister plenipotentiary from the States of America was not the least noticed. From this gentleman the Eye of Majesty and the Court glanced on Lord _____; to whose united Labours this Country stands indebted for the loss of a large territory and a divided and interrupted Commerce."

Adams to Jefferson

Bath Hotel Westminster June 7. 1785.

DEAR SIR

I have received yours of 25. May, and thank you for the News of my Son, and for the News of Paris. I wished to have seen the Queens Entrance into Paris, but I saw the Queen of England on Saturday, the Kings Birth day, in all her Glory. It is paying very dear to be a King or Queen to pass One such a day in a year. To be obliged to enter into Conversation with four or five hundred, or four or five Thousand People of both Sexes, in one day and to find Small Talk enough for the Purpose, adapted to the Taste and Character of every one, is a Task which would be out of all Proportion to my Forces of Mind or Body. The K and Q. speak to every Body. I stood next to the Spanish Minister [Don Bernardo del Campo], with whom his Majesty conversed in good French, for half or Quarter of an Hour, and I did not loose any Part of the discourse, and he said several, clever Things enough. One was Je suis convaincu que le plus grand Ennemy du Bien, est le mieux. You would have applied it as I did, to the Croud of Gentlemen present who had advised his Majesty, to renounce the Bien for the Mieux in America, and I believe he too had that Instance in his mind. Thursday I must be presented to the Queen, who I hope will say as many pretty Things to me, as the K. did.

You would die of Ennui here, for these Ceremonies are more numerous and continue much longer here than at Versailles.

I find I shall be accablé with Business and Ceremony together, and I miss my fine walks and pure Air at Auteuil. The Smoke and Damp of this City is ominous to me. London boasts of its Trottoir, but there is a space between it and the Houses through which all the Air from Kitchens, Cellars, Stables and Servants Appartements ascends into the Street and pours directly on the Passenger on Foot. Such Whiffs and puffs assault you every few Steps as are enough to breed the Plague if they do not Suffocate you on the Spot.

For Mercy Sake stop all my Wine but the Bourdeaux and Madeira, and Frontenac. And stop my order to Rouen for 500 Additional Bottles. I shall be ruined, for each Minister is not permitted to import more than 5 or 600 Bottles which will not more than cover what I have at the Hague which is very rich wine and my Madeira Frontenac and Bourdeaux at Auteuil. Petit will do the Business. Regards to Coll. Humphreys and Mr. Williamos. Adieu.

JOHN ADAMS

Franklin and Jefferson to Adams

Passy June 15, 1785.

SIR

Among the instructions given to the Ministers of the United States for treating with foreign powers, was one of the 11th. of May 1784. relative to an individual of the name of John Baptist Pecquet. It contains an acknowlegement on the part of Congress of his merits and sufferings by friendly services rendered to great numbers of American seamen carried prisoners into Lisbon, and refers to us the delivering him these acknowlegements in honourable terms and the making him such gratification as may indemnify his losses and properly reward his zeal. This person is now in Paris and asks whatever return is intended for him. Being in immediate want of money he has been furnished with ten guineas. He expressed desires of some appointment either for himself or son at Lisbon, but has been told that none such are in our gift, and that nothing more could be done for him in that line than to mention to Congress that his services will merit their recollection, if they should make any appointment there analogous to his talents. He sais his expences in the relief of our prisoners have been upwards of fifty Moidores. Supposing that, as he is poor, a pecuniary gratification will be most useful to him, we propose, in addition to what he had received, to give him a hundred and fifty guineas or perhaps 4000. livres, and to write a joint letter to him expressing the sense Congress entertain of his services. We pray you to give us your sentiments on this subject by return of the first post, as he is waiting here, and we wish the aid of your [coun]sels therein. We are to acknowlege the receipt of your letter of June 3. 1785 informing us of your reception at the court of London.

Adams to Franklin and Jefferson

Bath Hotel Westminster June 20. 1785.

GENTLEMEN

Let me request of you, to turn your Attention as soon as possible to the Subject of a Treaty of Commerce between the United States of America and Great Britain, and transmit to me, a Project that you would advise me to propose in the first Instance. For my own Part I like the Plan agreed on with Prussia so well, that I must request you to send me a Copy of it, and with such Changes as you may advise me to adopt I should be for proposing that. With great Respect etc.

Adams to Franklin and Jefferson

Westminster June 20. 1785

GENTLEMEN

I have just received your Favour of the 15 and have the Honour to agree entirely with you in sentiment respecting Gratification to be given to Mr. John Baptist Pecquet and the Letter to be written to him. I have the Honour etc.

Jefferson to Abigail Adams

Paris June 21. 1785

DEAR MADAM

I have received duly the honor of your letter, and am now to return you thanks for your condescension in having taken the first step for settling a correspondence which I so much desired; for I now consider it as *settled* and proceed accordingly. I have always found it best to remove obstacles first. I will do so therefore in the present case by telling you that I consider your boasts of the splendour of your city and of it's superb hackney coaches as a flout, and declaring that I would not give the polite, self-denying, feeling, hospitable, goodhumoured people of this country and their amability in every point of view, (tho' it must be confessed our streets are somewhat dirty, and our fiacres rather indifferent) for ten such races of rich, proud, hectoring, swearing, squibbing, carnivorous animals as those among whom you are; and that I do love this *people* with all my heart, and think that with a better religion and a better form of government and their present governors their condition and country would be most enviable. I pray you to observe that I have used the term *people* and that this is a noun of the masculine as well as feminine gender. I must add too that we are about reforming our fiacres, and that I expect soon an Ordonance that all their drivers shall wear breeches unless any difficulty should arise whether this is a subject for the police or for the general legislation of the country, to take care of. We have lately had an incident of some consequence, as it shews a spirit of treason, and audaciousness which was hardly thought to exist in this country. Some eight or ten years ago a Chevalier _____ was sent on a message of state to the princess of _____ of _____ of (before I proceed an inch further I must confess my profound stupidity; for tho' I have heard this story told fifty times in all it's circumstances, I declare I am unable to recollect the name of the ambassador, the name of the princess, and the nation he was sent to; I must therefore proceed to tell you the naked story, shorn of all those precious circumstances) some chevalier or other was sent on some business or other to some princess or other. Not succeeding in his negociation, he wrote on his return the following song.[30]

Ennivré du brillant poste
Que j'occupe récemment,
Dans une chaise de poste
Je me campe fierement:
Et je vais en ambassade
Au nom de mon souverain
Dire que je suis malade,
Et que lui se porte bien.

Avec une joue enflée
Je debarque tout honteux:
La princesse boursoufflée,
Au lieu d'une, en avoit deux;
Et son altesse sauvage
Sans doute a trouvé mauvais
Que j'eusse sur mon visage
La moitié de ses attraits.

Princesse, le roi mon maitre
M'a pris pour Ambassadeur;
Je viens vous faire connoitre
Quelle est pour vous son ardeur.
Quand vous seriez sous le
   chaume,
Il donneroit, m'a-t-il dit,
La moitié de son royaume
Pour celle de votre lit.

La princesse à son pupitre
Compose un remerciment:
Elle me donne une epitre
Que j'emporte lestement,
Et je m'en vais dans la rue
Fort satisfait d'ajouter
A l'honneur de l'avoir vue
Le plaisir de la quitter.

30. Printed in the *Journal de Paris*, May 31, 1785.

This song run through all companies and was known to every body. A book was afterwards printed, with a regular license, called 'Les quatres saisons litteraires' which being a collection of little things, contained this also, and all the world bought it or might buy it if they would, the government taking no notice of it. It being the office of the Journal de Paris to give an account and criticism of new publications, this book came in turn to be criticised by the redacteur, and he happened to select and print in his journal this song as a specimen of what the collection contained. He was seised in his bed that night and has been never since heard of. Our excellent journal de Paris then is suppressed and this bold traitor has been in jail now three weeks, and for ought any body knows will end his days there. Thus you see, madam, the value of energy in government; our feeble republic would in such a case have probably been wrapt in the flames of war and desolation for want of a power lodged in a single hand to punish summarily those who write songs. The fate of poor Pilatre de Rosiere will have reached you before this does, and with more certainty than we yet know it. This will damp for a while the ardor of the Phaetons of our race who are endeavoring to learn us the way to heaven on wings of our own. I took a trip yesterday to Sannois and commenced an acquaintance with the old Countess d'Hocquetout. I received much pleasure from it and hope it has opened a door of admission for me to the circle of literati with which she is environed. I heard there the Nightingale in all it's perfection: and I do not hesitate to pronounce that in America it would be deemed a bird of the third rank only, our mockingbird, and foxcoloured thrush being unquestionably superior to it. The squibs against Mr. Adams are such as I expected from the polished, mild tempered, truth speaking people he is sent to. It would be ill policy to attempt to answer or refute them. But counter-squibs I think would be good policy. Be pleased to tell him that as I had before ordered his Madeira and Frontignac to be forwarded, and had asked his orders to Mr. Garvey as to the residue, which I doubt not he has given, I was afraid to send another order about the Bourdeaux lest it should produce confusion. In stating my accounts with the United states, I am at a loss whether to charge house rent or not. It has always been allowed to Dr. Franklin. Does Mr. Adams mean to charge this for Auteuil and London? Because if he does, I certainly will, being convinced by experience that my expences here will otherwise exceed my allowance. I ask this information of you, Madam, because I think you know better than Mr. Adams what may be necessary and right for him to do in occasions of this class. I will beg the favor of you to present my respects to Miss Adams. I have no secrets to communicate to her in cypher at this moment, what I write to Mr. Adams being mere commonplace stuff, not meriting a communication to the Secretary. I have the honour to be with the most perfect esteem Dr. Madam Your most obedient and most humble servt.,

TH: JEFFERSON

Jefferson to Adams

Paris June 22. 1785.

DEAR SIR

My last to you was of the 2d. inst. since which I have received yours of the 3d. and 7th. I informed you in mine of the substance of our letter to Baron Thulemeyer. Last night came to hand his acknolegement of the receipt of it. He accedes to the method proposed for signing, and has forwarded our dispatch to the king. I inclose you a copy of our letter to Mr. Jay to go by the packet of this month. It contains a state of our proceedings since the preceding letter which you had signed with us. This contains nothing but what you had concurred with us in, and as Dr. Franklin expects to go early in July for America, it is probable that the future letters must be written by you and myself. I shall therefore take care that you be furnished with copies of every thing which comes to hand on the joint business.

What is become of this Mr. Lambe? I am uneasy at the delay of that business, since we know the ultimate decision of Congress. Dr. Franklin having a copy of the Corps Diplomatique has promised to prepare a draught of a treaty to be offered to the Barbary states; as soon as he has done so we will send it to you for your corrections. We think it will be best to have it in readiness against the arrival of Mr. Lambe on the supposition that he may be addressed to the joint ministers for instructions.

I asked the favour of you in my last to chuse two of the best London papers for me, one for each party. The D. of Dorset has given me leave to have them put under his address, and sent to the office from which his despatches come. (I think he called it Cleveland office, or Cleveland row or by some such name: however I suppose it can easily be known there.) Will Mr. Stockdale undertake to have these papers sent regularly, or is this out of the line of his business? Pray order me also any really good pamphlets which come out from time to time, which he will charge to me. I have the honour to be with sentiments of real respect and affection Dr. Sir Your most obedient and most humble servt.,

TH: JEFFERSON

Jefferson to Abigail Adams

Paris July 7. 1785.

DEAR MADAM

I had the honour of writing you on the 21st. of June, but the letter being full of treason has waited a private conveiance. Since that date there has been received for you at Auteuil a cask of about 60. gallons of wine. I would have examined it's quality and have ventured to decide on it's disposal, but it is in a cask within a cask, and therefore cannot be got at but by operations which would muddy it and disguise it's quality. As you probably know what it is, what it cost, etc. be so good as to give me your orders on the subject and they shall be complied with.

Since my last I can add another chapter to the history of the redacteur of the Journal de Paris. After the paper had been discontinued about three weeks, it appeared again, but announcing in the first sentence a change-ment de domicile of the redacteur, the English of which is that the redac-tion of the paper had been taken from the imprisoned culprit, and given to another. Whether the imprisonment of the former has been made to cease, or what will be the last chapter of his history I cannot tell. I love energy in government dearly. It is evident it was become necessary on this occasion, and that a very daring spirit has lately appeared in this country. For notwithstanding the several examples lately made of suppressing the London papers, suppressing the Leyden gazette, imprisoning Beaumarchais, and imprisoning the redacteur of the journal, the author of the Mercure of the last week has had the presumption, speaking of the German news-papers, to say 'car les journaux de ce pays-la ne sont pas forcés de s'en tenir à juger des hemistiches, ou à annoncer des programes academiques.' [31] Probably he is now suffering in a jail the just punishments of his insolent sneer on this mild government, tho' as yet we do not know the fact.

The settlement of the affairs of the Abbé Mably is likely to detain his friends Arnoud and Chalut in Paris the greatest part of the summer. It is a fortunate circumstance for me, as I have much society with them. What mischeif is this which is brewing anew between Faneuil hall and the na-tion of God-dem-mees? Will that focus of sedition be never extinguished? I apprehend the fire will take thro' all the states and involve us again in the displeasure of our mother country. I have the honour to be with the most perfect esteem Madam Your most obedt. and most humble servt.,

TH: JEFFERSON

31. "For the newspapers of that country are not compelled to rely on verses or to publish academic programs."

Jefferson to Adams

Paris July 7. 1785.

DEAR SIR

This will accompany a joint letter inclosing the draught of a treaty, and my private letter of June 22, which has waited so long for a private conveiance. We daily expect from the Baron Thulemeyer the French column for our treaty with his sovereign. In the mean while two copies are preparing with the English column which Doctr. Franklin wishes to sign before his departure, which will be within four or five days. The French, when received, will be inserted in the blank column of each copy. As the measure of signing at separate times and places is new, we think it necessary to omit no other circumstance of ceremony which can be observed. That of sending it by a person of confidence and invested with a character relative to the object, who shall attest our signature here, yours in London and Baron Thulemeyer's at the Hague, and who shall make the actual exchanges, we think will contribute to supply the departure from the usual form in other instances. For this reason we have agreed to send Mr. Short on this business, to make him a Secretary pro hac vice, and to join Mr. Dumas for the operations of exchange etc. As Dr. Franklin will have left us before Mr. Short's mission will commence, and I have never been concerned in the ceremonials of a treaty, I will thank you for your immediate information as to the papers he should be furnished with from hence. He will repair first to you in London, thence to the Hague, and so return to Paris.—What is become of Mr. Lambe? Supposing he was to call on the Commissioners for instructions, and thinking it best these should be in readiness, Dr. Franklin undertook to consult well the Barbary treaties with other nations, and to prepare a sketch which we should have sent for your correction. He tells me he has consulted those treaties, and made references to the articles proper for us, which however he shall not have time to put into form, but will leave them with me to reduce. As soon as I see them you shall hear from me.—A late conversation with an English gentleman here makes me beleive, what I did not believe before, that his nation think seriously that Congress have no power to form a treaty of commerce. As the explanations of this matter which you and I may separately give may be handed to their minister, it would be well that they should agree. For this reason, as well as for the hope of your shewing me wherein I am wrong, and confirming me where I am right, I will give you my creed on the subject. It is contained in these few principles. By the

Confederation Congress have no power given them in the first instance over the commerce of the states. But they have a power given them of entering into treaties of commerce, and these treaties may cover the whole feild of commerce, with two restrictions only. 1. That the states may impose equal duties on foreigners as natives, and 2. that they may prohibit the exportation or importation of any species of goods whatsoever. When they shall have entered into such treaty the superintendance of it results to them, all the operations of commerce which are protected by it's stipulations, come under their jurisdiction, and the power of the states to thwart them by their separate acts ceases. If Great Britain asks then why she should enter into treaty with us, why not carry on her commerce without treaty? I answer, because till a treaty is made no Consul of hers can be received (his functions being called into existence by a convention only, and the states having abandoned the right of separate agreements and treaties) no protection to her commerce can be given by Congress, no cover to it from those checks and discouragements with which the states will oppress it, acting separately and by fits and starts. That they will act so till a treaty is made, Great Britain has had several proofs, and I am convinced those proofs will become general. It is then to put her commerce with us on systematical ground, and under safe cover, that it behoves Great Britain to enter into treaty. And I own to you that my wish to enter into treaties with the other powers of Europe arises more from a desire of bringing all our commerce under the jurisdiction of Congress, than from any other views. Because, according to my idea, the commerce of the United states with those countries not under treaty with us, is under the jurisdiction of each state separately, but that of the countries which have treated with us is under the jurisdiction of Congress, with the two fundamental restraints only, which I have before noted.—I shall be happy to receive your corrections of these ideas as I have found in the course of our joint services that I think right when I think with you. I am with sincere affection Dear Sir Your friend and servt.,

TH: JEFFERSON

P.S. Monsr. Houdon has agreed to go to America to take the figure of General Washington. In case of his death between his departure from Paris and his return to it we may lose 20,000 livres. I ask the favour of you to enquire what it will cost to ensure that sum, on his life, in London, and to give me as early an answer as possible that I may order the insurance if I think the terms easy enough. He is I beleive between 30 and 35 years of age, healthy enough, and will be absent about 6 months.

Franklin and Jefferson to Adams

Passy July 8. 1785.

SIR

We duly received your letter of the 20th. of June and now in consequence thereof send you a draught of a treaty which we should be willing
to have proposed to the court of London. We have taken for our ground
work the original draught proposed to Denmark, making such alterations
and additions only as had occurred in the course of our negociations with
Prussia and Tuscany and which we thought were for the better. These
you will find in the 4th. 9th. 13th. and 25th. articles,[32] and are such as met
your approbation when we were considering those treaties. Nevertheless
we shall be happy to concur with you in any thing better which you may
wish to propose either in the original draught or the amendments. Particularly we wish it were possible to convince the British court that it
might be for their interest to continue their former bounties on the productions of our country on account of their quality, and of the nature of
the returns, which have always been in manufactures and not in money.

We have the honour to be with sentiments of the highest respect Sir
Your most obedt. and most humble servts.

Jefferson to Adams

Paris July 11. 1785.

DEAR SIR

Doctr. Franklin sets out this morning for Havre from whence he is to
cross over to Cowes there to be taken on board Capt. Truxen's ship bound
from London to Philadelphia. The Doctor's baggage will be contained in
150. or 200 boxes etc. We doubt that the laws of England will not permit
these things to be removed from one vessel into another; and it must be
attended with great difficulty, delay and expence should he be obliged to
enter them regularly merely to pass them from one vessel to another. Will
you be so good as to interest yourself (if it be necessary) to obtain a passport for these things or other letters which may protect them in the transfer from one vessel to another. The Doctor being extremely engaged in
the moment of departure I informed him that Mr. Harrison was setting
out for London today and that I would by him sollicit your interference

32. The full text of the proposed treaty is in JA's letter-book; the enclosure, with
alterations in the text of articles 4, 9, 13, 22, 24, and 25, is in Boyd, VIII, 274-75.

in this matter. You will judge best whether the orders had better be delivered to capt. Truxent or sent to Cowes. I rather think the last best, as they would put it in his power to land and store them and to discharge the vessel which carries them. Whatever is done should be speedily done. I am with sincere esteem Dr. Sir Your friend and servt.,

TH: JEFFERSON

Adams to Jefferson

Grosvenor Square Westminster, the Corner of
Duke and Brook Streets July 16th. 1785

DEAR SIR

I have been so perplexed with Ceremonials, Visits, Removals and eternal applications from Beggars of one Species and another, besides the real Business of my Department, that I fear I have not answered your favour of the second of June, which I received in Season. I have received from Mr. Garvey all but my wine and have written him to day to forward that and will run the risque of it, as I believe I shall easily obtain an order to receive it without paying duties. Petits Note of Expences [173 f. 8] which you paid, you either omitted to send me or I have lost it in the Confusion of a Removal, so that I must trouble you to send it again.

As to News Papers, I should advise you to apply to the Comte de Vergennes or Mr. Rayneval or Mr. Gennet the Premier Commis of the Bureau des Interpretes, who, I presume will readily order your Gazettes to come with their own, through the same Channel, free of Expence for Postage. The father of the present Mr. Gennet was so good as to oblige me in this way in the year 1780.

I wrote to you and Dr. Franklin on the 20th. of June, requesting you to send me a Project of a Treaty of Commerce with this Court, and proposed that agreed on with Prussia as the Model. Let me beg your answer to this as soon as possible.

The Doctor is to embark at Spithead or the Isle of White, on board of Captain Truckston as he tells me.

The proceedings at Boston make a Sensation here.[33] Yours most affectionately,

JOHN ADAMS

33. The merchants of Boston on April 15 and the mechanics on May 3 pledged themselves to make no purchases of British goods. Navigation acts were passed by the legislatures of Massachusetts and New Hampshire on June 23. Merrill Jensen, *The New Nation: A History of the United States during the Confederation, 1781-1789* (N. Y., 1950), 292-94.

Adams to Jefferson

Grosvenor Square July 18th. 1785

DEAR. SIR

Your favours of June 22d. and July 7 and 11th. are before me. The delay of Mr. Lamb's arrival is unfortunate, but I think with you that the sooner a project of Treaties is prepared the better, and I will give the earliest attention to it whenever you shall send it. I shall go this morning to Stockdale, to talk with him about sending you the News Papers, and Pamphlets through the Channell of Cleveland Row, i.e. Lord Carmarthens office.

I agree with pleasure to the appointment made by the Doctor and you of Mr. Short, to carry the treaty through London to the Hague, and in joining Mr. Dumas with him in making the Exchange. A Letter to him and another to Mr. Dumas signed by you and me, as the Doctor is gone, would be sufficient Authority: But I shall have no objection of giving each of them a more formal Commission under our Hands and seals, to be our Secretaries specially *pro hac Vice*. He must carry our original Commission to shew to the Baron De Thulemeyer and a Copy of it attested by Colo. Humphries to deliver him, and Mr. Dumas and he should see the Prussian Commission and receive an attested Copy of that. I do not think of any other Papers necessary.

I have given to Lord Carmarthen long ago, an Explanation of the power of Congress to form Treaties of Commerce, exactly conformable to that which you gave the English Gentleman, but I did not extend it to the Case of Consuls. He asked me no questions concerning Consuls, and I did not think it proper for me to say any thing on that subject, not having any Instructions. But I am not easy on that head. Mr. Temple talks of going out in three or four weeks, but I am very apprehensive he will meet with the difficulties you foresee.

I will enquire about insuring 20,000 Livres on the Life of Mr. Houdon. I have written to Mr. Frazier, the Under Secretary of State in Lord Carmarthens office, concerning Dr. Franklins Baggage, have stated the Circumstances as you State them to me, and have solicited the necessary Facilities. I hope for a favourable answer. Truxtun is to depart from hence on Thursday, and I will let him know the answer I may have.

I don't like the symptoms. Galloway, Deane, Chalmers, Watson are too much in favor. The Lottery for the Tories,[34] *although perhaps in Part*

34. The British State Lottery of 1785 was authorized by Parliament on recommendation of Prime Minister William Pitt in order to pay loyalist claims without additional taxation.

*inevitable, has been introduced with such pompous demonstrations of af-
fection and approbation as are neither wise, nor honest. There is too much
attention to the Navy, and there is another step, which allarms my apprehensions. Hanover is joining Prussia against the Views of the two
Imperial Courts at least in Bavaria.* Keep this as secret as the grave, but
search it to the botom where you are. *Does this indicate a Doubt Whether
our Business with De Thulemeyer* may be delayed? Does it indicate a
design in the *British Cabinet, to be Neutral* in order to be more *at Leisure
to deal with us? Can it be a Secret Understanding between St. James's
and Versailles? The disigns of ruining, if they can our carrying Trade, and
annihilating all our Navigation, and Seamen is too apparent.*[35] Yours
sincerely,

JOHN ADAMS

Adams to Jefferson

Grosvenor Square July 24th. 1785

DEAR SIR

I have a Letter from the Baron De Thulemeier of the 19th. and a Copy
of his Letter to you of the same date.[36] I hope now in a few Day's to take
Mr. Short by the hand in Grosvenor Square and to put my hand to the
treaty. I think no time should be lost. We will join Mr. Dumas with Mr.
Short in the Exchange if you please.

I applyed as you desired, and obtained the interposition of the Lords
Commissioners of the treasury, and the Commissioners of the Customs for
the transhipping of Dr. Franklin's Baggage. We have heared of the
Doctor's arrival at Rouen, but no further.

*The Britons Alliens Duty is a very burthensome Thing, and they may
carry it hereafter as far upon Tobacco, Rice Indigo and twenty other
Things, as they do now upon oil. To obviate this, I think of substituting
the words* "natural born Citizens of the United States," *and* "natural born
subjects of Great Britain," *instead of* "the most favoured Nation." *You
remember We first proposed to offer this to all Nations, but upon my ob-
jecting that the English would make their ships French or Sweedish or
Dutch etc. to avail themselves of it, without agreeing to it, on their Part,*

---

35. Italicized passages were written in code.
36. On July 24, 1785, JA wrote to De Thulemeier, "It is with great Pleasure I learn
that the Articles of the Treaty between his Prussian Majesty and the United States
are all agreed on mutual Satisfaction." Quoted in Boyd, VIII, 311*n*.

we altered it to the footing of "Gentis Amicissimae ["of the most-favored nation"]." But if the English will now agree to it, we shall secure ourselves against many odious Duties, and no ill Consequence can arise. It is true the French Dutch Sweeds and Prussians will of Course claim the Advantage, but as they must in return allow Us the same Advantage, so much the better. Let me know if any Objection occurs to you.[37]

There is a Bill before Parliament to prevent smuggling Tobacco, in which the restrictions are very rigorous, but cannot be effected. Two thirds of the Tobacco consumed in this Kingdom, I am told is Smuggled. How can it be otherwise, when the impost is five times the original Value of the Commodity. If one Pound in five escapes nothing is lost. If two in five, a great profit is made.

The Duty is 16d. pr. pound and tobacco sells for three pence. Yet all applications for lowering the Duty are rejected. Yours most affectionately,

JOHN ADAMS

Jefferson to Adams

Paris July 28. 1785.

DEAR SIR

Your favors of July 16. and 18. came to hand the same day on which I had received Baron Thulemeier's inclosing the ultimate draught for the treaty. As this draught, which was in French, was to be copied into the two instruments which Doctr. Franklin had signed, it is finished this day only. Mr. Short sets out immediately. I have put into his hands a letter of instructions how to conduct himself, which I have signed, leaving a space above for your signature. The two treaties I have signed at the left hand, Dr. Franklin having informed me that the signatures are read backwards. Besides the instructions to Mr. Short I signed also a letter to Mr. Dumas associating him with Mr. Short. These two letters I made out as nearly as I could to your ideas expressed in your letter of the 18th. If any thing more be necessary, be so good as to make a separate instruction for them signed by yourself, to which I will accede. I have not directed Mr. Dumas's letter. I have heretofore directed to him as 'Agent for the U.S. at the Hague' that being the description under which the journals of Congress speak of him. In his last letter to me is this paragraph. 'Mon nom à la Haie est assez connu, surtout au bureau de la poste, pour que mes lettres me

37. This paragraph was written in code.

soient rendus exactement, quand il n'y auroit d'autre direction.' [38] From this I conclude that the address I have used is not agreeable, and perhaps may be wrong. Will you be so good as to address the letter to him and to inform me how to address him hereafter? Mr. Short carries also the other papers necessary. His equipment for his journey requiring expences which cannot come into the account of ordinary expences, such as clothes etc. what allowance should be made him? I have supposed somewhere between a guinea a day and 1000 dollars a year which I beleive is the salary of a private secretary. This I mean as over and above his travelling expences. Be so good as to say, and I will give him an order on his return. The danger of robbery has induced me to furnish him with only money enough to carry him to London. You will be so good as to procure him enough to carry him to the Hague and back to Paris.

The Confederation of the K. of Prussia with some members of the Germanic body for the preservation of their constitution, is I think beyond a doubt. The Emperor has certainly complained of it in formal communications at several courts. By what can be collected from diplomatic conversation here I also conclude it tolerably certain that the Elector of Hanover has been invited to accede to the confederation and has done or is doing it. You will have better circumstances however, on the spot, to form a just judgment. Our matters with the first of these powers being now in conclusion, I wish it was so with the elector of Hanover. I conclude from the general expressions in your letter that little may be expected. Mr. Short furnishing so safe a conveyance that the trouble of the cypher may be dispensed with, I will thank you for such details of what has passed as may not be too troublesome to you.

The difficulties of getting books into Paris delayed for some time my receipt of the Corps diplomatique left by Dr. Franklin. Since that we have been engaged with expediting Mr. Short. A huge packet also brought by Mr. Mazzei has added to the causes which have as yet prevented me from examining Dr. Franklin's notes on the Barbary treaty. It shall be one of my first occupations. Still the possibility is too obvious that we may run counter to the instructions of Congress of which Mr. Lambe is said to be the bearer. There is a great impatience in America for these treaties. I am much distressed between this impatience, and the known will of Congress on the one hand, and the incertainty of the details committed to this tardy servant.

The D. of Dorset sets out for London tomorrow. He says he shall be absent two months. Some whisper that he will not return and that Ld. Carmarthen wishes to come here. I am sorry to lose so honest a man as the

38. "My name at the Hague is well enough known, especially at the post office, so that my letters should be delivered punctually, when no other address is given."

Duke. I take the liberty to ask an answer about the insurance of Houdon's life.

Congress is not likely to adjourn this summer. They have passed an ordinance for selling their lands.[39] I have not received it.

What would you think of the inclosed Draught [40] to be proposed to the courts of London and Versailles? I would add Madrid and Lisbon, but that they are still more desperate than the others. I know it goes beyond our powers; and beyond the powers of Congress too. But it is so evidently for the good of all the states that I should not be afraid to risk myself on it if you are of the same opinion. Consider it if you please and give me your thoughts on it by Mr. Short: but I do not communicate it to him nor any other mortal living but yourself. Be pleased to present me in the most friendly terms to the ladies and believe me to be with great esteem Dear Sir Your friend and servant,

TH: JEFFERSON

You say nothing in your letter about your wine at Auteuil. I think I sent you Petit's bill for I do not find it among my papers. It's amount was 173^{tt} [livres] 8s.

Jefferson to Adams

Paris July 31. 1785.

DEAR SIR

I was honoured yesterday with yours of the 24th. instant. When the *1st. article* of *our instructions* of May 7. 1784. was *under debate in Congress*, it was *proposed* that *neither party* should make *the other pay* in *their ports greater duties than* they *paid* in the *ports* of the *other*. One *objection* to this was *it's impracticability*, another *that it* would *put it* out *of our power to lay* such *duties* on *alien importation* as might *encourage importation* by *natives*. *Some members* much *attached* to *English policy* thought such a *distinction* should actually be *established*. *Some* thought the *power* to do it should be *reserved* in *case any* peculiar circumstances should *call for it, tho* under the present or *perhaps any* probable *circumstances they* did not *think* it would be *good policy* ever to *exercise* it. The

39. The Ordinance of May 20, 1785, establishing the public land system of the United States.

40. A draft treaty proposing reciprocal rights for citizens of one nation traveling in another. As Julian P. Boyd asserts, "If successfully carried out, it would have altered the very nature of the union and of the society of nations." First printed in Boyd, VIII, 317-19, 319-20*n*. See also above, 15.

footing gentis amicissimi was therefore *adopted* as you see in the *instruction*. As far as my enquiries enable me to judge *France and Holland* make no *distinction of duties between Aliens and natives*. I also rather believe that the *other states of Europe* make *none, England* excepted, to whom this *policy*, as that of her *navigation act, seems peculiar*. The question then *is*, *Should* we *disarm ourselves* of the *power to* make this *distinction against all nations* in order to *purchase an exemption* from the *Alien duties* in *England* only; for if we *put her importations* on the *footing of native*, all other *nations with whom we treat will* have a *right to claim the same*. I think we *should, because against other nations* who make no *distinction* in their *ports between us* and their *own subjects*, we ought *not to* make a *distinction in ours*. And *if the English* will *agree in like manner to* make none, we *should with equal reason abandon* the *right* as against *them*. I think all the *world would gain* by *setting commerce* at perfect *liberty*. I remember that when we were *digesting* the *general form of our treaty* this *proposition to put foreigners* and *natives on the same footing* was *considered*: and we were *all three (Dr. F.)* as *well as you* and *myself in favor of it. We* finally however *did not admit* it partly from the *objection* you *mention, but* more *still* on account of *our instructions. But tho'* the *English proclamation* had *appeared* in *America* at the time of *framing these instructions* I think it's *effect as to alien duties* had *not yet been experienced* and therefore was *not attended* to. *If it* had been *noted* in the *debate I am* sure that the *annihilation of our whale trade* would have been *thought too great a price to pay* for the *reservation of* a *barren power* which a *majority of the members* did not propose *ever to exercise tho* they were willing to *retain it. Stipulating equal rights for foreigners and natives we* obtain more in *foreign ports than* our *instructions required*, and *we* only *part* with, in *our own ports*, a *power* of which *sound policy* would *probably* for *ever forbid the exercise*. Add to this that *our treaty will be* for a very *short term*, and *if any* evil be *experienced under it*, a *reformation will soon* be in *our power. I am therefore* for *putting* this among *our original propositions* to the *court of London. If* it should *prove* an *insuperable obstacle with them, or if* it should *stand* in the way of *a greater advantage, we* can *but abandon* it in the *course* of the *negociation.*

In my copy of the cypher, on the Alphabetical side, numbers are wanting from 'Denmark' to 'disc' inclusive, and from 'gone' to 'governor' inclusive. I suppose them to have been omitted in copying. Will you be so good as to send them to me from yours by the first safe conveyance? Compliments to the ladies and to Colo. Smith from Dr. Sir Your friend and servant,[41]

Th: Jefferson

41. Italicized passages were written in code.

Adams to Jefferson

Grosvenor Square Augt. 4. 1785.

MY DEAR SIR

Yesterday our Friend Mr. Short arrived. Mr. Dumas had never any Commission from Congress, and therefore can have no Title under the United States. He never had any other Authorization than a Letter from Dr. Franklin and another from the Committee of Secret Correspondence, in the year 1775. I wish he had a regular Commission. I direct my Letters to Monsieur C. W. F. Dumas a la Haye, only. I should advise you to allow Mr. Short a Guinea a day except Sundays, which will amount to something near your Ideas.

Houdons Life may be insured for five Per Cent, two for the Life and three for the Voyage. I mentioned it at Table with several Merchants; they all agreed that it would not be done for less. But Dr. Price, who was present undertook to enquire and inform me. His answer is, that it may be done at an office in Hackney for five Per Cent. He cannot yet say for less, but will endeavour to reduce it a little. You may write to the Doctor to get it done, and he will reduce it, if possible. I will let you know by Mr. Short, how far I have ventured in conformity to the Propositions you inclose, knowing your sentiments before, but I think We had better wait sometime before We propose them any where else.

Mr. Samuel Watson a Citizen of the U. States, and settled at Charlestown S.C. as a Merchant, sailed from thence about two years ago, for the Havannah, and has not been heard of since, till lately a Gentleman from the Havannah has reported that a Mr. Watson from Charlestown was taken in the Bay of Mexico and carried into Carthagena, from thence sent to the Castle of St. Juan, de Ullua la Vera Cruz and afterwards sent to Trascala, where it is supposed he is at present. His Father and numerous Relations are very anxious for his Fate, and earnestly beg that you would interest yourself with the Comte D'Aranda and Mr. Charmichael for his Release, but if that cannot be had in full that you would endeavour to procure his removal to old Spain, that his Friends may hear from him, and gain Intelligence respecting the Property he may have left in Carolina. I have written to Charmichael, and intend to speak to Don Del Campo.

Pray send me the Arrêt against English Manufactures and every other new Arrêt, which may any Way affect the United States. It is confidently given out here that our Vessells are not admitted into the French W. Indias.

Has there been any new Arret, since that of August 1784? [42] Can you discover the Cause, of the great Ballance of Exchange in favour of England, from France, Spain, Holland, etc. as well as America? And whether this Appearance of Prosperity will continue? I think that at the Peace, the British Merchants sent their Factors abroad with immense quantities of their Manufactures, the whole Stock they had on hand. These Factors have sold as they could, and bought Remittances especially Bills of Exchange as they could, i.e. very dear, so that the loss on the Exchange is that of the British Merchant, and consequently that this appearance is not so much in favour of England. Spain I expect will follow the Example of France in prohibiting Brit. Manufactures, at least if Del Campo does not make a commercial Treaty with Woodward who is appointed to treat with him. But the Diplomaticks are of opinion nothing will be done with him, nor with Crawford. The two Years expire in January. If Crawford is likely to do any Thing be so good as to let me know it.

The words "Ship and Sailor," still turn the Heads of this People. They grudge to every other People, a single ship and a single seaman. The Consequence of this Envy, in the End, will be the loss of all their own. They seem at present to dread American Ships and Seamen more than any other. Their Jealousy of our Navigation is so strong, that it is odds if it does not stimulate them to hazard their own Revenue. I am, my dear Sir, with Sincere Esteem your Friend,

JOHN ADAMS

Jefferson to Adams

Paris Aug. 6. 1785.

DEAR SIR

I now inclose you a draught of a treaty for the Barbary states,[43] together with the notes Dr. Franklin left me. I have retained a presscopy of this draught, so that by referring to any article, line and word in it you can propose amendments and send them by the post without any body's being able to make much of the main subject. I shall be glad to receive any alterations you may think necessary as soon as convenient, that this matter may be in readiness. I inclose also a letter containing intelligence from

42. The Arrêt of Aug. 30, 1784, established seven free ports in the French West Indies and extended the list of imports permitted in American vessels, with some exceptions. L. C. Wroth and G. L. Annan, eds., *Acts of French Royal Administration ...prior to 1791* (N. Y., 1930), no. 1980.

43. "Draught of a Treaty of Amity and Commerce," printed in Boyd, VIII, 347-53.

Algiers. I know not how far it is to be relied on. My anxiety is extreme indeed as to these treaties. What are we to do? We know that Congress have decided ultimately to treat. We know how far they will go. But unfortunately we know also that a particular person has been charged with instructions for us, these five months who neither comes nor writes to us. What are we to do? It is my opinion that if Mr. Lambe does not come in either of the packets (English or French) now expected, we ought to proceed. I therefore propose to you this term, as the end of our expectations of him, and that if he does not come we send some other person. Dr. Bancroft or Capt. Jones occur to me as the fittest. If we consider the present object only, I think the former would be most proper: but if we look forward to the very probable event of war with those pirates, an important object would be obtained by Capt. Jones's becoming acquainted with their ports, force, tactics etc. Let me know your opinion on this. I have never mentioned it to either, but I suppose either might be induced to go. Present me affectionately to the ladies and Colo. Smith and be assured of the sincerity with which I am Dr. Sir Your friend and servt.,

TH: JEFFERSON

Adams to Jefferson

Grosvenor Square Westminster Aug. 7. 1785

DEAR SIR

As to the Cask of Wine at Auteuil, it is not paid for. If you will pay for it and take it, you will oblige me. By a sample of it, which I tasted it is good Wine, and very, extreamly cheap.

I am happy to find We agree so perfectly in the Change which is made in the Project. The Dye is cast. The Proposal is made. Let them ruminate upon it.

I thought of proposing a Tariff of Duties, that We might pay no more in their Ports than they should pay in ours. But their Taxes are so essential to their Credit, that it is impossible for them to part with any of them, and We should not choose to oblige ourselves to lay on as heavy ones. We are at Liberty to do it, however, when We please.

If the English will not abolish their Aliens Duty, relatively to us, We must establish an Alien Duty in all the United States. An Alien Duty against England alone will not answer the End. She will elude it by employing Dutch, French, Sweedish, or any other ships, and by frenchifying, dutchifying, or Sweedishizing her own Ships. If the English will persevere in excluding our Ships from their West India Islands, Canada, Nova Scotia, and Newfoundland, and in demanding any Alien Duty of us in their Ports within the Realm, and in refusing to amercian built Ships the Priviledges of british built Ships, We must take an higher Ground, a Vantage Ground. We must do more than lay on Alien Duties. We must take measures by which the Increase of Shipping and Seamen will be not only encouraged, but rendered inevitable. We must adopt in all the States the Regulations which were once made in England 5. Ric. 2. c. 3., and ordain that no American Citizen, or Denizen, or alien friend or Ennemy, shall ship any Merchandise out of, or into the United States and navigated with an American Captain and three fourths American Seamen. I should be sorry to adopt a Monopoly. But, driven to the necessity of it, I would not do Business by the Halves. The French deserve it of us as much as the English; for they are as much Ennemies to our Ships and Mariners. Their Navigation Acts are not quite so severe as those of Spain, Portugal and England, as they relate to their Colonies I mean. But they are not much less so. And they discover as strong a Lust to annihilate our navigation as any body.

Or might We modify a little? Might We lay a Duty of ten per Cent on all Goods imported in any but ships built in the United States, without saying any Thing about Seamen?

If We were to prohibit all foreign Vessells from carrying on our Coasting Trade, i.e. from trading from one State to another, and from one Port to another in the same State, We should do Something, for this Commerce will be so considerable as to employ many Ships and many Seamen, of so much the more Value to us as they will be always at home and ready for the Defence of their Country. But if We should only prohibit Importations, except in our own Bottoms or in the Bottoms of the Country or Nation of whose Growth or Production the Merchandises are, We should do nothing effectual against Great Britain. She would desire nothing better than to send her Productions to our Ports in her own Bottoms and bring away ours in return.

I hope the Members of Congress and the Legislatures of the States will study the British Acts of Navigation, and make themselves Masters of their Letter and Spirit, that they may judge how far they can be adopted by us, and indeed whether they are sufficient to do Justice to our Citizens in their Commerce with Great Britain.

There is another Enquiry which I hope our Countrymen will enter upon, and that is, what Articles of our Produce will bear a Duty upon Exportation? All such Duties are paid by the Consumer, and therefore are so much clear gain. Some of our Commodities will not bear any such

Duties; on the contrary, they will require Encouragement by Bounties: But I suspect that Several Articles would bear an handsome Impost.

We shall find our Commerce a complicated Machine and difficult to manage, and I fear We have not many Men, who have turned their Thoughts to it. It must be comprehended by Somebody in its System and in its detail, before it will be regulated as it should be. With great and Sincere Esteem I am dear Sir, your most obedient,

JOHN ADAMS

The Vacancy in your alphabet may be thus filled from points to points inclusive 1506. 970. 331. 504. 1186. 1268. 356. 517. 754. 1085. 269. 148. 205. 1318. 1258. 942. 712. 75. 246. 127. 609. 885. 1461. 837. 1327. and secondly, in like manner 472. 560. 820. 83.—Now give *me* leave. You make use of the number 1672. It has no meaning in my Cypher. Indeed there is a vacancy from 1596 to 1700 inclusive. When you have filled them up as you proposed I should thank you for a Copy by the first safe Conveyance etc.

Jefferson to Adams

Paris Aug. 10. 1785.

DEAR SIR

Your favor of the 4th. inst. came to hand yesterday. I now inclose you the two Arrets against the importation of foreign manufactures into this kingdom. The cause of the balance against this country in favor of England as well as it's amount is not agreed on. No doubt the rage for English manufactures must be a principal cause. The speculators in Exchange say also that those of the circumjacent countries who have a balance in their favor against France remit that balance to England from France. If so it is possible that the English may count this balance twice: that is, in summing their exports to one of those states, and their imports from it, they count the difference once in their favour: then a second time when they sum the remittances of cash they receive from France. There has been no arret relative to our commerce since that of Aug. 1784. and all the late advices from the French West Indies are that they have now in their ports always three times as many vessels as there ever were before, and that the increase is principally from our States. I have now no further fears of that arret's standing it's ground. When it shall become firm I do not think it's extension desperate. But whether the placing it on the firm basis of treaty be practicable is a very different question. As far as it is possible to judge from appearances I conjecture that Crawford will do nothing. I infer this from some things in his conversation, and from an expression of the Count de Vergennes in a conversation with me yesterday. I pressed upon him the importance of opening their ports freely to us in the moment of the oppressions of the English regulations against us and perhaps of the suspension of their commerce. He admitted it but said we had free ingress with our productions. I enumerated them to him and shewed him on what footing they were and how they might be improved. We are to have further conversations on the subject. I am afraid the voiage to Fontaine-bleau will interrupt them. From the enquiries I have made I find I cannot get a very small and indifferent house there for the season (that is, for a month) for less than 100. or 150 guineas. This is nearly the whole salary for the time and would leave nothing to eat. I therefore cannot accompany the court there, but I will endeavor to go occasionally there from Paris. They tell me it is the most favourable scene for business with the Count de Vergennes, because he is then more abstracted from the domestic applications. Count D'Aranda is not yet returned from the waters of Vichy. As soon as he returns I will apply to him in the case of Mr. Watson. I will pray you to insure Houdon's life from the 27th. of last month to his return to Paris. As he was to stay in America a month or two, he will probably be about 6 months absent: but the 3 per cent for the voiage being once paid I suppose they will ensure his life by the month whether his absence be longer or shorter. The sum to be insured is fifteen thousand livres tournois. If it be not necessary to pay the money immediately there is a prospect of exchange becoming more favourable. But whenever it is necessary be so good as to procure it by selling a draught on Mr. Grand which I will take care shall be honoured. Compliments to the ladies and am Dr. Sir Your friend and servt.,

TH: JEFFERSON

Jefferson to Adams

Paris Aug. 17. 1785.

DEAR SIR

I received yesterday your favor of the 7th. *This was 4. days later than* Mr. Short's of the *same date*. It *had evidently been opened. We must* therefore consider *both governments as possessed of it's contents.* I write you a line at this moment merely to inform you that *Mr. Barclay is willing* to *go to treat with* the *Barbary states if we desire it* and that *this will* not *take him from any employment here.* It will *only retard his voiage to America. Let me know your sentiments hereon.* The number 1672. is an error in the alphabetical side of the cypher. Turn to the numerical side and in the 11th. column and 72d. line you will see the number it should have been and what it was meant to signify. Correct your alphabetical side accordingly if it is wrong as mine was. We are told this morning that the *Cardinal Prince* of *Rohan* is *confined* to *his chamber* under *guard* for *reflections* on the *Queen who was present herself* in *council on his examination,* the first *time she* was ever *there* and the first *instance* of so *high an Ecclesiastical character* under actual *force.* Adieu. Your friend and servt.,[44]

TH: JEFFERSON

Adams to Jefferson

Grosvenor Square August 18. 1785

DEAR SIR

I have received your Favour of the 6. Aug. with the Notes and Project inclosed.

How can we send another Person? We have not in our Full Power authority to Substitute. Will not the Emperor and the Regencies feel their Dignity offended if a Person appears without a Commission from Congress? Do you mean that he should only agree upon the Terms and transmit them to Us to be signed? If you think this Method will do, I have no objection to either of the Persons you mention—nor to Mr. Short. Dr. Bancroft is the greatest Master of the French Language. If We conclude to send either he should take an attested Copy at least of all our Commissions for Africa, and a Letter and Instructions from Us. If there is any Truth in any of the Reports of Captures by the Algerines, Lambes Vessell may be taken by them.

Whoever is sent by us should be instructed to correspond constantly with us, and to send, by whatever conveyance he may find, whether thro' Spain France England Holland or otherwise, Copies of his Letters to us to Congress. He should be instructed farther to make dilligent Inquiry concerning the Productions of those Countries which would answer in America, and those of the United States which might find a Market in Barbary, and to transmit all such Information to Congress as well as to Us.

I have read over the Project with Care. The 17th. Article appears to be carried farther than our Countrymen will at present be willing to go. I presume the three last words of the third Line of this 17. Article must be

44. Italicized passages were written in code.

left out; and in the fourth line, the 7. 8. 9. 10. 11. and 12. Words; and in the Sixth Line the first, Second, third, fourth, and fifth Words.[45]

You have seen by this Time our Massachusetts Navigation Act, and the Reasonings and Dispositions of all the States tend the same Way at present, so that we must conform our Proceedings, as I suppose, to their Views. My Regards to Messrs. Humphreys, Mazzai, Williamos, etc. and believe me ever yours,

JOHN ADAMS

Mr. Short left us on Tuesday. Dr. Bancroft is just come in. This Letter will be delivered to you by Mr. James Smith, a Gentleman of South Carolina, a Relation of Mrs. Adams, whom I beg leave to introduce to you and recommend to your Civilities.

Abigail Adams to Jefferson

London Grosvenor Square August 21 1785

DEAR SIR

The Gentleman who is so kind as to convey this to you is from Carolina, his name is Smith. He is a distant relation of mine, tho I have not the pleasure of much acquaintance with him. He has resided in England some time, and bears a good Character here. Give me leave Sir to introduce him to your notice.

Mr. Short left us last Tuesday for the Hague. I did myself the honour of writing to you by him.

I find by the last papers from New York that Mr. Rutledge is appointed minister at the Hague; in the room of Mr. Livingstone who declined the embassy. There is no mention made of a secretary.

You will probably see our Massachusetts Navigation act before this reaches you; it has struck the hireling scriblers dumb. There has been less abuse against the Americans in the papers since the publication of it; than for a long time before.

Ireland has exerted herself, and Pharoah and his host are overthrown. The Courier of Europe will doubtless give you the debates. The July packet arrived last week, tho she left New York the seventh of July. She brought not a line of publick dispatch. A private Letter or two for Col. Smith, the contents of which we cannot know; as he is absent upon a Tour to Berlin.

I was much disapointed to find that my son had not arrived when the

45. The omissions from Article 17 advised by JA are shown in the text as printed in Boyd, VIII, 350.

packet saild. As the French packet sails sometime after the English, I am not without hopes that I may hear by that, and I will thank you sir to give me the earliest intelligence if she brings any account of the May packet.

Be so good as to present my Regards to Col Humphries. Mr. Short gives us some encouragement to expect him here this Winter. My Love to Miss Jefferson, to whom also my daughter desires to be remember'd. Our good old Friends the Abbes, I would tender my Regards. If I could write French, I would have scribled a line to the Abbe Arnou.

I think Madam Helvetius must be very melancholy now Franklin as she used to call him is gone. It is said here by a Gentleman lately from Philadelphia, that they determine to elect the Doctor president upon his arrival, as Mr. Dickinsons office expires in october.

In my Letter by Mr. Short I had taken the Liberty to request you to procure for me two or 3 articles, and to convey them by Col. Smith who talks of returning by way of Paris. But if he should not visit you, Mr. Smith when he returns will be so good as to take charge of them for me. But this I shall know in the course of a few weeks, and will take measures accordingly. I am sir with Sentiments of Esteem Your Humble Servant,

ABIGAIL ADAMS

Adams to Jefferson

Grosvenor Square Aug. 23. 1785

DEAR SIR

Last night, I received your Favour of the 17. If both Governments are possessed of the Contents of my letter of the 7th. by opening it in the Post Office, much good may those Contents do them. They both know they have deserved it. I hope it will convince them of their Error, and induce them to adopt more liberal Principles toward Us. I am for answering their Utmost Generosity with equal and indeed with greater Generosity. But I would not advise my Country to be the Bubble of her own Nobleness of Sentiment.

The Spirited Conduct of Ireland, I think will assist me, here. The News of the Reception in the Irish Parliament of the 20 Resolutions together with the Efforts in America towards a Navigation Act have raised my Hopes a good deal. But our States must mature their Plan and persevere in it, in order to effect the Work. In time, and with a Steady pursuit of our Purpose, I begin to think We shall prevail.

If Mr. Barclay will undertake the Voyage, I am for looking no farther. We cannot find a Steadier, or more prudent Man. He should look out for some Clerk or Companion who can write French and understands Italian.

When Dr. Price returns from his August Excursion to some Watering Place, I will get him to make the Insurance upon Houdons Life, on the best Terms he can. Adieu. Yours sincerely,

JOHN ADAMS

Jefferson to Abigail Adams

Paris Sep. 4. 1785.

DEAR MADAM

I was honoured with your letter of Aug. 21. by Mr. Smith who arrived here on the 29th. I am sorry you did not repeat the commission you had favoured me with by Mr. Short as the present would have been an excellent opportunity of sending the articles you wished for. As Mr. Short's return may yet be delayed, will you be so good as to write me by post what articles you desired, lest I should not otherwise know in time to send them by either of the Mr. Smiths. The French packet brought me letters from Mr. Jay and Dr. Ramsay only. They were dated July 13. They do not mention the arrival of your son. Dr. Ramsay's letter was on a particular subject, and Mr. Jay's letter was official. He may have arrived therefore, tho these letters do not mention it. However as he did not sail till June, and Westernly winds prevail in the summer I think the 13th. of July was too early to expect him to have arrived. I will certainly transmit you information of his arrival the moment I know it.

We have little new and interesting here. The Queen has determined to wear none but French gauzes hereafter. How many English looms will this put down? You will have seen the affair of the Cardinal de Rohan so well detailed in the Leyden gazette that I need add nothing on that head. The Cardinal is still in the Bastille. It is certain that the Queen has been compromitted without the smallest authority from her: and the probability is that the Cardinal has been duped into it by his mistress Madme. de la Motte. There results from this two consequences not to his honour, that he is a debauchee, and a booby. The Abbés are well. They have been kept in town this summer by the affairs of the Abbé Mably. I have at length procured a house in a situation much more pleasing to me than my present. It is at the grille des champs Elysees, but within the city. It suits me in every circumstance but the price, being dearer than the one I am now in. It has a clever garden to it. I will pray you to present my best respects to Miss Adams and to be assured of the respect and esteem with which I have the honour to be Dear Madam Your most obedient and most humble servt.,

TH: JEFFERSON

Jefferson to Adams

Paris Sep. 4. 1785.

DEAR SIR

On receipt of your favors of Aug. 18. and 23. I conferred with Mr. Barclay on the measures necessary to be taken to set our treaty with the pyratical states into motion through his agency. Supposing that we should begin with the emperor of Marocco, a letter to the emperor and instructions to Mr. Barclay seemed necessary. I have therefore sketched such outlines for these as appear to me to be proper.[46] You will be so good, as to detract, add to, or alter them as you please, to return such as you approve under your signature, to which I will add mine. A person understanding English, French and Italian, and at the same time meriting confidence, was not to be met with here. Colo. Franks understanding the two first languages perfectly, and a little Spanish instead of Italian, occurred to Mr. Barclay as the fittest person he could employ for a Secretary. We think his allowance (exclusive of his travelling expences and his board which will be paid by Mr. Barclay in common with his own) should be between 100 and 150 guineas a year. Fix it where you please between these limits. What is said in the instructions to Mr. Barclay as to his own allowance was proposed by himself. My idea as to the partition of the whole sum to which we are limited (80,000 D.) was that one half of it should be kept in reserve for the Algerines. They certainly possess more than half of the whole power of the Pyratical states. I thought then that Marocco might claim the half of the remainder, that is to say one fourth of the whole. For this reason in the instructions I propose 20,000 D. as the limits of the expences of the Marocco treaty. Be so good as to think of it, and to make it what you please. I should be more disposed to enlarge than abridge it on account of their neighborhood to our Atlantic trade. I did not think that these papers should be trusted through the post office, and therefore, as Colo. Franks is engaged in the business, he comes with

46. "Documents pertaining to the Mission of Barclay and Lamb to the Barbary States," Boyd, VIII, 610-24.

them. Passing by the diligence the whole expence will not exceed 12 or 14 guineas. I suppose we are bound to avail ourselves of the co-operation of France. I will join you therefore in any letter you think proper to write to the Count de Vergennes. Would you think it expedient to write to Mr. Carmichael to interest the interposition of the Spanish court? I will join you in any thing of this kind you will originate. In short be so good as to supply whatever you may think necessary. With respect to the money Mr. Jay's information to you was that it was to be drawn from Holland. It will rest therefore with you to avail Mr. Barclay of that fund either by your draughts, or by a letter of credit to the bankers in his favour to the necessary amount. I imagine the Dutch Consul at Marocco may be rendered an useful character in the remittances of money to Mr. Barclay while at Marocco.

You were apprised, by a letter from Mr. Short, of the delay which had arisen in the execution of the treaty with Prussia.[47] I wrote a separate letter of which I inclose you a copy, hoping it would meet one from you and set them again into motion. I have the honour to be with the highest respect Dear Sir Your most obedient and most humble servt.,

TH: JEFFERSON

Jefferson to Adams

Paris Sep. 4. 1785.

DEAR SIR

Mr. Mazzei, during the war was employed by the state of Virginia to procure them loans of money in Europe. He thinks that in allowing him for his expences they have allowed less than they actually were. You knew him in Paris, and knew of the journies which he made. I would thank you for the best guess you can make of what his expences may have been, according to the stile in which you observed him to live. My object is to have justice done him, if it has not been done, being assured that if the state has failed in this point, it has been from a want of evidence and that they will rectify their error if they find they have committed one. I am with the highest esteem Dr. Sir Your friend and servant,

TH: JEFFERSON

47. De Thulemeier objected to an English column in the treaty, and TJ informed Dumas and Short that "we should agree to consider the French column as the original if the Baron de Thulemeyer thinks himself bound to insist upon it." *Ibid.*, 459.

Jefferson to Adams

Paris Sep. 4. 1785.

DEAR SIR

Since writing my letter of this morning I have seen Mr. Grand and had a conversation with him on the subject of the interest due here. He is pressed on that subject. By a letter he received not long since from the Commissioners of the treasury it seems their intention that he should pay this interest out of the money in Holland, yet they omitted to give him any authority to ask for any of that money. I thought it possible they might have written to you on the subject and told him I would take the liberty of asking whether you had been desired to do any thing. It is a little unfortunate that our credit should be losing ground for default of paiment while money is understood to be lying dead, and sufficient for that purpose. The Commissioners themselves made this reflection in their letter. If you can give us any information on this subject I will thank you. I am with much esteem Dr. Sir Your friend and servt.,

TH: JEFFERSON

Adams to Jefferson

Grosvenor Square Westminster Septr. 4. 1785

DEAR SIR

I have received three Letter[s] of the Tenor and Date of the within. I cannot find in any Gazetteer or geographical Dictionary any Such Place as Roscoff, and I can make nothing of the Story.[48] I hope you have more Skill in Divination.

I have no Letters from Congress, nor any Answer from the Ministry.

Pray what are the Sentiments in France upon the American Acts of Navigation? And what has been the Success of the French Whale Fishery?

48. The case of Lister Asquith of Baltimore, owner of the schooner *William and Catherine*, which put into a Breton port on Aug. 8, 1785, in distress. Since her cargo was exclusively tobacco, it was seized as an illegal entry. Asquith, along with five others on board, was arrested by agents of the Farmers' General (the tobacco monopoly) and imprisoned. Asquith appealed to TJ in Paris who applied to Vergennes on their behalf, Nov. 14, 1785. Boyd, VIII, 477-78; IX, 31-38.

How many Ships have they sent out this Year? The Britons have introduced into theirs a Spirit of Gambling, by giving a Bounty of 500 £ to the Ship which has the greatest Success; 400 £ to the next. This will make many Adventurers and give a temporary Activity to the Business: But I rely upon it both the French and English Essays will fall through. My Reason for thinking so is, because the Business in itself is not profitable, and, excepting the four Vessells which may obtain the Bounties, the others upon an Avarage will be loosers. I know that my Countrymen in the best Times, with all their frugality, with all their Skill, and with their particular manner of conducting the Business could but barely live, and the Fishery was valuable to Us, only as a Remittance. The English are Sacrificing the Bread of thousands of their best Manufacturers to the interested Schemes of a very few Individuals and to a narrow Prejudice and a little Jealousy: but I dont believe the Delusion will be durable. Time will Shew, both them and the French, that it is better to buy our Oil and Candles and Fins, and pay for them in Buttons and Ribbons. If they dont discover their Error, We will lay on Duties upon Buttons and Ribbons, equal to the Alien Duties, and grant them out again in Bounties to our Whalemen.

We must not, my Friend, be the Bubbles of our own Liberal Sentiments. If We cannot obtain reciprocal Liberality, We must adopt reciprocal Prohibitions, Exclusions, Monopolies, and Imposts. Our offers have been fair, more than fair. If they are rejected, we must not be the Dupes. With great Esteem, dear Sir, yours,

JOHN ADAMS

Abigail Adams to Jefferson

London Septr. 6 1785

DEAR SIR

I cannot omit by this opportunity acquainting you that on Sunday the August packet arrived in which came Mr. Church and brought us Letters from our son to our no small joy. He arrived the 17 of july after a very tedious passage. He was however in good Health and Spirits. Mr. Adams has at Length received some Letters from the president, from Mr. Jay and a private Letter from Mr. Gerry, together with some newspapers and journals of Congress. The papers contain nothing very material. Mr. Osgood, Mr. Walter Livingston and Mr. Arthur Lee are the commissioners of the Treasury. Mr. Lee was chosen a few days before the sailing of the packet and was just gone from New York. It is said that the commissioners will have a difficult task to bring order out of the confusion in which the late financier left the office. Mr. Rutledge had not accepted his appointment when the gentlemen wrote. Mr. Jay writes that about the 29 of May Lambe sent for the papers from Congress, that they were sent, and that he saild soon after.

They are very anxious in America with respect to the posts,[49] especially since a reinforcement of troops have been sent out. The merchants say that the trade is worth annually 50.000 pounds sterling.

From the present movements here, there is no great prospect of obtaining them by fair means. *The prospect here,* is not the pleasentest in the World. But I must recollect this is to go by the post. Mr. A. is very buisy writing to New York as Mr. Storer is going out in a few days. He desires me to inform you that he would take any dispatches you may have provided you could trust them here. Mr. Storer was formerly private Secretary to Mr. Adams. I will tuck this in one corner of Mr. A's Letter. Yours etc.

Adams to Jefferson

Grosvr. Square 11th. Septemr. 1785.

DEAR SIR

In answer to your enquiry in your letter of the 4th. inst. I can only say that I knew Mr. Matzei at Paris and that he made long journeys. But in what stile he lived and at what expence he travelled I know not. He always made a genteel appearance without any unnecessary show, and kept good Company wherever he went. I observed this in Paris and heard of it in Holland. In Italy it could not be otherwise, for he is well known and esteemed there as I have always heard and particularly within these few days from the Genoese Ambassador and General Paoli; both of whom enquired of me, very respectfully, after Mr. Mazzei, at the Drawing Room, of their own motion. Knowing as you and I do how little way a thousand pounds go, in expences of living, if I were to guess at his expences, altho' he had not a house and train of Servants to maintain, nor a table that I know of, yet, considering the indispensible article of Cloaths, Carriage, Postage and Stationary, as well as the ordinary expences of Apartments, travelling and all the rest, I could not undertake to pay his way for a less Sum. I am, dear Sir, Yrs: etc: etc.

49. The western posts of defense and the fur trade, Detroit, Michilimackinac, Oswego, Niagara, etc., were still occupied by the British, contrary to the peace treaty of 1783. Samuel F. Bemis, *Jay's Treaty: A Study in Commerce and Diplomacy* (N. Y., 1923), 1-20.

Adams to Jefferson

Grosvenor Square Westminster Septr. 11. 1785.

Dear Sir

In Answer to your Favour of September 4. I am sorry to inform you that I have not received one line from the Commissioners of the Treasury, nor from Congress, nor any of their Ministers, respecting the Interest due in France. It is possible Messieurs Willinks and Van Staphorsts may, or possibly the orders may have been suspended to be sent by the Minister to the Hague, when they can find one who will venture to Europe under the present Regulations.

The System of having no Ministers in Europe has involved our Country in so many Inconveniences that I fancy it will go out of Fashion. It would be well to send Consuls, I think, who, upon Permission to trade, would serve without Salaries, if We cannot afford the salaries of Ministers. I am with great Respect, sir, your Friend and Servant,

JOHN ADAMS

Adams to Jefferson

Grosvenor Square Septr. 15. 1785

Dear Sir

I have received your Letter of the fourth instant by Colonel Franks, with a Project of a Letter to the Emperor of Morocco, and several other Papers.

I have had this Letter, fairly copied, with very few and very inconsiderable Alterations and have signed it. I have left room enough, at the Beginning, for you to insert, or leave Mr. Barclay to insert, the Emperors Titles and Address, which may be done, with the most certainty in Morocco.

By the Treaty We have with Holland, the States General have agreed, upon Requisition, to second our negotiations in the most favourable manner, by means of their Consuls. I would have prepared a Memorial and Requisition to that Purpose and have sent it to the Hague, But such a Memorial would publish to all the World Mr. Barclays Mission. I Shall wait for your Advice, and if you think proper, I will Still Send a Memorial.

But I am inclined to think We had better wait till We receive from Mr. Barclay in Morocco some account of his Prospects.

The best Argument Mr. Barclay can use, to obtain Treaties upon moderate Terms, is that We have absolutely as yet no Ships in the Mediterranean Sea, and shall have none untill Treaties are made. That our Seamen will not go there, untill Treaties are made. That therefore the Algerines will have no Chance of taking any American Vessells, any where but in the Atlantic, and there they can expect to take but very few, at a vast Expence of Corsairs, and exposed to our Privateers and Frigates.

Treaties of Peace are very unpopular, with the People of Algiers. They say it is taking from them all the Opportunities of making Profits by Prizes for the sake of inriching the Dey by Presents. The Probability then that our Trade would be more beneficial to the People, than the Few Prizes they would have a chance to make, by going at a vast Expence out of the Mediterranean and spreading themselves over the Ocean in quest of our ships, exposed to our Frigates and the Men of War of Portugal, etc. would be the best Reason for the Dey to use with the People. The common Argument is the Bombardments and Depredations with which their Ennemies threaten them by their Fleets and Squadrons, which commonly accompany the Embassy. Mr. Barclay will be very naked in this respect. With great Respect, your most obedient

John Adams

Adams to Jefferson

Grosvenor Square Septr. 16. 1785

Dear [Sir]

At the desire of the Baron De Poellnitz, I do myself the Honour to introduce him to you. This Nobleman you know married a Daughter of the Earl of Bute once the Wife of Earl Piercy. They have lived some time in New York. He goes to France to meet his Lady who arrived there sometime since.

Coll. Franks will leave Us tomorrow. There are abroad so many infamous Fictions concerning the Captures made by the Algeriens, that I still hope the Report of their Advertizing American Vessells and Cargoes for sale, is without a better foundation. With great Esteem Your Friend and Servant,

John Adams

Adams to Jefferson

Grosvenor Square 18 Sepr. 1785

Dear Sir

Inclosed, you have in Confidence some Compliments. Give me in confidence your Opinion of them. Is there any thing said by me which I ought not to have said? Is there any expression exceptionable? Have I compromised myself or the public in any thing? more than ought to be—

The Custom of making a Speech is so settled, that not only, the Secretary of State and the Master of the Ceremonies, but some of the Foreign Ministers, took the pains to inform me it was indispensable; otherwise being sensible of the difficulty of being complaisant enough without being too much, I intended to have delivered my Credentials, without saying more, than that they were Credentials to his Majesty from the United States. Your Friend.

Jefferson to Adams

Sep. 19. 1785. Paris.

Lambe is *arrived. He brings new full powers* to *us* from *Congress* to *appoint persons* to *negotiate with* the *Barbary states,* but *we* are to *sign* the *treaties. Lambe has* not *even a recommendation* from *them* to *us,* but it seems clear that *he would* be *approved* by *them. I told him* of *Mr. Barclay's appointment* to *Marocco* and *proposed Algiers* to *him. He agrees. A small alteration* in the *form* of *our dispatches* will be *necessary,* and of *course* another *courier shall* be *dispatched* to *you* on the *return* of *Colo. Franks,* for *your pleasure herein.*[50]

Jefferson to Adams

Paris Sep. 24. 1785.

Dear Sir

My letter of Sep. 19. written the morning after Mr. Lamb's arrival here, would inform you of that circumstance. I transmit you herewith copies of the papers he brought to us on the subject of the Barbary treaties. You

50. Italicized passages were written in code.

will see by them that Congress has adopted the very plan which we were proposing to pursue. It will now go on under less danger of objection from the other parties. The receipt of these new papers therefore has rendered necessary no change in matter of substance in the dispatches we had prepared. But they render some formal changes necessary. For instance in our letter of credence for Mr. Barclay to the Emperor of Marocco, it becomes improper to enter into those explanations which seemed proper when that letter was drawn; because Congress in their letter enter into that explanation. In the letter to the Ct. de Vergennes it became proper to mention the new full powers received from Congress and which in some measure accord with the idea communicated by him to us from the M. de Castries. These and other formal alterations, which appeared necessary to me, I have made, leaving so much of the original draughts approved and amended by you as were not inconsistent with these alterations. I have therefore had them prepared fair to save you the trouble of copying; yet wherever you chuse to make alterations you will be so good as to make them; taking in that case the trouble of having new fair copies made out.

You will perceive by Mr. Jay's letter that Congress had not thought proper to give Mr. Lamb any appointment. I imagine they apprehended it might interfere with measures actually taken by us. Notwithstanding the perfect freedom which they are pleased to leave to us on his subject, I cannot feel myself clear of that bias which a presumption of their pleasure gives, and ought to give. I presume that Mr. Lamb met their approbation, because of the recommendations he carried from the Governor and state of Connecticut, because of his actual knowlege of the country and people of the states of Barbary, because of the detention of these letters from March to July, which considering their pressing nature would otherwise have been sent by other Americans who in the mean time have come from N. York to Paris; and because too of the information we received by Mr. Jarvis. These reasons are not strong enough to set aside our appointment of Mr. Barclay to Marocco: that I think should go on, as no man could be sent who would enjoy more the confidence of Congress. But they are strong enough to induce me to propose to you the appointment of Lamb to Algiers. He has followed for many years the Barbary trade and seems intimately acquainted with those states. I have not seen enough of him to judge of his abilities. He seems not deficient as far as I can see, and the footing on which he comes must furnish a presumption for what we do not see. We must say the same as to his integrity; we must rely for this on the recommendations he brings, as it is impossible for us to judge of this for ourselves. Yet it will be our duty to use such reasonable cautions as are in our power. Two occur to me. 1. To give him a clerk capable of assisting and attending to his proceedings and who, in case he thought any thing was going amiss, might give us information. 2. Not to give a credit on Van Staphorst and Willinck, but let his draughts be made on yourself, which with the knowlege you will have of his proceedings, will enable you to check them, if you are sensible of any abuse intended. This will give you trouble; but as I have never found you declining trouble when it is necessary, I venture to propose it. I hope it will not expose you to inconvenience as by instructing Lamb to insert in his draughts a proper usance you can in the mean time raise the money for them by drawing on Holland. I must inform you that Mr. Barclay wishes to be put on the same footing with Mr. Lamb as to this article and therefore I return you your letter of Credit on Van Staphorsts & co. As to the 1st. article there is great difficulty. There is no body at Paris fit for the undertaking who would be likely to accept of it. I mean there is no American, for I should be anxious to place a native in the trust. Perhaps you can send us one from London. There is a Mr. Randolph there from New York whom Mr. Barclay thinks might be relied on very firmly for integrity and capacity. He is there for his health: perhaps you can persuade him to go to Algiers in pursuit of it. If you cannot, I really know not what will be done. It is impossible to propose to Bancroft to go in a secondary capacity. Mr. Barclay and myself have thought of Cairnes at l'Orient as a dernier resort. But it is incertain, or rather improbable that he will undertake it. You will be pleased in the first place to consider of my proposition to send Lamb to Algiers, and in the next all the circumstances before detailed as consequences of that. The inclosed letter from Richard O'Bryan furnishes powerful motives for commencing, by some means or other, the treaty with Algiers more immediately than would be done if left on Mr. Barclay. You will perceive by that that two of our vessels with their crews and cargoes have been carried captive into that port. What is to be done as to those poor people? I am for hazarding the supplementory instruction to Lamb which accompanies these papers. Alter it or reject it as you please. You ask what I think of claiming the Dutch interposition. I doubt the fidelity of any interposition too much to desire it sincerely. Our letters to this court heretofore seemed to oblige us to communicate with them on the subject. If you think the Dutch would take amiss our not applying to them, I will join you in the application. Otherwise the fewer are apprised of our proceedings the better. To communicate them to the States of Holland is to communicate them to the whole world.

Mr. Short returned last night and brought the Prussian treaty duly executed in English and French. We may send it to Congress by the Mr. Fitzhughs going from hence. Will you draw and sign a short letter for that purpose? I send you a copy of a letter received from the

M. Fayette. In the present unsettled state of American commerce, I had as lieve avoid all further treaties except with American powers. If Count Merci therefore does not propose the subject to me, I shall not to him, nor do more than decency requires if he does propose it. I am with great esteem Dr. Sir your most obedient humble servt.,

TH: JEFFERSON

Jefferson to Adams

Paris Sep. 24. 1785.

DEAR SIR

I have received your favor of the 18th. inclosing your compliments on your presentation. The sentiments you therein expressed were such as were entertained in America till the Commercial proclamation, and such as would again return were a rational conduct to be adopted by Gr. Britain. I think therefore you by no means compromitted yourself or our country, nor expressed more than it would be our interest to encourage, if they were disposed to meet us. I am pleased however to see the answer of the king. It bears the marks of suddenness and surprize, and as he seems not to have had time for reflection we may suppose he was obliged to find his answer in the real sentiments of his heart, if that heart has any sentiment. I have no doubt however that it contains the real creed of an Englishman, and that the word which he has let escape is the true word of the ænigma, "The moment I see such sentiments as yours prevail and a disposition to give this country *the preference*, I will etc." All this I stedfastly beleive. But the condition is impossible. Our interest calls for a perfect equality in our conduct towards these two nations; but no preferences any where. If however circumstances should ever oblige us to shew a preference, a respect for our character, if we had no better motive, would decide to which it should be given. My letters from members of Congress render it doubtful whether they would not rather that full time should be given for the present disposition of America to mature itself and to produce a permanent improvement in the federal constitution, rather than, by removing the incentive, to prevent the improvement. It is certain that our commerce is in agonies at present, and that these would be relieved by opening the British ports in the W. Indies. It remains to consider whether a temporary continuance under these sufferings would be paid for by the amendment it is likely to produce. However I beleive there is no fear that Great Britain will puzzle us by leaving it in our choice to hasten or delay a treaty.

Is insurance made on Houdon's life? I am uneasy about it, lest we should hear of any accident. As yet there is no reason to doubt their safe passage. If the insurance is not made I will pray you to have it done immediately.

As I have not received any London newspapers as yet I am obliged to ask you what is done as to them, lest the delay should proceed from some obstacle to be removed. There is a Mr. Thompson at Dover who has proposed to me a method of getting them post free: but I have declined resorting to it till I should know in what train the matter is actually. I have the honour to be with the most perfect esteem Dear Sir Your friend and servt,.

TH: JEFFERSON

Jefferson to Abigail Adams

Paris Sep. 25. 1785.

DEAR MADAM

Mr. Short's return the night before last availed me of your favour of Aug. 12. I immediately ordered the shoes you desired which will be ready tomorrow. I am not certain whether this will be in time for the departure of Mr. Barclay or of Colo. Franks, for it is not yet decided which of them goes to London. I have also procured for you three plateaux de dessert with a silvered ballustrade round them, and four figures of Biscuit. The former cost 192^{tt}, the latter 12^{tt} each, making together 240 livres or 10. Louis. The merchant undertakes to send them by the way of Rouen through the hands of Mr. Garvey and to have them delivered in London. There will be some additional expences of packing, transportation and duties here. Those in England I imagine you can save. When I know the amount I will inform you of it, but there will be no occasion to remit it here. With respect to the figures I could only find three of those you named, matched in size. These were Minerva, Diana, and Apollo. I was obliged to add a fourth, unguided by your choice. They offered me a fine Venus; but I thought it out of taste to have two at table at the same time. Paris and Helen were presented. I conceived it would be cruel to remove them from their peculiar shrine. When they shall pass the Atlantic, it will be to sing a requiem over our freedom and happiness. At length a fine Mars was offered, calm, bold, his faulchion not drawn, but ready to be drawn. This will do, thinks I, for the table of the American Minister in

London, where those whom it may concern may look and learn that though Wisdom is our guide, and the Song and Chase our supreme delight, yet we offer adoration to that tutelar god also who rocked the cradle of our birth, who has accepted our infant offerings, and has shewn himself the patron of our rights and avenger of our wrongs. The groupe then was closed, and your party formed. Envy and malice will never be quiet. I hear it already whispered to you that in admitting Minerva to your table I have departed from the principle which made me reject Venus: in plain English that I have paid a just respect to the daughter but failed to the mother. No Madam, my respect to both is sincere. Wisdom, I know, is social. She seeks her fellows. But Beauty is jealous, and illy bears the presence of a rival—but, Allons, let us turn over another leaf, and begin the next chapter. I receive by Mr. Short a budget of London papers. They teem with every horror of which human nature is capable. Assassinations, suicides, thefts, robberies, and, what is worse than assassination, theft, suicide or robbery, the blackest slanders! Indeed the man must be of rock, who can stand all this; to Mr. Adams it will be but one victory the more. It would have illy suited me. I do not love difficulties. I am fond of quiet, willing to do my duty, but irritable by slander and apt to be forced by it to abandon my post. These are weaknesses from which reason and your counsels will preserve Mr. Adams. I fancy it must be the quantity of animal food eaten by the English which renders their character insusceptible of civilisation. I suspect it is in their kitchens and not in their churches that their reformation must be worked, and that Missionaries of that description from hence would avail more than those who should endeavor to tame them by precepts of religion or philosophy. But what do the foolish printers of America mean by retailing all this stuff in our papers? As if it was not enough to be slandered by one's enemies without circulating the slanders among his friends also.

To shew you how willingly I shall ever receive and execute your commissions, I venture to impose one on you. From what I recollect of the diaper and damask we used to import from England I think they were better and cheaper than here. You are well acquainted with those of both countries. If you are of the same opinion I would trouble you to send me two sets of table cloths and napkins for 20 covers each, by Colo. Franks or Mr. Barclay who will bring them to me. But if you think they can be better got here I would rather avoid the trouble this commission will give. I inclose you a specimen of what is offered me at 100. livres for the table cloth and 12 napkins. I suppose that, of the same quality, a table cloth 2. aunes wide and 4. aunes long, and 20 napkins of 1. aune each, would cost 7. guineas.—I shall certainly charge the publick my house rent and court taxes. I shall do more. I shall charge my outfit. Without this I can never get out of debt. I think it will be allowed. Congress is too reasonable to expect, where no imprudent expences are incurred, none but those which are required by a decent respect to the mantle with which they cover the public servants, that such expences should be left as a burthen on our private fortunes. But when writing to you, I fancy myself at Auteuil, and chatter on till the last page of my paper awakes me from my reverie, and tells me it is time to assure you of the sincere respect and esteem with which I have the honour to be Dear Madam your most obedient and most humble servt.,

TH: JEFFERSON

P.S. The cask of wine at Auteuil, I take chearfully. I suppose the seller will apply to me for the price. Otherwise, as I do not know who he is, I shall not be able to find him out.

3

"As We are poor We ought to be Œconomists"

THE MOST critical diplomatic question confronting Adams and Jefferson was that of trade relations. In a report to Foreign Secretary Jay on October 11, 1785, Jefferson summarized the situation with respect to commercial treaties negotiated by the American commissioners. The treaty with Prussia had been concluded in July; discussions with other nations were in process, but the results were not assured.[1] In bargaining for the trade so desperately needed, the diplomats would have to take as firm a stand as possible. But always the ebb and flow of power politics must be closely watched.

Both Adams and Jefferson knew that the true test of American diplomacy would come in negotiations with Great Britain and France. To Jay, in the same report, Jefferson observed that "England shews no disposition to treat." As for France he thought that even if her ministers should "be able to keep the ground of the arret of August 1784, against the clamours of her merchants, and should they be disposed hereafter to give us more, it is not probable she will bind herself to it by treaty, but keep her regulations dependent on her own will." [2] This proved to be an accurate prediction.

Although the American treaty of amity and commerce with France guaranteed most-favored-nation treatment, discrimination against Americans strained friendly relations between the two countries. Jefferson sought to preserve amicable relations "by approaching the condition of their citizens reciprocally to that of *natives*, as a better

1. TJ to Jay, Oct. 11, 1785, Boyd, VIII, 608.
2. On the Arrêt of Aug. 1784, see above, 49, n. 42.

ground of intercourse than that of *the most favoured nation*." [3] Since
the navigation acts of Massachusetts, New Hampshire, and other states
affected French trade adversely, Jefferson found them embarrassing;
furthermore, it was difficult to explain technicalities of American law
that threatened to deny the French heirs of General Edward Oglethorpe their claims in Georgia.[4]

During months of frustrating negotiation as the envoys of a weak
Republic, one accomplishment must have reassured Adams and Jefferson as "œconomists." American spermaceti oil and candles were admitted to French markets, though for a limited period. Before the
Revolution, this had been a lucrative but highly competitive business,
based upon the famous whaling industry of Nantucket and whale-oil
distribution by the merchants of Rhode Island and Massachusetts. The
product of highest quality was spermaceti oil from the sperm whale,
and spermaceti candles, a by-product of great popularity. No nation
had competed successfully in this industry with the New Englanders;
their merchants had even achieved a sort of trade association to which
they adhered for brief periods.[5]

But the whale fishery had been demoralized during the War for
Independence and the chief markets in Great Britain and her island
colonies had been swept away. In the process of post-war reorganiza-
tion, confronted by prohibitive British duties on oil, the New Englanders turned to France.[6] In the fall of 1785 Thomas Boylston, a "solid
capitalist" of Boston, was endeavoring through diplomatic channels
to introduce a cargo of spermaceti oil into France with remission of
duties. About the same time Nathaniel Barrett, agent for several Boston
merchants, was seeking a general agreement for developing the trade
in France. His proposal impressed Jefferson more favorably than Boylston's which was on an individual basis.[7] As a New Englander Adams
became enthusiastic over the prospects of illuminating French cities
"with our fine White Sperma Coetic Oil, and their Churches and

3. TJ to Vergennes, Nov. 20, 1785, Boyd, IX, 51.
4. TJ to Governor of Georgia, Dec. 22, 1785, *ibid.*, 120-21; TJ to JA, Feb. 7, 1786,
below, 118.
5. Jefferson, "Observations on the Whale Fishing," Boyd, XIV, 242-54; James B.
Hedges, *The Browns of Providence Plantations: Colonial Years* (Cambridge, 1952),
Chap. V.
6. Hedges, *Browns of Providence*, 295-96, 309-10; Louis Gottschalk, *Lafayette between the American and the French Revolution (1783-1789)* (Chicago, 1950), 221.
7. TJ to JA, Nov. 19, Dec. 10, 1785, below, 94, 104-5.

Families with our beautifull Sperma Coeti Candles." [8] Through the good offices of Lafayette, who had direct approach to M. Tourtille Sangrain, sole contractor for public lighting in Paris and other cities, Jefferson negotiated the removal of the duties on spermaceti oil for one year and secured French credit for the Boston merchants to buy the oil and ship it to France.[9]

To secure an equitable arrangement with Britain, however, seemed impossible. Adams hoped that preferences given to the French might force the issue; indeed he went so far as to suggest that "the thirteen States must each pass a Navigation Act," though only against British merchandise.[10] Jefferson preferred to transfer this power to Congress to assure more effective retaliation and perhaps bring about a commercial treaty with America's best pre-war customer.[11] The stubborn stand of the British embittered both ministers, for it challenged the political independence of the United States by means of economic pressure. "In this Country," wrote Mrs. Adams wryly from London, "there is a great want of many French comodities, Good Sense, Good Nature, Political Wisdom and benevolence." [12]

Despite their failure to conclude a commercial treaty with England, Adams and Jefferson could report some progress in their negotiations, in addition to the treaty with Prussia. When Congress commissioned Jefferson in 1784, it authorized a commercial treaty with Austria. Franklin had made an earlier gesture, but the Emperor had been waiting for an American minister to initiate the conversation.[13] During Lafayette's visit to Vienna in September 1785 he assumed the role of unofficial envoy of good will, suggesting "liberal treaties, that would oppen the door to American importations in order to pay for Austrian goods." [14] But the Emperor moved so slowly that the two-year-old commission from Congress expired before a final agreement could be reached.

More promising were Adams's negotiations with the Portuguese envoy extraordinary, the Chevalier de Pinto, in London. At Adams's

8. JA to TJ, Nov. 1, 1785, below, 87; JA to De Thulemeier, July 24, 1785, Boyd, VIII, 311.
9. TJ to JA, Dec. 27, 1785, and JA to TJ, Jan. 19, 1786, below, 111, 116; Gottschalk, *Lafayette*, 165-67, 205, 208-9, 211. See also below, Chap. 6.
10. JA to TJ, Oct. 3 and 24, 1785, below, 77-78, 86.
11. TJ to JA, Sept. 24, 1785, above, 68; TJ to JA, Nov. 19, 1785, below, 94-95.
12. AA to TJ, Nov. 24, 1785, below, 100.
13. TJ to JA, Jan. 12, 1786, below, 114.
14. Lafayette to TJ, Sept. 4, 1785, Boyd, VIII, 478-79; Gottschalk, *Lafayette*, 190-91.

request, Jefferson sent a detailed compilation of commodities that could be conveniently exchanged.[15] Portugal's objections to the British Navigation Acts made her more susceptible to American inducements; indeed, if etiquette had not forbidden making the first move, Portugal would have sent a minister to the United States. By March 1786 the project of a treaty was in the making and Jefferson had gone to London to collaborate with Adams on the spot.[16] There they could compare notes on their diplomatic problems.

Adams had already cautioned Jefferson that "We must not, my Friend, be the Bubbles of our own Liberal Sentiments." [17] The evidence is unmistakable that these molders of the new nation's foreign policy early sensed the dangers of European entanglement and sounded the first warning.

Adams to Jefferson

Grosvenor Square Sept. 25. 1785.

DEAR SIR

The Bearer of this Letter Mr. Thomas Boylston, is one of the clearest and most Solid Capitalists, that ever raised himself by private Commerce in North America. He Seems to be desirous of assisting us, in introducing the knowledge and use of our white Sperma Cœti Oil, into France. His Judgment and Abilities to carry through whatever he undertakes may be depended on. Let me beg your Attention to him. With great Esteem, I have the Honour to be, Sir your most obedient and most humble Servant,

JOHN ADAMS

Adams to Jefferson

Grosvenor Square Octr. 2. 1785.

DEAR SIR

Coll. Franks arrived Yesterday afternoon, with your Favour of Septr. 24.—I have signed all the Papers as you sent them, not perceiving any

15. TJ to JA, Nov. 27, 1785, below, 100-3.
16. Boyd, IX, 410 ff.
17. JA to TJ, Sept. 4, 1785, above, 61.

Alteration necessary. I am afraid, that our Agent to Algiers going without any military Power will not succeed; as the Danger of having their Town bombarded, or their Vessells taken, is the Principal Argument which the Dey has to use with the People, to reconcile them to a Peace. However We must try the Experiment. I have received a Letter from Mr. Stephen Sayre, dated N. York 25. Aug. inclosing another of 23. of Aug. signed by Messrs. Gerry, King, Hardy, Monroe, and Grayson recommending strongly Mr. Sayre to you and me, to be employed as Agent to Morocco, Algiers and the other Powers, and inclosing another Letter to you, probably to the same Effect. This Letter I now inclose to you. It is but a day or two that these Letters have been received by me. Franks is gone to see if Mr. Randolph [i.e., Randall] can be prevailed on to go. If he cannot, will you join Sayre with Lamb? If you will, insert his Name in the Papers. Mr. Lamb will meet Mr. Sayre at Madrid, where I suppose he now is. But if he is not, Lamb must not wait for him a Moment. I should very readily undertake the Trouble, of having Bills drawn upon me, both by Mr. Barclay and Mr. Lamb, if the good of the Service could be promoted by it. But you are sensible there must be a Loss, in transferring Money, from Amsterdam to London: Yet the Advantage may ballance it.

You are diffident of Interpositions: but it is possible We may carry this too far. I think Mr. Barclay and Mr. Lamb would do well, to visit all the foreign Consulls, every one of whom will I am persuaded, shew them Civilities, and do nothing at all to obstruct their negotiations. They will not dare to do it, without orders, and no Cabinet in Europe I verily believe, would venture to give such orders. It will not be from Governments, that We shall receive opposition. Agents of Insurance offices in London or of Merchants trading in Fish etc. in the Mediterranean, may stimulate the Corsairs by exaggerated Representations of our Wealth and the Riches of our Prizes, but that is all. As nothing can be more hostile to the United States, than any Endeavours to embarrass, obstruct or counteract them in their Endeavours to form Treaties of Peace with the Barbary Powers, I wish you would impress it upon Mr. Barclay and Mr. Lamb, to be attentive to this, and obtain Proofs; and if the Consul or Agent of any foreign Power should be found and proved to do any Thing against Us, that they transmit to Us the earliest account of it with the Evidence. Congress would no doubt order a formal Complaint to be made against him to his Court, and in this way he would be held up publicly to the Execrations of all Mankind, and probably be punished by his Master.

Oct. 5 [i.e., 6] We have prevailed upon John [i.e., Paul] Randal Esqr. to go with Mr. Lamb, so that Sayre I suppose must be out of the Question, especially as We know not that he is arrived in Europe. I should think that much time may be saved, by Mr. Lambs going directly to Marseilles, and from thence over to Algiers but if you think there will be a greater Advantage, in seeing the Algerine Envoy at Madrid, or the Comte de Spilly, if he negotiated the late Treaty for Spain, I shall submit entirely to your better Judgment.

As our Commission authorizes us, I suppose it will be construed that it requires us to constitute the Agents by Writing under our Hands and Seals: I have accordingly made out four Commissions, which if you approve you will sign and seal, as I have done. I have written Letters to Mr. Barclay and Mr. Lamb authorizing them to draw upon me. These Letters you will please to sign, as the signature of both of us will be necessary.[18] You will be so good as to write also to Messrs. Wilhem and Jan Willink and Nicholas & Jacob Vanstaphorst of Amsterdam, giving your Approbation and Consent to their Paying the Bills to be drawn upon me by Barclay and Lamb, otherwise they may think my Authority alone, imperfect. I am Sir your most obedient and humble Servant,

JOHN ADAMS

Adams to Jefferson

Grosvenor Square Octr. 3. 1785

DEAR SIR

You have undoubtedly hit upon, the true Word of the Riddle. Yet there was no riddle, nor any clear meaning. It is impossible for any Country to give to another, more decided Proofs of Preference, than our thoughtless Merchants have since the Peace given to this, in matters of Commerce. He had seen this Preference sufficiently prevail. This alone then could not be his Meaning. If he meant a political Preference, an Alliance, such as Hartley was perpetually harping upon, he will wait till Doomsday, and it will never come. We ought to have no Prefferences nor Partialities. But this must be understood upon Condition, that this Country uses us, as well as France. If she does not, I am for giving France the Preference. I would wait with Patience and give full Time to deliberate, but if finally this Court will not act a reasonable and equitable Part, I would enter into still closer and stronger connections with France, both commercial and political. I would enter into Treaty, that certain French Manufactures should pay in the U.S. but half or a quarter of the Duties

18. Commissions, letters of credence, instructions, etc., to Barclay and Lamb, in Boyd, VIII, 611-17.

imposed upon English. French ships should have priviledges from which English should be excluded, and I would enter into an Alliance, offensive and defensive. But more of this hereafter.

I went out, eight days ago, to Dr. Price to get him to have the Insurance done.

October 5. Dr. Price called upon me this morning, but had unfortunately wholly forgot the Insurance on Heudon's Life. But I gave him an extract of your Letter to me, and promised to pay the Money for the Premium at any Moment. I am afraid that Certificates of Heudons State of Health will be required, and the Noise of Algerine Captures may startle the Insurers. The Doctor However will get it done if he can, and as low as possible.

I went to Stockdale with your Letter. He says he sent some News Papers by Mr. Short and by a Friend since, and will send by Franks. He applied to the office, he says in Cleaveland Row but could not get them sent that way. But he will call on the Duke of Dorsett, and get his Permission. If your Correspondent at Dover [Thomas Thompson] however can convey them to you free of Postage you had better agree with him. But after all your surest way would be to apply to the Comte de Vergennes, or Mr. Gennet, the Premier Comis du Bureau des Interpretes. In any other way your Papers will be liable to frequent Interruptions. I found that the only sure way, in the year 1780, after many fruitless Projects and Endeavours for several months. Yours affectionately,

JOHN ADAMS

Jefferson to Adams

Paris Oct. 5. 1785.

SIR

The Chevalier Dolomieu of the order of Malta, who served in the army of Count Rochambeau in America being to pass into England, I take the liberty of introducing him to you. An acquaintance with him in America enables me to assure you of his merit; his politeness and good understanding will of themselves recommend him to your esteem. I have the honour to be with the highest respect Sir Your most obedient and most humble servt.,

TH: JEFFERSON

Abigail Adams to Jefferson

London October 7th. 17[85]

DEAR SIR

Your very polite favour was handed me by Colo. Franks. I am much obliged to you for the execution of the several commissions I troubled you with. Be assured sir that I felt myself Honourd by your commands, tho I have only in part executed them. For I could not find at any store table Cloths of the dimensions you directed. The width is as you wisht, but they assure me that four yds. and three quarters are the largest size ever used here which will cover a table for 18 persons. To these Cloths there are only 18 Napkins, and to the smaller size only twelve. I was the more ready to credit what they said, knowing that I had been obliged to have a set of tables made on purpose for me in order to dine 16 or 18 persons. These rooms in general are not calculated to hold more and it is only upon extraordinary occasions that you meet with that number at the tables here. The Marquis of Carmarthan who occasionally dines the Foreign ministers, and has a House furn[ishe]d him by his Majesty, cannot entertain more than 15 at once, and upon their Majesties Birth days, he is obliged to dine his company at his Fathers the Duke of Leeds's. The person where I bought the Cloth offerd to have any size made, that I wisht for, and agreed to take eight pounds ten shillings for 20 Napkins and a cloth 5 yds. long. I gave Seven for this which I send, and shall wait your further directions. I took the precaution of having them made and marked to Secure them against the custom House, and hope they will meet your approbation. I think them finer than the pattern, but it is difficult judging by so small a Scrap. I have also bought you two pairs of Nut crackers for which I gave four Shillings. We [find them so?] convenient that I thought they would be equally so to [you. The]re is the article of Irish linen which is much Superiour here to any that is to be had in France, and cheeper I think. If you have occasion for any you will be so good as to let me know. It cannot easily pass without being made. But that could be easily done. Only by sending a measure, at the rate of 3 Shilling and six pence per yd. by the peice, the best is to be had. As we are still in your debt, the remainder of the money shall be remitted you or expended here as you direct. Mr. Adams supposed there might be something of a balance due to him in the settlement of a private account with Mr. Barclay, which he has orderd paid to you. He will also pay the money here for the insurence of Mr. Hudons Life, by which means what ever remains due to you can be easily settled.

Haveing finishd the article of Business, I am totally foild at that of Compliment. Sure the air of France, conspired with the Native politeness and Complasance of the writer to usher into the World Such an assemblage of fine things. I shall value the warrior Deity the more for having been your choise, and he cannot fail being in taste in a Nation which has given us such proofs of their Hostility; forgiveness of injuries is no part of their Character, and scarcly a day passes without a Boxing match; even in this Square which is calld the polite and Court end of the city, my feelings have been repeatedly shock'd to see Lads not more than ten years old striped and fighting untill the Blood flow'd from every part, enclosed by a circle who were claping and applauding the conquerer, stimulating them to continue the fight, and forceing every person from the circle who attempted to prevent it. Bred up with such tempers and principals, who can wonder at the licentiousness of their Manners, and the abuse of their pens. Their arrows do not wound, they rebound and fall harmless [...] but amidst their boasted freedom of the press, one must bribe [...] to get a paragraph inserted in favour of America, or her Friends. Our Country has no money to spair for such purposes; and must rest upon her own virtue and magnimimity. So we may too late convince this Nation that the Treasure which they knew not how to value, has irrecoverably past into the possession of those who were possesst of more policy and wisdom.

I wish I might flatter myself with the hope of seeing you here this winter. You would find a most cordial welcome from your American Friends, as well as from some very distinguishd literary Characters of this Nation.

My best regards to Miss Jefferson, to Col. Humphries, to Mr. Short, or any other Friends or acquaintance who may inquire after Your Friend and humble Servant,

A ADAMS

My daughter presents her respectfull regards to you and compliments to the rest of the Gentlemen.

Jefferson to Abigail Adams

Paris Oct. 11. 1785.

DEAR MADAM

Your favor of the 7th. was put into my hands the last night and as I received at the same time dispatches from Mr. Adams which occasion a great deal to be done for Congress to be sent by the Mr. Fitzhughs who set out tomorrow morning for Philadelphia as Mr. Preston the bearer of this does for London, I have only time to thank you for your kind attention to my commission and your offer of new service. Your information as to the shirt linen draws a new scene of trouble on you. You had better have held your tongue about it: but as it is, you must submit to what cannot now be prevented and take better care hereafter. You will think it some apology for my asking you to order me a dozen shirts of the quality of the one sent, when I assure you they made me pay for it here 10 livres and a half the aune, which is at the rate of 6/6 sterl. the yard. I will pray you to chuse me linen as nearly as possible of the same quality because it will enable me to judge of the comparative prices of the two countries. There will probably be Americans coming over from London here in the course of the winter who will be so kind as to bring the shirts to me, which being ready made will escape the custom houses. I will not add to your trouble that of a long apology. You shall find it in the readiness and zeal with which I shall always serve you. But I find that with your friends you are a very bad accountant, for after purchasing the table linen, and mentioning the insurance money on Houdon's life, you talk of what will still remain due to me. The truth is that without this new commission I should have been enormously in your debt. My present hurry does not permit me to state the particulars, but I will prove it to you by the first opportunity. And as to the balance which will be due from me to Mr. Adams should he have no occasion of laying it out here immediately I will transmit it by some safe hand. I have not yet seen the table linen you were so kind as to buy for me, but I am sure it is good. The merchant here promises to shew me some of a new supply he has, which will enable me to judge somewhat of the two manufactures and prices. The difference must be considerable tho' to induce me to trouble you. Be so good as to present my respects to Miss Adams and to accept assurances of the esteem and respect with which I have the honour to be Dear Madam Your most obedient and most humble servt.,

Th: Jefferson

Jefferson to Adams

Paris Oct. 11. 1785.

Dear Sir

Colo. Franks and Mr. Randolph [i.e., Randall] arrived last night. This enables me to send copies of all the Barbary papers to Congress by the Mr. Fitzhughs, together with the Prussian treaty. They wait till tomorrow for this purpose.

Considering the treaty with Portugal as among the most important to the U.S. I some time ago took occasion at Versailles to ask the Portuguese Ambassador [de Sousa Coutinho] if he had yet received an answer from his court on the subject of our treaty. He said not, but that he would write again. His Secretaire d'Ambassade called on me two days ago and translated into French as follows a paragraph of a letter from his minister to the Ambassador. 'Relativement à ce que V. E. nous a fait part de ce qu'elle avoit parlé avec le ministre de l'Amerique, cette puissance doit etre dejà persuadée par d'effets la maniere dont ses vaisseaux ont eté accueillis içi: et par consequence sa majesté auroit beaucoup de satisfaction à entretenir une parfaite harmonie et bonne correspondence *entre* [19] les memes etats unis. Mais il seroit à propos de commencer par la nomination reciproque des deux parties des personnes qui, au moins avec la caractere d'Agens, informeroient reciproquement leurs constituents de ce qui pourroit conduire à la connoissance des interets des deux nations sans prejudice de l'un ou de l'autre. C'est le premier pas qu'il paroit convenable de donner pour conduire à la fin proposée.' [20] By this I suppose they will prefer proceeding as Spain has done,[21] and that we may consider it as definitive of our commission to them. I communicate it to Congress that they may take such other measures for leading on a negotiation as they may think proper.

You know that the 3d. article of instructions of Oct. 29. 1783. to the Ministers for negotiating peace, directed them to negociate the claim for the prizes taken by the Alliance and sent in to Bergen, but delivered up by the court of Denmark: [22] you recollect also that this has been deferred in order to be taken up with the general negotiation for an alliance. Capt.

19. TJ interpreted this word in a marginal note: "qu. *avec*.," as he did also in his letter to Jay, Oct. 11, quoting this French translation. Boyd, VIII, 604, 609. This was consistent with TJ's desire, expressed to JA on July 7, "of bringing all our commerce under the jurisdiction of Congress."

20. "With respect to what Your Excellency has told us of the discussion with the American minister, that power should already be convinced by the facts, the manner in which its vessels have been received here, and that consequently Her Majesty would take great satisfaction in maintaining perfect harmony and good correspondence *with* the United States. But it would be proper to begin with the reciprocal nomination by the two parties of persons who, at least in the character of agents, would each inform their principals what could lead to a knowledge of the interests of the two nations without prejudice to either. This is the first step it would seem fitting to take in order to lead to the end proposed."

21. Don Diego de Gardoqui had been commissioned as Spanish chargé d'affaires in the United States, Sept. 27, 1784; his opposite number in Spain was William Carmichael.

22. The American frigate *Alliance*, accompanying the *Bonhomme Richard*, Captain John Paul Jones, had captured two British privateers during the famous voyage of 1779. Lincoln Lorenz, *John Paul Jones* (Annapolis, 1943), 278-79. See JA to TJ, Nov. 4, 1785, and TJ to JA, Nov. 19, 1785, below, 88-89, 96-97.

Jones desiring to go to America proposed to me that he should leave the sollicitation of this matter in the hands of Doctor Bancroft, and to ask you to negotiate it through the minister of Denmark at London. The delay of Baron Waltersdorf [23] is one reason for this. Your better acquaintance with the subject is a second. The Danish minister here being absent is a third: and a fourth and more conclusive one is that, having never acted as one of the commissioners for negotiating the peace I feel an impropriety in meddling with it at all, and much more to become the principal agent. I therefore told Capt. Jones I would sollicit your care of this business. I beleive he writes to you on the subject. Mr. Barclay sets out in two or three days. Lamb will follow as soon as the papers can be got from this ministry. Having no news, I shall only add assurances of the esteem with which I am Dear Sir Your friend and servant,

TH: JEFFERSON

Jefferson to Adams

Paris Oct. 18. 1785.

DEAR SIR

Your letter of the 10th. came safely to hand and I delivered the one therein inclosed to Mr. Grand. It was a duplicate of one he had before received. You will have heard of the safe arrival of Doctr. Franklin in America. Strange we do not hear of that of Otto and Doradour. If you know of the safe arrival of the packet in which they went, pray communicate it to me, as Madame de Doradour, who is ill in Auvergne, is greatly uneasy for her husband. Our dispatches to the Westward are all gone. Those to the Southward will go this week. This goes by post which will account for it's laconicism. I must however add my respects to the ladies and assurances to yourself of the esteem with which I am Dear Sir Your most obedient humble servt.,

TH: JEFFERSON

23. De Walterstorff had discussed a Danish treaty of amity and commerce with the American commissioners in Paris and took a draft treaty to Denmark in Feb. 1785, but no agreement was reached. American Commissioners to President of Congress, Feb. [9], 1785, Boyd, VII, 646-47; TJ to John Jay, May 12, 1786, *ibid.*, IX, 514-15.

Abigail Adams to Jefferson

London October 19 1785

DEAR SIR

Mr. Fox a young gentleman from Philadelphia who came recommended by Dr. Rush to Mr. Adams, will have the Honour of delivering you this Letter. We requested him to call upon Mr. Stockdale for your papers etc.

Mr. Adams is unwell, and will not be able to write you by this opportunity. I am to acquaint you sir that Dr. Price has transacted the business respecting Mr. Hudon. The Money is paid, but the policy is not quite ready but the Doctor has promised that it shall be sent in a few days, when it will be forwarded to you.

In your English papers you will find an extract of a Letter from Nova Scotia, representing the abuse said to be received by a Captain Stanhope at Boston, the commander of the Mercury. The account is as false—if it was not too rough a term for a Lady to use, I would say false as Hell, but I will substitute, one not less expresive and say, false as the English.

The real fact is this. One Jesse Dumbar, a native of Massachusetts, and an inhabitant of a Town near Boston and one Isaac Lorthrope were during the War taken prisoners and from one ship to an other were finally turnd over to this Captain Stanhope, commander of the Mercury, who abused him and the rest of the prisoners, frequently whiping them and calling them Rebels. The ship going to Antigua to refit, he put all the prisoners into Jail and orderd poor Jesse a dozen lashes for refusing duty on Board his ship. This Mr. Dumbar felt as an indignity and contrary to the Law of Nations. Peace soon taking place Jesse returnd Home, but when Stanhope came to Boston, it quickened Jesses remembrance and he with his fellow sufferer went to Boston and according to his deposition, hearing that Captain Stanhope was walking in the Mall, he went theither at noon day and going up to the Captain asked him if he knew him, and rememberd whiping him on Board his Ship. Having no weapon in his hand, he struck at him with his fist, upon which Captain Stanhope stept back and drew his sword. The people immediately interposed and gaurded Stanhope to Mr. Mortens door, Dumbar and his comrade following him, and at Mr. Mortens door he again attempted to seize him, but then the high sheriff interposed and prevented further mischief, after which they all went to their several homes. This Mr. Stanhope calls assassination and complains that the *News papers* abuse him. He wrote a Letter to the Govenour demanding protection. The Govenour replied by telling him that if he had been injured the Law was open to him and would redress him upon which he wrote a very impudent abusive Letter to Mr. Bowdoin, so much so that Mr. Bowdoin thought proper to lay the whole correspondence before Congress, and Congress past some resolves in consequence and have transmitted them with copies of the Letters to be laid before Mr. Stanhopes master.

Dumbars Deposition was comunicated in a private Letter by Mr. Bowdoin himself to Mr. Adams, so that no publick use can be made of it, but the Govenour was sensible that without it the Truth would not be known.[24]

Is Col. Smith in Paris? Or have we lost him? Or is he so mortified at the king of Prussias refusing him admittance to his Reviews, that he cannot shew himself here again? This is an other English Truth, which they are industriously Circulating. I have had, however, the pleasure of contradicting the story in the most positive terms, as Col. Smith had enclosed us the copy of his own Letter and the answer of his Majesty, which was written with his own hand. How mean and contemptable does this Nation render itself?

Col. Franks I hope had the good fortune to carry your things safely to you, and that they will prove so agreeable as to induce you to honour again with your commands Your Friend and Humble Servant,

Abigail Adams

Compliments to the Gentlemen of your family and love to Miss Jefferson. Mr. Rutledge has refused going to Holland. I fancy foreign embassies upon the present terms are no very tempting objects.

Adams to Jefferson

Grosvenor Square Octr. 24. 1785

Dear Sir

Mr. Preston arrived here, two days ago, but had lost his Letters. I hope he had none of Consequence. He dont remember he had any for me. He tells me from you, that the Doctor is arrived at Philadelphia which I am glad to hear, and those oracles of Truth the English Newspapers tell us, he had an honourable Reception, which I should not however have doubted, if I had not any such respectable Authority for it.

24. TJ's account of the Stanhope affair is in Boyd, IX, 4-7.

The Insurance is made upon Houdons Life for Six Months from the 12 of October. I have paid Thirty two Pounds Eleven shillings Præmium and Charges, which you will please to give me Credit for. I could not persuade them to look back, as they say, they never ensure but for the future and from the date of the Policy. I suppose it will be safest to keep the Receipt and Policy here, for fear of Accidents.

I begin to be uneasy about our Funds. The Draughts upon Willinks & Co. and the Expences of the Negotiations in Barbary, will exhaust the little that remains, and unless We have fresh supplies, We shall all be obliged to embark, in the first ships We can find before next March, for Want of bread. I hope you will press this subject in your Letters to America. Rutledge declines,[25] and you will not wonder at it. I dont believe Congress will find any other Man, who will venture abroad upon the present Plan. The Doctor was lucky to get out of the Scrape, in Season. You and I shall soon wish ourselves at home too.

I have a Letter from Thulemeier, that he has received from the King [of Prussia] a Ratification of the Treaty, and is ready to exchange it. I hope you will request of Congress a prompt Ratification on their Part, that one affair at least may be finished. I see no comfortable hopes here. We hold Conferences upon Conferences, but the Ministers either have no Plan or they button it up, closer than their Waistcoats. The thirteen States must each pass a Navigation Act, and heavy Duties upon all British Merchandizes, so as to give a clear Advantage to their own and the Manufactures of France and Germany, Prussia and Russia, or we shall be a long time weak and poor.

This will be delivered you by Dr. Rodgers a Son of Dr. Rodgers of New York a young Gentleman of Merit. I am Sir with the greatest Esteem your Friend and Sert.,

JOHN ADAMS

Abigail Adams to Jefferson

London october 25 1785

SIR

I should not so soon have ventured to interrupt your more important avocations by an other Scrible, having writen you a few Days since, if it was not to inform you of the loss of your Letters by Mr. Preston. He says that when he landed at Dover, he was very sick, and that he could not accompany his trunk to the custom House, into which for *Security* he had

25. John Rutledge declined to serve as minister to the United Dutch Provinces.

put his Letters. But upon his arrival here he found he had lost them; so that unless your Letter should contain any thing for the English newspapers I fear I shall never know its contents. The gentleman deliverd me a little bundle, by the contents of which I conjecture What you design, but must request you to repeat your orders by the first opportunity, that I may have the pleasure of punctually fulfilling them.

A Dr. Rogers from America will convey this to you with the Newspapers in which you will see the Letters I mentiond in my last between Governour Bowdoin and Captain Stanhope. Lord George Gordon appears to interest himself in behalf of his American Friends, as he stiles them, but neither his Lordships Friendship or enmity are to be coveted.

Mr. Adams writes you by this opportunity. I have directed a Letter to Mr. Williamos to be left in your care. Am very sorry to hear of his ill state of Health.

We hear nothing yet of Col. Smith, know not where he is, as we find by the Gentlemen last arrived that he is not at Paris. I am sir with Sentiments of respect and esteem Your etc,

AA

Adams to Jefferson

Grosvenor Square Nov. 1. 1785.

DEAR SIR

Your Favour of the 18th. did not reach me, till last night. I am glad the Doctor has arrived safe and in so good health, and would fain hope he may contribute to compose the jarring Parties in Pensilvania, as well as assist in improving the Union of the States. Mrs. Rucker has a Letter from her Sister at New York, which mentions the Arrival of Mr. Otto, so that I think Madame la Comtess de Doradour may be satisfied that the Comte her Husband is arrived.

I have been told that the Court of France has contracted with an House at Nantes for supplying their Navy, with American Masts. As this is an affair somewhat interesting, to Great Britain as well as to France and the United States, I should be obliged to you for the Particulars. I wish the Report may be true, and that it may be soon followed by Arrangements for illuminating their Cities with our fine White Sperma Cœti Oil, and their Churches and Families with our beautifull Sperma Cœti Candles. Pray what is the Reason that the Virginians dont learn to sort their Tobacco at home, that they may be able to furnish the French with such Parts of their Produce as are adapted to that Markett, without obliging the Farmers general to think of going to Holland, or coming to England to purchase them. There is a considerable Loss to our Country, in Freight, Insurance, Commissions and Profits, arising from this indirect Commerce and you know as We are poor We ought to be Œconomists: but if we were rich it would not be wise nor honourable to give away our Wealth without Consideration and Judgment.

General Arnold is gone out to Hallifax, with a Vessell and Cargo, of his own, upon what kind of Speculation I know not. Some say that not associating with British Officers, not being able to bear a Life of Inactivity, and having a young Family to provide for, he is gone to seek his Fortune. Whether it is a political Maneuvre or not, I wish that Mr. Deane, Mr. Irvin, Mr. Chalmers and Mr. Smith, were gone with him. The Doctrine of these Gentlemen is that this Country and her Commerce are so essential to the U. States that they cannot exist without them, and that the States can never unite in any measures of Retaliation, nor in any Plan to encourage their own Navigation Acts, and they find Persons enough who have an ardent Passion to believe what is so conformable to their Wishes. If our Country is so situated that she must consent that G. Britain shall carry all our own Produce, to the West India Islands, to Canada, to Nova Scotia, to Newfoundland and to Europe too, We must be humble. When We are willing they should carry half our own Produce, it is not very modest for them to insist upon carrying all.

It is reported that the Ariel has been sent out, express, since the News of the Hurricane, to carry orders for admitting American Vessells to the English West India Islands: but for what time and under what restrictions I know not.

Captain Bell arrived at Philadelphia, on the 14. Sept. the same day with Dr. F. and is said to have made a good Voyage. This is the third Ship from India, and Insurance is making here upon four oth[er ships bo]und the same Way. The former could not be insured under tw[elve Per] Cent. These are done at Seven. My dear Sir Adieu,

JOHN ADAMS

Adams to Jefferson

Grosvenor Square Nov. 4. 1785

DEAR SIR

Mr. Preston has at last found and sent me your Letter. Dr. Bancroft spoke to me, about Commodore Jones's Demand upon Denmark: but upon looking into the Papers we found that the Commodore is recommended by Congress wholly to the Minister at the Court of Versailles, so that We were apprehensive our Powers would be disputed. The Danish Minister however was not here; I offered to ʔo with Dr. Bancroft to the Charge D'Affairs, and speak to him upon the Subject. But the Doctor thought it would be safest to follow the Intentions of Congress, and write to Jones to request you to speak to the Chargé D'Affairs of Denmark at Paris. I know nothing of the subject more than you. The offer of 10,000 £ was made to Dr. Franklin alone. All that you or I can do is to speak or write to the Minister or Chargé D'Affairs and receive his Answer. The Surrender of the Prizes to the English was an Injury to Jones and his People and to the U. States and ought to be repaired.

Will you be so good as to send me the Ordonnance du Roi of 18 Sept., establishing Bounties upon Salt Fish of the French Fisheries and Imposts upon foreign Fish in the Marketts of the French Islands and in Spain, Portugal and Italy?

The Portuguese Minister told me yesterday that his Court did not choose to treat in France, but I have learned from another Quarter that he has written for and expects full Power to treat here. This you will keep to yourself. As soon as any Proposals are made to me, I will send them to you. But I am every day more and more sensible, We must confine our Exports to our own ships, and therefore shall be afraid to let any more foreign ships into our Ports, without a rich equivalent for it. We must encourage our Manufactures too. All foreign nations are taking an ungenerous Advantage of our Symplicity and philosophical Liberality. We must take heed.

I dont doubt that all the Courts of Europe would join my Friends the Abbes,[26] in their Prayer that We may be perpetually poor, not indeed like them with a desire that We may be perpetually virtuous, but that Europeans may have all the Profit of American Labour.—Our Countrymen I fancy, have more wit, if they have not so much Wisdom as Philosophers with them or so much Patience under insidious Policy, as Courtiers would be glad to find in them. With the most cordial Esteem, your Friend and Sert.,

John Adams

26. Abbé Gabriel Bonnot de Mably, who had died on April 23, 1785; Abbé Chalut and Abbé Arnoux maintained a summer residence at Passy, where JA had been their guest.

Adams to Jefferson

Grosvenor Square November 5th. 1785

DEAR SIR

The Chevalier de Pinto, Envoy Extraordinary and Minister Plenipotentiary, from Portugal, after a long absence by leave of his Court is lately arrived here from Lisbon. Upon several occasions, when I met him at Court and upon visits, he told me that he had orders from his Court to confer with me upon the Project of a Treaty between the United States and Portugal, but he [nev]er descended to Particulars till yesterday, when he called upon me and s[aid] that before he left Lisbon his Court had learned that I was in England and had charged him to enter into conference with me, concerning that Project of a Treaty, which had been transmitted to his Court by the Comt de Lusi [i.e., Sousa]. That the Portuguese Ministry, notwithstanding their high Esteem for their Ambassador in France, knowing that he lived in the Country, and was in distress, did not choose that the Negotiation should be any longer conducted by him, but had committed the Project to their Envoy at the Court of England and had instructed him to assure me that the Court of Lisbon was sincerely desirous of entering into a Treaty of Commerce with the United States of America, a Power with which it was more convenient for Portugal to Trade than any other. But there were some things in the Plan proposed which were inadmissible, particularly the Americans could never be admitted into the Brazils. It was impossible, it was the invariable maxim of their Court to exclude all Nations from those Territories, and having himself served for some years as Governor General of one of the Brazils he knew it was a Policy from which his Court could never upon any Consideration depart, that it was a great compliment to him to be prefered to the Comt de Lusi for the Conduct of such a Negotiation, that he made no Pretentions to such merit, but readily acknowledged the superiority of the Ambassador; but it was the pleasure of his Court and he had no right to dispute it.

I answered, that I had no authority to treat, but in conference with Mr. Jefferson, the Minister Plenipotentiary of the United States at the Court of Versailles; that the full Powers to treat with Portugal, was to Mr. Jefferson and me jointly; that I could conclude nothing without his Concurrence, nor Carry on any Conferences without Communicating them to him; to this I supposed he could have no objection. He said none at all.

His first instruction was he said to confer with me concerning the Mutual Wants and several Productions of our Countries which might be the objects of Commerce. His Countrymen wanted he said Grain.— I asked if they did not want Flour? He said he was not precisely instructed concerning Flour, but they had Mills in Portugal which they wished to employ. I replied that in every Negotiation, I thought there ought to be a mutual Consideration of each others profits and Losses advantages and disadvantages, so that the result might be equitable and give sattisfaction on both sides; that a Commerce founded upon Compacts made upon this Principle would be carried on with more Pleasure, and to better effect; that we had Mills which we wished to employ, as well as Portugal, and Mills as Costly and as Good as those of any Nation. In this respect our pretentions were mutual and equal, but there were other Particulars in which without any benefit to Portugal the loss to the United States would be very great. The Commodity was more difficult to preserve in Grain than in Flour. It was more exposed to the Insect, and to heat both at home and upon the Passage, by which means the loss upon Wheat was much greater than that upon Flour; that it would not be equitable then, for Portugal to receive Wheat to the exclusion of Flour; that this was a point of so much Importance that it would facilitate the Treaty and encourage the Commerce, if his Court should think fit to agree to receive our Flour. He said he had not precise instructions but he would write to his Court particularly upon this Point.— The next article wanted by the Portuguese was Lumber of various sorts, particularly staves for Pipes in large Quantities. They wanted also Shiptimber, Pitch, Tar and turpentime, Pot Ash for their Manufactures of Glass, Iron, Masts Yards and Beausprits, Furrs, Ginseng and above all salt Fish. The Consumption of this article in Portugal he said was immense and he would avow to me that the American salt Fish was prefered to any other on account of its Quality. Here you see said the Chevalier de Pinto is a Catalogue of Articles, which the Portuguese will want in larger or smaller Quantities: now what are the Articles you can take in America in Exchange? It behoves my Nation to inquire what they can supply yours with, otherwise the ballance in your favour may be to ruinous to us. It happens unluckily for Portugal that the Americans have no Occasion for our Principal Commodities which are Tobacco, Rice, Indigo and the Produce of the Brazils.

I replied, that the United States had been used to take Considerable Quantities of Maderia, Lisbon and Port Wines, Fruits, Olive Oil, Salt etc. He asked why we could not take Tea, from Lisbon? They imported from the East large quantities, and very good. The English East India Company had purchased of them this year Teas to the amount of forty thousand Pounds, and he thought they could sell it to us cheaper than we bought it elsewhere. They could supply us likewise with all other East India Goods.

Perhaps we intended to supply ourselves by a direct Trade to India: he was glad to hear that our first Enterprises had succeeded: but if we continued to take any Part of our Consumption from Europe, they could supply us as cheap as any other Nation. Sugar too, the Produce of the Brazils, they could furnish to us of as good quality as English or French and much cheaper. If we should think of Manufactures amongst ourselves they could supply us with Wool of the same quality with the Spanish, and Coton in any quantities we might want. If we made Chocolate, they could sell us Cocoa; indeed they had Woolen Manufactures and could afford us Cloth as good and as cheap as other Nations.

These were things I replied in which the Merchants on both sides should speculate. If the United States should proceed in the Plan already begun of encouraging their own Manufactures, the raw Materials of Wool and Coton would be in demand, and if they persevered in their Measures for encouraging their own Navigation they would want large quantities of Hemp, Sail Cloth etc. from the Baltic, and for what I knew they might find their account in taking sugars, Coton, Cocoa etc. at Lisbon to Carry as remittances to Petersbourg and Stockholm. They might even upon some occasions Purchase Tobacco, Rice and Indigo, for the same markett as well as the Mediterranean, if that scene should be open to our ships. But all these things would depend upon the Facilities given to our Commodities by the Treaty. Nothing would contribute so much to promote the Trade as their receiving our Flour without Duties or Discouragements. Our ready built ships too, were an Article of Importance to us.— He said he did not know that our ready built ships were prohibited. I asked if they could not take our White sperma Ceati oil, to burn in their Lamps or for any other uses. He said no, they had such an abundance of Oil made in the Country of Olives which grew there, that they had no occasion for their own sperma Ceati Oil which they sold to Spain; they had now a very pretty sperma Ceati Whale Fishery which they had learn'd of the New Englanders and Carried on upon the Coast of the Brazils. I asked if they could not take our sperma Ceati Candeles and burn them in their Churches. He said they made some Wax in Portugal and some in the Brazils but he would own to me it was not enough for their Consumption. The surplus they bought in Italy and Barbary at a dear rate.

At length I observed to the Chavelier that Portugal abounded in two articles which would be extremely agreeable and convenient to my Fellow Citizens in which she might allways Ballance Accounts with us to our intire sattisfaction, whether she would take more or less of their Comodities. These were Gold and Silver, than which no kind of Merchandise was in greater demand or had a higher reputation.— The Chavel[ier] thought the taste of his Countrymen so much like ours that they had rather pay us in any thing else.

I added if the Conduct of the Court of St. James should oblige the United States to make a navigation Act their Commerce with Portugal must increase. A Navigation Act? says he, why there is not a Nation in Europe that would suffer a Navigation Act to be made in any other, at this day. The English Navigation Act was made in times of Ignorance When few Nations Cultivated Commerce and no Court but this understood or cared any thing about it. But at present all Courts were attentive to it. For his part if he were Minister in Portugal he would not hesitate to exclude from her Ports the Ships of any Nation that should make such an a[ct].

I replied that I did not mean a Navigation act against any Nation but this: but if the English persevered in inforcing their Act against us, We could do no other than make one against them. The Chavelier said we should be perfectly in the right: the Courts of Europe had a long time cried out against this Act of the English. If it were now to begin, it would not be submitted to. This observation is just, it may be carried further. I dont beleive the British Navigation Act can last long, as least I am persuaded if America has spirit enough, Umbone repellere Umbonem [27]— that all other Nations will soon follow her Example, and the apprehension of this would be alone sufficient, if thinking Beings Governed this Island to induce them to silence America by giving her sattisfaction. But they rely upon our Disunion and think it will be time enough when We shall have shewn them that we can agree.

The Chavelier Concluded the Conference by saying that he would write to his Court for further information and instructions, and as I understood him for full Powers. But before he went away, he said he had Orders from his Court to inquire of me what were the sentiments of Congress upon the Head of Ministers and Consuls, whether they would send a Minister and Consul to Lisbon. His Court had a Mind to send some body to the United States, But Etiquette required that Congress should send in return to Portugal. I answered that in the Project of a Treaty which was in His Possession there was an Article that each Party should have a right to send Consuls, so that when the Treaty was concluded Portugal would be at Liberty to send when she would. As to Ministers I had no instructions, but there could be no doubt that if their Majesties of Portugal thought proper to send an Ambassador of any denomination he would be received by Congress with all the respect due to his Character and his sovereign. He said if there was a treaty there ought to be Ministers. I could not make answer to this particular for want of instructions, but

27. "To ward off the thrust of a shield with one's own shield."

Congress had as yet but few Ministers abroad and indeed they had not found many Gentlemen disposed to quit the delight of their own Families and Connections and the Esteem of their Fellow Citizens for the sake of serving in Europe, and here ended the Conversation. Your Friend,

JOHN ADAMS

Jefferson to Adams

Paris Nov. 19. 1785.

DEAR SIR

I wrote to you on the 11th. of Octob. by Mr. Preston and again on the 18th. of the same month by post. Since that yours of Sep. 25. by Mr. Boylston, Oct. 24. Nov. 1. and Nov. 4. have come safe to hand. I will take up their several subjects in order. Boylston's object was first to dispose of a cargo of sperma ceti oyl which he brought to Havre. A secondary one was to obtain a contract for future supplies. I carried him to the M. de la fayette. As to his first object we are in hopes of getting the duties taken off which will enable him to sell his cargo. This has led to discussions with the ministers which give us a hope that we may get the duties taken off in perpetuum. This done, a most abundant market for our oyl will be opened by this country, and one which will be absolutely dependant on us, for they have little expectation themselves of establishing a succesful whale fishery. Perhaps it is possible they may only take the duties off of those oils which shall be the produce of associated companies of French and American merchants. But as yet nothing certain can be said.

I thank you for the trouble you have taken to obtain insurance on Houdon's life. I place the 32 £-11 s to your credit, and not being able as yet to determine precisely how our accounts stand, I send a sum by Colo. Smith which may draw the scales towards a balance.

The determination of the British cabinet to make no equal treaty with us, confirms me in the opinion expressed in your letter of Oct. 24. that the U.S. must pass a navigation act against Great Britain and load her manufactures with duties so as to give a preference to those of other countries: and I hope our assemblies will wait no longer, but transfer such a power to Congress at the sessions of this fall. I suppose however it will only be against Great Britain, and I think it will be right not to involve other nations in the consequences of her injustice. I take for granted the commercial system wished for by Congress was such an one as should leave commerce on the freest footing possible. This was the plan on which we prepared our general draught for treating with all nations. Of those with whom we were to treat, I ever considered England, France, Spain and Portugal as capitally important; the first two on account of their American possessions, the last for their European as well as American. Spain is treating in America, and probably will give us an advantageous treaty. Portugal shews dispositions to do the same. France does not treat. It is likely enough she will chuse to keep the staff in her own hands. But in the mean time she gave us an access to her W. Indies, which tho' not all we wished was yet extremely valuable to us: this access indeed is much wounded by the late arrets of the 18th. and 25th. of September, which I inclose to you.[28] I consider these as a reprisal for the navigation acts of Massachusets and New Hampshire. The minister has complained to me officially of these acts as a departure from the reciprocity stipulated by the treaty. I have assured him that his complaints shall be communicated to Congress, and in the mean time observed that the example of discriminating between foreigners and natives had been set by the Arret of Aug. 1784. and still more remarkeably by those of Sep. 18. and 25. which in effect are a prohibition of our fish in their islands. However it is better for us that both sides should revise what they have done. I am in hopes this country did not mean these as permanent regulations. Mr. Bingham, lately from Holland, tells me the Dutch are much dissatisfied with those acts. In fact I expect the European nations in general will rise up against an attempt of this kind, and wage a general commercial war against us. They can do too well without all our commodities except tobacco, and we cannot find elsewhere markets for them. The selfishness of England alone will not justify our hazarding a contest of this kind against all Europe. Spain, Portugal, and France have not yet shut their doors against us: it will be time enough when they do to take up the commercial hatchet. I hope therefore those states will repeal their navigation clauses except as against Great Britain and other nations not treating with us.

I have made the enquiries you desire as to American shiptimber for this country. You know they sent some person (whose name was not told us) to America to examine the quality of our masts, spars etc. I think this was young Chaumont's business. They have besides this instructed the officer who superintends their supplies of masts, spars etc. to procure good quantities from our Northern states, but I think they have made no contract: on the contrary that they await the trials projected, but with a determination to look to us for considerable supplies if they find our timber answer. They have on the carpet a contract for live oak from the Southern states.

28. The Arrêt of September 25 dealt with duties on codfish imported into the French West Indies. Wroth and Annan, eds., *Acts of French Royal Administration*, no. 2013.

You ask why the Virginia merchants do not learn to sort their own tobaccoes? They can sort them as well as any merchants whatever. Nothing is better known than the quality of every hogshead of tobacco from the place of it's growth. They know too the particular qualities required in every market. They do not send their tobaccoes therefore to London to be sorted, but to pay their debts: and tho they could send them to other markets and remit the money to London, yet they find it necessary to give their English merchant the benefit of the consignment of their tobacco to him (which is enormously gainful) in order to induce him to continue his indulgence for the balance due.

Is it impossible to persuade our countrymen to make peace with the Nova scotians? I am persuaded nothing is wanting but advances on our part; and that it is in our power to draw off the greatest proportion of that settlement, and thus to free ourselves from rivals who may become of consequence. We are at present co-operating with Gr. Br. whose policy it is to give aliment to that bitter enmity between her states and ours which may secure her against their ever joining us. But would not the existence of a cordial friendship between us and them be the best bridle we could possibly put into the mouth of England?

With respect to the Danish business you will observe that the instructions of Congress, article 3. of Octob. 29. 1783. put it entirely into the hands of the *ministers plenipotentiary of the U.S. of A. at the court of Versailles empowered to negotiate a peace or to any one or more of them.* At that time I did not exist under this description. I had received the permission of Congress to decline coming in the spring preceding that date. On the 1st. day of Nov. 1783. that is to say two days after the date of the instruction to the Commissioners Congress recommended J. P. Jones to the Minister Plenipotentiary of the U.S. at Versailles as agent to sollicit under his direction the paiment of all prizes taken in Europe under his command. But the object under their view at that time was assuredly the money due from the court of Versailles for the prizes taken in the expedition by the Bon homme Richard, the Alliance etc. In this business I have aided him effectually, having obtained a definitive order for paying the money to him, and a considerable proportion being actually paid him. But they could not mean by their resolution of Nov. 1. to take from the Commissioners powers which they had given them two days before. If there could remain a doubt that this whole power has resulted to you, it would be cleared up by the instruction of May. 7. 1784. article 9. which declares 'that these instructions be considered as supplementory to those of Octob. 29. 1783. and not as revoking except where they contradict them.' Which shews they considered the instructions of Octob. 29. 1783. as still in full force. I do not give you the trouble of this discussion to save myself the trouble of the negociation. I should have no objections to this part: but it is to avoid the impropriety of meddling in a matter wherein I am unauthorised to act, and where any thing I should pretend to conclude with the court of Denmark might have the appearance of a deception on them. Should it be in my power to render any service in it, I shall do it with chearfulness, but I repeat it that I think you are the only person authorised.

I received a few days ago the Nuova minuta of Tuscany which Colo. Humphrys will deliver you. I have been so engaged that I have not been able to go over it with any attention. I observe in general that the order of the articles is entirely deranged, and their diction almost totally changed. When you shall have examined it if you will be so good as to send me your observations by post, in cypher, I will communicate with you in the same way and try to mature this matter.

The deaths of the Dukes of Orleans and Praslin will probably reach you through the channel of the public papers before this letter does. Your friends the Abbés are well and always speak of you with affection. Colo. Humphries comes to pass some time in London. My curiosity would render a short trip thither agreeable to me also, but I see no probability of taking it. I will trouble you with my respects to Doctr. Price. Those to Mrs. Adams I witness in a letter to herself. I am with very great esteem Dr. Sir Your most obedient and most humble servt.,

Th: Jefferson

Jefferson to Abigail Adams

Paris Nov. 20. 1785.

Dear Madam

I have been honoured with your two letters of Octob. 19. and 25. by Mr. Fox and Doctor Rodgers since the date of my last. I am to thank you for your state of Stanhope's case. It has enabled me to speak of that transaction with a confidence of which I should otherwise have been deprived by the different state of it in the public papers and the want of information from America. I have even endeavored to get it printed in a public paper to counteract the impressions of the London papers and Mercure de France. I do not yet know however whether it will be admitted.—Your letter to Mr. Williamos I immediately sent to him. The illness which had long confined him, proved in the end to be mortal. He died about ten days ago.

Mr. Adams's letter of the 4th. instant informs me that Mr. Preston had at length found my letter to him. I hope he has also found, or that he will in time find that which I took the liberty of writing to you. It was to pray you to order me a dozen shirts, of exactly the quality of the one sent, to be made in London. I gave for that 10tt-10s the aune, and wished to be able to judge of the comparative prices in the two countries. The several commissions you have been so good as to execute for me, with what Mr. Adams has paid for insuring Houdon's life leave me considerably in your debt. As I shall not get so good an opportunity of making a remittance, as by Colo. Smith, I trouble him with thirty two Louis for you. This I expect may place us in the neighborhood of a balance. What it is exactly I do not know. I will trouble you to give me notice when you receive your plateaux de dessert, because I told the marchand I would not pay him till you had received them; he having undertaken to send them. I give you so much trouble that unless you find some means of employing me for yourself in return I shall retain an unpleasant load on my mind. Indeed I am sensible this balance will always be against me, as I want more from London than you will do from Paris. True generosity therefore will induce you to give me opportunities of returning your obligations.

Business being now got through I congratulate you on the return of Colo. Smith. I congratulate you still more however on the extreme worth of his character, which was so interesting an object in a person connected in office so nearly with your family. I had never before had an opportunity of being acquainted with him. Your knowlege of him will enable you to judge of the advantageous impressions which his head, his heart, and his manners will have made on me.

I begin to feel very sensibly the effect of the derangement of the French packets. My intelligence from America lately has become more defective than it formerly was. The proceedings of Congress and of the assemblies there this winter will be very interesting.

The death of the Duc d'Orleans has darkened much the court and city. All is sable. No doubt this is a perfect representation of their feelings, and particularly of those of the Duc de Chartres to whom an additional revenue of four millions will be a paultry solace for his loss. News from Madrid give much to fear for the life of the only son of the Prince of Asturias.

Colo. Humphries comes to take a view of London. I should be gratified also with such a trip, of which the pleasure of seeing your family would make a great part. But I foresee no circumstances which could justify, much less call for, such an excursion. Be so good as to present my respects to Miss Adams and to be assured yourself of the sincerity of the esteem with which I have the honour to be Dear Madam Your most obedient and most humble servt.,

TH: JEFFERSON

Abigail Adams to Jefferson

Grosvenor Square Novr. 24th. 1785.

Sir

I hope if the Marquiss de la Fayette is returned to Paris he may be able to give us some account of Colln. Smith for whom we are not a little anxious, having no intelligence from him since the begining of September when he wrote that he should tarry at Berlin till the reviews were over which would be by the 20th. of that month and then should make the utmost expedition to Paris where his stay would be six days or six Hours according to the intelligence he should meet with there from Mr. Adams. Ten weeks have since elapsed and not a Line or Syllable respecting him has come to hand. In all that time we have been daily and hourly expecting his return. We should have been still more anxious, if the Spanish Minister had not informed us that by a Letter which he received from Colln. Miranda early in Septemr. he wrote him that he had some thoughts of going to Vienna. Colln. Miranda's friends are allarmed about him and have been here to inquire if we could give any account of him. We are now daily more and more anxious because we cannot account for Coll. Smiths long absence but by sickness or some disaster, and even then we ought to have heard from him or of him. You will be so good Sir as to give us every information in your Power as soon as may be.

We suppose you have made an excursion to Fontainbleau by our not having heard from you for a long time. Mr. Preston found the Letters he supposed to have been taken out of his Trunk, amongst his Linnen ten days after his arrival. Your orders shall be executed to the best of my abilities.

Inclosed is a Letter which I found a few days ago respecting the Wine which you was so kind as to take. Mr. Adams is uncertain whether he requested you to Pay to Mr. Bonfeild on his order 319 Livres for a Cask of Wine which he procured for him and of which he never received any account untill his arrival here. If Mr. Barclay has not done it Mr. Adams would be obliged to you to pay it for him.

A Vessell arrived this week from New York and brings papers to the 16 of Octr. They contain nothing material. A Letter from Mr. Jay informs us that no Minister was yet appointed to the Hague, but that Mr. Izard and Mr. Madison were in Nomination, that the rage for New States was very prevalent, which he apprehended would have no good effect. He wished the Ministers abroad to bear testimony against it in their Letters to Congress.

In this Country there is a great want of many French comodities, Good Sense, Good Nature, Political Wisdom and benevolence. His Christian Majesty would render essential service to His Britanick Majesty if he would permit Cargoes of this kind to be exported into this Kingdom against the next meeting of Parliament.

The Treaty lately concluded between France and Holland and the Conduct of England with respect to America proves Her absolute deficiency in each Article. Compliments to the Gentlemen of your Family from Sir your Humble Servant,

A ADAMS

Jefferson to Adams

Paris Nov. 27. 1785.

DEAR SIR

Your favor of the 5th. came to hand yesterday, and Colo. Smith and Colo. Humphries (by whom you will receive one of the 19th. from me) being to set out tomorrow, I hasten to answer it. I sincerely rejoice that Portugal is stepping forward in the business of treaty, and that there is a probability that we may at length do something under our commissions which may produce a solid benefit to our constituents. I as much rejoice that it is not to be negociated through the medium of the torpid uninformed machine [29] at first made use of. I conjecture from your relation of the conference with the Chevalier de Pinto that he is well informed and sensible. So much the better. It is one of those cases (perhaps no others exist) where the better the interests of the two parties are understood, the broader will be the bottom on which they will connect them.

To the very judicious observations on the subjects of the conference which were made by you, I have little to add.

1. Flour. It may be observed that we can sell them the flour ready manufactured for much less than the wheat of which it is made. In carrying to them wheat, we carry also the bran, which does not pay it's own freight. In attempting to save and transport wheat to them, much is lost by the weavil, and much spoiled by heat in the hold of the vessel. This loss must be laid on the wheat which gets safe to market, where it is paid by the consumer. Now this is much more than the cost of manufacturing it with us, which would prevent that loss. I suppose the cost of manufacturing does not exceed seven per cent on the value. But the loss by the weavil,

29. Count de Sousa de Coutinho, Portuguese ambassador at Versailles.

and damage on ship board amount to much more. Let them buy of us as much wheat as will make a hundred weight of flour. They will find that they have paid more for the wheat than we should have asked for the flour, besides having lost the labour of their mills in grinding it. The obliging us therefore to carry it to them in the form of wheat, is a useless loss to both parties.

Iron. They will get none from us. We cannot make it in competition with Sweden or any other nation of Europe where labour is so much cheaper.

Wines. The strength of the wines of Portugal will give them always an almost exclusive possession of a country where the summers are so hot as in America. The present demand will be very great if they will enable us to pay for them; but if they consider the extent and rapid population of the United states they must see that the time is not distant when they will not be able to make enough for us, and that it is of great importance to avail themselves of the prejudices already established in favor of their wines and to continue them by facilitating the purchase. Do this and they need not care for the decline of their use in England. They will be independant of that country.

Salt. I do not know where the Northern states supplied themselves with salt, but the Southern ones took great quantities from Portugal.

Cotton and wool. The Southern states will take manufactures of both: the Northern will take both the manufactures and raw materials.

East-India goods of every kind. Philadelphia and New York have begun a trade to the East Indies. Perhaps Boston may follow their example. But their importations will be sold only to the country adjacent to them. For a long time to come the states south of the Delaware will not engage in a direct commerce with the East Indies. They neither have nor will have ships or seamen for their other commerce. Nor will they buy East India goods of the Northern states. Experience shews that the states never bought foreign goods of one another. The reasons are that they would, in so doing, pay double freight and charges, and again that they would have to pay mostly in cash what they could obtain for commodities in Europe. I know that the American merchants have looked with some anxiety to the arrangements to be taken with Portugal in expectation that they could get their E. India articles on better and more convenient terms, and I am of opinion Portugal will come in for a good share of this traffic with the Southern states, if they facilitate our paiments.

Coffee. Can they not furnish us of this article from Brazil?

Sugar. The Brazil sugars are esteemed with us more than any other.

Chocolate. This article when ready made, and also the Cacao becomes so soon rancid, and the difficulties of getting it fresh have been so great in America that it's use has spread but little. The way to increase it's consumption would be to permit it to be brought to us immediately from the country of it's growth. By getting it good in quality, and cheap in price, the superiority of the article both for health and nourishment will soon give it the same preference over tea and coffee in America, which it has in Spain where they can get it by a single voiage, and of course while it is sweet. The use of the sugars, coffee, and cotton of Brazil would also be much extended by a similar indulgence.

Ginger and spices from the Brazils, if they had the advantage of a direct transportation might take place of the same articles from the E. Indies.

Ginseng. We can furnish them with enough to supply their whole demand for the E. Indies.

They should be prepared to expect that in the beginning of this commerce more money will be taken by us, than after a while. The reasons are that our heavy debt to Gr. Britain must be paid before we shall be masters of our own returns, and again that habits of using particular things are produced only by time and practice.

That as little time as possible may be lost in this negociation I will communicate to you at once my sentiments as to the alterations in the draught sent them,[30] which will probably be proposed by them, or which ought to be proposed by us, noting only those articles.

Art. 3. They will probably restrain us to their dominions in Europe. We must expressly include the Azores, Madeiras, and Cape du verd islands some of which are deemed to be in Africa. We should also contend for an access to their possessions in America according to the gradation in the 2d. article of our instructions of May 7. 1784. But if we can obtain it in no one of these forms, I am of opinion we should give it up.

Art. 4. This should be put into the form we gave it in the draught sent you by Doctr. Franklin and myself for Great Britain.[31] I think we had not reformed this article when we sent our draught to Portugal. You know the Confederation renders the reformation absolutely necessary; a circumstance which had escaped us at first.

Art. 9. Add from the British draught the clause about wrecks.

Art. 13. The passage 'Nevertheless etc. to run as in the British draught.

Art. 18. After the word 'accident' insert 'or wanting supplies of provisions or other refreshments,' and again instead of 'take refuge' insert 'come' and after 'of the other' insert 'in any part of the world.' The object of this is to obtain leave for our whaling vessels to refit and refresh on the coast of the Brazils, an object of immense importance to that class of our

30. "Project of a Treaty Submitted by the American commissioners," Boyd, IX, 412-21; and "Observations by the Portuguese Minister," *ibid.*, 424-26.
31. *Ibid.*, VIII, 274.

vessels. We must acquiesce under such modifications as they may think necessary for regulating this indulgence, in hopes to lessen them in time, and to get a pied-à-terre in that country.

Art. 19. Can we get this extended to the Brazils? It would be precious in case of a war with Spain.

Art. 23. Between 'places' and 'whose' insert 'and in general all others' as in the British draught.

Art. 24. for 'necessaries' substitute 'comforts.'

Art. 25. add 'but if any such Consuls shall exercise commerce etc. as in the British draught.

We should give to Congress as early notice as possible of the reinstitution of this negociation, because in a letter by a gentleman who sailed from Havre the 10th. inst. I communicated to them the answer of the Portuguese minister through the Ambassador here, which I sent to you. They may in consequence be taking other arrangements which might do injury. The little time which now remains of the continuance of our commissions should also be used with the Chevalr. de Pinto to hasten the movements of his court.

But all these preparations for trade with Portugal will fail in their effect unless the depredations of the Algerines can be prevented. I am far from confiding in the measures taken for this purpose. Very possibly war must be recurred to. Portugal is in war with them. Suppose the Chevalier de Pinto was to be sounded on the subject of an union of force, and even a stipulation for contributing each a certain force to be kept in constant cruize. Such a league once begun, other nations would drop into it one by one. If he should seem to approve it, it might then be suggested to Congress, who, if they should be forced to try the measure of war, would doubtless be glad of such an ally. As the Portuguese negociation should be hastened, I suppose our communications must often be trusted to the post, availing ourselves of the cover of our cypher. I am with sincere esteem Dear Sir Your friend and servt.,

TH: JEFFERSON

Adams to Jefferson

Grosvenor Square Dec. 2. 1785.

DEAR SIR

Mr. Nathaniel Barrett, a Gentleman of a respectable Family in Boston, of a fair Character and long Experience in Trade, will have the Honour to deliver you this Letter. He comes to France for the express Purpose of negotiating with proper Persons concerning the Proposals of Monsieur Tourtille de Sangrain, relative of Sperma Cœti oil. I beg Leave to recommend him and his Business to your Attention. I mean this however as mere matter of Form, as I know very well, that your Zeal for the Support of our Whale Fishery, would have been Introduction enough for Mr. Barrett to you, without any Interference of mine. With great Respect and Esteem, I have the Honour to be Dear Sir, your most obedient and most humble Servant,

JOHN ADAMS

Jefferson to Adams

Paris Dec. 10. 1785.

DEAR SIR

On the arrival of Mr. Boylston I carried him to the Marquis de la Fayette, and received from him communications of his object. This was to get a remission of the duties on his cargo of oil, and he was willing to propose a future contract. I proposed however to the Marquis, when we were alone, that instead of wasting our efforts on individual applications, we had better take it up on general ground, and, whatever could be obtained, let it be common to all. He concurred with me. As the jealousy of office between ministers does not permit me to apply immediately to the one in whose department this was, the Marquis's agency was used. The result was to put us on the footing of the Hanseatic towns, as to whale oil, and to reduce the duties to 11^{tt}-5s for 520 lb. French, which is very nearly two livres on the English hundred weight, or about a guinea and a half the ton. But the oil must be brought in American or French ships, and the indulgence is limited to one year. However as to this I expressed to Ct. de Vergennes my hopes that it would be continued, and should a doubt arise, I should propose at the proper time to claim it under the treaty on the footing gentis amicissimi. After all, I beleive Mr. Boylston has failed of selling to Sangrain, and, from what I learn, through a little too much hastiness of temper. Perhaps they may yet come together or he may sell to somebody else.

When the general matter was thus arranged, a Mr. Barrett arrived here from Boston with letters of recommendation from Govr. Bowdoin, Cushing and others. His errand was to get the whale business here put on a general bottom, instead of the particular one which had been settled you know the last year for a special company. We told him what was done.

He thinks it will answer, and proposes to settle at L'Orient for conducting the sales of the oil and the returns. I hope therefore that this matter is tolerably well fixed as far as the consumption of this country goes. I know not as yet to what amount that is; but shall endeavor to find out how much they consume, and how much they furnish themselves. I propose to Mr. Barrett that he should induce either his state or individuals to send us a sufficient number of boxes of the Spermaceti candle, to give one to every leading house in Paris, I mean to those who lead the ton: and at the same time to deposit a quantity for sale here and advertize them in the Petites affiches.[32] I have written to Mr. Carmichael to know on what footing the use and introduction of the whale oil is there, or can be placed. I have the honour to be with very sincere esteem Dear Sir Your most obedient humb. servt.,

TH: JEFFERSON

Jefferson to Abigail Adams

Paris Dec. 11. 1785.

DEAR MADAM

Expecting Baron Polnitz to call every moment, I have only time to acknolege the receipt of your favor of Nov. 24. and to answer you on the subject of the bill for 319 livres drawn by Mr. Adams in favor of Mr. Bonfeild. I had never heard of it before, and Mr. Barclay calling on me this morning I asked of him if he knew any thing of it. He says that such a bill was presented to him, and he desired them not to send it back but to let it lie till he could write to Mr. Adams. He wrote. Not having Mr. Adams's answer in his pocket he can only say that from that he was discouraged from paying it by Mr. Adams's expressing a doubt whether he had not desired me to pay it. The bill therefore went back without my having ever heard a tittle of it. I told Mr. Barclay I would write immediately to Mr. Bondfeild to send it to me on an assurance that I would pay it on sight. But he desired I would not; that he would immediately see to the paiment of it, and that it would be a convenience to him to be permitted to do it, as he had a balance of Mr. Adams's in his hands. I could have urged the same reason, but he had the regular authority. Between us therefore you may count on the settlement of this matter, and always on me for that of any other with which you will please to entrust

32. *Annonces, affiches, et avis divers, ou journal général de France,* an eight-page daily edited by Abbé Aubert. E. Hatin, *Bibliographie de la presse périodique française* (Paris, 1866), 19.

me, and which may give me an opportunity of proving to you the sincere esteem with which I have the honor to be Dear Madam your most obedient humble servt.,

TH: JEFFERSON

Jefferson to Adams

Paris Dec. 11. 1785.

DEAR SIR

Baron Polnitz not going off till to-day enables me to add some information which I receive from Mr. Barclay this morning. You know the immense amount of Beaumarchais' accounts with the U.S.[33] and that Mr. Barclay was authorized to settle them. Beaumarchais had pertinaciously insisted on settling them with Congress. Probably he received from them a denial: for just as Mr. Barclay was about to set out on the journey we destined him Beaumarchais tendered him a settlement. It was thought best not to refuse this, and that it would produce a very short delay. However it becomes long, and Mr. Barclay thinks it will occupy him all this month. The importance of the account, and a belief that nobody can settle it so well as Mr. Barclay, who is intimately acquainted with most of the articles, induce me to think we must yeild to this delay. Be so good as to give me your opinion on this subject. I have the honour to be with very great esteem Dear Sir Your most obedient and most humble servt.,

TH: JEFFERSON

P.S. Pray contrive the inclosed letter to Colo. Monroe. It must not pass through the hands of the English post officers.

Adams to Jefferson

Grosvenor Square Decr. 13. 1785.

DEAR SIR

I have received a Letter from my Friend General Warren of Milton Hill near Boston, acquainting me, that Congress have it in Contemplation to appoint their Ministers Consuls General, or rather to give them Author-

33. For military supplies provided by his firm, Roderique Hortalez & Co., with capital advanced by the kings of France and Spain. Bemis, *Diplomacy of the American Revolution*, 27, 37-39.

ity to appoint Consuls, and that you are to have the nomination of that officer for Lisbon, that his son Winslow Warren, went sometime ago and settled at Lisbon, partly upon some Encouragement of some Members of Congress that he might have that Place, and requesting me to write you upon the Subject.

I sincerely hope, as far as it concerns myself that Congress, instead of giving me the Appointment of any, may do the Business themselves. For there can be no Employment more disagreable than that of weighing Merit, by the Grain and Scruple, because the world very seldom form an opinion of a Man precisely the same with his own, and therefore the Scales will always be objected to, as not justly ballanced. It is worse than the Business of a Portrait Painter, as Men are generally better Satisfied with their own Talents and Virtues, than even with their Faces. I fancy you will not be delighted with this Amusement more than myself, but if we are ordered upon this service, I suppose we must do it. In which Case, I only pray you to remember that Mr. Warren now at Lisbon is a Candidate. I have known him from his Infancy, from his very Cradle. He is an ingenious and as far as I have observed a modest Man. His Education, Connections and Course of Life, having been bred to Trade, has been such that his Qualifications for the Place may be supposed to be as good as any who will probably apply for it, or accept of it. Coll. Otis his Grandfather, the famous James Otis his Unkle, his other Unkles, and his Father, have been to my knowledge, for these five and twenty Years, among the firmest and steadiest supporters of the American Cause. I declare, I dont believe there is one Family upon Earth to which the United States are so much indebted for their Preservation from Thraldom. There was scarcely any Family in New England had such Prospects of Opulence and Power under the Royal Government. They have sacrificed them all. It is true, and I know you will act upon the Maxim, that the Public Good alone is the Criterion, but it is equally true that the public Good requires that such conspicuous and exemplary Services and Sacrifices, should not be neglected, and therefore Considerations of this Sort ever did, and ever will and ever ought in some degree to influence Mankind. I know of no other Candidate. Probably there will be several, and I know you will decide upon the purest Principles and with mature deliberation, and therefore I shall not only acquiesce in but defend your Decision, tho it may be against my young Friend the son of a very old and much beloved one. I am with usual Esteem, dear Sir, your Sincere Friend and very humble Servant,

JOHN ADAMS

Abigail Adams to Jefferson

Grosvenor Square Decemr. 20th. 1785

DEAR SIR

Your favours by Colln. Smith and by the Baron Polintz came safe to hand. As you have justly estimated the Worth and merit of the former, you will easily suppose we were very glad to see him, and equally so to wellcome Colln. Humphryes upon English Ground. I hope his reception here will be as agreeable to him as he expected. He will inform you I dare say that he has seen both the Lions, and His Majesty.

You will find by the publick Papers what favourites we are at Court. The Prince of Wales supping with us, Mr. Adams holding frequent conferences with His Majesty, and yesterday going to Windsor for the same purpose. It is said by some that these are Ministerial manoeuvres to keep up the stocks. A Paragraph of this kind has certainly been attended with that effect. Others say it is to seek out the minds of the People with respect to a Treaty with America, of which if I dared to give my opinion, I should say that some simptoms have lately appeard tending to that point. But this is said in confidence Sir, as I must not betray secrets.

The affair of Capt. Stanhope has been officially taken up and his Conduct much disapproved of by the Lords of the Admirality, as Congress are informed by an official reply to them. Mr. A. has also received an answer to his Demand of the Citizens of the United States sent to the East Indies, "that orders were immediately issued for their discharge." It is not probable that any thing very material will take place till the meeting of Parliament.

The Pacquet arrived last week from New York, in which came Passenger Monsieur Houdon. He returns to Paris the latter End of this week. There were no official Dispatches, and only a private Letter or two to the second of November, but as Mr. A. writes you I will leave Politicks with which I really have no business, and talk of that which more properly belongs to me.

The Commission you honourd me with will be compleat to send by the return of Colln. Humphryes. I received my Plateau safe about ten days since. It is a very good one and I am much obliged by your kind attention to it. The Deities however shewed that they were subject to Humane frailty and got a few Limbs dislocated in their Tour.

If Mr. Barclay will be so good as to settle with Mr. Bonfeild Mr. Adams will be obliged to him. Coll. Smith delivered me the Louis's you sent by him, and when Colln. Humphryes returns I will forward you the account of my stewardship.

Compliments to Mr. Short. We are sorry to hear of his indisposition. I once found great benefit in the Dissorder which he complains of by taking an oz. of Castile soap and a pint of Bristol Beer dividing it into three portions; and takeing it three Mornings, fasting.

I wish you could make it convenient to let Miss Jefferson come and pass a few Months with us here. I do not yet dispair of seeing you in England and in that Case you will certainly bring her with you. I am Sir your most obedient servt.,

A Adams

Adams to Jefferson

Grosvenor Square Decr. 20. 1785

Dear Sir

Mr. Barretts Arrival at Paris, is a lucky Event, and his appointment by the Merchants in Boston a judicious step; but I am not so clear in the Choice he makes of L'Orient to reside in. Paris, or even Havre, seems to me a better situation, Paris in preference to all others. If Boylstone would Act in concert with him, his Capital would be equal to every Thing which relates to the Business: But he is a Singular Character, irritable, fiery, avaricious, parcimonious, to a degree, that made me always doubtfull whether he would succeed; besides his Age and Ignorance of the Language. It is to be regretted that his Cargo cannot be put into the Hands of Sangrain because it is a great Object, to bring that Gentleman into an Acquaintance with the Qualities of the white Sperma Cœti Oil, and into a Course of Experiments of its Use. The first Point to be gained, is to shew that this Oil, considering all its Properties, may be used in the Reverberes [34] cheaper than the Olive Oil, Neatsfoot Oil, or Linseed Oil, or whatever other Substance goes to the Composition of that with which they now enlighten their Cities. We must engage Œconomy, as an Advocate in our Cause, or we shall finally loose it. The Marquis tells me, the Duty is reduced to 7. Liv. 10.s. the Barrique of 520 Weight. You state it at 11.tt 10.s. I should be glad to be exact in this Information, and to know which is right. But, 11:tt 10s the Barrique, even as you state it, is so much less than 18.£ 3.s Sterling the Ton, the Allien Duty paid here that one would think it must turn all the Trade to France, as I hope it will, and as it certainly will if the French Government encourage the Attempt. If an American Merchant can fix himself at Paris and remain a Man of Business, and not become infected with a Rage for Amusements, he might by correspond-

34. French *reverbère*, a reflecting lamp.

ing with all the great Cities of the Kingdom soon do a great deal, towards introducing an extensive Trade between the United States and the French.

I am extreamly sorry for the Accident, which has retarded Mr. Barclay, but I think with you that We must submit to it, for a reasonable Time. But I hope Mr. Barclay will not suffer himself to be delayed one moment unnecessarily. If any Pretences or Excuses for postponing are contrived, I hope he will break away from them all. It is a horrid Thing, that Business so essential should have been neglected so long.

The Chevr. De Pinto is sick, which will unluckily retard our affair with him. But I will quicken it as soon and as much as I can. With great Esteem I am, dear Sir your most obedient Servant,

JOHN ADAMS

Jefferson to Abigail Adams

Paris Dec. 27. 1785.

DEAR MADAM

I am this day honoured with your favor of the 20th. and an opportunity offering to acknolege it immediately, I do not fail to embrace it. I thank you for the intelligence it contains. You refered me to Mr. Adams for news; but he gives me none; so that I hope you will be so good as to keep that office in your own hands. I get little from any other quarter since the derangement of the French packets.

I condole with you sincerely on the dismemberment of the gods and goddesses, and take some blame to myself for not having detained them for Colo. Smith who would have carried them safely. Can I be instrumental in repairing the loss? I will promise not to trust to a workman another time.

Mr. Short is on the recovery. I will take care to communicate to him your prescription, as soon as he returns from St. Germain's. All your friends here are well. The Abbés always desire me to remind you of them. What shall I do for news to tell you? I scratch my head in vain. Oh! true. The new opera of Penelope by Marmontel and Piccini succeeds. Mademoiselle Renaud, of 16. years of age sings as no body ever sung before. She is far beyond Madme. Mara in her own line of difficult execution. Her sister of 12 years of age will sing as well as she does. Having now emptied my budget I have the honour of presenting my respects to Miss Adams and of assuring you of the sincere esteem with which I have the honour to be Dear Madam Your most obedient and most humble servt.,

TH: JEFFERSON

Jefferson to Adams

Paris Dec. 27. 1785.

Dear Sir

Your favors of the 13th. and 20th. were put into my hands today. This will be delivered you by Mr. Dalrymple, secretary to the legation of Mr. Craufurd. I do not know whether you were acquainted with him here. He is a young man of learning and candor, and exhibits a phaenomenon I never before met with, that is, a republican born on the North side of the Tweed.

You have been consulted in the case of the Chevalr. de Mezieres nephew to Genl. Oglethorpe, and are understood to have given an opinion derogatory of our treaty with France. I was also consulted, and understood in the same way. I was of opinion the Chevalier had no right to the estate, and as he had determined the treaty gave him a right, I suppose he made the inference for me that the treaty was of no weight. The Count de Vergennes mentioned it to me in such a manner that I found it was necessary to explain the case to him, and shew him that the treaty had nothing to do with it. I inclose you a copy of the explanation I delivered him.[35]

Mr. Boylston sold his cargo to an Agent of Monsieur Sangrain. He got for it 55. livres the hundred weight. I do not think that his being joined to a company here would contribute to it's success. His capital is not wanting. Le Couteux has agreed that the Merchants of Boston sending whale oil here, may draw on him for a certain proportion of money, only giving such a time in their draughts as will admit the actual arrival of the oil into a port of France for his security. Upon these draughts Mr. Barrett is satisfied they will be able to raise money to make their purchases in America.—The duty is 7^{tt}-10 on the barrel of 520 lb. French, and 10. sous on every livre, which raises it to 11^{tt}-5, the sum I mentioned to you. France uses between 5. and 6. millions of pounds weight French, which is between 3. and 4000 tons English. Their own fisheries do not furnish one million and there is no probability of their improving. Sangrain purchases himself upwards of a million. He tells me our oil is better than the Dutch or English, because we make it fresh, whereas they cut up the whale and bring it home to be made, so that it is by that time entered into fermentation. Mr. Barrett says that 50. livres the hundred weight will pay the prime cost and duties and leave a profit of 16. per cent to the merchant. I hope that England will within a year or two be obliged to come here to buy whale oil for her lamps.

35. For TJ's amplification of subjects discussed with Vergennes, see Boyd, IX, 107-10; also *ibid.*, 120-22, on TJ's suggestions to Georgia.

I like as little as you do to have the gift of appointments. I hope Congress will not transfer the appointment of their Consuls to their ministers. But if they do, Portugal is more naturally under the superintendance of the minister at Madrid, and still more naturally under the minister at Lisbon, where it is clear they ought to have one. If all my hopes fail, the letters of Govr. Bowdoin and Cushing, in favor of young Mr. Warren, and your more detailed testimony in his favor, are not likely to be opposed by evidence of equal weight in favor of any other.

I think with you too that it is for the public interest to encourage sacrifices and services by rewarding them, and that they should weigh to a certain point in the decision between candidates.

I am sorry for the illness of the Chevalr. Pinto. I think that treaty important: and the moment to urge it is that of a treaty between France and England.

Lamb, who left this place the 6th. of Nov. was at Madrid the 10th. of this month. Since his departure Mr. Barclay has discovered that no copies of the full powers were furnished to himself, nor of course to Lamb. Colo. Franks has prepared copies which I will endeavor to get to send by this conveiance for your attestation: which you will be so good as to send back by the first safe conveiance and I will forward them. Mr. Barclay and Franks being at this moment at St. Germain's, I am not sure of getting the papers in time to go by Mr. Dalrymple. In that case I will send them by Mr. Bingham.

Be so good as to present me affectionately to Mrs. and Miss Adams, to Colos. Smith and Humphries and accept assurances of the esteem with which I am Dear Sir Your friend and servt.,

Th: Jefferson

P.S. Be pleased to forward the inclosed, sealing that to Congress after you have read it.

Jefferson to Adams

Paris Jan. 12. 1786.

Sir

You were here the last year when the interest due to the French officers was paid to them, and were sensible of the good effect it had on the credit and honor of the U.S. A second year's interest is become due. They have presented their demands. There is not money here to pay them, the pittance remaining in Mr. Grand's hands being only sufficient to pay current expences three months longer. The dissatisfaction of these officers is extreme, and their complaints will produce the worst effect.[36] The treasury board has not ordered their paiment, probably because they knew there would not be money. The amount of their demands is about 42,000 livres and Mr. Grand has in his hands but twelve thousand. I have thought it my duty under this emergency to ask you whether you could order that sum for their relief from the funds in Holland? If you can, I am persuaded it will have the best of effects.

The imperial Ambassador took me apart the other day at Count d'Aranda's, and observed to me that Doctr. Franklin about eighteen or twenty months ago had written to him a letter proposing a treaty of commerce between the Emperor and the U.S. that he had communicated it to the Emperor and had answered to Doctor Franklin that they were ready to enter into arrangements for that purpose: but that he had since that received no reply from us. I told him I knew well that Doctor Franklin had written as he mentioned, but that this was the first mention I had ever heard made of any answer to the letter, that on the contrary we had always supposed it was unanswered and had therefore expected the next step from him. He expressed his wonder at this and said he would have the copy of his answer sought for and send it to me. However, he observed that this matter being now understood between us, the two countries might proceed to make the arrangements. I told him the delay had been the more unlucky as our powers were now near expiring. He said he supposed Congress could have no objections to renew them, or perhaps to send some person to Brussels to negotiate the matter there. We remitted all further discussion till he should send me a copy of his letter. He has not yet done it, and I doubt whether he has not forgotten the substance of his letter which probably was no more than an acknowlegement of the receipt of Dr. Franklin's and a promise to transmit it to his court. If he had written one proposing conferences, it could never have got safe to Doctor Franklin. Be this as it will he now makes advances, and I pray you to write me your sentiments immediately as to what is best to be done on our part. I will endeavor to evade an answer till I can hear from you. I have the honor to be with the highest respect and esteem Dear Sir, your most obedient and most humble servant,

Th: Jefferson

36. These were French officers who had served in the Continental Army and held certificates under the Commutation Act of 1783, promising full pay for five years in the form of 6 per cent securities. In 1784 Congress authorized new certificates with interest payable at Mr. Grand's in Paris. On the amount due, about $8,200, the Confederation was defaulting. One of these officers, the Chevalier de Segond, filed a typical complaint with TJ in Jan. 1787, which he forwarded to Secretary Jay. Jensen, *New Nation*, 76-82; TJ to Commissioners of the Treasury, Jan. 26, 1786, Boyd, IX, 227; Segond to TJ, Jan. 17, 1787, *ibid.*, XI, 53.

Jefferson to Adams

Paris. Jan. 12. 1786.

DEAR SIR

I had just closed the preceding letter when M. de Blumendorf the Imperial Secretary of legation called on me with the answer to Doctr. Franklin. It was that of Sep. 28. 1784 which you remember as well as myself, wherein Count Merci informed us the Emperor was disposed to enter into commercial arrangements with us and that he would give orders to the Government of the Austrian Netherlands to take the necessary measures. I observed to M. de Blumendorff that this answer shewed the next step was to come from them. He acknoleged it, but said these orders having been for the Netherlands only, they had waited in expectation of others for comprehending Hungary, Bohemia and the Austrian dominions in general, and that they still expect such instructions. I told him that while they should be expecting them, I would write to you on the subject, as it was necessary for us to act jointly in this business. I think they are desirous of treating, and will urge it. I shall be anxious therefore to receive your sentiments on the subject; and renew the assurances of the esteem with which I am Dear Sir, Your friend and servt.,

TH: JEFFERSON

Adams to Jefferson

Grosvenor Square Jan. 19. 1786

DEAR SIR

I am favoured with yours of 27. Decr. and am obliged to you for what you said to the Count De Vergennes in the Case of the Chevalier De Mezieres. You may always very safely depend upon it, that I never have given and never shall give any opinion against the Letter or Spirit of the Treaty with France. In this Case I have never given any opinion at all. Indeed I have never been consulted. The Marquis De Belgarde, with whom I had a Slight Acquaintance at the Hague, called upon me here after the Death of Gen. Oglethorpe, and desired that Mr. Granville Sharp might call upon me and shew me some Papers relative to the Generals Lands in Georgia and S. Carolina. Mr. Sharpe called accordingly, but shewed me no Papers. I never looked nor enquired into the Case, but advised both to write and send a Power of Attorney to our old Friend Edward Rutledge, who was able to give them the best Advice and Information and all the Assurance which the Law allows in their Claim. The Treaty with France never occurred to me, nor was suggested to me in the Conference, nor did I ever give any opinion on any Question concerning it. I have never written a Line to America about it, nor put pen to Paper. The Supposition that any opinion of yours in private Conversation, or of mine if any such had been given which never was, should influence Courts and Juries in Georgia or Carolina, is ridiculous. The Case, as you state it, indeed appears to be unconnected with the Treaty entirely, and if Sound Sense can remove a Prejudice, what you have said upon it, will put an End to the Jealousy.

Does the Count de Vergennes pretend that the United States of America, are bound by their Treaty with France never to lay a Duty on French Vessells? The Mass. and N.H. Navigation Laws, leave French ships, Subjects and Merchandizes upon the Footing Gentis Amicissimae. And does the Treaty require more?

I have been informed by Richard Jackson Esqr., whose Fame is known in America, that a Question has been referred to a Number of the first Lawyers common and civil, among whom he was one, "Whether the Citizens of the United States born before the Revolution, were still entituled in the British Dominions to the Rights of British Subjects." Their unanimous Determination was that Such as were born before, the Signature of the Definitive Treaty of Peace, are still to be considered as British Subjects, if they claim the rights, in the British Dominions. This Decision was I believe more upon Analogy, and Speculation, than upon any Established Principle or Precedent, since ours is I believe a new Case. How it has been determined in America I know not. But I believe not the same way. However the Lawyers and Judges may determine it, I wish the Assemblies may adopt it as a Rule respecting Estates held before the Seperation since a Generosity of this Kind will be more for their Honour and their Interest, as I conceive than a rigorous Claim of an Escheat however clear in Law.

The Chevalier De Pinto informs me, that he has written to his Court for Explanations upon some Points, and expects an Answer in a few Days. When it arrives he will call upon me. In the mean time, he says his Court is solicitous to send a Minister to America: but that Ettiquette forbids it, unless Congress will agree to send one to Lisbon. They would send a Minister to N. York if Congress would return the Compliment, but if Congress will not send a Minister Plenipotentiary they wish to send a Resident, or even a Chargé des Affaires, but Ettiquette will not permit this unless Congress will send a Resident or Chargé D'Affaires to Portugal.

Is it really expected or intended that Eden shall do more than Crawford did? Pray let me know, if there is any Probability of a Treaty, in Earnest, between France and England?

Mr. Barrett has it seems succeeded very well. And Boylston too. If this last has made thirty Per Cent Profit, I will answer for it, that he alone will prevent the Expiration of our Whale Trade and the Depopulation of Nantuckett. He is an admirable Patriot when thirty per Cent can be made by serving his Country. Our Nantuckett and Cape Codd Men and our Boston Merchants are much to blame for having neglected so long the French Markett for their oil and Fins, and for remaining so long in Ignorance of it.

Perhaps the Difference between our White Sperma Cœti Oil and the Ordinary Train Oil of the Dutch and English is not yet sufficiently known to Mr. Sangrain. The Dutch I believe take no Sperma Cœti Whales, and it is but lately that the English have taken any, and they are able to take them now, only with our Skippers, Oarsmen and Endsmen. These we shall soon get back from them if our States are cunning enough to repeal the Refugee Laws, and if France is wise enough to encourage the Exportation of her own Produce and Manufactures by receiving ours in Payment.

Mr. Voss from Virginia has just now called upon me and shewn me a State of the Debt of that Commonwealth which is very consolatory. It is dated 12. Nov. 1785. and signed B. Stark, H. Randolph and J. Pendleton. The whole Debt at that Period was only 928,031 £: 9s: 0d. The annual Interest 55,649 £ 15s: 3d. Pension List annually 6,000 £ Officers of Government Ditto 29,729 £. Criminal Prosecution ditto 5,509. Thus it appears that 96,878 £: 15s: 3d. annually will pay the whole Interest of their Debt and all the Charges of Government.

Virginia by this may sing O be joyfull.

On the 19. Nov. The [Virginia] Lower House resolved to invest Congress with full Power to regulate Trade, and in the mean time that all Commerce should cease with the British Colonies in the West Indies and North America, and that all ships of foreign Nations with whom we have not Treaties of Commerce should be prohibited from importing any Thing but the Productions of their own Country. It seems they revoked these Resolutions again, because the House was thin, but with design to take them up in another day. This perhaps may not be done till next year. But it is a strong Symptom of what is coming. Mr. Voss gives a comfortable account of the Trade in Peltries as well as Grain and Tobacco. Every Vessell that arrives brings fresh Comfort, and I fancy our Commerce with the East Indies will be effectually secured by the Reception of Mr. Pitts Bill. Mr. Voss tells me, that the British Debts will not be permitted to be sued for untill the Treaty is complied with, by the English by the Evacuation of the Posts and Payment for the Negroes.[37] Ld. Carmarthen told me yesterday, that he was labouring at an Answer to my Memorial concerning the Posts and that he should compleat it, as soon as he could get all the Information he was looking for concerning the British Debts, for that Complaints had been made by the Creditors here to Ministry. I am glad that I am to have an Answer. For whatever Conditions they may tack to the Surrender of the Posts, We shall find out what is broiling in their Hearts, and by degrees come together. An Answer, though it might be a rough one, would be better than none. But it will not be rough. They will smooth it as much as they can and I shall transmit it to Congress who may again pass the smoothing plain over it. I expect it will end in an Accommodation, but it will take Eighteen months more time to finish it. With great Esteem yours,

JOHN ADAMS

Adams to Jefferson

Grosvenor Square Jan. 28. 1786

DEAR SIR

I have received yours of the 12, but yesterday, and wish it were in my Power to order the Interest due to the French Officers to be paid; but it is not. They must remain unpaid, be the Consequence what it may untill Congress or the Board of Treasury order it. Indeed, I dont know how your Subsistence and mine is to be paid after next month. Mr. Grand will be likely to advance yours, but from whence mine is to come I know not.

I am clearly for treating with the Emperors Ambassador immediately, and even for the Netherlands only, although it would be better to extend it to all the rest of his Dominions. Why will not the Prussian Treaty answer for the Model. I pray you to proceed in the Business, as fast as you please. Treaties commercial with the two Imperial Courts cannot possibly do us any harm that I can conceive.

This Letter goes by Mr. Joy, whom I pray you to attend to a little. He wishes to go to the East Indies, with views of promoting a Trade between the United States and that Country. In great Haste yours forever,

JOHN ADAMS

37. See AA to TJ, Sept. 6, 1785, above, 61-62, n.49.

Jefferson to Adams

Paris Feb. 7. 1786.

DEAR SIR

I am honored with yours of Jan. 19. Mine of Jan. 12. had not I suppose at that time got to your hands as the receipt of it is unacknoleged. I shall be anxious till I receive your answer to it.

I was perfectly satisfied, before I received your letter, that your opinion had been misunderstood or misrepresented in the case of the Chevalier de Mezieres. Your letter however will enable me to say so with authority. It is proper that it should be known that you had not given the opinion imputed to you, tho' as to the main question it is become useless, Monsieur de Reyneval having assured me that what I had written on that subject had perfectly satisfied the Ct. de Vergennes and himself that this case could never come under the treaty. To evince still further the impropriety of taking up subjects gravely on such imperfect information as this court had, I have this moment received a copy of an act of the Georgia assembly placing the subjects of France as to real estates on the footing of natural citizens and expressly recognizing the treaty. Would you think any thing could be added after this to put this question still further out of doors? A gentleman of Georgia [38] assures me General Oglethorpe did not own a foot of land in the state.—I do not know whether there has been any American determination on the question whether American citizens and British subjects born before the revolution can be aliens to one another? I know there is an opinion of Ld. Coke's in Calvin's case that if England and Scotland should in a course of descent pass to separate kings, those born under the same sovereign during the union would remain natural subjects and not aliens. Common sense urges strong considerations against this, e.g. natural subjects owe allegiance. But we owe none.—Aliens are the subjects of a foreign power. We are subjects of a foreign power.—The king by the treaty acknoleges our independance; how then can we remain natural subjects.—The king's power is by the constitution competent to the making peace, war and treaties. He had therefore authority to relinquish our allegiance by treaty.—But if an act of parliament had been necessary, the parliament passed an act to confirm the treaty, etc. etc. So that it appears to me that in this question fictions of law alone are opposed to sound sense.

38. John McQueen, formerly of Charleston, S. C., who made extensive land purchases in Georgia. W. C. Hartridge, ed., *The Letters of Don Juan McQueen to His Family, 1791-1807* (Columbia, S. C., 1943), xxv-vi.

I am in hopes Congress will send a minister to Lisbon. I know no country with which we are likely to cultivate a more useful commerce. I have pressed this in my private letters.

It is difficult to learn any thing certain here about the French and English treaty. Yet, in general, little is expected to be done between them. I am glad to hear that the Delegates of Virginia had made the vote relative to English commerce, tho they afterwards repealed it. I hope they will come to again. When my last letters came away they were engaged in passing the revisal of their laws, with some small alterations. The bearer of this, Mr. Lyons, is a sensible worthy young physician, son of one of our Judges, and on his return to Virginia. Remember me with affection to Mrs. and Miss Adams, Colos. Smith and Humphreys and be assured of the esteem with which I am Dr. Sir your friend and servant,

Th: Jefferson

Abigail Adams to Jefferson, with Enclosure

London, Grosvenor Square, Feb. 11th, 1786.

Col. Humphries talks of leaving us on Monday. It is with regret, I assure you, Sir, that we part with him. His visit here has given us an opportunity of becoming more acquainted with his real worth and merit, and our friendship for him has risen in proportion to our intimacy. The two American Secretaries of Legation would do honor to their country placed in more distinguished stations. Yet these missions abroad, circumscribed as they are in point of expenses, place the ministers of the United States in the lowest point of view of any envoy from any other Court; and in Europe every being is estimated, and every country valued, in proportion to their show and splendor. In a private station I have not a wish for expensive living, but, whatever my fair countrywomen may think, and I hear they envy my situation, I will most joyfully exchange Europe for America, and my public for a private life. I am really surfeited with Europe, and most heartily long for the rural cottage, the purer and honester manners of my native land, where domestic happiness reigns unrivalled, and virtue and honor go hand in hand. I hope one season more will give us an opportunity of making our escape. At present we are in the situation of Sterne's starling.[39]

39. A caged starling appears in Lawrence Sterne's *Sentimental Journey and the Journal to Eliza*, ed. by Ernest Rhys (Everyman's Library edn.; N. Y., [1926?]), 76-80.

Congress have by the last dispatches informed this Court that they expect them to appoint a minister. It is said (not officially) that Mr. Temple is coldly received, that no Englishman has visited him, and the Americans are not very social with him. But as Colonel Humphries will be able to give you every intelligence, there can be no occasion for my adding any thing further than to acquaint you that I have endeavored to execute your commission agreeably to your directions. Enclosed you will find the memorandum. I purchased a small trunk, which I think you will find useful to you to put the shirts in, as they will not be liable to get rubbed on the journey. If the balance should prove in my favor, I will request you to send me 4 ells of cambric at about 14 livres per ell or 15, a pair of black lace lappets—these are what the ladies wear at court—and 12 ells of black lace at 6 or 7 livres per ell. Some gentleman coming this way will be so kind as to put them in his pocket, and Mrs. Barclay, I dare say, will take the trouble of purchasing them for me; for troubling you with such trifling matters is a little like putting Hercules to the distaff.

My love to Miss Jefferson, and compliments to Mr. Short. Mrs. Siddons is acting again upon the stage, and I hope Colonel Humphries will prevail with you to cross the Channel to see her. Be assured, dear Sir, that nothing would give more pleasure to your friends here than a visit from you, and in that number I claim the honor of subscribing myself.

A. ADAMS

4 pair of shoes for Miss Adams, by the person who made Mrs. A.'s, 2 of satin and 2 of spring silk, without straps, and of the most fashionable colors.

ENCLOSURE

Memorandum of purchases made for TJ reading as follows:

	£	s.	d.
To 2 peices of Irish linen at 4s. pr. yd.	8	14s.	od.
To making 12 Shirts at 3s per Shirt	1	16	0
To buttons thread silk	0	3	0
To Washing	0	3	6
A Trunk	1	1	0
	11	17	6

The Louis I parted with at 20 shillings

Adams to Jefferson

Grosvenor Square Feb. 17. 1786.

DEAR SIR

I was sometime in doubt, whether any Notice Should be taken of the Tripoline Ambassador [Abdurrahman]; but receiving Information that he made Enquiries about me, and expressed a Surprise that when the other foreign Ministers had visited him, the American had not; and finding that He was a universal and perpetual Ambassador, it was thought best to call upon him. Last Evening, in making a Tour of other Visits, I Stopped at his Door, intending only to leave a Card, but the Ambassador was announced at Home and ready to receive me. I was received in State. Two great Chairs before the Fire, one of which was destined for me, the other for his Excellency. Two Secretaries of Legation, men of no Small Consequence Standing Upright in the middle of the Room, without daring to Sitt, during the whole time I was there, and whether they are not yet upright upon their Legs I know not. Now commenced the Difficulty. His Excellency Speaks Scarcely a Word of any European Language, except Italian and Lingua Franca, in which, you know I have Small Pretensions. He began soon to ask me Questions about America and her Tobacco, and I was Surprized to find that with a pittance of Italian and a few French Words which he understands, We could so well understand each other. "We make Tobacco in Tripoli," said his Excellency "but it is too Strong. Your American Tobacco is better." By this Time, one of his secretaries or *upper servants* brought two Pipes ready filled and lighted. The longest was offered me; the other to his Excellency. It is long since I took a Pipe but as it would be unpardonable to be wanting in Politeness in so ceremonious an Interview, I took the Pipe with great Complacency, placed the Bowl upon the Carpet, for the Stem was fit for a Walking Cane, and I believe more than two Yards in length, and Smoaked in aweful Pomp, reciprocating Whiff for Whiff, with his Excellency, untill Coffee was brought in. His Excellency took a Cup, after I had taken one, and alternately Sipped at his Coffee and whiffed at his Tobacco, and I wished he would take a Pinch in turn from his Snuff box for Variety; and I followed the Example with Such Exactness and Solemnity that the two secretaries, appeared in Raptures and the superiour of them who speaks a few Words of French cryed out in Extacy, Monsieur votes etes un Turk. —The necessary Civilities being thus compleated, His Excellency began upon Business; asked many Questions about America: the soil Climate

Heat and Cold, etc. and said it was a very great Country. But "Tripoli is at War with it." I was "Sorry to hear that." "Had not heard of any War with Tripoli." "America had done no Injury to Tripoli, committed no Hostility; nor had Tripoli done America any Injury or committed any Hostility against her, that I had heard of." True said His Excellency "but there must be a Treaty of Peace. There could be no Peace without a Treaty. The Turks and Affricans were the souvereigns of the Mediterranean, and there could be no navigation there nor Peace without Treaties of Peace. America must treat as France and England did, and all other Powers. America must treat with Tripoli and then with Constantinople and then with Algiers and Morocco." Here a Secretary brought him some Papers, one of which a Full Power in French from the Pacha, Dey and Regency of Tripoli, as Ambassador, to treat with all the Powers of Europe, and to make what Treaties he pleased and to manage in short all the foreign Affairs of his Country, he delivered me to read. He was ready to treat and make Peace. If I would come tomorrow or next day, or any other day and bring an Interpreter, He would hear and propose Terms, and write to Tripoli and I might write to America, and each Party might accept or refuse them as they should think fit. How long would it be before one could write to Congress and have an Answer? Three months. This was rather too long but he should stay here sometime. When I had read his French Translation of his Full Power He Shewed me the original in his own Language. You perceive that his Excellency was more ready and eager to treat than I was as he probably expected to gain more by the Treaty. I could not see him Tomorrow nor next day but would think of it.

I must now my dear sir beg of you to send me a Copy of the Project of a Treaty sent [to Morocco] by Mr. Barclay and Mr. Lamb, as I had not time to take one, when it was here. You will please to write me your Thoughts and Advice upon this Occasion. This is a Sensible Man, well known to many of the foreign Ministers who have seen him before, in Sweeden, at Vienna, in Denmark etc. He has been so much in Europe that he knows as much of America, as anybody; so that nothing new will be suggested to him or his Constituents by our having Conferences with him. It seems best then to know his Demands. They will be higher I fear, than we can venture.

The King told one of the foreign Ministers in my hearing at the Levee, that the Tripoline Ambassador refused to treat with his Ministers and insisted upon an Audience. But that all he had to say was that Tripoli was at Peace with England and desired to continue so. The King added all he wants is, a Present, and his Expences born to Vienna or Denmark.

The Relation of my Visit is to be sure very inconsistent with the Dignity of your Character and mine, but the Ridicule of it was real and the Drollery inevitable. How can We preserve our Dignity in negotiating with Such Nations? And who but a Petit Maitre would think of Gravity upon such an occasion.[40] With great Esteem your most obedient

JOHN ADAMS

Adams to Jefferson

Grosvenor Square Feb. 21. 1786.

DEAR SIR

I have desired Colonel Smith to go Express to Paris, to intreat you to come here without loss of Time. The Portuguese Minister has received his Instructions from his Court, and we may here together conduct and finish the Negotiation with him, I suppose in three Weeks. But there is another Motive more Important. There is here a Tripolitan Ambassador with whom I have had three Conferences. The Substance of what passed Colonel Smith will explain to you. Your Visit here will be imputed to Curiosity, to take a Look at England and pay your Respects at Court and to the Corps Diplomatick. There is nothing to be done in Europe, of half the Importance of this, and I dare not communicate to Congress what has passed without your Concurrence. What has been already done and expended will be absolutely thrown away and We shall be involved in a universal and horrible War with these Barbary States, which will continue for many Years, unless more is done immediately. I am so impressed and distressed with this affair that I will go to New York or to Algiers or first to one and then to the other, if you think it necessary, rather than it should not be brought to a Conclusion. Somebody must go to N. York, one of Us, or Humphries or Smith in order to perswade Congress of the Necessity of doing more. Then somebody must go to Holland to obtain the means, and then somebody perhaps to Algiers to make Use of them. The Tripolitan might be perswaded to go with him. I refer you to the Bearer for all other Particulars, and have the Honour to be with great Esteem your Friend,

JOHN ADAMS

40. JA sent a more prosaic account of his conference with the Tripolitan minister to Jay, Feb. 17, 1786, *Works*, VIII, 372-73.

Adams to Jefferson

Grosvenor Square Feb. 25. 1786

DEAR SIR

Give me Leave to introduce to you Mr. Samuel Hartley a Relation of the late Minister at Paris. He has Business at Paris which he will explain to you, whether you can be of any Service to him in that or not, your Civilities will be very agreeable to him and oblige Dear Sir your most humble Servant,

JOHN ADAMS

4

"Abate the ardor of those pyrates against us"

IN MARCH 1786 at the request of John Adams, Jefferson visited England on a mission which proved to be fruitless and frustrating diplomatically, though pleasant enough otherwise. The two friends made a tour of English gardens, Jefferson with Thomas Whately's *Observations on Modern Gardening* in hand, Adams with an eye to historic sites and the ostentatious luxury of country estates.[1] Jefferson must also have enjoyed frequent visits in the Adams household, where Colonel William Stephens Smith, secretary of the American legation, would soon take young Abigail as his bride. The Virginian sat for a portrait by Mather Brown and presented it to Adams, who returned the favor two years later when he sent Jefferson his own portrait by Brown.[2]

Not long after his arrival on March 11 Jefferson was presented at court, but the author of the Declaration of Independence met with a cold reception.[3] Later he referred caustically to George III as "truly the American Messias.... Twenty long years has he been labouring to drive us to our good." [4] That good, however, did not include an Anglo-American commercial treaty, for the project which the American commissioners submitted to the British ministry met only with delay and indifference.[5]

1. "Notes on a Tour of English Gardens," Boyd, IX, 369-73, 374-75n.
2. Boyd, XII, xxxvii; see frontispieces of Vols. I and II of the present work.
3. According to C. F. Adams, the King turned his back on both JA and TJ. C. F. Adams, "Life of John Adams," *Works,* I, 420; TJ, "Autobiography," Ford, I, 89.
4. TJ to AA, Aug. 9, 1786, below, 149.
5. TJ to Richard Henry Lee, April 22, 1786, and JA and TJ to John Jay, April 25, 1786, Boyd, IX, 398-99, 406-7.

The treaty with Portugal offered better prospects for success during Jefferson's six-week stay in England. Negotiations were completed with De Pinto, but the Portuguese government, faced with domestic difficulties and shifting allegiances abroad, failed to ratify. Nevertheless, Queen Maria I gave protection a few weeks later to American vessels from Algerine corsairs in the Atlantic.[6]

Perhaps the most intriguing aspect of Adams's and Jefferson's collaboration in London was their negotiations with the Barbary states. In initiating the move a year earlier for dealings with them, the American commissioners had sought the advice of the Comte de Vergennes, French foreign minister, who wisely recommended that they operate through agents sent to those countries rather than invite envoys to France at great expense. He even agreed guardedly to such assistance as he might discreetly provide.[7] Acting on this advice, Adams and Jefferson had dispatched Thomas Barclay, American consul general in France, to Morocco, and John Lamb, merchant and consul in Spain, to Algiers in October 1785.[8] The friendly attitude of the Spanish court, which William Carmichael, American chargé d'affaires, had been cultivating, smoothed Barclay's approach to the Emperor of Morocco in the spring of 1786. Lamb had already arrived in Algiers on March 25; but the outcome of the two missions was success on the one hand and failure on the other.

Thus far, indirect dealings with the Barbary powers had not conveyed realistically to the American commissioners the ruthless tactics that would give affront to their principles of morality. In London, however, they met one of the piratical envoys face to face. Abdurrahman, the Tripolitan ambassador, conferred with Adams in February 1786 before Jefferson's arrival and inspired one of the most amusing letters Adams ever wrote. He admitted unofficially to Jefferson that it was "very inconsistent with the Dignity of your Character and mine, but the Ridicule of it was real and the Drollery inevitable." In fact, Adams was so highly entertained that he seems to have misjudged His Excellency's willingness "to treat and make Peace," although he admitted that the sums demanded might be higher "than we can ven-

6. "Negotiations for a Treaty of Amity and Commerce with Portugal," *ibid.*, 410 ff; JA to TJ, June 29, 1786, Jan. 25, 1787, below, 138, 161-62.
7. JA to Franklin and TJ, March 20, 1785, above, 19-20.
8. "Documents Pertaining to the Mission of Barclay and Lamb to the Barbary States," Boyd, VIII, 610-24; Ray W. Irwin, *The Diplomatic Relations of the United States with the Barbary Powers, 1776-1816* (Chapel Hill, 1931), 26-32.

ture." [9] And so it turned out at the conference of the American commissioners with Abdurrahman in March. Perpetual peace was his objective, but at a price: "30,000 Guineas for his Employers and £3,000 for himself were the lowest terms . . . and this must be paid in Cash on the delivery of the treaty signed by his sovereign." [10]

After Jefferson returned to France at the end of April, he resumed his correspondence with Adams, much of it concerned with the Barbary pirates whose measure they had taken in London. In Morocco the friendly overtures of the Emperor dating back to the American Revolution, the good offices of the Spanish government, and Barclay's diplomatic acumen brought about a treaty with most-favored-nation provisions, mutual immunity of citizens from seizure, and exchange of prisoners of war in lieu of enslavement.[11] In contrast to this significant achievement (the treaty was ratified by Congress in July 1786), the Algerian negotiations lagged and the American agent was apparently a Lamb among wolves. The Dey of Algiers, head of the most powerful of the Barbary states, "would not speake of Peace" to Lamb, except on his own terms. He demanded an extortionate price for a treaty and insisted on an additional $59,496 for the release of twenty-one Americans held as prisoners.[12] Although Lamb was evidently a clumsy negotiator and raised false hopes among the prisoners, Adams, who had no high opinion of him, admitted that under the circumstances a better qualified appointee would have accomplished no more.[13] When Barclay suggested that he proceed from Morocco to Algiers to try to work diplomatic persuasion on the Dey, Adams and Jefferson vetoed the proposal, the latter reluctantly.[14]

"Money and fear," Vergennes had warned Jefferson, "are the only two agents at Algiers," [15] but the American ministers could neither offer enough money to the pirates nor make any real threats against them. Faced with the humiliation of their country and outraged by this vaunted lawlessness in an age that talked much of the law of

9. JA to TJ, Feb. 17, 1786, above, 121-22. Congress had appropriated $80,000 for bargaining with *all* the Barbary states.

10. American Commissioners to John Jay, March 28, 1786, Boyd, IX, 358.

11. "Treaty with Morocco," *ibid.,* X, 419-26 and *n.*

12. Lamb to American Commissioners, May 20, 1786, *ibid.,* IX, 549-52; Irwin, *Diplomatic Relations with Barbary Powers,* Chap. III.

13. Richard O'Bryen and Others to TJ, June 8, 1786, Boyd, IX, 614-22; JA to TJ, Jan. 25, 1787, below, 162.

14. JA to TJ, Sept. 11, 1786, and TJ to JA, Sept. 26, 1786, below, 153, 154.

15. TJ to JA, May 30, 1786, below, 132-33.

nations and the rights of citizens, Adams and Jefferson were obliged at least to advise Congress on alternative courses to pursue. Perturbed by the pretensions of the Barbary powers "to make war upon Nations who had done them no Injury," Jefferson recommended retaliatory war against the Algerians as more honorable and cheaper in the long run; [16] indeed, he expressed confidence in a highly improbable confederation with Portugal and Naples to blockade the port of Algiers and effect a just peace. Thus it was Jefferson who advocated the beginning of an American navy. Adams would support it, but he took a more practical view, pointing out that war would have to be conducted "with Vigor" and expressing doubts that Congress would do so in its straitened financial condition. For the present, he concluded, the United States had better pay tribute money to save her Mediterranean trade.[17]

Although Jefferson deferred to Adams's judgment, he proceeded to open negotiations for payments to the Order of Mathurins in France, whose good works for centuries had consisted of collecting and disbursing funds for the release of prisoners from Mediterranean pirates. Here the practical-minded and humanitarian Virginian, fundamentally hostile to the priesthood, turned to one of its orders for help in a desperate situation. But the French Revolution dissolved the Mathurins before they could relieve the prisoners, who had to endure their sufferings until the treaty of 1796 between the United States and Algiers.[18]

The ironical aspect of the Algerine crisis was, of course, the willingness of Europeans to condone piracy on the false assumption that the trade of one nation profited from the destruction of the trade of another. The Barbary states were weak bullies whose strongest support came from the great powers. This support of depredation and extortion, of cruelty and inhumanity, casts a grim reflection on the Age of the Enlightenment and its darker corners.

16. American Commissioners to John Jay, March 28, 1786, Boyd, IX, 358; TJ to JA, July 11, 1786, below, 142-43.

17. JA to TJ, July 31, 1786, below, 146-47.

18. TJ to JA, Jan. 11, 1787, and JA to TJ, Jan. 25, 1787, below, 160, 161-62; TJ to John Jay, Feb. 1, 1787, Boyd, XI, 101-2; Irwin, *Diplomatic Relations with Barbary Powers,* 44-46, 74-75.

Jefferson to Adams

Paris May 11. 1786.

DEAR SIR

I do myself the honour of inclosing to you letters which came to hand last night from Mr. Lamb, Mr. Carmichael and Mr. Barclay. By these you will perceive that our peace is not to be purchased at Algiers but at a price far beyond our powers. What that would be indeed Mr. Lamb does not say, nor probably knows. But as he knew our ultimatum, we are to suppose from his letter that it would be a price infinitely beyond that. A reference to Congress seems hereon to be necessary. Till that can be obtained Mr. Lambe must be idle to Algiers, Carthagena or elsewhere. Would he not be better employed in going to Congress? They would be able to draw from him and Mr. Randall the information necessary to determine what they will do, and if they determine to negotiate, they can reappoint the same, or appoint a new negotiator, according to the opinion they shall form on their examination. I suggest this to you as my first thoughts; an ultimate opinion should not be formed till we see Mr. Randall, who may be shortly expected. In the mean time, should an opportunity occur, favour me with your ideas hereon, that we may be maturing our opinions. I send copies of these three letters to Mr. Jay by the packet which sails from l'Orient the 1st. day of the next month.

On my return to Paris the Imperial ambassador informed me he had received full powers for treating with us. I repeated to him the information that ours would expire the 12th. of this month. He said he supposed Congress would have no objections to renew them, proposed that I should write to them on the subject, and in the mean time desired our project and observed that we might be proceeding to arrange the treaty, so as that it should be ready for signature on the arrival of our powers. I gave him a copy of our project, in which, taking the Danish one for the ground work, I made the alterations noted on the within paper; [19] being such as had occurred and met our approbation during the Prussian, Tuscan and Portuguese negotiations. I write to Congress an information of what has passed, and in the mean time shall take no other step till you favor me with your opinion whether we should proceed to prepare terms according to Count Merci's proposition.

I inclose you a copy of the queries [20] of which I had put an illegible one into your hands when in London.

19. Enclosure printed in Boyd, IX, 507-9 and *n*.
20. Probably the queries respecting American trade with the French colonies, *ibid.*, 134.

I beg to leave to present my most friendly respects to the ladies, and to yourself assurances of the esteem with which I have the honor to be Dear Sir your most obedient and most humble servant,

TH: JEFFERSON

Adams to Jefferson

Grosvenor Square May 16. 1786

MY DEAR FRIEND

Mr. Smith, a Son of the Lady you Saw here, who is a Sister of our old Acquaintances the Rutledges, will deliver you this Letter. He goes to reside Sometime in France. Mr. Jay, in a Letter of the 7. of April, writes me "We are well, 'tho not officially informed, that all the States have granted the Impost to Congress, except New York, in whose Legislature there is a Strong Party, against it." And this is all his Letter contains.

New York, I think must Soon come in. If not, all the Blame of Consequences must rest upon her, and She will find the Burthen of it, heavier than the Impost.

I need not ask your Civilities to our young Countryman, who takes this from my dear Sir your Friend and Sert.,

JOHN ADAMS

Jefferson to Adams

Paris May 17. 1787 [i.e., 1786]

DEAR SIR

This will be handed you by young Monsieur de Tronchin, son to a gentleman of that name here who is minister for the republic of Geneva, resident at this court. The son is now in England as a traveller.[21] He is personally unknown to me; but what I hear of him from others, together with my acquaintance with, and respect for, his father, induces me to recommend him to your notice. I do this the rather as it is proposed that he shall finish his travels by a trip to America, where the father has in contemplation to procure an establishment for some of his family. I have

---

21. TJ suggested that William Stephens Smith might introduce Tronchin to John Trumbull, the young American painter. *Ibid., 545.*

the honour to be with the greatest respect and esteem Dr. Sir your most obedient and most humble servt.,

TH: JEFFERSON

Adams to Jefferson

London May 23. 1786

DEAR SIR

I am honoured with yours of the 11th. with the enclosures from Mr. Lamb, Mr. Carmichael and Mr. Barclay. I am not surprized that Mr. Lamb has only discovered that our means are inadequate, without learning the Sum that would be Sufficient. Il faut marchander avec ces Gens la ["One must bargain with those people"]. They must be beaten down as low as possible. But We shall find at last the Terms very dear. The Algerines will never make Peace with us, untill We have Treaties finished with Constantinople, Tunis, Tripoli and Morocco. They always stand out the longest. Mr. Barclay will have no better fortune and I dont believe it worth while for him to wait a Moment to discover what sum will do.

I think with you, that it is best to desire Mr. Lamb immediately to return to Congress, and Mr. Randal too. It is Surprising that neither of them, has given Us more circumstantial Information, and that Mr. Randal has not come on to Paris and London. I think you will do well to write him to come forward without loss of time, and am glad You sent Copies of all the Letters to Mr. Jay. I concur with you entirely in the Propriety of your going on with the Comte de Merci, in the Negotiation and in transmitting to Congress the Plan you may agree upon,[22] that they may Send a new Commission if they judge proper.

I have a Letter from Mr. Randal at Madrid 4. May, but shall not answer it as I wish you to write in behalf of both of Us to return immediately to Paris and London. I have a Letter too from Isaac Stephens at Algiers the 15. of April. He Says the Price is 6000 Dollars for a Master, 4000 for a Mate, and 1500 for each Sailor. The Dey will not abate a 6d., he Says and will not have any Thing to Say about Peace with America. He Says "The People" i.e. the Sailors as I suppose, are carrying Rocks and Timber on their backs for nine miles out of the Country, over sharp Rocks and Mountains, That he has an Iron round his Leg, etc. He begs that We would pay the Money for their Redemption, without sending to Congress, but this is impossible. With great Regard I am sir your affectionate

JOHN ADAMS

22. For a commercial treaty with Emperor Joseph II.

Jefferson to Adams

Paris May 30. 1786.

DEAR SIR

In my letter of the 11th. instant I had the honour of inclosing you copies of letters relative to the Barbary affairs. Others came to hand three days ago, of some of which I now send you copies, and of the others the originals. By these you will perceive that Mr. Randall and Mr. Lamb were at Madrid, that the latter means to return to Alicant and send on a courier to us. Mr. Randall does not repeat that he shall come himself. When either he or the courier arrives we shall have information to decide on. But these papers have strengthened my idea of desiring them to repair to Congress. I am anxious to know your sentiments on this. These papers came in time for me to send copies to Mr. Jay by the packet which will sail from l'Orient the day after tomorrow.

The inclosed paper from the Academy of chirurgery was put into my hands to be forwarded to you. I have the honor to be with sentiments of the most perfect esteem and respect Dear Sir Your most obedient and most humble servt.,

TH: JEFFERSON

P.S. I shall be much obliged to Colo. Smith for a copy of the treaty with Portugal as soon as it is signed. I am of opinion we had better send Luzac a copy as soon as it is signed. What think you?

Jefferson to Adams

Paris May 30. 1786.

DEAR SIR

In my letter of this day I omitted to inform you that according to what we had proposed I have had a long consultation with the Count de Vergennes on the expediency of a Diplomatic mission to Constantinople. His information is that it will cost a great deal of money, as great presents are expected at that court and a great many claim them; and his opinion is that we shall not buy a peace one penny the cheaper at Algiers. He says that those people do indeed acknowlege a kind of vassalage to the Porte and avail themselves of it when there is any thing to be claimed; but regard it not at all when it subjects them to a duty; that money and fear are the two only agents at Algiers. He cited the example of Spain which tho under treaty with the Porte is yet obliged to buy a peace at Algiers at a most enormous price. This is the sum of his information. The Baron de Tott is gone to Flanders for the summer. I am with sincere respect and esteem Dr. Sir Your friend and servt,

TH: JEFFERSON

Adams to Jefferson

Grosvenor Square June 6. 1786

DEAR SIR

Yesterday I received your Favour of 30. May with its Inclosures. You have Since that day no doubt received my answer to yours of the 11th., in which I agreed perfectly with you in the Propriety of Sending Mr. Lamb to Congress without Loss of time. I am content to send Mr. Randal with him but had rather he Should come to you first and then to me, and embark in London after we shall have had opportunity from his Conversation to learn as much as we can.

The Comte de Vergennes is undoubtedly right in his Judgment that Avarice and Fear are the only Agents at Algiers, and that we shall not have Peace with them the cheaper, for having a Treaty with the Sublime Porte. But is he certain we can ever at any Price have Peace, with Algiers, unless we have it previously with Constantinople? And do not the Turks from Constantinople, send Rovers into the Mediterranean? And would not even Treaties of Peace with Tunis, Tripoli, Algiers and Morocco be ineffectual for the Security of our Mediterranean Trade, without a Peace with the Porte? The Porte is at present the Theater of the Politicks of Europe, and commercial Information might be obtained there.

The first Question is, what will it cost us to make Peace with all five of them? Set it if you will at five hundred Thousand Pounds Sterling, tho I doubt not it might be done for Three or perhaps for two.

The Second Question is, what Damage shall we suffer, if we do not treat.

Compute Six or Eight Per Cent Insurance upon all your Exports, and Imports. Compute the total Loss of all the Mediterranean and Levant Trade.

Compute the Loss of half your Trade to Portugal and Spain.

These computations will amount to more than half a Million sterling a year.

The third Question is what will it cost to fight them? I answer, at least half a Million sterling a year without protecting your Trade, and when you leave off fighting you must pay as much Money as it would cost you now for Peace.

The Interest of half a Million Sterling is, even at Six Per Cent, Thirty Thousand Guineas a year. For an Annual Interest of 30,000 £ st. then and perhaps for 15,000 or 10,000, we can have Peace, when a War would sink us annually ten times as much.

But for Gods Sake dont let us amuse our Countrymen with any further Projects of Sounding. We know all about it, as much ever we can know, untill we have the Money to offer. We know if we Send an Ambassador to Constantinople, he must give Presents. How much, the Comte de Vergennes can tell you better than any Man in Europe.

We are fundamentally wrong. The first Thing to be done is for Congress to have a Revenue. Taxes [and] Duties must be laid on by Congress or the Assemblies and appropriated to the Payment of Interest. The Moment this is done we may borrow a Sum adequate to all our Necessities. If it is not done in my Opinion you and I as well as every other Servant of the United States in Europe ought to go home, give up all Points, and let all our Exports and Imports be done in European Bottoms. My Indignation is roused beyond all Patience to see the People in all the United States in a Torpor, and see them a Prey to every Robber, Pirate and Cheat in Europe. Jews and Judaizing Christians are now Scheeming to buy up all our Continental Notes at two or three shillings in a Pound, in order to oblige us to pay them at twenty shillings a Pound. This will be richer Plunder than that of Algerines or Loyds Coffee House. My dear friend Adieu,

JOHN ADAMS

Jefferson to Adams

Paris June 16. 1786.

DEAR SIR

I inclose you the copy of a letter received from Mr. Barclay dated Cadiz May 23. by which you will perceive he was still on this side the Mediterranean. Has Mr. Lamb written to you? I hear nothing from him nor of him, since Mr. Carmichael's information of his arrival in Spain. Mr. Randall gave reason to expect that himself would come on. Yet neither himself nor any letters from him arrive. Perhaps they find conveyances for reporting to you the causes of their delay. I am anxious also to receive your opinion what is best to be done.

The Swedish Ambassador [Baron de Stael-Holstein] asked me some time ago to give him in writing my thoughts on the best method of rendering the island of St. Bartholomew useful in the commerce between Sweden and the U.S. He afterwards pressed this on me every time I saw him till I was obliged to do it. I gave it as my opinion that to render that island most instrumental to the commerce of Sweden and the U.S. and also most useful to Sweden in every other point of view, it should be made a free port without a single restriction. As he has pressed this matter so much, I suspect his court might have instructed him to do it, and might also direct their minister at London to get your opinion on the same point. This latter possibility induced me to trouble you with information of what had passed here.

I observe in the Leyden gazette of June 2. the extract of a letter dated Algiers Apr. 15. which says that on the 10th. of April an American vessel the Clementina Captain Palmer from Philadelphia was carried in there by a cruiser. There being other circumstances mentioned in the same letter relative to our affairs which I know to be true, I am afraid this capture is also true.

The king sets out on the 21st. inst. for Cherburg in order to animate by his notice the operations going on there. The Count d'Artois has lately been there. This is an astonishing effort of human industry. It is believed it will be among the best ports in the world and will contain the whole navy of France. Those threats of invasion on England heretofore made, may become real in a future war, besides the bridle which this fixes in the mouth of the Thames.

Present me affectionately to Mrs. and Miss Adams, assuring them of my friendly and respectful remembrance of them, and how much I regret that I am not of their party in visiting the gardens this summer; and accept yourself assurances of the esteem and regard with which I have the honor to be Dear Sir your most obedient humble servt,

TH: JEFFERSON

Jefferson to Adams

Paris June 23. 1786.

DEAR SIR

I hear of a conveyance which allows me but a moment to write to you. I inclose a copy of a letter from Mr. Lamb. I have written both to him and Mr. Randall agreeable to what we had jointly thought best. The

Courier de l'Europe gives us strange news of armies marching from the U.S. to take the posts from the English. I have received no public letters and not above one or two private ones from America since I had the pleasure of seeing you, so I am in the dark as to all these matters. I have only time left to address heaven with my good wishes for Mrs. Adams and Miss Adams, and to assure you of the sincere esteem with which I have the honour to be Dear Sir your most obedt. and most humble servt,

TH: JEFFERSON

Adams to Jefferson

London June 25. 1786

DEAR SIR

Last night I received yours of the 16. Mr. Lamb has not written to me. Mr. Randal I have expected every day, for a long time, but have nothing from him, but what you transmitted me. My opinion of what is best to be done, which you desire to know is, that Mr. Lamb be desired to embark immediately for New York, and make his Report to Congress and render his account, and that Mr. Randal be desired to come to you first and then to me, unless you think it better for him to embark with Lamb. It would be imprudent in us, as it appears to me to incurr any further Expence, by sending to Constantinople, or to Algiers, Tunis or Tripoli. It will be only so much Cash thrown away, and worse, because it will only increase our Embarrassment, make us and our Country ridiculous, and irritate the Appetite of these Barbarians already too greedy.—I have no News of the Clementine Captain Palmer.

The Sweedish Minister here [Baron de Nolken], has never asked me any Question concerning the Island of St. Bartholomew. I suspect there are not many confidential Communications made to him, from his Court; he has been here 20 or 30 years and has married an English Lady, and is a Fellow of the Royal Society. From these Circumstances he may be thought to be *too well* with the English. This is merely conjecture. Your Advice was the best that could be given.

The Kings Visit to Cherbourg will have a great Effect upon a Nation whose Ruling Passion is a Love of their Sovereign, and the Harbour may and will be of Importance. But the Expectation of an Invasion will do more than a Real one.

Mrs. Adams and *Mrs. Smith* [23] have taken a Tour to Portsmouth. We took Paines Hill in our Way out, and Windsor, in our Return; but the Country in general disappointed us. From Guilford to Portsmouth is an immense Heath. We wished for your Company, which would have added greatly to the Pleasure of the Journey. Pray have you visited the Gardens in France? How do you find them? Equal to the English? With great Regard I am dear Sir your Friend and humble Sert,

JOHN ADAMS

Adams to Jefferson

Grosvenor Square June 26. 1786

DEAR SIR

Sometime Since I received from Gov. Bowdoin some Papers relating to Alexander Gross, with an earnest desire that I would communicate them to the French Ambassador here. I did so and his Excellency was so good as to transmit them to the Comte De Vergennes. Mr. Bartholomy however advised me to write to you upon the Subject, that you might prevent it from being forgotten.

Inclosed is a Letter, which I received yesterday from Griffin Green at Rotterdam, with a Paper inclosed dated Dunkirk 15. June. 1786. relating to this unhappy Man. What can be done for his Relief I know not. Neither the Ransom Money nor the other Charges I Suppose can ever be paid, for Government never is expected to redeem such Hostages and his Relations are not able. If this is the Truth as I suppose it is, it would be better for the French Government and for the Persons interested, to set him at Liberty, than to keep him a Prisoner at Expence. [24]

Let me pray you to minute this affair among your Memorandums to talk of, with the Comte De Vergennes and Mr. Rayneval, when you are at Versailles. They will shew you the Papers, which have been transmitted them through the Comte D'Adhemar.

I wrote you on the 23d. of May ulto. and on the 6th. inst. which Letters I hope you have received. Yours,

JOHN ADAMS

23. Abigail Amelia Adams was married to Colonel William Stephens Smith on June 12, 1786, by the Bishop of St. Asaph. Janet Payne Whitney, *Abigail Adams* (Boston, 1947), 212-13; Edward E. Curtis, "Smith, William Stephens," *DAB*, XVII, 369.

24. The case of the unfortunate American seaman, Alexander Gross, is described in Robert Murdoch to TJ, June 29, 1786, Boyd, X, 79-80.

Adams to Jefferson

London June 29. 1786

DEAR SIR

Inclosed is a Letter to Mr. Lamb and another to Mr. Randall: [25] if you approve them please to Sign them and send them on. Why those Gentlemen have lingered in Spain I know not. I have long expected to hear of their Arrival in Paris. Possibly they wait for orders. If so, the inclosed will answer the End.

The Chev. De Pinto told me on Wednesday that he had orders from his Court to inform me, that the Queen had sent a Squadron to cruise in the Mouth of the Streights, and had given them orders to protect all Vessells belonging to the United States of America, against the Algerines equally with Vessells of her own Subjects. With much Affection yours,

JOHN ADAMS

Adams to Jefferson

London July 3. 1786.

DEAR SIR

Yours of the 23 of June is come to hand, with a Copy of Mr. Lambs of 6 June from Aranjuez.

There is no Intelligence from America of Armies marching to take the Posts from the English. The News was made as I Suppose against the opening of the Three Per Cents, and it had the intended Effect to beat down the Stocks a little.

Altho the Posts are important, the war with the Turks is more So. I lay down a few Simple Propositions.

1. We may at this Time, have a Peace with them, in Spight of all the Intrigues of the English or others to prevent it, for a Sum of Money.

2. We never Shall have Peace, though France, Spain, England and Holland Should use all their Influence in our favour without a Sum of Money.

25. American Commissioners to John Lamb, June 29, July 7, 1786, Boyd, X, 96-97; the letter to Randall was not forwarded because he arrived in Paris on July 2.

ABIGAIL ADAMS

Portrait by Ralph Earl, painted in England, *ca.* 1785
(See p. xxiii)

A view of the residence of the late President Adams at Quincy Mass.

ADAMS HOUSE, *Quincy, Massachusetts* Drawing by Sarah Apthorp, 1822

(See p. xxiii)

3. That neither the Benevolence of France nor the Malevolence of England will be ever able materially to diminish or Increase the Sum.

4. The longer the Negotiation is delayed, the larger will be the Demand.

From these Premisses I conclude it to be wisest for Us to negotiate and pay the necessary Sum, without Loss of Time. Now I desire you and our noble Friend the Marquis to give me your opinion of these four Propositions. Which of them do you deny? or doubt? If you admit them all do you admit the Conclusion? Perhaps you will Say, fight them, though it Should cost Us a great Sum to carry on the war, and although at the End of it we should have more Money to pay as presents. If this is your Sentiment, and you can persuade the Southern States into it, I dare answer for it that all from Pensylvania inclusively northward, would not object. It would be a good occasion to begin a Navy.

At present we are Sacrificing a Million annually to Save one Gift of two hundred Thousand Pounds. This is not good Œconomy. We might at this hour have two hundred ships in the Mediterranean, whose Freight alone would be worth two hundred Thousand Pounds, besides its Influence upon the Price of our Produce. Our Farmers and Planters will find the Price of their Articles Sink very low indeed, if this Peace is not made. The Policy of Christendom has made Cowards of all their Sailors before the Standard of Mahomet. It would be heroical and glorious in Us, to restore Courage to ours. I doubt not we could accomplish it, if we should set about it in earnest. But the Difficulty of bringing our People to agree upon it, has ever discouraged me.

You have Seen Mr. Randall before this no doubt, if he is not fallen Sick on the Road.

This Letter is intended to go by Mr. Fox. The Chev. De Pinto's Courier unfortunately missed a Packet, which delayed him and consequently the Treaty a Month. The Queen his Mistress, as I wrote you a few Days Since, has given orders to her Squadron cruising in the Streights to protect all Vessells belonging to the United States. This is noble and Deserves Thanks. Accept the Sincerest Assurances of Esteem and Affection from dear Sir your most obedient

JOHN ADAMS

Mrs. Adams having read this letter finds it deficient in not having added her best respects to Mr. Jefferson and sincere thanks for his petitions.[26]

26. Postscript in AA's hand.

Jefferson to Adams

Paris July 9. 1786.

DEAR SIR

I wrote you last on the 23d. of May.[27] Your favor of that date did not come to hand till the 19th. of June. In consequence of it I wrote the next day letters to Mr. Lamb and Mr. Randall, copies of which I have now the honour to inclose you. In these you will perceive I had desired Mr. Randall, who was supposed to be at Madrid, to return immediately to Paris and London, and to Mr. Lambe, supposed at Alicant, I recommended the route of Marseilles and Paris, expecting that no direct passage could be had from Alicant to America, and meaning on his arrival here to advise him to proceed by the way of London, that you also might have an opportunity of deriving from him all the information he could give. On the 2d. of July Mr. Randall arrived here and delivered me a letter from Mr. Lambe dated May 20. of which I inclose you a copy, as well as of another of June 5. which had come to hand some time before. Copies of these I have also sent to Mr. Jay. Yours of the 29th. of June by Dr. Bancroft and inclosing a draught of a joint letter to Mr. Lambe, came to hand on the 5th. inst. I immediately signed and forwarded it, as it left him more at liberty as to his route than mine had done. Mr. Randall will deliver you the present and supply the informations heretofore received. I think with you that Congress must begin by getting money. When they have this, it is a matter of calculation whether they will buy a peace, or force one, or do nothing.

I am also to acknolege the receipt of your favors of June 6. 25. and 26. The case of Grosse shall be attended to. I am not certain however whether my appearing in it may not do him harm by giving the captors a hope that our government will redeem their citizen. I have therefore taken measures to find them out and sound them. If nothing can be done privately I will endeavour to interest this government.

Have you no news yet of the treaty with Portugal? Does it hang with that court? My letters from N. York of the 11th. of May inform me that there were then 11. states present and that they should ratify the Prussian treaty immediately. As the time for exchange of ratifications is drawing to a close, tell me what is to be done, and how this exchange is to be made. We may as well have this settled between us before the arrival of the

27. TJ's last letter to JA is dated June 23; JA's letter to which he refers is dated May 23.

ratification, that no time may be lost after that. I learn through the Marechal de Castries that he has information of New York's having ceded the impost in the form desired by Congress, so as to close this business.[28] Corrections in the acts of Maryland, Pennsylvania, etc. will come of course. We have taken up again the affair of whale oil, that they may know in time in America what is to be done in it. I fear we shall not obtain any further abatement of duties; but the last abatement will be continued for three years. The whole duties paiable here are nearly 102 livres on the English ton, which is an atom more than four guineas according to the present exchange.

The monopoly of the purchase of tobacco for this country which had been obtained by Robert Morris had thrown the commerce of that article into agonies. He had been able to reduce the price in America from 40/ to 22/6 lawful the hundred weight, and all other merchants being deprived of that medium of remittance the commerce between America and this country, so far as it depended on that article, which was very capitally too, was absolutely ceasing. An order has been obtained obliging the farmers general to purchase from such other merchants as shall offer, 15,000 hogsheads of tobacco at 34, 36, and 38 livres the hundred according to the quality, and to grant to the sellers in other respects the same terms as they had granted to Robert Morris. As this agreement with Morris is the basis of this order I send you some copies of it [29] which I will thank you to give to any American (not British) merchants in London who may be in that line. During the year this contract has subsisted, Virginia and Maryland have lost 400,000 £ by the reduction of the price of their tobacco.

I am meditating what step to take to provoke a letter from Mrs. Adams, from whom my files inform me I have not received one these hundred years. In the mean time present my affectionate respects to her and be assured of the friendship and esteem with which I have the honour to be Dear Sir Your most obedient and most humble servt.,

TH: JEFFERSON

28. New York had rejected in effect the impost on May 4, 1786, by placing the collection and disposition of the funds in the hands of her own officers. On Feb. 15, 1787, the Assembly rejected the impost outright. Jensen, *New Nation*, 415-17.
29. Printed in Boyd, IX, 586-88

Jefferson to Adams

Paris July 11. 1786.

DEAR SIR

Our instructions relative to the Barbary states having required us to proceed by way of negotiation to obtain their peace, it became our duty to do this to the best of our power. Whatever might be our private opinions, they were to be suppressed, and the line marked out to us, was to be followed. It has been so honestly, and zealously. It was therefore never material for us to consult together on the best plan of conduct towards these states. I acknolege I very early thought it would be best to effect a peace thro' the medium of war. Tho' it is a question with which we have nothing to do, yet as you propose some discussion of it I shall trouble you with my reasons. Of the 4. positions laid down in your letter of the 3d. instant, I agree to the three first, which are in substance that the good offices of our friends cannot procure us a peace without paying it's price, that they cannot materially lessen that price, and that paying it, we can have the peace in spight of the intrigues of our enemies. As to the 4th. that the longer the negotiation is delayed the larger will be the demand, this will depend on the intermediate captures: if they are many and rich the price may be raised; if few and poor it will be lessened. However if it is decided that we shall buy a peace, I know no reason for delaying the operation, but should rather think it ought to be hastened. But I should prefer the obtaining it by war. 1. Justice is in favor of this opinion. 2. Honor favors it. 3. It will procure us respect in Europe, and respect is a safe-guard to interest. 4. It will arm the federal head with the safest of all the instruments of coercion over their delinquent members and prevent them from using what would be less safe. I think that so far you go with me. But in the next steps we shall differ. 5. I think it least expensive. 6. Equally effectual. I ask a fleet of 150. guns, the one half of which shall be in constant cruise. This fleet built, manned and victualled for 6. months will cost 450,000 £ sterling. It's annual expence is 300 £ sterl. a gun, including every thing: this will be 45,000 £ sterl. a year. I take British experience for the basis of my calculations, tho' we know, from our own experience, that we can do, in this way, for pounds lawful, what costs them pounds sterling. Were we to charge all this to the Algerine war it would amount to little more than we must pay if we buy peace. But as it is proper and necessary that we should establish a small marine force (even were we to buy a peace from the Algerines,) and as that force laid up in our dockyards would cost us half as much annually as if kept in order for service, we have a right to say that only 22,500 £ sterl. per ann. should be charged to the Algerine war. 6. It will be as effectual. To all the mis-managements of Spain and Portugal urged to shew that war against those people is ineffectual, I urge a single fact to prove the contrary where there is any management. About 40. year ago, the Algerines having broke their treaty with France, this court sent Monsr. de Massac with one large and two small frigates, he blockaded the harbour of Algiers three months, and they subscribed to the terms he dictated. If it be admitted however that war, on the fairest prospects, is still exposed to incertainties, I weigh against this the greater incertainty of the duration of a peace bought with money, from such a people, from a Dey 80. years old, and by a nation who, on the hypothesis of buying peace, is to have no power on the sea to enforce an observance of it.

So far I have gone on the supposition that the whole weight of this war would rest on us. But 1. Naples will join us. The character of their naval minister (Acton), his known sentiments with respect to the peace Spain is officiously trying to make for them, and his dispositions against the Algerines give the greatest reason to believe it. 2. Every principle of reason tells us Portugal will join us. I state this as taking for granted, what all seem to believe, that they will not be at peace with Algiers. I suppose then that a Convention might be formed between Portugal, Naples and the U.S. by which the burthen of the war might be quotaed on them according to their respective wealth, and the term of it should be when Algiers should subscribe to a peace with all three on equal terms. This might be left open for other nations to accede to, and many, if not most of the powers of Europe (except France, England, Holland and Spain if her peace be made) would sooner or later enter into the confederacy, for the sake of having their peace with the Pyratical states guarantied by the whole. I suppose that in this case our proportion of force would not be the half of what I first calculated on.

These are the reasons which have influenced my judgment on this question. I give them to you to shew you that I am imposed on by a semblance of reason at least, and not with an expectation of their changing your opinion. You have viewed the subject, I am sure in all it's bearings. You have weighed both questions with all their circumstances. You make the result different from what I do. The same facts impress us differently. This is enough to make me suspect an error in my process of reasoning tho' I am not able to detect it. It is of no consequence; as I have nothing to say in the decision, and am ready to proceed heartily on any other plan which may be adopted, if my agency should be thought useful. With respect to the dispositions of the states I am utterly uninformed. I cannot help thinking however that on a view of all circumstances, they might be united in either of the plans.

Having written this on the receipt of your letter, without knowing of any opportunity of sending it, I know not when it will go: I add nothing therefore on any other subject but assurances of the sincere esteem and respect with which I am Dear Sir your friend and servant,

TH: JEFFERSON

Adams to Jefferson

London July 16. 1786

DEAR SIR

Last night Mr. Randal arrived with yours of the 9th. If the Prussian Treaty arrives to you, I think you will do well to Send Mr. Short with it to the Hague and Exchange it with Thulemeier, and get it printed in a Pamphlet Sending a Sufficient Number to you and to me. If it comes to me and you approve, I will Send Some one or go myself.

The Chevr. De Pinto's Courier unfortunately missed a Packet by one Day, which obliged him to wait a month at Falmouth for another. The Chevalier was greatly chagrined at the Delay. He is much obliged for your Notes, and I Should be more so for another Copy, having Sent mine to my Brother Cranch, who writes me that your Argument in favour of American Genius, would have been much Strengthened, if a Jefferson had been Added to a Washington, a Franklin and a Rittenhouse. I wrote you lately that the Queen of Portugal had ordered her Fleet cruising in the Streights to protect all Vessells belonging to American Citizens equally with those of her own Subjects against the Algerines.

Boylstons Vessell Arrived in Boston, with Sugars, and he expects another Vessell hourly, with which he will go again to France. He desires me, to express his obligations to you and the Marquis, for your former Assistance. Coffin Jones has Sent a Vessell to L'Orient, with another Cargo of oil. The French Government would do well to encourage that Trade. If they do not, it will go elsewhere. It is in vain for French or English to think, that Sperma Cæti oil cannot find a Market but in their Territories. It may find a Market in every City that has dark nights, if any one will do as Boylston did, go and shew the People its qualities by Samples and Experiments. The Trade of America in oil and in any Thing else will labour no longer, than public Paper is to be sold under Par. While a Bit of Paper can be bought for five shillings that is worth twenty, all Capitals will be employed in that Trade, for it is certain there is no other that will yeild four hundred Per Cent Profit, clear of Charges and Risques.

As soon as this lucrative Commerce shall cease We shall see American Capitals employed in sending all where it will find a Market, that is all over Europe if France does not wisely monopolise it as she may, if she will. Inclosed is an oration of Dr. Rush. I am my dear Sir, your most obedient

JOHN ADAMS

Abigail Adams to Jefferson

London july 23. 1786

DEAR SIR

Mr. Trumble will have the honour of delivering this to you. The knowledge you have of him, and his own merit will ensure him a favourable reception. He has requested a Letter from me, and I would not refuse him, as it gives me an opportunity of paying my respects to a Gentleman for whom I entertain the highest esteem, and whose portrait dignifies a part of our room, tho it is but a poor substitute for those pleasures which we enjoy'd some months past.[30]

We console ourselves however by the reflection which tends to mollify our grief for our [depar]ted Friends; that they are gone to a better Country, an[d to a] Society more congenial to the benevolence of their minds.

I Supposed Sir that Col. Smith was your constant correspondent, and that his attention, left me nothing to inform you of. This Country produced nothing agreeable and our own appears to be takeing a Nap, as several vessels have lately arrived without a scrip, from any creature. By one of the papers we learn that Col. Humphries was safely arrived.

Perhaps neither of the Gentlemen may think to acquaint you, that the Lords of the admiralty have orderd home Captain Stanhopes Ship, and calld upon him for a justification of his conduct to Govenour Bowdoin, that having received what he offerd as such, they voted it not only unsatisfactory, but his conduct highly reprehensible. As such they have represented it to his Majesty, and Captain Stanhope will not be permitted to return to that Station again. Thus far we must give them credit.

30. The portrait of TJ by Mather Brown, painted during March-April 1786. See Vol. II, frontispiece, of the present work.

I suppose you must have heard the report respecting Col. Smith—that he has taken my daughter from me, a contrivance between him and the Bishop of St. Asaph. It is true he tenderd me a son as an equivilent and it was no bad offer. But I had three Sons before, and but one daughter. Now I have been thinking of an exchange with you Sir. Suppose you give me Miss Jefferson, and in some [fu]ture day take a Son in lieu of her. I am for Strengthening [the] federal union.

Will you be so good as to let petite apply to my shoe maker for 4 pr. of silke shoes for me. I would have them made with straps, 3 pr. of summer silke and one pr. blew sattin. Col. Trumble will deliver you a guiney for them. Whenever I can be of service to you here, pray do not hessitate to commission me. Be assured you confer a favour upon your Humble Servant,

A ADAMS

Adams to Jefferson

London July 31. 1786

DEAR SIR

I have received the Ratification of the Prussian Treaty, and next Thursday Shall Sett off for the Hague in order to exchange it with the Baron De Thulemeyer.

Your favour of the 11th. instant I have received. There are great and weighty Considerations urged in it in favour of arming against the Algerines, and I confess, if our States could be brought to agree in the Measure, I Should be very willing to resolve upon eternal War with them. But in Such a Case We ought to conduct the War with Vigour, and protect our Trade and People. The Resolution to fight them would raise the Spirits and Courage of our Countrymen immediately, and we might obtain the Glory of finally breaking up these nests of Banditti. But Congress will never, or at least not for years, take any such Resolution, and in the mean time our Trade and Honour suffers beyond Calculation. We ought not to fight them at all, unless we determine to fight them forever.

This thought is I fear, too rugged for our People to bear. To fight them at the Expence of Millions, and make Peace after all by giving more Money and larger Presents than would now procure perpetual Peace Seems not to be Œconomical.—Did Monsieur De Massac carry his Point without making the Presents? Did Louis 14. obtain his Point without making the Presents? Has not France made Presents ever Since? Did any

Nation ever make Peace with any one Barbary State, without making the Presents? Is there one Example of it? I believe not, and fancy you will find that even Massac himself made the Presents.

I agree in opinion of the Wisdom and Necessity of a Navy for other Uses, but am apprehensive it will only make bad worse with the Algerines. I will go all Lengths with you in promoting a Navy, whether to be applied to the Algerines or not. But I think at the Same time We should treat. Your Letter however has made me easier upon this Point.—Nevertheless I think you have rather undercalculated the Force necessary to humble the Algerines. They have now fifty Gun Boats, which being Small objects in Smooth Water, against great Ships in rough Water are very formidable. None of these existed in the time of Monsieur Massac. The Harbour of Algiers too is fortified all round, which it was not in Mr. Massac's time, which renders it more difficult and dangerous to attempt a Blockade.

I know not what dependence is to be had upon Portugal and Naples, in Case of a War with the Barbarians. Perhaps they might assist us in some degree.

Blocking Algiers would not obtain Peace with Morocco Tunis or Tripoli, so that our Commerce would still be exposed.

After all, tho I am glad We have exchanged a Letter upon the subject, I percieve that neither Force nor Money will be applied. Our States are so backward that they will do nothing for some years. If they get Money enough to discharge the Demands upon them in Europe, already incurred, I shall be agreably disappointed. A Disposition Seems rather to prevail among our Citizens to give up all Ideas of Navigation and naval Power, and lay themselves consequently at the Mercy of Foreigners, even for the Price of their Produce. It is their Concern, and We must submit, for your Plan of fighting will no more be adopted than mine of negotiating. This is more humiliating to me, than giving the Presents would be. I have a Letter from Mr. Jay of 7. July, by Packet, containing nothing but an Acknowledgment of the Receipt [of] our Letter of 25. of April.

N. Hampshire and R. Island have suspended their Navigation Acts and Massachusetts now left alone will suspend theirs, so that all will be left to the Convention, whose system, if they form one, will not be compleated, adopted and begin to operate under Several Years.

Congress have received the Answer which you saw, to my Memorial of 30 Nov.[31] and Mr. Ramsay writes me, he is not distressed at it, because it will produce a repeal of all the Laws, against recovering private Debts. With every Sentiment of Friendship I am yours,

JOHN ADAMS

31. "A Memorial from Mr. Adams respecting the Evacuation of the Posts, etc.," Nov. 30, 1785, Diplomatic Correspondence, 1783-1789, II, 542-43.

Jefferson to Adams

Paris Aug. 8. 1786.

DEAR SIR

Your favour of July 16. came duly to hand by Mr. Trumbul. With respect to the whale oil, tho' this country has shewn a desire to draw it hither, and for that purpose have reduced the duties to about four guineas on the English ton, yet I do not see a probability of a further reduction at this moment. It has been much pressed, and I expect every day to receive a final determination. Should it not be obtained now we have reason to expect some years hence an abatement of one third, as a promise was given to the people that the imposition of 10. sous per livre should not be renewed at the expiration of the term for which it was laid on, which will be about half a dozen years hence. I inclose you copies of letters received from Mr. Carmichael, O'Brian, and Lamb. Be so good as to say what answer we shall give the last about his settlement.[32] Shall we undertake the settlement? If so, where shall it be done? I will join in any thing you please as to this. Taking for granted, from a message delivered by Mr. Trumbul, that you are now in Holland, I will only add a request to send me some copies of the ratified treaty with Prussia (which will be I hope in both languages,) and assurances of the sincere esteem and respect with which I have the honour to be Dear Sir your most obedt. humble servt.,

TH: JEFFERSON

Jefferson to Abigail Adams

Paris Aug. 9. 1786.

DEAR MADAM

It is an age since I have had the honor of a letter from you, and an age and a half since I presumed to address one to you. I think my last was dated in the reign of king Amri, but under which of his successors you

32. Lamb wrote to TJ from Alicante, Spain, July 18, 1786, that because his "Indisposition" would not permit him to travel further, he must "begg a Settlement of my Reasonable Accounts Since I have been on this Journey...." He also desired to defend himself against accusations by "Gentelmen on my mission... [who] knowd nothing of my business in Algiers and of Course Could not write the Truth." Boyd, X, 151-52.

wrote, I cannot recollect. Ochosias, Joachar, Manahem or some such hard name. At length it is resumed: I am honoured with your favor of July 23. and I am at this moment writing an answer to it. And first we will dispatch business. The shoes you ordered, will be ready this day and will accompany the present letter. But why send money for them? You know the balance of trade was always against me. You will observe by the inclosed account that it is I who am to export cash always, tho' the sum has been lessened by the bad bargains I have made for you and the good ones you have made for me. This is a gaining trade, and therefore I shall continue it, begging you will send no more money here. Be so good as to correct the inclosed that the errors of that may not add to your losses in this commerce. You were right in conjecturing that both the gentlemen might forget to communicate to me the intelligence about Captn. Stanhope. Mr. Adams's head was full of whale oil, and Colo. Smith's of German politics (—but don't tell them this—) so they left it to you to give me the news. De tout mon coeur, I had rather receive it from you than them. This proposition about the exchange of a son for my daughter puzzles me. I should be very glad to have your son, but I cannot part with my daughter. Thus you see I have such a habit of gaining in trade with you that I always expect it.—We have a blind story here of somebody attempting to assassinate your king. No man upon earth has my prayers for his continuance in life more sincerely than him. He is truly the American Messias. The most precious life that ever god gave, and may god continue it. Twenty long years has he been labouring to drive us to our good, and he labours and will labour still for it if he can be spared. We shall have need of him for twenty more. The Prince of Wales on the throne, Lansdowne and Fox in the ministry, and we are undone! We become chained by our habits to the tails of those who hate and despise us. I repeat it then that my anxieties are all alive for the health and long life of the king. He has not a friend on earth who would lament his loss so much and so long as I should. —Here we have singing, dauncing, laugh, and merriment. No assassinations, no treasons, rebellions nor other dark deeds. When our king goes out, they fall down and kiss the earth where he has trodden: and then they go to kissing one another. And this is the truest wisdom. They have as much happiness in one year as an Englishman in ten.—The presence of the queen's sister enlivens the court. Still more the birth of the princess. There are some little bickerings between the king and his parliament, but they end with a sic volo, sic jubeo ["as I wish, so I rejoice"]. The bottom of my page tells me it is time for me to end with assurances of the affectionate esteem with which I have the honor to be, dear Madam, your most obedient and most humble servant,

Th: Jefferson

Mrs. Adams to Th:J.   Dr.

1785. June	2.	To paid Petit	173[tt] - 8s	
Aug.	17.	To pd. Mr. Garvey's bill	96 -16 - 6	
Nov.		To cash by Colo. Smith	768 - 0 - 0	
1786. Jan.	5.	To pd. Bazin for Surtout de dessert and figures etc.	264 -17 - 6	
Feb.	27.	To pd. for shoes for Miss Adams	24 -	
Mar.	5.	To pd. for sundries viz.		

12. aunes de dentelle	96.[tt]		
une paire de barbes	36.		
4. aunes of cambric	92.		
4. do.	60.	284 - 0 - 0	

(reckoning 24. livres at 20/
sterl.)   1611 - 2 - 0   being £67- 2- 7 ster

Mar. 9. To balance expences of journey
          between Mr. Adams and myself   8- 9- 4½

                                                         75-11-11½

Cr.

1785 Oct.	12.	By pd. insurance on Houdon's life		£32-11s- 0d
1786 Jan.	10.	By damask table cloth and napkins		7 - 0 - 0
		2. pr. nutcrackers		4 - 0

2 peices Irish linen	
@ 4/	£8 -14s
making 12. shirts	1 -16
buttons, thread, silk	3
washing	3 -6
a trunk	1 - 1

11-17 - 6

Apr. 9. By pd. for 9 yds. of muslin @ 11/   4-19 - 0
     12. By do. for 21 yds. Chintz @ 5/6   5-15 - 6
          By pd. for 25 yds.
            linen @ 4/   £5. ⎫ for Mr. Short 6- 6- 6
          for making 7. shirts 1-6-6 ⎭
          By pd. for altering 12. shirts   6 - 6
          Balance   6-11 -11½
                                                    75-11 -11½

Jefferson to Adams

Paris Aug. 13. 1786.

DEAR SIR

The inclosed came to hand this morning. Mr. Carmichael you observe,
and Mr. Barclay suppose something may yet be done at Algiers. It remains
for us to consider whether the conduct of the Dey of that country leaves
any room to hope that any negotiator can succeed without a great addition
to the price to which we are confined? And should we think in the negative, yet whether the expences of Mr. Barclay's going there may not be
compensated by additional information, by the possibility that he may get

at their ultimatum, by the importance of possessing Congress of this ultimatum, that knowing their ground, they may not suspend a decision. Spain having made it's peace with Algiers, we may see whether their interference can count as money, as it has done at Marocco. Hostilities too may possibly be suspended or slackened a while longer. These are all chances on which I acknolege I build very little; yet as nothing weighs against them but the expence of Mr. Barclay's journey, they might be tried. If you are of that opinion, send me the necessary papers for Mr. Barclay ready signed by you, and I will sign them and forward them.— There is lodged in Mr. Grand's hands money enough to support the diplomatic establishment of our country in Europe three months, on which your draughts and Colo. Smith's shall be honoured if you think proper to make them. I am with sincere esteem Dear Sir, your friend and servt.,

TH: JEFFERSON

Jefferson to Adams

Paris Aug. 27. 1786.

DEAR SIR

Your favour of July 31. was lately delivered me. The papers inform me you are at the Hague, and, incertain what stay you may make there, I send this by Mr. Voss who is returning to London by the way of Amsterdam. I inclose you the last letters from Mr. Barclay and Mr. Carmichael, by which we may hope our peace with Marocco is signed, thanks to the good offices of a nation which is honest, if it is not wise.[33] This event with the naval cruises of Portugal will I hope quiet the Atlantic for us. I am informed by authority to be depended on, that insurance is made at Lorient, on American vessels sailing under their own flag, against every event, at the price usually paid for risks of the sea alone. Still however the most important of our marts, the Mediterranean, is shut. I wrote you a proposition to accept Mr. Barclay's offer of going to Algiers. I have no hope of it's making peace; but it may add to our information, abate the ardor of those pyrates against us, and shut the mouths of those who might impute our success at Marocco and failure at Algiers to a judicious appointment to the one place and an injudicious one at the other. Let me hear from you as soon as possible on this, and if you accede to it send me all the necessary

33. Spain, whose foreign minister, Count Floridablanca, had encouraged Barclay and promised to provide him with a letter from the King of Spain to the Emperor of Morocco. Barclay to TJ, March 23, 1786, *ibid.*, IX, 352.

papers ready signed. I inclose you the article 'Etats Unis' of one of the volumes of the Encyclopedie, lately published.[34] The author, M. de Meusnier, was introduced to me by the D. de la Rochefoucault. He asked of me information on the subject of our states, and left with me a number of queries to answer. Knowing the importance of setting to rights a book so universally diffused and which will go down to late ages, I answered his queries as fully as I was able, went into a great many calculations for him, and offered to give further explanations where necessary. He then put his work into my hands. I read it, and was led by that into a still greater number of details by way of correcting what he had at first written,[35] which was indeed a mass of errors and misconceptions from beginning to end. I returned him his work and my details; but he did not communicate it to me after he had corrected it. It has therefore come out with many errors which I would have advised him to correct, and the rather as he was very well disposed. He has still left in a great deal of the Abbé Raynal, that is to say a great deal of falsehood, and he has stated other things on bad information. I am sorry I had not another correction of it. He has paid me for my trouble, in the true coin of his country, most unmerciful compliment. This, with his other errors, I should surely have struck out had he sent me the work, as I expected, before it went to the press. I find in fact that he is happiest of whom the world sais least, good or bad.—I think if I had had a little more warning, my desire to see Holland, as well as to meet again Mrs. Adams and yourself, would have tempted me to take a flying trip there. I wish you may be tempted to take Paris in your return. You will find many very happy to see you here, and none more so than, Dear Sir, your friend and servant,

TH: JEFFERSON

Adams to Jefferson

Grosvenor Square Septr. 11. 1786.

DEAR SIR

On my Return from Holland on the Sixth instant I found your Favours of the 8. and 13. Aug. On my Arrival at the Hague The Exchange of Ratifications was made on the 8. of August with The Baron De Thulemeier, and I had it Printed. It is only in French. Copies shall be Sent you

34. *Encyclopédie Méthodique* (1782-1833).
35. "The Article on the United States in the *Encyclopédie Méthodique*" (including TJ's answers to Démeunier's queries and his observations on Démeunier's manuscript), Boyd, X, 3-65.

as soon as I can find an Opportunity. We were present at Utrecht at the August Ceremony of Swearing in their new Magistrates. In no Instance, of ancient or modern History, have the People ever asserted more unequivocally their own inherent and unalienable Sovereignty.—But whatever Pleasure I might have in enlarging upon this Subject, I must forbear.

The Affair of Oil has taken a turn here. The Whale men both at Greenland and the southward, have been unsuccessful and the Price of Spermacæti Oil, has risen above fifty Pounds a Ton. Boy[l]ston's ship arrived with two or three hundred Ton, and finding he could pay the Duties and make a Profit of five and twenty Per Cent, he sold his Cargo here, instead [of] going again to France as he intended. This Circumstance will oblige the French Court, or the French Merchants or both to take other Measures, or they will loose this Trade. The Price of Oil will rise in Boston, so much that I am afraid Mr. Barrett's Contract must be fullfilled at an immense Loss.

As to Mr. Lambs Settlement, I still think he had better embark forthwith for New York from Spain. If he cannot he may transmit to you and me his Account, and remit to us the Ballance in favour of U.S.

Mr. Barclays Proposal, of going to Tunis and Tripoli, I suppose appears to you as it does to me, from what We learned from the Ambassador from Tripoli in London, to be unnecessary, at least till We hear farther from Congress. It seems to me too, very unlikely that any Benefit will be had from a Journey to Algiers. I wish to see the Treaty with Morocco, and to know the Particulars of that Affair, first. At present I believe We are taken in, and that We shall be plagued with Demands for annual Presents. I confess, I have no Faith in the Supposition that Spanish Interference has counted for Money, or at least that it will pass long for it.

If however you are clearly in favour of sending Mr. Barclay to Algiers, I will make out a Commission, and send it to you, for your Signature, Signed by my self, because I would not set up my own Judgment against yours, Mr. Carmichaels and Mr. Barclays: but I confess, at present I cannot see any Advantage in it, but on the contrary Several Disadvantages. Mr. Randall is gone to Congress, and We may expect their further orders, e'er long. With Sincere Affection I am, dear sir, your Friend and servant,

JOHN ADAMS

Inclosed is a Project of an Answer to Mr. Lamb,[36] if you approve it, you will sign and send it.

J.A.

36. Advising Lamb to "return to Congress for their further instructions as soon as possible, and . . . to embark from Spain by the first opportunity." American Commissioners to Lamb, [Sept. 26, 1786], *ibid.*, 407.

Jefferson to Adams

Paris Septr. 26th. 1786.

DEAR SIR

My last letter to you was dated the 27th. of August since which I have recieved yours of Sep. 11th. The letter to Mr. Lamb therein inclosed I immediately signed and forwarded. In mine wherein I had the honor of proposing to you the mission of Mr. Barclay to Algiers, I mentioned that my expectations from it were of a subordinate nature only. I very readily therefore recede from it in compliance with your judgment that this mission might do more harm than good. I accordingly wrote to Mr. Barclay that he was at liberty to return to this place, to London or to America, as he should think best. I now inclose you copies of such letters from him, Mr. Lamb and Mr. Carmichael as have come to hand since my last to you. I have had opportunities of making further enquiry as to the premium of insurance at L'Orient for Vessels bound to or from America, and I find that no additional premium is there required on account of the risque of capture by the Barbary States. This fact may be worth mentioning to American merchants in London.

We have been continually endeavoring to obtain a reduction of the duties on American whale oil: the prospect was not flattering. I shall avail myself of the information contained in your letter to press this matter further. Mr. Barrett is arrived here, and the first object for his relief is to obtain a dissolution of his former contract.

I will thank you for some copies of the Prussian treaty by the first opportunity and take the liberty of troubling you to forward the packets of letters which Mr. Smith the bearer of this will have the honor of delivering to you. I beg the favor of you to present my most respectful compliments to Mrs. Adams, and to be assured yourself of the sentiments of sincere esteem and respect with which I have the honor to be dear Sir, Your most obedient and humble Servant,

WSHORT FOR TH. JEFFERSON [37]

37. Letter and signature in Short's hand; TJ had dislocated his right wrist on Sept. 18. L. H. Butterfield, in *Wm. and Mary Quart.*, 3d ser., 5 (1948), 620-21.

Jefferson to Adams

Paris Octr. 23d. 1786

DEAR SIR

Your favor of Sept. the 11th. came to hand in due time and since that I have recieved the copies of the Prussian treaty you were so kind as to send me. I have recieved a short letter from Mr. Barclay dated Cadiz Septr. 25th. only announcing his arrival there and that he should proceed immediately to Madrid. At this latter place he would meet my letter informing him that we did not propose any thing further with the Piratical states at this time. The inclosed extract of a letter from Mr. Carmichael also mentions Mr. Barclay's arrival at Cadiz. A letter from Mr. Carmichael some time ago informed me that a bill had been drawn on him by Mrs. Lamb in America, by order as she said of Mr. Lamb; This gentleman not proposing to proceed either to New-York, London, or Paris to settle his accounts, I desired Mr. Carmichael, if any money remained yet in the hands of Mr. Lamb's banker at Madrid, to obstruct it's going out until he could give us information. His answer was that it was all withdrawn by Mr. Lamb. By some means or other I omitted to mention these circumstances to you at the time. I mention them now to explain the reasons of Mr. Carmichael's touching on that subject in the inclosed. We may now hourly expect from Mr. Barclay a copy of the preliminary treaty with Morocco. Is it your opinion that the definitive one [38] should be executed through his agency, or that of Colo. Franks or of any other person? I beg you to present my most friendly respects to Mrs. Adams and to be assured yourself of the esteem and attachment with which I have the honor to be Sir, your most obedient humble Servant,

TH: JEFFERSON

Jefferson to Adams

Paris Oct. 27. 1786.

DEAR SIR

I formerly had the honour of mentioning to you the measures I had taken to have our commerce with this country put on a better footing; and you know the circumstances which had occasioned the articles of whale oil and tobacco to be first brought forward. Latterly we got the

38. "Treaty with Morocco," text and notes, Boyd, X, 419-27.

committee, which had been established for this purpose, to take up the other articles, and on their report the King and council have come to the decisions explained in the inclosed letter from M. de Calonnes to me. The abandonment of revenues raised on articles of *importation* shews a friendly disposition. I have had thro this business a most zealous, and powerful auxiliary in the M. de La fayette, by whose activity it has been sooner and better done than I could otherwise possibly have expected. Tho you are free to shew the inclosed letter as you please, I would wish it to be kept out of the public papers two or three months. I am Dear Sir your affectionate friend and servant,

TH: JEFFERSON [39]

Adams to Jefferson

Grosvenor Square Nov. 30th. 1786

DEAR SIR

By Dr. Gibbon a young Gentleman of Philadelphia whom I beg Leave to introduce to you, I have the Honour to send you a few more Copies of the Prussian Treaty; and to inclose in this, a Resolution of Congress of September 26. annulling Mr. Lambs Commission and Instructions. Mr. Jay desires me to transmit it to him, and although I hope Mr. Lamb is on his Passage to New York or already arrived there, it is proper to send it along to Mr. Carmichael who will be so good as to convey it, if Mr. Lamb should not be departed. The favour of transmitting it to him let me ask of you.

You ask me in your last Letter my opinion who should be sent to exchange the Treaty with Morocco? I am content that either Mr. Barclay or Mr. Franks should go, or to leave it to Mr. Barclay to go in Person or send Mr. Franks as you shall judge best. But I wonder the Treaty has not arrived, to you.

Dont be allarmed at the late Turbulence in New England.[40] The Massachusetts Assembly had, in its Zeal to get the better of their Debt, laid on a Tax, rather heavier than the People could bear; but all will be well, and this Commotion will terminate in additional Strength to Government.

With great and Sincere Esteem, I have the Honour to be, Sir your most obedient and humble Servant,

JOHN ADAMS

39. Written with TJ's left hand.
40. Shays's Rebellion. See below, Chap. 5.

Jefferson to Abigail Adams

Paris [Nov. 1786]

DEAR MADAM

I am never happier than when I am performing good offices for good people; and the most friendly office one can perform is to make worthy characters acquainted with one another. The good things of this life are scattered so sparingly in our way that we must glean them up as we go. Yourself and Madame de Corny then must avail yourselves of the short time she will remain in London to make each other happy. A good heart and a good head will ensure her a place in your esteem. I have promised it to her: and she has yet a better title, a high respect for your character. I asked her to carry me in her pocket, that I might have the pleasure of bringing you together in person; but on examining the treaty of commerce, she found I should be contraband; that there might be a search—and seizure—and that the case would admit very specially of embarras. So instead of my having the honour of presenting her to you, she will have that of putting this into your hands, and of giving you assurances of her esteem and respect, with which permit me to mingle those of, dear Madam, your most obedient and most humble servant,

TH: JEFFERSON

Jefferson to Adams

Paris Dec. 20. 1786.

DEAR SIR

Colo. Franks will have the honor of delivering you the treaty with the emperor of Marocco, and all it's appendages. You will perceive by Mr. Barclay's letters that it is not necessary that any body should go back to Marocco to exchange ratifications. He sais however that it will be necessary that Fennish receive some testimony that we approve the treaty: and as, by the acts of Congress, our signature is necessary to give validity to it, I have had duplicates of ratification prepared, which I have signed, and now send you. If you approve and sign them send one back to me to be forwarded to Fennish thro' Mr. Carmichael. Perhaps a joint letter should be written to Fennish; if you think so, be so good as to write and sign one and send it with the ratification and I will sign and forward it. The other ratification is to go to Congress. Colo. Franks wishes to proceed with the papers to that body. He should do it I think immediately, as Mr. Jay in a letter to me of Oct. 26. says that Congress have heard thro' the French Chargé des affaires that the treaty was signed, and they wonder they have not heard it from us.

I inclose you a copy of a letter from Mr. Lamb: by which you will perceive he does not propose to quit Alicant. I will forward the resolution of Congress to Mr. Carmichael which was inclosed of yours of Nov. 30. to see if that will move him. As the turn of this resolution admits a construction that Congress may think our original appointment of him censurable, I have, as in justice I ought, in a letter to Mr. Jay, taken on myself the blame of having proposed him to you, if any blame were due. I have inclosed him a copy of my letter to you of Sep. 24. 1785. Mr. Barclay has proposed to go to Alicant to settle Lamb's accounts, and has asked to be strengthened with our authority. If Lamb will obey the resolve of Congress it will be better to let him go and settle his account there. But if he will not go back, perhaps it might not be amiss for Mr. Barclay to have instructions from us to require a settlement, those instructions to be used in that case only. If you think so, be so good as to write a joint letter and send it to me. But this, if done at all, should be done immediately. How much money has Lamb drawn?—I have suggested to Mr. Jay the expediency of putting the Barbary business into Carmichael's hands, or sending some body from America, in consideration of our separate residence and our distance from the scene of negociation.

I had seen, without alarm, accounts of the disturbances in the East. But Mr. Jay's letter on the subject had really affected me. However yours sets me to rights. I can never fear that things will go far wrong where common sense has fair play. I but just begin to use my pen a little with my right hand, but with pain. Recommending myself therefore to the friendship of Mrs. Adams I must conclude here with assurances of the sincere esteem of Dr. Sir your friend and servant,

TH: JEFFERSON

Should a Mr. Maury of Virginia, but now a merchant of Liverpool, present himself to you, I recommend him to your notice as my old schoolfellow, and a man of the most solid integrity.

Jefferson to Abigail Adams

Paris Dec. 21. 1786.

DEAR MADAM

An unfortunate dislocation of my right wrist has for three months deprived me of the honor of writing to you. I begin now to use my pen a little, but it is in great pain, and I have no other use of my hand. The swelling has remained obstinately the same for two months past, and the joint, tho I beleive well set, does not become more flexible. I am strongly advised to go to some mineral waters at Aix in Provence, and I have it in contemplation.—I was not alarmed at the humor shewn by your country-men. On the contrary I like to see the people awake and alert. But I re-ceived a letter which represented it as more serious than I had thought. Mr. Adams however restores my spirits; I believe him and I thank him for it. The good sense of the people will soon lead them back, if they have erred in a moment of surprize.—My friends write me that they will send my little daughter [41] to me by a Vessel which sails in May for England. I have taken the liberty to tell them that you will be so good as to take her under your wing till I can have notice to send for her, which I shall do express in the moment of my knowing she is arrived. She is about 8. years old, and will be in the care of her nurse, a black woman, to whom she is confided with safety. I knew your goodness too well to scruple the giving this direction before I had asked your permission. I beg you to accept assurances of the constant esteem with which I have the honor to be Dear Madam your most obedient and most humble servt.,

TH: JEFFERSON

Jefferson to Adams

Paris Jan. 11. 1787

DEAR SIR

Mr. Jay, in his last letter to me, observes that they hear nothing further of the treaty with Portugal. I have taken the liberty of telling him that I will write to you on the subject, and that he may expect to hear from you

41. Mary ("Polly") Jefferson (b. Aug. 1, 1778).

on it by the present conveyance. The Chevalier del Pinto being at London, I presume he has, or can inform you why it is delayed on their part. I will thank you also for the information he shall give you.

There is here an order of priests called the Mathurins, the object of whose institution is the begging of alms for the redemption of captives. About 18. months ago they redeemed 300, which cost them about 1500 livres a peice. They have agents residing in the Barbary states, who are constantly employed in searching and contracting for the captives of their nation, and they redeem at a lower price than any other people can. It occurred to me that their agency might be engaged for our prisoners at Algiers. I have had interviews with them, and the last night a long one with the General of the order. They offer their services with all the benignity and cordiality possible. The General told me he could not expect to redeem our prisoners as cheap as their own, but that he would use all the means in his power to do it on the best terms possible, which will be the better as there shall be the less suspicion that he acts for our public. I told him I would write to you on the subject, and speak to him again. What do you think of employing them, limiting them to a certain price, as 300 dollars for instance, or any other sum you think proper? He will write immediately to his instruments there, and in two or three months we can know the event.[42] He will deliver them at Marseilles, Cadiz, or where we please, at our expence. The money remaining of the fund destined to the Barbary business may I suppose be drawn on for this object. Write me your opinion if you please, on this subject, finally, fully, and immediately, that, if you approve the proposition, I may enter into arrangements with the General before my departure for the waters of Aix, which will be about the beginning of February. I have the honour to be with very sincere esteem and respect Dear Sir your most obedient and most humble servt.,

Th: Jefferson

Jefferson to Adams

Paris Jan. 19. 1787.

Sir

Colo. Franks having occasion for fifty pounds sterling to enable him to pursue his journey to London and New York, Mr. Grand has furnished him with that sum, for the reimbursement whereof I have drawn on you

42. See TJ to JA, Dec. 31, 1787, below, 220.

in his favor, and have to pray you to honour that draught and to charge it against the fund appropriated to the negociations with Marocco, as expended in that business. I have the honour to be with the most perfect esteem and respect, Sir, Your most obedient and most humble servt.,

Th: Jefferson

Adams to Jefferson

Grosvenor Square Jan. 25. 1787

Dear Sir

I have received your Letters of December 20. and Jan. 11. by Coll. Franks. The whole of the Business shall be dispatched, and Coll. Franks sent to Congress as you propose, as soon as possible. I have prepared a Draught of a joint Letter to Mr. Barclay and signed it, concerning Mr. Lamb, and shall inclose it to you with this. As to the Treaty with Portugal, the Chevalier De Pinto's Courier whom he sent off when you were here, is still in Lisbon. He is a confidential Domestick of De Pinto and calls every day, at the Ministers office in Lisbon but can get no answer. De Pinto is very uneasy, makes apologies when he sees me, but can do no more. He says Mr. De Melo has been sick and the Queen in the Country, and that Falkner could obtain no audience for these Causes till December. —I suppose the Treaty of Commerce between France and England has astonished Portugal, and divided the Court into Parties, so that neither administration can be settled, nor a system adopted relative to Spain France, England or America. Congress are always informed of Facts as soon as they happen, and it is not to be expected that we should write Letters every Day to tell them, that Events have not happened. As to the Reasons why the Treaty is not signed, they know at New York as well as you and I know, or even as De Pinto knows them.

The charitable, the humane, the Christian Mathurins deserve our kindest Thanks, and we should be highly obliged to them if they could discover at what Price, our Countrymen may be redeemed: but I dont think we have Authority to advance the Money without the further orders of Congress. There is no Court, or Government, that redeems its Citizens unless by a Treaty of Peace. This is left to private Connections and benevolent Societies. If Congress redeem these, it will be a Precedent for all others, and although I might in Congress vote for Setting the Precedent, and making it a Rule, Yet I dont think that as Subordinate Ministers We have a Right to do it. The Money remaining, must in February be applied to the Payment of Interest, and We must absolutely come to a full Stop in all Expences relating to Barbary Matters untill further orders of Congress. Lamb has drawn on me for Three thousand two hundred and twelve Pounds, twelve shillings. Mr. Barclay has drawn a great sum, £4020..0..0 according to the Minutes inclosed.

If Congress thought the original appointment of Lamb censurable they had reason. But you and I were not censurable. We found him ready appointed to our hands. I never saw him nor heard of him.—He ever was and still is as indifferent to me, as a Mohawk Indian. But as he came from Congress with their Dispatches of such importance, I supposed it was expected We should appoint him.—There is no harm done.—If Congress had sent the ablest Member of their own Body, at such a Time and under such pecuniary Limitations he would have done no better. With great and sincere Esteem I have the honour to be, dear Sir, your most obedient and most humble Servant,

JOHN ADAMS

5

"The first principle of a good government"

L IFE AND HISTORY are full" of political lessons, too often disregarded, Adams wrote Jefferson in October 1787.[1] On both sides of the Atlantic the world was stirring with great events. The *ancien régime* of France was tottering on the brink of revolution. Vergennes, vigilant defender of the Bourbon monarchy, who at times lent a sympathetic though enigmatic ear to American interests, had died in February. Thus a strategic link had been severed in the diplomatic chain of command accessible to Jefferson. In Philadelphia the Federal Convention was in secret session throughout the summer, debating the political future of the American nation, and news of the momentous results would not reach the diplomats in Europe until November. In Massachusetts the climax and anticlimax of Shays's Rebellion provided the most exciting and sobering information, as well as one of the reasons for John Adams to compose an essay on government that grew into a three-volume work.[2]

The letters exchanged by the Adamses and Jefferson were full of these great events as well as family incidents cherished by all three participants. Adams confessed to Jefferson that the "intimate Correspondence with you . . . is one of the most agreable Events in my Life."[3] Jefferson's friendship with Abigail Adams was a source of reflective contentment for him. In July 1786 he wrote her husband that he hoped "to provoke a letter from Mrs. Adams" from whom, he

1. JA to TJ, Oct. 9, 1787, below, 202.
2. C. F. Adams, "Life of John Adams," *Works*, I, 430-32; Marion L. Starkey, *A Little Rebellion* (N. Y., 1955), *passim*.
3. JA to TJ, March 1, 1787, below, 177.

added, "I have not received one these hundred years." [4] She soon resumed the correspondence of news and banter with Mr. Jefferson. Since Colonel Smith "has taken my daughter from me," she proposed that Jefferson exchange one of his daughters for one of her sons. "I am for Strengthening [the] federal union," she reminded him. [5]

That summer, through his artist friend John Trumbull, Jefferson met Mrs. Maria Cosway and fell in love with her. Born in Italy of an English family, Maria Hadfield, a student of art and music, had contracted a marriage of convenience with the artist Richard Cosway, who was somewhat jealous of his wife's attainments as an artist in her own right. It is not surprising that the forty-three-year-old American widower was vulnerable to the charms of this intellectual and artistic young woman of twenty-seven. Their association, though brief, was delightful, and remembrance of it was sustained in their lifelong, though intermittent, correspondence. [6] A month of frequent companionship was suddenly interrupted by an accident on September 18 which dislocated Jefferson's right wrist, probably during a fence-jumping incident while walking along the Seine with Maria. [7] Although severe pain in the wrist sobered him emotionally and forced him to use his left hand, he felt impelled to write the tender twelve-page letter of October 12 to Maria, then in Antwerp, containing the well known dialogue between the Head and the Heart. [8] The Head had prevailed in the man of reason who seldom allowed his self-discipline to get out of control, but not until the Heart had almost won full sway.

No mention of Maria Cosway occurs in the letters between Jefferson and Mrs. Adams. He did not write to her during the months of attention paid to the charming young artist, nor during his recovery from the physical pain and emotional disturbance he had suffered. At length, on December 21, he sent Mrs. Adams an incomplete explanation: "An unfortunate dislocation of my right wrist has for three months deprived me of the honor of writing to you." [9] The

4. TJ to JA, July 9, 1786, above, 141.
5. AA to TJ, July 23, 1786, above, 146.
6. Malone, *Jefferson*, II, Chap. V; Helen D. Bullock, *My Head and My Heart* ... (N. Y., 1945).
7. TJ to Maria Cosway, [Oct. 5, 1786], Boyd, X, 431-32 and *n.;* see Chap. 4 above, 154, n. 37.
8. TJ to Maria Cosway, Oct. 12, 1786, Boyd, X, 443-53, 453-54*n.;* Malone, *Jefferson*, II, 73-78.
9. TJ to AA, Dec. 21, 1786, above, 159.

reticence which Jefferson consistently maintained concerning the intimate details of personal and family affairs suggests that his feelings for Maria Cosway were too deeply held to risk expression of them even to Mrs. Adams. Jefferson corresponded with Maria in London, where the Cosways made their home, and during the autumn of 1787, while Maria was visiting in Paris, they saw each other occasionally. She broke their last appointment on the morning of her departure and thus there was no final farewell.[10]

During the winter of 1786-87 Jefferson's thoughts were on his little daughter Polly whom Virginia kinsmen were to send in a vessel bound for England the next spring. He hoped Mrs. Adams would "take her under your wing" until he could send for her, and Mrs. Adams readily consented.[11] When Polly arrived in London in June, she quickly won Mrs. Adams's affection.[12] Since Jefferson had only recently returned from a spring tour of southern France and northern Italy, accumulation of business made it inadvisable for him to defer affairs of state so soon again in order to meet his daughter. After the long voyage from Virginia, Polly expressed disappointment (and Mrs. Adams sympathized with her) that her father had not come for her but instead had sent Petit, his maître d'hôtel, "a man whom she cannot understand."[13] She had become devoted to Mrs. Adams and was reluctant to leave her. "If I must go I will," wept Polly, "but I cannot help crying so pray dont ask me to."[14] On July 15 the faithful Petit delivered her safely to her father in Paris. He expressed his own feeling of gratitude as well as his daughter's in promptly reporting her arrival to Mrs. Adams.[15]

Abigail Adams's personal pleasure was marred by the disturbing news of insurgency in her native state, to which she reacted more violently than did her husband. Adams was inclined at first to minimize it by explaining that the Assembly, "to get the better of their Debt, [had] laid on a Tax, rather heavier than the People could bear; but all will be well. . . ."[16] By late January the news was more alarming

10. Bullock, *My Head and My Heart*, Chap. VI.
11. TJ to AA, Dec. 21, 1786, above, 159; AA to TJ, Jan. 29, 1787, below, 169.
12. AA to TJ, June 26 and 27, 1787, below, 178, 179.
13. AA to TJ, July 6, 1787, below, 183-84.
14. AA to TJ, July 10, 1787, below, 184.
15. TJ to AA, July 16, 1787, below, 188. See Dumas Malone, "Polly Jefferson and Her Father," *Va. Quart. Rev.*, 7 (1931), 81-95.
16. JA to TJ, Nov. 30, 1786, above, 156.

and Mrs. Adams more apprehensive that the rebels would be "sapping the foundation [of the Commonwealth], and distroying the whole fabrick at once." [17] If reports of Shays's Rebellion were exaggerated in Massachusetts, small wonder that the degree of violence and lawlessness was magnified among those who, at a much greater distance, deplored this challenge to republican government. The cry for paper money, the stopping of the courts, the demand for repudiation of debts, the threat of mob rule, agitated Mrs. Adams to a high pitch; but Jefferson translated the episode into "a little rebellion," "the spirit of resistance to government . . . so valuable on certain occasions." [18] Although his reply must have shocked Mrs. Adams (she wrote no more to him on the subject until nine months later), the spirit of resistance won much needed reforms. If the Massachusetts General Court had not been so obtuse, it might have spared the state Shays's Rebellion, in which insurgents and militia faced each other reluctantly and bloodshed was almost accidental, in which mercy was in readiness and pardon not too long forthcoming.[19]

When the first news of the disturbance in Massachusetts reached London in the fall of 1786, John Adams remarked prophetically, "This Commotion will terminate in additional Strength to Government." [20] In early October he had begun work on his *Defence of the Constitutions of the United States*, provoked by a combination of factors: his omnivorous reading of ancient and modern history; his admiration for the English constitution and the balanced government it sustained, in contrast to the highly centralized government of France, so much praised by most of the *philosophes* of the Enlightenment; and his desire to defend the system of balanced or "mixed" government of the American states. He aimed to refute the philosopher Turgot's charge that they had slavishly imitated the English brand from which the Revolution could have freed them.[21] The challenge to republican government in Massachusetts only made Adams's task the more urgent. His native Commonwealth had produced one of the better revolutionary constitutions in terms of separation of powers

17. AA to TJ, Jan. 29, 1787, below, 168.
18. AA to TJ, Jan. 29, 1787, below, 168; TJ to AA, Feb. 22, 1787, below, 173; Boyd, XI, 175*n*.
19. Robert J. Taylor, *Western Massachusetts in the Revolution* (Providence, 1954), Chaps. VII-VIII; Starkey, *A Little Rebellion*, Chaps. XVI-XIX.
20. JA to TJ, Nov. 30, 1786, above, 156.
21. "Preface," by C. F. Adams, *Works*, IV, 273-74.

(he had been its chief author); there were others—Pennsylvania's or Virginia's—that badly needed revising, if not rewriting; but the people, with all the imperfection of man's nature, must recognize the virtues of their government. "The best republics will be virtuous, and have been so," Adams declared; "but we may hazard a conjecture, that the virtues have been the effect of the well ordered constitution, rather than the cause." Such a constitution should decentralize power and set up a proper balance between each of the components—legislature, executive, and judiciary.[22]

Adams's *Defence* was an erudite study of comparative government —of ancient republics and Italian city aristocracies—pointing up the conclusion that "the United States of America have exhibited, perhaps, the first example of governments erected on the simple principles of nature," applied in concrete terms of their written constitutions. Since Adams was personally acquainted with most of the framers of these documents, his present purpose was "to lay before the public a specimen of that kind of reading and reasoning which produced the American constitutions." [23]

The first volume of his work proved to be more timely than he anticipated, for copies were circulating in the United States not long before the Federal Convention assembled in June. Jefferson predicted that the book "will do great good in America. It's learning and it's good sense will I hope make it an institute for our politicians, old as well as young." [24] His judgment was confirmed by Benjamin Rush, a member of the Convention, who reported the volume made such an impression that "there is little doubt of our adopting a vigorous and compounded federal legislature." [25]

Composition of the *Defence*, interspersed with Adams's diplomatic responsibilities, was completed in about fifteen months. It was a hasty job, unrevised before publication, and he was apologetic about it. The early commendation he received moved him to disclaim being a great scholar.[26] On receipt of the second volume in September 1787,

22. "Defence of the Constitutions," *Works*, VI, 219; C. F. Adams, "Life of John Adams," *ibid.*, I, 426, 427.
23. "Defence," *Works*, IV, 292, 293-94.
24. TJ to JA, Feb. 23, 1787, below, 174.
25. Rush to Richard Price, June 2, 1787, L. H. Butterfield, ed., *Letters of Benjamin Rush* (Princeton, 1951), I, 418.
26. JA to TJ, March 1, 1787, below, 176; JA to Richard Cranch, Jan. 15, 1787, *Works*, I, 432; Zoltan Haraszti, *John Adams and the Prophets of Progress* (Cambridge, 1952), 46-48, Chap. IX.

Jefferson supported Adams's belief in distribution of powers as "the first principle of a good government." [27] But Adams's own generation refused to recognize him as a creative political scientist.

Abigail Adams to Jefferson

London Janry. 29th. 1787

MY DEAR SIR

I received by Col. Franks your obliging favour and am very sorry to find your wrist still continues lame; I have known very salutary effects produced by the use of British oil upon a spraind joint. I have sent a servant to see if I can procure some. You may rest assured that if it does no good: it will not do any injury.

With regard to the Tumults in my Native state [28] which you inquire about, I wish I could say that report had exagerated them. It is too true Sir that they have been carried to so allarming a Height as to stop the Courts of justice in several Counties. Ignorant, wrestless desperadoes, without conscience or principals, have led a deluded multitude to follow their standard, under pretence of grievances which have no existance but in their immaginations. Some of them were crying out for a paper currency, some for an equal distribution of property, some were for annihilating all debts, others complaning that the Senate was a useless Branch of Government, that the Court of common pleas was unnecessary, and that the sitting of the General Court in Boston was a grievence. By this list you will see the materials which compose this rebellion, and the necessity there is of the wisest and most vigorus measures to quell and suppress it. Instead of that laudible spirit which you approve, which makes a people watchfull over their Liberties and alert in the defence of them, these mobish insurgents are for sapping the foundation, and distroying the whole fabrick at once.—But as these people make only a small part of the state, when compared to the more sensible and judicious, and altho they create a just allarm and give much trouble and uneasiness, I cannot help flattering myself that they will prove sallutary to the state at large, by leading to an investigation of the causes which have produced these commotions. Luxury and extravagance both in furniture and dress had pervaded all orders of our Countrymen and women, and was hastning fast to sap their independance by involving every class of citizens in distress, and accumulating debts upon them which they were unable to discharge.

27. TJ to JA, Sept. 28, 1787, below, 199.
28. Shays's Rebellion.

Vanity was becoming a more powerfull principal than patriotism. The lower order of the community were prest for taxes, and tho possest of landed property they were unable to answer the demand, whilst those who possest money were fearfull of lending, least the mad cry of the mob should force the Legislature upon a measure very different from the touch of Midas.[29]

By the papers I send you, you will see the beneficial effects already produced. An act of the Legislature laying duties of 15 per cent upon many articles of British manufacture and totally prohibiting others—a number of Vollunteers Lawyers physicians and Merchants from Boston made up a party of Light horse commanded by Col. Hitchbourn, Leit. Col. Jackson and Higgenson, and went out in persuit of the insurgents and were fortunate enough to take 3 of their principal Leaders, Shattucks Parker and Page. Shattucks defended himself and was wounded in his knee with a broadsword. He is in Jail in Boston and will no doubt be made an example of.

Your request my dear sir with respect to your Daughter shall be punctually attended to, and you may be assured of every attention in my power towards her.

You will be so kind as to present my Love to Miss Jefferson, compliments to the Marquiss and his Lady. I am really conscience smitten that I have never written to that amiable Lady, whose politeness and attention to me deserved my acknowledgment.

The little balance which you stated in a former Letter in my favour, when an opportunity offers I should like to have in Black Lace at about 8 or 9 Livres pr. Ell. Tho late in the Month, I hope it will not be thought out of season to offer my best wishes for the Health, Long Life and prosperity of yourself and family, or to assure you of the Sincere Esteem and Friendship with which I am Your's etc. etc.,

A. ADAMS

Jefferson to Adams

Paris Feb. 6. 1787

DEAR SIR

Your favors by Colo. Franks have come safely to hand. He will set out from hence the 8th. inst. the packet being to sail from Havre the 10th. I

---

29. In AA's draft of this letter the following paragraph appears at this point: "The disturbances which have taken place have roused from their Lethargy the Supine and the Indolent animated the Brave and taught wisdom to our Rulers." Boyd, XI, 87, n. 7.

inclose you the copy of a letter lately received from Mr. Barclay, and of the paper it inclosed.[30] In a letter from Mr. Carmichael is a postscript dated Dec. 25. in the following words 'since writing the preceding, the Portuguese Ambassador has pressed me to hint that the present moment is favorable to push our treaty with his court.' In the body of the letter he sais 'the Ct. d'Expilly has promised me to continue his attention to our prisoners during his stay at Algiers, and I have also engaged the Consul of Spain who remains there on his return to take care of them. Advances have been made for their support which ought to be refunded.' I suppose that these advances have been made by order of Mr. Lamb, and that, his powers being at an end, it will be incumbent on us to take measures on that subject. The Count de Vergennes is extremely ill. His disease is gouty. We have for some days had hopes it would fix itself decidedly in the foot. It shews itself there at times, as also in the shoulder, the stomach etc. Monsr. de Calonnes is likewise ill: but his complaints are of a rheumatic kind which he has often had before. The illness of these two ministers has occasioned the postponement of the Assembly of the Notables to the 14th. and probably will yet postpone it. Nothing is yet known of the objects of that meeting. I send you a pamphlet giving a summary account of all the meetings of a general nature which have taken place heretofore. The treaty between Russia and this country is certainly concluded; but it's contents are not yet known. I shall set out for the waters of Aix [-en-Provence] on the 15th. instant, so that I am unable to say when and whence I shall have the honour of addressing you again. But I take measures for the conveying to me on my road all letters, so that should any thing extraordinary require it, I can at all times be recalled to Paris in a fortnight. I shall hope to hear from you at times as if I were in Paris. I thank you much for the valuable present of your book.[31] The subject of it is interesting and I am sure it is well treated. I shall take it on my journey that I may have time to study it. You told me once you had had thoughts of writing on the subject of hereditary aristocracy. I wish you would carry it into execution. It would make a proper sequel to the present work. I wish you all possible happiness and have the honour to be with sentiments of sincere esteem and affection, Dear Sir, your most obedient and most humble servant,

TH: JEFFERSON

30. Printed in Boyd, XI, 20-22; see also *ibid.*, 119*n.*
31. JA, *Defence of the Constitutions of the United States* (London, 1787), [Vol. I].

MONTICELLO Watercolor of the west front, by Mrs. William Thornton, *ca.* 1804

(See p. xxiv)

THOMAS JEFFERSON
Plaster bust by Jean Antoine Houdon
(See p. xxiv)

Jefferson to Adams

Paris Feb. 14. 1787

DEAR SIR

As I propose to write you on business by Mr. Cairnes who will set out in a few days for London, the object of the present letter is only to inform you that the Count de Vergennes died yesterday morning and that the Count de Montmorin is appointed his successor: and further to beg the favor of you to forward the inclosed by the first vessel from London. I set out on my journey on Sunday the 18th. I have the honour to be with sentiments of very sincere affection and respect Dear Sir Your most obedient and most humble servt.,

TH: JEFFERSON

Jefferson to Adams

Paris Feb. 20. 1787.

DEAR SIR

I am now to acknoledge the receipt of your favor of Jan. 25. Colo. Franks sailed in the packet of this month from Havre for New York. This arrangement of the packets opens a direct communication between Paris and America, and if we succeed as I expect we shall in getting Honfleur made a freeport, I hope to see that place become the deposit for our Whale oil, rice, tobacco and furs, and that from thence what is not wanted in this country may be distributed to others.   You remember giving me a letter of credit on Messrs. Willink and Staphorst for 1000 guineas to pay for the swords and medals. When the swords were finished I drew on the Vandemjvers [i.e., Vandenyver frères] with whom the money was deposited for 6500 livres to pay for the swords. They paid it. A medal is now finished, and others will very soon be: but these gentlemen say they must have fresh orders. In the mean time the workmen complain. Will you be so good as to draw in favor of Mr. Grand on Willink etc. for the balance of the thousand guineas (which is about the sum that will be necessary) and send the bill to Mr. Grand, who in my absence will negotiate it and pay the workmen. I inclose you Vandemjers answer.   The meeting of the Notables on Thursday and the necessity of paying my court to our new minister will detain me till Friday and perhaps till Tuesday next. Nothing is known yet of the objects of this assembly. I inclose you two new pamphlets relative to it: and will inform you of whatever I can discover relative to it during my stay.

I learn with real pain the resolution you have taken of quitting Europe. Your presence on this side the Atlantic gave me a confidence that if any difficulties should arise within my department, I should always have one to advise with on whose counsels I could rely. I shall now feel bewidowed. I do not wonder at your being tired out by the conduct of the court you are at. But is there not room to do a great deal of good for us in Holland in the department of money? No one can do it so well as yourself. But you have taken your resolution I am sure on mature consideration, and I have nothing to offer therefore but my regrets. If any thing transpires from the Notables before my departure worth communication, you shall yet hear from me. In the mean time believe me to be with sincere esteem and respect Dr. Sir your most obedt. and most humble servt.,

TH: JEFFERSON

Adams to Jefferson

Grosvenor Square Feb. 20. 1787

DEAR SIR

Dr. Gordon who is about publishing his Proposals for printing his History desires a Letter to you.—I told him that he might depend upon your good offices without any Letter, but as no harm will be done by complying with his Desire I beg Leave to introduce him, and to recommend his History to your Patronage in France. With equal affection, Esteem and respect, I have the Honour to be, Sir your most obedient humble Servant,

JOHN ADAMS

Jefferson to Abigail Adams

Paris Feb. 22. 1787.

DEAR MADAM

I am to acknolege the honor of your letter of Jan. 29. and of the papers you were so good as to send me. They were the latest I had seen or have yet seen. They left off too in a critical moment; [32] just at the point where the Malcontents make their submission on condition of pardon, and before the answer of government was known. I hope they pardoned them. The spirit of resistance to government is so valuable on certain occasions, that I wish it to be always kept alive. It will often be exercised when wrong, but better so than not to be exercised at all. I like a little rebellion now and then. It is like a storm in the Atmosphere. It is wonderful that no letter or paper tells us who is president of Congress, tho' there are letters in Paris to the beginning of January. I suppose I shall hear when I come back from my journey, which will be eight months after he will have been chosen. And yet they complain of us for not giving them intelligence. Our Notables assembled to-day, and I hope before the departure of Mr. Cairnes I shall have heard something of their proceedings worth communicating to Mr. Adams. The most remarkeable effect of this convention as yet is the number of puns and bon mots it has generated. I think were they all collected it would make a more voluminous work than the Encyclopedie. This occasion, more than any thing I have seen, convinces me that this nation is incapable of any serious effort but under the word of command. The people at large view every object only as it may furnish puns and bon mots; and I pronounce that a good punster would disarm the whole nation were they ever so seriously disposed to revolt. Indeed, Madam, they are gone. When a measure so capable of doing good as the calling the Notables is treated with so much ridicule, we may conclude the nation desperate, and in charity pray that heaven may send them good kings.— The bridge at the place Louis XV. is begun. The hotel dieu is to be abandoned and new ones to be built. The old houses on the old bridges are in a course of demolition. This is all I know of Paris. We are about to lose the Count d'Aranda, who has desired and obtained his recall. Fernand Nunnez, before destined for London is to come here. The Abbés Arnoux and Chalut are well. The Dutchess Danville somewhat recovered from the loss of her daughter. Mrs. Barrett very homesick, and fancying herself otherwise sick. They will probably remove to Honfleur. This is all our news. I have only to add then that Mr. Cairnes has taken charge of 15. aunes of black lace for you at 9 livres the aune, purchased by Petit and therefore I hope better purchased than some things have been for you; and that I am with sincere esteem Dear Madam your affectionate humble servt.,

TH: JEFFERSON

32. In Shays's Rebellion.

Jefferson to Adams

Paris Feb. 23. 1787

DEAR SIR

The Notables met yesterday. The king opened the assembly with a short speech, wherein he expressed his inclination to consult with them on the affairs of his kingdom, to receive their opinions on the plans he had digested, and to endeavor to imitate the head of his family Henry IV. whose name is so dear to the nation. The speech was affectionate. The Guarde des sceaux [33] spoke about 20 minutes, complimented the Clergy, the Noblesse, the Magistrates and tiers etats. The Comptroller general spoke about an hour. He enumerated the expences necessary to arrange his department when he came to it, he said his returns had been minutely laid before the king, he took a review of the preceding administrations, and more particularly of Mr. Neckar's, he detailed the improvements which had been made, he portrayed the present state of the finances, and sketched the several schemes proposed for their improvement; he spoke on a change in the form of the taxes, the removal of the interior custom houses to the frontiers, provincial administrations and some other objects. The assembly was then divided into Committees. To-day there was to be another grand assembly, the plans more fully explained and referred to the discussion of the Committees. The grand assembly will meet once a week and vote individually.   The propriety of my attending the first audience day of Count Montmorin, which will not be till the 27th. retards my departure till then.

I have read your book with infinite satisfaction and improvement. It will do great good in America. It's learning and it's good sense will I hope make it an institute for our politicians, old as well as young. There is one opinion in it however, which I will ask you to reconsider, because it appears to me not entirely accurate, and not likely to do good. Pa. 362. 'Congress is not a legislative, but a diplomatic assembly.' Separating into parts the whole sovereignty of our states, some of these parts are yeilded to Congress. Upon these I should think them both legislative and executive; and that they would have been judiciary also, had not the Confederation required them for certain purposes to appoint a judiciary. It has accordingly been the decision of our courts that the Confederation is a part of the law of the land, and superior in authority to the ordinary laws, because it cannot be altered by the legislature of any one state. I doubt whether

33. Principal judicial officer of the kingdom of France.

they are at all a diplomatic assembly. On the first news of this work, there were proposals to translate it. Fearing it might be murdered in that operation, I endeavored to secure a good translator. This is done, and I lend him my copy to translate from.[34] It will be immediately announced to prevent others attempting it. I am with sincere esteem and respect Dear Sir Your most obedt. and most humble servt.,

TH: JEFFERSON

Jefferson to Adams

Paris Feb. 28. 1787.

DEAR SIR

The inclosed letter is come to hand since I had the honour of addressing you last.[35] Will you be so good as to forward a copy to Mr. Jay? The assembly of Notables is held to secrecy, so that little transpires and this floats among so much incertain matter that we know not what can be depended on. 80. millions more of annual revenue and provincial assemblies are the certain objects. The giving to the protestants a civil state will be effected without recurrence to the Notables. I am now in the moment of my departure and have therefore only time to add assurances of the esteem and respect with which I have the honor to be Dear Sir your most obedient humble servt.,

TH: JEFFERSON

Adams to Jefferson

London March 1. 1787

DEAR SIR

I am much obliged to you for your favours of Feb. 20. and 23 by Mr. Carnes, and the curious Pamphlets.

Opening a direct Communication between Paris and America will facilitate the Trade of the two Countries, very much, and the new Treaty between France and England, will promote it still more. John Bull dont

34. First French edition published by Buisson: *Defense des constitutions americaines* ... (1792) with "Notes et Observations" by Jacques-Vincent Delacroix; but it is not certain that he was the "good translator" referred to by TJ.
35. Barclay to American Commissioners, Feb. 10, 1787, Boyd, XI, 132-33.

see it, and if he dont see a Thing at first, you know it is a rule with him ever after wards to swear that it dont exist, even when he does both see it and feel it.

I have this moment written to Messrs. Willinks and Vanstaphorsts to remit to you or Mr. Grand in your absence, what remains to be received to make up the Thousand Guineas for the Swords and Medals, you having before drawn for 6500 Livres tournois, as part of them.

My Resolution of Quitting Europe, has been taken upon mature deliberation: but really upon motives of Necessity, as much at least as Choice. —Congress cannot consistent with their own honour and Dignity, renew my Commission to this Court—and I assure you, I should hold it so inconsistent with my own honour and Dignity little as that may be, that if it were possible for Congress to forget theirs I would not forget mine, but send their Commission back to them, unless a Minister were sent from his Britannic Majesty to Congress.

As to a Residence in Holland, that Climate is so destructive to my health, that I could never bear it: and I am sure it would be fatal to her, on whom depends all the satisfaction that I have in Life. No Consideration would tempt me to think of removing to that Country with my Family.

For a Man who has been thirty Years rolling like a stone never three years in the same Place, it is no very pleasant Speculation, to cross the seas with a Family, in a State of Uncertainty what is to be his fate; what reception he shall meet at home; whether he shall set down in private Life to his Plough; or push into turbulent Scenes of Sedition and Tumult; whether be sent to Congress, or a Convention or God knows what.—If it lay in my Power, I would take a Vow, to retire to my little Turnip yard, and never again quit it.—I feel very often a violent disposition to take some Resolution and swear to it. But upon the whole, it is best to preserve my Liberty to do as I please according to Circumstances.

The approbation you express in general of my poor Volume, is a vast consolation to me. It is an hazardous Enterprize, and will be an unpopular Work in America for a long time.—When I am dead, it may be regretted that such Advice was not taken in the season of it.—But as I have made it early in life and all along a Rule to conceal nothing from the People which appeared to me material for their Happiness and Prosperity, however unpopular it might be at the time, or with particular Parties, I am determined not now to begin to flatter popular Prejudices and Party Passions however they may be countenanced by great authorities.

The Opinion you Object to p. 362, "that Congress is not a legislative but a diplomatic assembly" I should wish to have considered as a Problem, rather for Consideration, than as an opinion: and as a Problem too, relative to the Confederation as it now stands, rather than to any other Plan that may be in Contemplation of the States. It is a most difficult Topick, and no Man at a distance can judge of it, so well as those in America. If the Book Should be translated into french, I wish you would insert this, in a Note. You have laid me under great obligation, by taking the trouble to Secure a Good Translator.—If the Thing is worth translating at all, it will not surely bare to loose any Thing by the Translation.—But will not the Government proscribe it?—If I should get well home, and Spend a few Years in Retirement, I shall pursue this subject, somewhat further: but I hope never to be left, again, to publish so hasty a Production as this. A Work upon the Subject you mention, *Nobility in general,* which I once hinted to you a wish to see handled at large would be too extensive and Splendid for my means and Forces. It would require many Books which I have not, and a more critical Knowledge both of ancient and modern Languages than at my Age a Man can aspire to.—There are but two Circumstances, which will be regretted by me, when I leave Europe. One is the oppertunity of Searching any questions of this kind, in any books that may be wanted, and the other will be the Interruption of that intimate Correspondence with you, which is one of the most agreable Events in my Life. There are four or five Persons here, with whom I hold a friendly Intercourse and shall leave with some degree of Pain but I am not at home in this Country. With every affectionate and friendly Sentiment I am and shall be in this world and the future yours,

JOHN ADAMS

Adams to Jefferson

London April 18. 1787

DEAR SIR

Mr. Mortimer the Bearer of this Letter, is a Gentleman of Letters, and although little known to me, is recommended by some of my Friends as a worthy, though unfortunate Man. He is represented to be a Friend to Liberty, and Humanity, and as such I beg leave to introduce him to you, and to ask for him any friendly Advice or Aid you may be able to afford him in his Views, of litterary Employment as a Teacher of Languages, or otherwise. With great Regard I am, my dear Sir always yours,

JOHN ADAMS

Abigail Adams to Jefferson

London june 26 1787

DEAR SIR

I have to congratulate you upon the safe arrival of your Little Daughter [Polly] whom I have only a few moments ago received. She is in fine Health and a Lovely little Girl I am sure from her countanance, but at present every thing is strange to her, and she was very loth to try New Friends for old. She was so much attachd to the Captain and he to her, that it was with no small regret that I seperated her from him, but I dare say I shall reconcile her in a day or two. I tell her that I did not see her sister cry once. She replies that her sister was older and ought to do better, besides she had her pappa with her. I shew her your picture. She says she cannot know it, how should she when she should not know you. A few hours acquaintance and we shall be quite Friends I dare say. I hope we may expect the pleasure of an other visit from you now I have so strong an inducement to tempt you. If you could bring Miss Jefferson with you, it would reconcile her little Sister to the thoughts of taking a journey. It would be proper that some person should be accustomed to her. The old Nurse whom you expected to have attended her, was sick and unable to come. She has a Girl about 15 or 16 with her,[36] the Sister of the Servant you have with you. As I presume you have but just returnd from your late excursion, you will not put yourself to any inconvenience or Hurry in comeing or sending for her. You may rely upon every attention towards her and every care in my power. I have just endeavourd to amuse her by telling her that I would carry her to Sadlers Wells.[37] After describing the amusement to her with an honest simplicity, I had rather says she see captain Ramsey one moment, than all the fun in the World.

I have only time before the post goes, to present my compliments to Mr. Short. Mr. Adams and Mrs. Smith desire to be rememberd to you. Captain Ramsey has brought a Number of Letters. As they may be of importance to you to receive them we have forwarded them by the post. Miss Polly sends her duty to you and Love to her Sister and says she will try to be good and not cry. So she has wiped her eyes and layd down to sleep. Believe me dear Sir affectionately yours etc etc,

A ADAMS

36. Sally Hemings (*b.* 1773).

37. Sadler's Wells in Clerkenwell near London dates back to 1683 as a spa. In the eighteenth century it became an amusement park, with athletic contests, dancing, trained-animal acts, and musical programs. Warwick Wroth and Arthur E. Wroth, *The London Pleasure Gardens of the Eighteenth Century* (London and N. Y., 1896), 43-53.

Abigail Adams to Jefferson

London june 27 1787

DEAR SIR

I had the Honour of addressing you yesterday and informing you of the safe arrival of your daughter. She was but just come when I sent of my letter by the post, and the poor little Girl was very unhappy being wholy left to strangers. This however lasted only a few Hours, and Miss is as contented to day as she was misirable yesterday. She is indeed a fine child. I have taken her out to day and purchased her a few articles which she could not well do without and I hope they will meet your approbation. The Girl who is with her is quite a child, and Captain Ramsey is of opinion will be of so little Service that he had better carry her back with him. But of this you will be a judge. She seems fond of the child and appears good naturd.

I sent by yesterdays post a Number of Letters which Captain Ramsey brought with him not knowing of any private hand, but Mr. Trumble has just calld to let me know that a Gentleman sets off for paris tomorrow morning. I have deliverd him two Letters this afternoon received, and requested him to wait that I might inform you how successfull a rival I have been to Captain Ramsey, and you will find it I imagine as difficult to seperate Miss Polly from me as I did to get her from the Captain. She stands by me while I write and asks if I write every day to her pappa? But as I have never had so interesting a subject to him to write upon [...] I hope he will excuse the hasty scrips for the [scanty?] intelligence they contain, and be assured Dear Sir that I am with sentiments of sincere esteem your Humble Servant,

A ADAMS

Jefferson to Abigail Adams

Paris July 1. 1787.

A thousand thanks to you, my dear Madam, for your kind attention to my little daughter. Her distresses I am sure must have been troublesome to you: but I know your goodness will forgive her, and forgive me too for having brought them on you. Petit now comes for her. By this time she will have learned again to love the hand that feeds and comforts her, and have formed an attachment to you. She will think I am made only to tear her from all her affections. I wish I could have come myself. The pleasure of a visit to yourself and Mr. Adams would have been a great additional inducement. But, just returned from my journey, I have the arrearages of 3. or 4. months all crouded on me at once. I do not presume to write you news from America, because you have it so much fresher and frequenter than I have. I hope all the disturbances of your country are quieted and with little bloodshed. What think you of present appearances in Europe? The Emperor and his subjects? The Dutch and their half king, who would be a whole one? in fine the French and the English? These new friends and allies have hardly had time to sign that treaty which was to cement their love and union like man and wife, before they are shewing their teeth at each other. We are told a fleet of 6. or 12 ships is arming on your side the channel; here they talk of 12 or 20, and a camp of 15,000 men. But I do not think either party in earnest. Both are more laudably intent on arranging their affairs.—Should you have incurred any little expences on account of my daughter or her maid, Petit will be in a condition to repay them. If considerable, he will probably be obliged to refer you to me, and I shall make it my duty to send you a bill immediately for the money. Count Sarsfeild sets out for London four days hence. At dinner the other day at M. de Malesherbe's he was sadly abusing an English dish called Gooseberry tart. I asked him if he had ever tasted the cranberry. He said, no. So I invited him to go and eat cranberries with you. He said that on his arrival in London he would send to you and demander á diner. I hope Mrs. Smith and the little grandson are well. Be so good as to present me respectfully to her. I have desired Colo. Smith to take a bed here on his return. I will take good care of him for her, and keep him out of all harm. I have the honour to be with sentiments of sincere esteem and respect Dear Madam your most obedient and most humble servt.,

TH: JEFFERSON

Jefferson to Adams

Paris July 1. 1787.

DEAR SIR

I returned about three weeks ago from a very useless voiage. Useless, I mean, as to the object which first suggested it, that of trying the effect of the mineral waters of Aix en Provence on my hand. I tried these because recommended among six or eight others as equally beneficial, and because they would place me at the beginning of a tour to the seaports of Marseilles, Bourdeaux, Nantes and Lorient which I had long meditated, in hopes that a knowlege of the places and persons concerned in our commerce and the information to be got from them might enable me sometimes to be useful. I had expected to satisfy myself at Marseilles of the causes of the difference of quality between the rice of Carolina and that of Piedmont which is brought in quantities to Marseilles. Not being able to do it, I made an excursion of three weeks into the rice country beyond the Alps, going through it from Vercelli to Pavia about 60 miles. I found the difference to be, not in the management as had been supposed both here and in Carolina, but in the species of rice, and I hope to enable them in Carolina to begin the Cultivation of the Piedmont rice and carry it on hand in hand with their own that they may supply both qualities, which is absolutely necessary at this market. I had before endeavored to lead the depot of rice from Cowes to Honfleur and hope to get it received there on such terms as may draw that branch of commerce from England to this country. It is an object of 250,000 guineas a year. While passing thro' the towns of Turin, Milan and Genoa, I satisfied myself of the practicability of introducing our whale oil for their consumption and I suppose it would be equally so in the other great cities of that country. I was sorry that I was not authorized to set the matter on foot. The merchants with whom I chose to ask conferences, met me freely, and communicated fully, knowing I was in a public character. I could however only prepare a disposition to meet our oil merchants. On the article of tobacco I was more in possession of my ground, and put matters into a train for inducing their government to draw their tobaccos directly from the U.S. and not as heretofore from G.B. I am now occupied with the new ministry here to put the concluding hand to the new regulations for our commerce with this country, announced in the letter of M. de Calonnes which I sent you last fall. I am in hopes in addition to those, to obtain a suppression of the duties on Tar, pitch, and turpentine, and an extension of the privileges of American *whale* oil, to their *fish* oils in general. I find that the quantity of Codfish oil brought to Lorient is considerable. This being got off hand (which will be in a few days) the chicaneries and vexations of the farmers on the article of tobacco, and their elusions of the order of Bernis,[38] call for the next attention. I have reason to hope good dispositions in the new ministry towards our commerce with this country. Besides endeavoring on all occasions to multiply the points of contact and connection with this country, which I consider as our surest main-stay under every event, I have had it

38. Named for Calonne's chateau, where on May 24, 1786, a meeting of the "American Committee" was held, both Calonne and Vergennes being present, to put Franco-American commerce on a better footing. TJ to JA, July 9, Oct. 27, 1786, above, 141, 155-56; *Diplomatic Correspondence, 1783-1789,* I, 764-65.

much at heart to remove from between us every subject of misunderstanding or irritation. Our debts to the king, to the officers, and the farmers are of this description. The having complied with no part of our engagements in these draws on us a great deal of censure, and occasioned a language in the Assemblées des notables very likely to produce dissatisfaction between us. Dumas being on the spot in Holland, I had asked of him some time ago, in confidence, his opinion on the practicability of transferring these debts from France to Holland, and communicated his answer to Congress, pressing them to get you to go over to Holland and try to effect this business.[39] Your knowlege of the ground and former successes occasioned me to take this liberty without consulting you, because I was sure you would not weigh your personal trouble against public good. I have had no answer from Congress, but hearing of your journey to Holland have hoped that some money operation had led you there. If it related to the debts of this country I would ask a communication of what you think yourself at liberty to communicate, as it might change the form of my answers to the eternal applications I receive. The debt to the officers of France carries an interest of about 2000 guineas, so we may suppose it's principal is between 30. and 40,000. This makes more noise against [us] than all our other debts put together.

I send you the arrets which begin the reformation here, and some other publications respecting America: together with copies of letters received from Obryon and Lambe.[40] It is believed that a naval armament has been ordered at Brest in correspondence with that of England. We know certainly that orders are given to form a camp in the neighborhood of Brabant, and that Count Rochambeau has the command of it. It's amount I cannot assert. Report says 15,000 men. This will derange the plans of oeconomy. I take the liberty of putting under your cover a letter for Mrs. Kinloch of South Carolina, with a packet,[41] and will trouble you to enquire for her and have them delivered. The packet is of great consequence, and therefore referred to her care, as she will know the safe opportunities of conveying it. Should you not be able to find her, and can forward the packet to it's address by any very safe conveiance I will beg you to do it. I have the honour to be with sentiments of the most perfect friendship and esteem Dear Sir your most obedient and most humble servant,

TH: JEFFERSON

39. C. W. F. Dumas to TJ, Jan. 23, 1787, Boyd, XI, 62-65.

40. O'Bryen to TJ, April 28, 1787, and Lamb to TJ, May 20, 1787, *ibid.*, 321-22, 368-69.

41. TJ to Anne Cleland Kinloch, July 1, 1787, with "a small parcel of Piedmont rice, addressed to Mr. [William] Drayton chairman of the committee of the South Carolina society for promoting and improving agriculture." *Ibid.*, 520-21.

Abigail Adams to Jefferson

London july 6 1787

MY DEAR SIR

If I had thought you would so soon have sent for your dear little Girl, I should have been tempted to have kept her arrival here, from you a secret. I am really loth to part with her, and she last evening upon Petit's arrival, was thrown into all her former distresses, and bursting into Tears, told me it would be as hard to leave me as it was her Aunt Epps. She has been so often deceived that she will not quit me a moment least she should be carried away. Nor can I scarcely prevail upon her to see Petit. Tho she says she does not remember you, yet she has been taught to consider you with affection and fondness, and depended upon your comeing for her. She told me this morning, that as she had left all her Friends in virginia to come over the ocean to see you, she did think you would have taken the pains to have come here for her, and not have sent a man whom she can-not understand. I express her own words. I expostulated with her upon the long journey you had been, and the difficulty you had to come and upon the care kindness and attention of Petit, whom I so well knew. But she cannot yet hear me. She is a child of the quickest sensibility, and the maturest understanding, that I have ever met with for her years. She had been 5 weeks at sea, and with men only, so that on the first day of her arrival, she was as rough as a little sailor, and then she been decoyed from the ship, which made her very angry, and no one having any Authority over her; I was apprehensive I should meet with some trouble. But where there are such materials to work upon as I have found in her, there is no danger. She listend to my admonitions, and attended to my advice and in two days, was restored to the amiable lovely Child which her Aunt had formed her. In short she is the favorite of every creature in the House, and I cannot but feel Sir, how many pleasures you must lose by committing her to a convent. Yet situated as you are, you cannot keep her with you. The Girl she has with her, wants more care than the child, and is wholy incapable of looking properly after her, without some superiour to direct her.

As both Miss Jefferson and the maid had cloaths only proper for the sea, I have purchased and made up for them, such things as I should have done had they been my own, to the amount of Eleven or 12 Guineys. The particulars I will send by Petit.

Captain Ramsey has said that he would accompany your daughter to

Paris provided she would not go without him, but this would be putting you to an expence that may perhaps be avoided by Petits staying a few days longer. The greatest difficulty in familiarizing her to him, is on account of the language. I have not the Heart to force her into a Carriage against her will and send her from me almost in a Frenzy; as I know will be the case, unless I can reconcile her to the thoughts of going and I have given her my word that Petit shall stay untill I can hear again from you. Books are her delight, and I have furnishd her out a little library, and she reads to me by the hour with great distinctness, and comments on what she reads with much propriety.

Mrs. Smith desires to be remembered to you, and the little Boy [42] his Grandmama thinks is as fine a Boy as any in the Kingdom. I am my dear sir with Sentiments of Esteem Your Friend and Humble Servant,

A ADAMS

Jefferson to Abigail Adams

Paris July 10. 1787.

DEAR MADAM

This being the day on which, according to my calculation, my daughter would be crossing the channel, I had calculated the course from Dover to Calais and was watching the wind when your favour of the 6th. was put into my hands. That of June 27. had been received four days ago. I perceived that that had happened which I had apprehended, that your goodness had so attached her to you that her separation would become difficult. I had been in hopes that Petit would find means to rival you, and I still hope he will have done it so as that they may be on their way here at present. If she were to stay till she should be willing to come, she would stay till you cease to be kind to her, and that, Madam, is a term for which I cannot wait. Her distress will be in the moment of parting and I am in hopes Petit will soon be able to lessen it.—We are impatient to hear what our federal convention are doing. I have no news from America later than the 27th. of April. Nor is there any thing here worth mentioning. The death of Mr. Saint James and flight of M. de Calonnes are perhaps known to you. A letter of M. de Mirabeau to the K. of Prussia is handed about by the Colporteurs. I will endeavor to find an opportunity of sending it

42. William Steuben Smith (b. April 30, 1787), son of Colonel William Stephens Smith and Abigail Adams Smith.

to Mr. Adams.—Your kind advances for my daughter shall be remitted you by Colo. Smith when he returns or some other good opportunity. I have the honor to be with sentiments of gratitude for your goodness and with those of perfect esteem Dr. Madam your most obedt. humble servt.,

TH: JEFFERSON

Abigail Adams to Jefferson, with Enclosure

London july 10th. 1787

DEAR SIR

When I wrote you last I did not know that petit had taken places in the Stage and paid for them. This being the case I have represented it to your little daughter and endeavourd to prevail with her to consent to going at the time appointed. She says if I must go I will, but I cannot help crying so pray dont ask me to. I should have taken great pleasure in presenting her to you here, as you would then have seen her with her most engageing countanance. Several lines of an old song frequently occur to me as different objects affect her.

> What she thinks in her Heart
> You may read in her Eyes
> For knowing no art
> She needs no disguise.

I never saw so intelligent a countanance in a child before, and the pleasure she has given me is an ample compensation for any little services I have been able to render her. I can easily conceive the earnest desire you must have to embrace so lovely a child after so long a seperation from her. That motive, and my own intention of setting out next week upon a journey into the County of Devonshire, has prevaild with me to consent to parting with her so soon, but most reluctantly I assure you. Her temper, her disposition, her sensibility are all formed to delight. Yet perhaps at your first interview you may find a little roughness but it all subsides in a very little time, and she is soon attached by kindness. I inclose a memorandum of the articles purchased [I have? be]en a little particular, that you might know how I [have dispose]d of the money. If at any time I can be of service in this [respec]t it will give me pleasure. I have desired petit to Buy me 12 Ells of black lace at 8 Livres pr. Ell and 1 dozen of white and one of coulourd Gloves. You will be so good as to place them to my account and Col. Smith will take them when he returns.

As to politicks, to avoid touching so disagreeable a subject, I send you the Boston news papers received by the last vessels.

Mrs. Paridise has just left me and desires to be rememberd to you. She is just upon the eve of departure for virginia. Whether he can be prevaild upon to go on Board altho their passage is taken, and every thing in readiness, is very uncertain. She is determined at all Hazards. He most assuredly will get a Seat in Kings Bench if he stays behind. His affairs are daily worse and worse. Mr. Adams will write you. He has not a portrait that he likes to send you. Mr. Trumble talks of taking one. If he succeeds better than his Brethren, Mr. Adams will ask your acceptance of it. You will be so good as to let me hear from my dear little Girl by the first post after her arrival. My Love to her sister whom I congratulate upon such an acquisition.

I have not been able to find Mrs. Kinlock yet, but hope too. If I should not, Mr. Heyward is going to carolina in a few days and I will send the package by him. All your other Letters were deliverd as directed.

With Sentiments of the highest Esteem I am dear sir your Humble Servant,

A ADAMS

I have received of petit six Louis d'ors. [I do not know] what the exchange is. But the remainder you wi[ll be so good] as to let him purchase me some lace and Gloves with the remainder.

ENCLOSURE

Memorandum of articles by Mrs. Adams for Miss Jefferson and Maid

	£	s	d
Paid for bringing the Trunks from Tower Hill		5	6
Four fine Irish Holland frocks	3	10	
5 yd. white dimity for shirts		15	
4 yd. checked muslin for a frock	1	10	
3 yd. lace Edging to trim it		6	6
To making the frock		5	
3 yd. flannel for under coats		7	6
A Brown Bever Hat and feathers		13	
2 pr. leather Gloves		2	4
5 yd. diaper for arm Cloths		5	10
6 pr. cotton Stockings		13	6
3 yd. blue sash Ribbon		3	
To diaper for pockets linning tape			
cloth for night caps etc		5	6
To a comb and case, comb Brush, tooth Brush		1	6

For the Maid Servant

12 yds. calico for 2 short Gowns and coats	1	5	6
4 yd half Irish linen for Aprons		7	4
3 pr Stockings		6	
2 yd linning		2	
1 Shawl handkerchief		4	6
paid for washing		6	8
Sterling	10	15	8
	11	16	2[43]

Received Six Louis d'ors of petit.

A ADAMS

Adams to Jefferson

Grosvenor Square July 10, 1787

DEAR SIR

I received with great Pleasure your favour of the first.—Your Excursion I dare answer for it, will be advantageous in many respects to our Country. —The object of mine to Holland was to procure Money, and I had the good fortune to obtain as much as was necessary for the then present Purpose: but it was not in Consequence of any orders from Congress, and therefore I am under some Apprehension for fear my Loan should not be ratified with so much Promptitude as I wish. If Congress ratify my Loan they will be able to pay the 2000 Guineas to the officers you mention, and to pay the Principal Sum too, if they please.—I have no doubt that Congress might borrow Money in Holland to pay off the Debt to France, if the States would lay on a Duty, to pay the Interest.—If you will venture to draw upon Willinks and Van Staphorsts, I Suppose you may have the Money to pay the French officers their Interest. But perhaps you would choose to have a previous order of Congress or the Board of Treasury.

I am extreamly sorry, that you could not come for your Daughter in Person, and that we are obliged to part with her so soon. In my Life I never saw a more charming Child. Accept of my Thanks, for the Pamphlets and Arrets.—Tell Mazzei, he cannot conceive what an Italian I am become.—I read nothing else, and if he writes to me it must be in that Language: but he must remember to make his Letters, so plain, that I can

43. Correction of AA's total is in TJ's hand.

see them. In writing English he is obliged to write so slow that his Characters are visible; but in Italian such is the Rapidity of his Eloquence, that I must get a Solar Microscope, if he is not upon his guard. You too, write Italian, and if you like it, you will oblige me: but I am not yet presumptuous enough to write a Line in any Thing but rugged American. I am, my dear Sir with perfect Friendship yours,

JOHN ADAMS

Jefferson to Abigail Adams

Paris July 16. 1787.

DEAR MADAM

I had the happiness of receiving yesterday my daughter in perfect health. Among the first things she informed me of was her promise to you, that after she should have been here a little while she would go back to pay you a visit of four or five days. She had taken nothing into her calculation but the feelings of her own heart which beat warmly with gratitude to you. She had fared very well on the road, having got into favor with gentlemen and ladies so as to be sometimes on the knee of one sometimes of another. She had totally forgotten her sister, but thought, on seeing me, that she recollected something of me. I am glad to hear that Mr. and Mrs. Paradise are gone or going to America. I should have written to them, but supposed them actually gone. I imagined Mr. Hayward gone long ago. He will be a very excellent opportunity for sending the packet to Mr. Drayton. Petit will execute your commissions this morning, and I will get Mr. Appleton to take charge of them. He sets out for London the day after tomorrow. The king and parliament are at extremities about the stamp act, the latter refusing to register it without seeing accounts etc. M. de Calonne has fled to the Hague. I had a letter from Colo. Smith dated Madrid June 30. He had been detained by the illness of his servant, but he was about setting out for Lisbon.[44] My respects attend his lady and Mr. Adams, and eternal thanks yourself with every sentiment of esteem and regard from Dear Madam your most obedient and most humble servt,

TH: JEFFERSON

44. To present to the Queen of Portugal Congress's letter of thanks for giving protection to American vessels. William Stephens Smith to TJ, June 30, 1787, Boyd, XI, 511-12 and n.

Jefferson to Adams

Paris July 17. 1787.

DEAR SIR

I have been duly honoured with your's of the 10th. inst. and am happy to hear of the success of your journey to Amsterdam. There can be no doubt of it's ratification by Congress. Would to heaven they would authorize you to take measures for transferring the debt of this country to Holland before you leave Europe. Most especially is it necessary to get rid of the debt to the officers. Their connections at court are such as to excite very unfavorable feelings there against us, and some very hard things have been said (particularly in the Assemblée des Notables) on the prospects relative to our debts. The paiment of the interest to the officers would have kept them quiet: but there are two years now due to them. I dare not draw for it without instructions, because in the instances in which I have hitherto ventured to act uninstructed, I have never been able to know whether they have been approved in the private sentiments of the members of Congress, much less by any vote. I have pressed on them the expediency of transferring the French debts to Holland, in order to remove every thing which may excite irritations between us and this nation. I wish it may be done before this ministry may receive ill impressions of us. They are at present very well disposed. I send you by Mr. Appleton some pamphlets and have the honour to be with sentiments of very cordial esteem and respect Dear Sir your affectionate humble servant,

TH: JEFFERSON

Jefferson to Adams

Paris July 23. 1787.

DEAR SIR

Frouillé, the bookseller here who is engaged in having your book translated and printed, understanding that you were about publishing a sequel to it, has engaged me to be the channel of his prayers to you to favor his operation by transmitting hither the sheets of the sequel as they shall be printed; and he will have them translated by the same hand, which is a good one.

It is necessary for me to explain the passage in Mr. Barclay's letter of July 13th.[45] of which he writes me he had sent you a duplicate, wherein

45. Barclay to American Commissioners, *ibid.*, 582-83.

he mentions that I had given him a full dispensation from waiting on you in London. Mr. Barclay was arrested in Bourdeaux for debt and put into prison. The parliament released him after five days on the footing of his being Consul and minister from the U.S. to Marocco. His adversaries applied here to deprive him of his privilege. I spoke on the subject to the minister. He told me that the character of Consul was no protection at all from private arrest, but that he would try to avail him of the other character. I found however that the event might be doubtful, and stated the whole in a letter to Mr. Barclay, observing at the same time that I knew of nothing which rendered it necessary for him to come to *Paris* before his departure for America. He determined therefore to go to America immediately which indeed was his wisest course, as he would have been harrassed immediately by his creditors.—Our funds here have been out some time and Mr. Grand is at the length of his tether in advancing for us. He has refused very small demands for current occasions, and I am not clear he will not refuse my usual one for salary. He has not told me so, but I am a little diffident of it. I shall know in a few days. Whether he does or not, I cannot approve of his protesting small and current calls. Having had nothing to do with any other banker, I cannot say what their practice is: but I suppose it their practice to advance for their customers, when their funds happen to be out, in proportion to the sums which they pass thro' their hands. Mr. Grand is a very sure banker, but a very timid one, and I fear he thinks it possible that he may lose his advances for the United states. Should he reject my draught, would there be any prospect of it's being answered in Holland, merely for my own and Mr. Short's salaries, say 4500 livres a month?—You will have heard that the emperor has put troops into march on account of the disturbances in Brabant. The situation of affairs in Holland you know better than I do. How will they end?—I have the honour to be with sentiments of the most perfect esteem and respect Dear Sir your most obedient and most humble servt.,

TH: JEFFERSON

Jefferson to Adams

Paris July 28. 1787.

DEAR SIR

I take the liberty of troubling you with the inclosed bill of exchange for £46-17-10 sterling, rather than engage Mrs. Smith in so disagreeable a business. It will arrive in time I hope to cover the one drawn by General

Sullivan on Colo. Smith,[46] who certainly ought not to have been involved in the business.—The parliament are obstinately decided against the stamp tax. Their last remonstrance is said to be a master peice of good sense and firmness. We have it from the Imperial Ambassador that his master has marched 45,000 men against his resisting subjects. I have the honour to be with sincere sentiments of esteem and respect Dear Sir Your most obedient and most humble servt.,

TH: JEFFERSON

Adams to Jefferson

Grosvenor Square, London Aug. 25. 1787

DEAR SIR

On my return from an Excursion to Devonshire with my Family, where we have been to fly from the Putrefaction of a Great City in the Summer heat, I had the Pleasure to find your favours of 17. and 23. of July.

A Million of Guilders are borrowed on a new Loan in Holland, and I went over lately to Subscribe the obligations, a Punctillio which the Brokers were pleased to think indispensible, to gratify the Fancies of the Money Lenders. But as I had no fresh Authority from Congress, nor any particular new Instructions, I have been and am Still under Serious Apprehensions of its meeting with obstacles in the way of its Ratification.— If it is ratified, Congress may if they please, pay the Interest and Principal too, out of it, to the French officers.—I presume that if Mr. Grand Should refuse your Usual draughts for your Salary Messrs. Willinks and Vanstaphorsts, will honour them to the amount of yours and Mr. Short's Salaries, without any other Interposition than your Letter. But if they Should make any difficulty, and it Should be in my Power to remove it, you may well Suppose, I shall not be wanting. To be explicit, I will either advise or order the Money to be paid, upon your Draught as may be necessary, So that I pray you to make your Mind perfectly easy on that Score.

46. General John Sullivan of New Hampshire had organized a hunting expedition in March 1787 to obtain specimens of moose, caribou, deer, and elk, at TJ's request, so that he might send them to the naturalist Georges L. Buffon, whose theory of degenerate fauna in America TJ had refuted in his *Notes on the State of Virginia*. The shipment was delayed so long that it was October 1 before TJ could transmit to Buffon "these spoils . . . [that] may have the merit of adding any thing new to the treasures of nature which [have] so fortunately come under your observation, and of which she seems [to] have given you the keys." Sullivan should have submitted his charges directly to TJ. See Sullivan's letters to TJ, in April and May 1787, Boyd, XI, 295-96, 321, 326, 359, 384; and TJ's letters of Sept. 28, Oct. 1, 4, 5, 1787, *ibid.*, XII, 192-93, 194-95, 202, 208-9.

Mr. Barclay, I agree with you, took the wisest Course, when he embarked for America, tho it will lay me under Difficulties in Settling my affairs finally with Congress.

The French Debt, and all the Domestic Debt of the United States might be transferred to Holland, if it were judged necessary or profitable, and the Congress or Convention would take two or three preparatory Steps. All the Perplexities, Confusions and Distresses in America arise not from defects in their Constitutions or Confederation, not from a want of Honour or Virtue, So much as from downright Ignorance of the Nature of Coin, Credit and Circulation.—While an annual Interest of twenty, thirty and even fifty Per Cent, can be made, and a hope of augmenting Capitals in a Proportion of five hundred Per Cent is opened by Speculations in the Stocks, Commerce will not thrive. Such a State of Things would annihilate the Commerce, and overturn the Government too in any nation in Europe.

I will endeavour to Send you a Copy, with this Letter of the Second volume of the Defence etc. If Frouillé the Bookseller has a Mind to translate it he may, but it may not Strike others as it does Americans. Three Editions of the first volume have been printed in America.[47] The Second volume contains three long Courses of Experiments in Political Philosophy, every Tryal was intended and contrived to determine the Question whether Mr. Turgots System would do. The Result you may read. It has cost me a good deal of Trouble and Expence to Search into Italian Rubbish and Ruins. But enough of pure Gold and Marble has been found to reward the Pains. I shall be Suspected of writing Romances to expose Mr. Turgots Theory. But I assure you, it is all genuine History. The vast Subject of Confederations remains: but I have neither head, heart, hands, Eyes, Books, or Time, to engage in it. Besides it ought not to be Such an hasty Performance as the two volumes already ventured before the Public. With perfect Esteem, your Sincere Friend,

JOHN ADAMS

Jefferson to Abigail Adams

Paris Aug. 30. 1787.

DEAR MADAM

I have omitted writing sooner to you in expectation that Colo. Smith would have taken this in his route: but receiving now information from

47. The first American editions of JA's *Defence of the Constitutions of the United States,* Vol. I, appeared in Philadelphia and New York in 1787; the third in Boston in 1788. See TJ to JA, Feb. 23, 1787, and JA to TJ, March 1, 1787, above, 174-75, 176-77.

him that he embarks from Lisbon, I avail myself of the opportunity by
Mr. Payne of thanking you for the disbursements you were so kind as to
make for my daughter in London, and of stating to you our accounts as
follows.

	£	s	d
Disbursements of Mrs. Adams as summed up in her state of them	10	15	8
Error in addition to her prejudice	1	0	6
	11	16	2
Cash paid by Petit to Mrs. Adams, viz. 6. Louis d'ors @ 19/6	5	17	
Paid by do. for black lace 75.^{tt} which at the same exchange is	3	1	
Do. for 2. doz. pr. gloves 37^{tt} — 12s	1	10	6
Balance due to Mrs. Adams	1	7	8
	11	16	2

which balance I will beg the favor of Colo. Smith to pay you, and to debit
me with.   I am afraid, by the American papers, that the disturbances in
Massachusets are not yet at an end. Mr. Rucker, who is arrived here, gives
me a terrible account of the luxury of our ladies in the article of dress. He
sais that they begin to be sensible of the excess of it themselves, and to
think a reformation necessary. That proposed is the adoption of a national
dress. I fear however they have not resolution enough for this. I rejoice in
the character of the lady who accompanies the Count de Moustier to
America, and who is calculated to reform these excesses as far as her
example can have weight. Simple beyond example in her dress, tho neat,
hating parade and etiquette, affable, engaging, placid, and withal beautiful, I cannot help hoping a good effect from her example. She is the
Marquise de Brehan, sister in law to the Count de Moustier, who goes
partly on account of a feeble health, but principally for the education of
her son (of 17. years of age) which she hopes to find more masculine there
and less exposed to seduction. The Count de Moustier is of a character
well assorted to this. Nothing niggardly, yet orderly in his affairs, genteel
but plain, loving society upon an easy not a splendid tone, unreserved,
honest, and speaking our language like a native. He goes with excellent
notions and dispositions, and is as likely to give satisfaction as any man
that could have been chosen in France.[48] He is much a whig in the politics
of his own country. I understand there is a possibility that Congress will
remove to Philadelphia.—My daughter talks of you often and much, still

48. On the dissatisfaction caused by the Count de Moustier and the Marquise de
Brehan in the United States, see Malone, *Jefferson*, II, 197-98.

fancies she is to pay you the visit she promised. In the mean time she is very contented in the Convent with her sister. Both join me in compliments to Mrs. Smith and in assurances to yourself of the attachment and respect which I have the honour to proffer for them as well as for, dear Madam, your most obedient and most humble servant,

TH: JEFFERSON

Jefferson to Adams

Paris Aug. 30. 1787.

DEAR SIR

Since your favor of July 10. mine have been of July 17. 23 and 28. The last inclosed a bill of exchange from Mr. Grand on Tessier for £46-17-10 sterl. to answer Genl. Sullivan's bill for that sum. I hope it got safe to hand, tho' I have been anxious about it as it went by post and my letters thro' that channel sometimes miscarry.

From the separation of the Notables to the present moment has been perhaps the most interesting interval ever known in this country. The propositions of the Government, approved by the Notables, were precious to the nation and have been in an honest course of execution, some of them being carried into effect, and others preparing. Above all the establishment of the Provincial assemblies, some of which have begun their sessions, bid fair to be the instrument for circumscribing the power of the crown and raising the people into consideration. The election given to them is what will do this. Tho' the minister who proposed these improvements seems to have meant them as the price of the new supplies, the game has been so played as to secure the improvements to the nation without securing the price. The Notables spoke softly on the subject of the additional supplies, but the parliament took them up roundly, refused to register the edicts for the new taxes, till compelled in a bed of justice [49] and prefered themselves to be transferred to Troyes rather than withdraw their opposition. It is urged principally against the king, that his revenue is 130. millions more than that of his predecessor was, and yet he demands 120. millions further. You will see this well explained in the 'Conference entre un ministre d'etat et un Conseiller au parlement' which I send you with some other small pamphlets. In the mean time all tongues in Paris

49. A court session attended by the king in person or by a prince of the blood as his immediate representative.

(and in France as it is said) have been let loose, and never was a license of speaking against the government exercised in London more freely or more universally. Caracatures, placards, bon mots, have been indulged in by all ranks of people, and I know of no well attested instance of a single punishment. For some time mobs of 10; 20; 30,000 people collected daily, surrounded the parliament house, huzzaed the members, even entered the doors and examined into their conduct, took the horses out of the carriages of those who did well, and drew them home. The government thought it prudent to prevent these, drew some regiments into the neighborhood, multiplied the guards, had the streets constantly patrolled by strong parties, suspended privileged places, forbad all clubs, etc. The mobs have ceased: perhaps this may be partly owing to the absence of parliament. The Count d'Artois, sent to hold a bed of justice in the Cour des Aides,[50] was hissed and hooted without reserve by the populace; the carriage of Madame de (I forget the name) in the queen's livery was stopped by the populace under a belief that it was Madame de Polignac's whom they would have insulted, the queen going to the theater at Versailles with Madame de Polignac was received with a general hiss. The king, long in the habit of drowning his cares in wine, plunges deeper and deeper; the queen cries but sins on. The Count d'Artois is detested, and Monsieur [Louis, Comte de Provence] [51] the general favorite. The Archbishop of Thoulouse is made Ministre principale, a virtuous, patriotic and able character. The Marechal de Castries retired yesterday notwithstanding strong sollicitations to remain in office. The Marechal de Segur retired at the same time, prompted to it by the court. Their successors are not yet known. M. de St. Prist goes Ambassador to Holland in the room of Verac transferred to Switzerland, and the Count de Moustier goes to America in the room of the Chevalier de la Luzerne who has a promise of the first vacancy. These nominations are not yet made formally, but they are decided on and the parties are ordered to prepare for their destination. As it has been long since I have had a confidential conveiance to you, I have brought together the principal facts from the adjournment of the Notables to the present moment which, as you will perceive from their nature, required a confidential conveyance.[52] I have done it the rather because, tho' you will have heard many of them and seen them in the public papers, yet floating in the mass of lies which constitute the atmospheres of London and Paris, you may not have been sure of their truth: and I have mentioned every truth of any consequence to enable you to

50. The Cour des Aides (excises), established in 1543, had jurisdiction in suits relating to tax revenues.
51. The King's eldest brother, later Louis XVIII.
52. Thomas Paine, who was carrying letters to London. Boyd, XII, 69n.

stamp as false the facts pretermitted. I think that in the course of three months the royal authority has lost, and the rights of the nation gained, as much ground, by a revolution of public opinion only, as England gained in all her civil wars under the Stuarts. I rather believe too they will retain the ground gained, because it is defended by the young and the middle aged, in opposition to the old only. The first party increases, and the latter diminishes daily from the course of nature. You may suppose that under this situation, war would be unwelcome to France. She will surely avoid it if not forced by the courts of London and Berlin. If forced, it is proba- ble she will change the system of Europe totally by an alliance with the two empires, to whom nothing would be more desireable. In the event of such a coalition, not only Prussia but the whole European world must receive from them their laws. But France will probably endeavor to preserve the present system if it can be done by sacrifising to a certain degree the pretensions of the patriotic party in Holland. But of all these matters you can judge, in your position, where less secrecy is observed, better than I can. I have news from America as late as July 19. Nothing had then transpired from the Federal convention. I am sorry they began their deliberations by so abominable a precedent as that of tying up the tongues of their members. Nothing can justify this example but the in- nocence of their intentions, and ignorance of the value of public discus- sions. I have no doubt that all their other measures will be good and wise. It is really an assembly of demigods. Genl. Washington was of opinion they should not separate till October. I have the honour to be with every sentiment of friendship and respect Dear Sir Your most obedient and most humble servant,

TH: JEFFERSON

Adams to Jefferson

Grosvenor Square Sepr. 6 1787

DEAR SIR

I am Sorry to give you the trouble of this Commission: but I fear it will not be effectually done but by you, and therefore let me beg the favour of you to send for Mr. de La Blancherie and withdraw my Sub- scription to the Society of whose affairs he has the direction, and put a stop to his sending me the Nouvelles de la Republique des Lettres et Des Arts. He persuaded me at the Hague to Subscribe and paid him a years Subscription. The society continued One year and then ceased and I thought I had done with it forever: but since I have been in England now and then a Bundle of those Gazettes are pourd in upon me. I have no use for them, and sometimes I am put to an enormous expence of Postage. I am now determined at all Events to put a stop to it forever and pray you to take Measures for that purpose by paying him off and taking his Receipt, and by delivering him the inclosed Letter which Contains a Renunciation of my Subscription.

With great Esteem I am etc etc.

P.S. When I subcribed I understood it to be for one year only, and accordingly paid him the four Guineas. But I suppose he will now pretend that I am bound by that Subscription to pay for the Subsequent years. I will not dispute this with him, tho I am not bound in Law or Honour. One year the Society and Paper ceased since which it has been revived two years, or nearly so that he may pretend that I am eight Louis D'ors in Arrear. Pay him this if you please and no more, and I will repay you immediately. But at all Events I will be cleared from all Connection with this Man and his society and Nouvelles for the future.

J A

Abigail Adams to Jefferson

London Septr. 10th

DEAR SIR

Your obliging favours of july and August came safe to Hand. The first was brought during my absence on an excursion into the Country. I was very happy to find by it, that you had received your daughter safe, and that the dear Girl was contented. I never felt so attached to a child in my Life on so short an acquaintance. Tis rare to find one possessd of so strong and lively a sensibility. I hope she will not lose her fine spirits within the walls of a convent, to which I own I have many, perhaps false prejudices.

Mr. Appleton deliverd my Lace and gloves safe. Be so good as to let petit know that I am perfectly satisfied with them. Col. Smith has paid me the balance [which] you say was due to me, and I take your word for it, but [I do] not know how. The Bill which was accepted by Mr. Adams [in] the absence of Col. Smith, I knew would become due, in our absence, and before we could receive your orders. The money was left with Brisler our Servant, who paid when it was presented. On our return we found the Bill which you had drawn on Mr. Tessier, but upon presenting it he refused to pay it, as he had not received any letter of advise tho it was then more than a month from its date, but he wrote immediatly to Mr. Grand, and by return of the next post, paid it.

With regard to your Harpsicord, Col. Smith who is now returnd, will take measures to have it sent to you. I went once to Mr. Kirkmans to inquire if it was ready. His replie was, that it should be ready in a few days, but [that he had] no orders further than to report when it [was done. I told him] to write you, but he seemd to think he had done all [that was] required of him. The Canister addrest to Mr. Drayton [was] delivered to Mr. Hayward with special directions, and he assured me he would not fail to deliver it.

The ferment and commotions in Massachusetts has brought upon the surface abundance of Rubbish; but still there is some sterling metal in the political crusible. The vote which was carried against an emission of paper money by a large majority in the House, shews that they have a sense of justice; which I hope will prevail in every department of the State. I send a few of our News papers, some of which contain sensible speculations.

To what do all the political motions tend which are agitating France Holland and Germany? Will Liberty finally gain the assendency, or arbitrary power strike her dead.

Is the report true that is circulated here, that Mr. Littlepage has a commission from the King of poland to his most Christian Majesty?!

We have not any thing from Mr. Jay later than 4th of july. There was not any congress then, or expected to be any untill the convention rises at Philadelphia.[53]

Col. Smith I presume will write you all the politicks of the Courts he has visited, and I will not detain you longer than to assure you that I am at all times Your Friend and Humble Servant,

A A

Adams to Jefferson

London Septr. 16, 1787

DEAR SIR

Give me Leave to introduce to you Mr. John Brown Cutting, who will need no other Recommendation, than his own Genius. Let me beg your acceptance, too of a Sett of my Defence etc. and let me know your Opinion of the Second volume, and whether it is worth my while to write a third upon Confederations etc. Yours most Sincerely,

JOHN ADAMS

---

53. The Federal Convention adjourned Sept. 17, 1787. Max Farrand, ed., *The Records of the Federal Convention of 1787* (rev. edn.; New Haven, 1937), II, 649.

Jefferson to Adams

Paris Sep. 28. 1787.

DEAR SIR

I received your favors by Mr. Cutting, and thank you sincerely for the copy of your book. The departure of a packet-boat, which always gives me full emploiment for some time before, has only permitted me to look into it a little. I judge of it from the first volume which I thought formed to do a great deal of good. The first principle of a good government is certainly a distribution of it's powers into executive, judiciary, and legislative, and a subdivision of the latter into two or three branches. It is a good step gained, when it is proved that the English constitution, acknowleged to be better than all which have proceeded it, is only better in proportion as it has approached nearer to this distribution of powers. From this the last step is easy, to shew by a comparison of our constitutions with that of England, how much more perfect they are. The article of Confederations is surely worthy of your pen. It would form a most interesting addition to shew what have been the nature of the Confederations which have existed hitherto, what were their excellencies and what their defects. A comparison of ours with them would be to the advantage of ours, and would increase the veneration of our countrymen for it. It is a misfortune that they do not sufficiently know the value of their constitutions and how much happier they are rendered by them than any other people on earth by the governments under which they live.—You know all that has happened in the United Netherlands.[54] You know also that our friends Van Staphorsts will be among the most likely to become objects of severity, if any severities should be exercised. Is the money in their hands entirely safe? If it is not, I am sure you have already thought of it. Are we to suppose the game already up, and that the Stadtholder is to be reestablished, perhaps erected into a monarch, without this country lifting a finger in opposition to it? If so, it is a lesson the more for us. In fact what a crowd of lessons do the present miseries of Holland teach us? Never to have an hereditary officer of any sort: never to let a citizen ally himself with kings: never to call in foreign nations to settle domestic differences: never to

54. The Patriot party had curtailed severely the powers of the Stadholder, William V of Orange, and insulted his wife, sister of the King of Prussia. When, in false expectation of help from France, the Patriots refused to make reparation, the Prussian Army under the Duke of Brunswick invaded the Netherlands on September 13 and, with the surrender of Amsterdam on October 10, completed occupation of the country. Petrus Johannes Blok, *History of the People of the Netherlands* (N. Y. and London, 1912), V, 244-53.

suppose that any nation will expose itself to war for us etc. Still I am not without hopes that a good rod is in soak for Prussia, and that England will feel the end of it. It is known to some that Russia made propositions to the emperor and France for acting in concert; that the emperor consents and has disposed four camps of 180,000 men from the limits of Turkey to those of Prussia. This court hesitates, or rather it's premier hesitates; for the queen, Monmorin and Breteuil are for the measure. Should it take place, all may yet come to rights, except for the Turks, who must retire from Europe; and this they must do were France Quixotic enough to undertake to support them. We I hope shall be left free to avail ourselves of the advantages of neutrality: and yet much I fear the English, or rather their stupid king, will force us out of it. For thus I reason. By forcing us into the war against them they will be engaged in an expensive land war as well as a sea war. Common sense dictates therefore that they should let us remain neuter: ergo they will not let us remain neuter. I never yet found any other general rule for foretelling what they will do, but that of examining what they ought not to do.—You will have heard doubtless that M. Lambert is Comptroller general, that the office of Directeur general du tresor royal has been successively refused by Monsr. de la Borde and Monsr. Cabarrus; that the Conte de Brienne, brother of the Archbishop, is minister of war, and the Count de la Luzerne minister of Marine. They have sent for him from his government in the West Indies. The Chevalier de la Luzerne has a promise of the first vacant Embassy. It will be that of London if Adhemar can be otherwise disposed of. The Chevalier might have had that of Holland if he would. The Count de Moustier will sail about the middle of next month. Count d'Aranda leaves us in a few days. His successor is hourly expected.—I have the honor to be with my best respects to Mrs. Adams, and sentiments of perfect esteem and regard to yourself dear Sir your most obedient and most humble servant,

TH: JEFFERSON

P.S. Since writing the above, I learn through a *very* [55] *good* [*channel*] *that this court is deci*[*ded*] *and is ar*[*ran*]*ging with the* [*two empires*]. Perhaps as a proof of this we may soon *see them recall their officers in the* [*Dutch serv*]*ice.*

55. This and subsequent words in italics were written in code. Syllables and words in brackets (supplied) are conjectured readings by the editors of *The Papers of Thomas Jefferson;* Boyd, XIII, 190.

Jefferson to Abigail Adams

Paris Octob. 4. 1787.

DEAR MADAM

By Mr. Cutting I have an opportunity of acknoleging the receipt of your favor of Sep. 10th. inclosing one for my daughter Polly. When she received it she flushed, she whitened, she flushed again, and in short was in such a flutter of joy that she could scarcely open it. This faithful history of her sensibility towards you must stand in lieu of her thanks which she has promised me she will write you herself: but at this moment she is in the convent where she is perfectly happy. By Mr. Cutting you will also receive the 5. aunes of cambric which Colo. Smith desired me to have purchased for you at 12. livres the aune. I am sorry you were put to the trouble of advancing the money for Mr. Sullivan's bill. I thought myself sure that Mr. Grand's bill would reach you in time, and did not know he had omitted to advise Mr. Teissier of it. He is always afraid to give to any body a complete power to call on him for money. Mr. Littlepage is here under a secret commission from the King of Poland. Possibly it may become a permanent one. I thank you for the American newspapers, and am glad to find that good sense is still uppermost in our country. Great events are I think preparing here: and a combination of force likely to take place which will change the face of Europe. Mr. Grenville has been very illy received. The annunciation by Mr. Eden that England was arming, was considered as an insult: after this and the King of Prussia's entrance on the territories of Holland, Mr. Grenville's arrival with conciliatory propositions is qualified with the title of 'une insulte tres gratuite.' I am not certain that the final decision of this country is yet taken. Perhaps the winter may be employed in previous arrangements unless any thing takes place at sea to bring on the rupture sooner. The Count de Gortz told me yesterday that the Prussian troops would retire from Holland the moment the states of Holland should make the expected reparation of the insult to the Princess. May not the scene which is preparing render it necessary for Mr. Adams to defer the return to his own country? I have the honor to be with very sincere sentiments of esteem and respect Dear Madam your most obedient and most humble servant,

TH: JEFFERSON

Adams to Jefferson

Grosvenor Square Oct. 9. 1787

DEAR SIR

I sent you a Copy of my second volume by Mr. Barthelemy the French Chargé here now Minister, with a Letter about Money matters. In your favour of Sept. 28. you dont mention the receipt of them.—I have indeed long thought with Anxiety of our Money in the hands of our Friends, whom you mention, and have taken the best Precaution in my Power, against Accidents. I do not consider the Game as up. But a disgrace has happened, which is not easy to get rid of.—Disgrace is not easily washed out, even with blood. Lessons my dear Sir, are never wanting. Life and History are full. The Loss of Paradise, by eating a forbidden apple, has been many Thousand years a Lesson to Mankind; but not much regarded. Moral Reflections, wise Maxims, religious Terrors, have little Effect upon Nations when they contradict a present Passion, Prejudice, Imagination, Enthusiasm or Caprice. Resolutions never to have an hereditary officer will be kept in America, as religiously as that of the Cincinnati was in the Case of General Greens son.[56] Resolutions never to let a Citizen ally himself with things will be kept untill an Opportunity presents to violate it. If the Duke of Angoleme, or Burgundy, or especially the Dauphin should demand one of your beautiful and most amiable Daughters in Marriage, all America from Georgia to New Hampshire would find their Vanity and Pride, so agreably flattered by it, that all their Sage Maxims would give way; and even our Sober New England Republicans would keep a day of Thanksgiving for it, in their hearts. If General Washington had a Daughter, I firmly believe, she would be demanded in Marriage by one of the Royal Families of France or England, perhaps by both, or if he had a Son he would be invited to come a courting to Europe.—The Resolution not to call in foreign Nations to settle domestic differences will be kept untill a domestic difference of a serious nature shall break out.—I have long been settled in my own opinion, that neither Philosophy, nor Religion, nor Morality, nor Wisdom, nor Interest, will ever govern nations or Parties, against their Vanity, their Pride, their Resentment or Revenge, or

56. Immediately after General Nathanael Greene's funeral at Savannah, June 20, 1786, members of the Georgia Society of the Cincinnati convened and resolved, out of respect to the late general, that his eldest son, George Washington Greene, be admitted to the Society, to take his seat on reaching the age of eighteen. G. W. Greene, *Life of Nathanael Greene* (N. Y., 1871), III, 535-36.

their Avarice or Ambition. Nothing but Force and Power and Strength can restrain them. If Robert Morris should maintain his Fortune to the End, I am convinced that some foreign Families of very high rank will think of Alliances with his Children. If the Pen Family should go to America, and engage in public affairs and obtain the Confidence of the People, you will see Connections courted there. A Troop of Light Horse from Philadelphia meeting Dick Pen in New Jersey, will strike the Imaginations of Princes and Princesses. How few Princes in Europe could obtain a Troop of Light Horse to make them a Compliment of Parade. In short my dear Friend you and I have been indefatigable Labourers through our whole Lives for a Cause which will be thrown away in the next generation, upon the Vanity and Foppery of Persons of whom we do not now know the Names perhaps.—The War that is now breaking out will render our Country, whether she is forced into it, or not, rich, great and powerful in comparison of what she now is, and Riches Grandeur and Power will have the same effect upon American as it has upon European minds. We have seen enough already to be sure of this. A Covent Garden Rake will never be wise enough to take warning from the Claps caught by his Companions. When he comes to be poxed himself he may possibly repent and reform. Yet three out of four of them become even by their own sufferings, more shameless instead of being penitent.

Pardon this freedom. It is not Melancholly: but Experience and believe me without reserve your Friend, O tempora— *oh mores*

JOHN ADAMS.

Adams to Jefferson

London Oct. 28. 1787

DEAR SIR

Mr. Daniel Parker will have the Honour to deliver you this. He is an intelligent American, and well informed as any Man you will see from hence. I beg leave to introduce him to you.

Let me thank you for your late Letter and the important State Papers inclosed with it.

I have ordered to your Address, a dozen Copies of my Boudoir [57] for the Marquis, who desired Mr. Appleton and Mr. Paine to have them sent. I have called it a Defence of the American Constitutions, because it is a

57. His pouting room or his study? See Boyd, XII, 293*n*.

Resistance to an Attack of Turgot. The two volumes are confined to one Point, and if a City is defended from an Attack made on the North Gate, it may be called a Defence of the City, although the other three Gates, the East West and South Gates were so weak, as to have been defenceless, if they had been attacked.—If a Warriour should arise to attack our Constitutions where they are not defencible, I'l not undertake to defend them. Two thirds of our States have made Constitutions, in no respect better than those of the Italian Republicks, and as sure as there is an Heaven and an Earth, if they are not altered they will produce Disorders and Confusion.

I can tell you nothing of Politicks. All the world is astonished at the Secrecy of Mr. Pitt. Great Preparations for War, yet the World can find no Ennemy nor Object. Carmarthen "hopes the Scudd will blow over, and even that the Quarrell between the Port and Russia will be made up. While a Fire is burning in any quarter of Europe, no one can tell when or where it may Spread." The General Understanding is that the U.S. are to be let alone, and they have given general orders to the Navy, to let American Vessells and Seamen alone. They will have their hands full, I believe, and there is little Plunder to be made of Americans, so that we may be quiet,—as long as they will let us.—But our Countrymen will do well to think of the Possibility of Danger and of the means of Defence. A war would cost us more than we have of Cash or Credit, but if we should be attacked we must defend, Money or no Money, Credit or no Credit. Whether John Bull has Command enough of his Passions to see us punctually fulfill our Treaties, as we must do, without being transported with rage, you who know him can tell as well as I.—We know this Gentlemans hasty Temper so well that I think we may very safely wish for the Continuance of Peace, between France and him, even upon Selfish Principles, tho' our Commerce and Navigation would be greatly promoted by a War, if we can keep out of it.

I tremble and agonize for the suffering Patriots in Holland. You may judge to what Lengths the Spight extends against them, by a formal Complaint of their High Mightinesses against Dumas, and a Requisition to me, to employ him no longer but to appoint some other Person in my absence. It is not I am well persuaded as Agent for the United States, but as a Friend of France or of the Patriotic Party against the Statholder, that he has unfortunately incurred this Censure and Displeasure. Yet as Mr. Dumas holds not his Character or Authority from me, I can do nothing, but transmit the Papers to Congress. With great Esteem, I have the honour to be dear Sir, your most obedient Servant,

JOHN ADAMS

6

"On... Guard against the immeasurable avarice of Amsterdam"

IN THE HISTORY of the American Republic as well as in the careers of its two ministers to the courts of western Europe, the years 1788-89 marked the end of an era. This was, in fact, the end of an era in the Western world. In February 1787 Jefferson learned that Adams had requested Congress to relieve him of his office so that he might return home.[1] To Jefferson this was most unwelcome news, for he relied on Adams for advice and felt more confidence in his own diplomatic maneuvers because he respected Adams's judgment and longer experience. At the same time he was sympathetic with Adams's desire to depart, for he did "not wonder at your being tired out by the conduct of the court you are at."[2] Jefferson had diagnosed the case correctly; but, fortunately for him and his country, Adams was not released until the spring of 1788. In the interim he was able to contribute something toward meeting the financial obligations of the United States through his previous connections in Holland.

The American debt to France, incurred during the Revolutionary War, had continued unpaid and now interest payments were in arrears. If, however, the American Republic was a debtor nation, the French monarchy was much worse off, with failing revenues aggravated by a restrictive mercantile policy and an extravagant court. Since the United States was still allied with France, Jefferson was sorely embarrassed by the vociferous complaints of French officers whom Congress had failed to pension for their services in the War for

1. W. S. Smith to TJ, Jan. 29, 1787, Boyd, XI, 91.
2. TJ to JA, Feb. 20, 1787, above, 172.

Independence, though legally and morally bound to do so. This damage to American prestige was more injurious to Jefferson's sensibilities than the shortage of his own salary at the hands of the same impecunious Congress.[3] Nevertheless, the young United States, an expanding nation with vast undeveloped resources, was a good financial risk; and Dutch bankers with money to lend recognized America's need as their opportunity.[4]

In the late spring of 1787, without authorization from Congress but in the face of interest payments due June 1, Adams secured a Dutch loan of $400,000 at 5 per cent and, to please the brokers, he went to Holland to sign the obligations. The bonds were not to be issued until approved by Congress. He believed that the domestic debt of the United States as well as its debt to France might be transferred to Holland, if Congress would only take action; indeed, he maintained that the distress and confusion in America resulted mainly "from downright Ignorance of the Nature of Coin, Credit and Circulation." [5] His proposal for transfer was turned down, although the new 5 per cent loan was approved. In January 1788 the twelve-year loan of 1776, the first obtained from private capital during the war (51,000 florins or $20,400), came due to Fizeau & Company in Holland. Would the Amsterdam bankers provide funds for a new loan to pay off the old debt? "Mr. Van staphorst" (of Van Staphorst & Willinck), Adams assured Jefferson, "will have no objection to an handsome Commission, for paying off, the Debt"; in fact, the moneylenders would probably be satisfied with interest payments until Congress could refinance the loans.[6] Adams proved to be somewhat overoptimistic in his expectation. When the banker Willinck insisted on an order from the Treasury of the United States, Jefferson, "willing to participate with you in any risk," [7] looked to Adams to take the lead in these financial negotiations.

The situation was complicated by the fact that much of the domestic as well as the foreign debt of the United States had been bought up at low rates by speculators, supported by collusion between certain

3. TJ to JA, July 17 and 23, 1787, above, 189-90; see also Boyd, XI, 699-700n., and TJ to Abbé Morellet, Oct. 24, 1787, *ibid.*, XII, 286-87.

4. See P. J. van Winter, *Het Aandeel van den Amsterdamschen Handel aan den Opbouw van het Amerikaansche Gemeenebest* (Hague, 1927).

5. JA to TJ, Aug. 25, 1787, above, 191-92; Jefferson, "Autobiography," Ford, I, 116-17.

6. JA to TJ, Dec. 25, 1787, below, 219.

7. TJ to JA, Dec. 12 and 31, 1787, Jan. 13, 1788, below, 215-16, 220, 221.

Americans and Europeans; and the prospects of improved credit under the new Constitution of the United States, now in process of ratification, encouraged the moneylenders. But European confidence in the American people was more than matched by that of Jefferson who declared that he "had rather trust money in their hands than in that of any government on earth." [8]

With Adams departing shortly for America, the burden of this financial problem would rest solely on his Virginia colleague. Fortunately they were able to join forces for a few days in Amsterdam in March 1788 and negotiate a new loan to meet interest payments and other expenses until the new government could get under way.[9] It was distasteful business dealing with speculators, who took every advantage of their superior bargaining power; yet Adams sensed their respect for American credit: "The Amsterdammers love Money too well, to execute their Threats." [10] The bankers were not genuinely interested in getting subscriptions to the new loan beyond the extent that payment of their own interest charges would be assured; therefore after his return to Paris, Jefferson directed his thoughts to a plan for funding the debt over a period of years, the scheduled payments to be derived from duties on imports. Although he failed to get support for the scheme from the expiring Congress of the Confederation, he did anticipate Hamilton's plan adopted by the Congress of the new government, and Jefferson's proposals, recently discovered among his papers, add another cubit to his stature as a practical student of finance.[11]

Among the perennial commercial problems that occupied the ministers of a trading nation struggling for favorable status, the whale-oil fishery came to the fore again in 1788. Jefferson prepared himself to meet the issue. In seeking to recover the markets lost during the War for Independence,[12] the Nantucket whalers were susceptible to offers from both France and Britain, although they were not inclined to change their nationality. Since the war, the British had made a vigorous effort to capture the oil business, but "les Nantuckois," now in distress,

8. TJ to C. W. F. Dumas, Feb. 9, 1787, Boyd, XI, 128.
9. TJ to John Jay, March 13 and 16, 1788, *ibid.*, XII, 661, 671-73.
10. JA to TJ, Feb. 12, 1788, below, 225.
11. TJ's assessment of the debt problem and his attempt to solve it in the face of prevailing opposition and indifference in America and Europe are forcefully presented by Julian P. Boyd in the editorial note to "Proposals for Funding the Foreign Debt," Boyd, XIV, 190-97; "Jefferson's Plan," [Oct. 1788], *ibid.*, 201-9.
12. See above, Chap. 5.

proved more sensitive to French blandishments than to English. In 1786 the port of Dunkirk was opened to William Rotch of Nantucket and his associates. Then in December 1787 the French allowed an abatement of duties on American oil, an affront to the British who retaliated by providing government premiums for underselling the French markets. When the Dunkirk fishermen raised a loud protest, the French answer was the Arrêt (decree) of September 28, 1788, banning the oil trade with all nations. Since *European* oil had not been specified in the decree, *American* was not excepted. This threat of disaster to American interests stirred Jefferson to action. Within a few weeks he gathered pertinent data and documents and composed his substantial *Observations on the Whale Fishery*. This was followed shortly by a "Report to the Ministry" and the Arrêt of December 7, restoring the privileges of American whale oil.[13] Jefferson had not only scored an important gain for American trade; he had also won an advantage over the British insofar as it could be enforced.[14] And he had produced a valuable historical document on whaling in his *Observations*.

If the specific accomplishments of Jefferson and Adams for the United States were of limited duration, one must remember that the bargaining power of a weak republic held a low rating among kings, except to tip the scales in their own game of diplomacy. How could the American Confederation's hand be strengthened? Its ministers abroad provided the answer on numerous occasions, as Jefferson did in the spring of 1786: "I am in hopes our letters will give a new spi[rit] to the proposition for investing Congress with the regulation of our commerce." [15] It was commercial issues that led delegates from a few states to assemble at Annapolis in September of that year, providing the prelude to the Federal Convention in Philadelphia in 1787.

It seems almost an injustice, an inappropriate course of events, that neither Adams nor Jefferson was a member of the Federal Convention, that "assembly of demigods," as Jefferson called it.[16] He deplored its secret sessions, and though he was attached to "the good, old, and

13. "Documents Concerning the Whale Fishery," editorial note, Boyd, XIV, 217-25; *Observations on the Whale Fishery* [Paris, 1788], anonymous, without title page or imprint, 18 pages, printed by Jacques-Gabriel Clousier, text in *ibid.*, 242-54; "Report to the Ministry," *ibid.*, 256-67; "Arret, 7 December 1788," *ibid.*, 268-69; TJ to JA, Dec. 5, 1788, below, 232-33.
14. TJ to Jay, Jan. 14, 1789, Boyd, XIV, 447; TJ to JA, Jan. 14, 1789, below, 234-35.
15. TJ to William Carmichael, May 5, 1786, Boyd, IX, 449.
16. TJ to JA, Aug. 30, 1787, above, 196.

venerable fabrick," the Articles of Confederation,[17] he later hailed the new Constitution as "unquestionably the wisest ever yet presented to men." [18] At his inaugural in 1797, President Adams pointed out, "I first saw the Constitution of the United States in a foreign country. Irritated by no literary altercation, animated by no public debate, heated by no party animosity, I read it with great satisfaction.... In its general principles and great outlines it was conformable to such a system of government as I had ever most esteemed...." [19] This was written ten years afterward, with the retrospect of eight years' experience in the operation of the government. However, as we have seen,[20] his *Defence of the Constitutions* of the several states had arrived in Philadelphia in time to lend serious weight to the argument on behalf of balanced government for the United States of America.

When Adams first read the Constitution, he feared the aristocracy implicit in the Senate rather more than he did the power of the presidency, although he wanted assurance that the latter was properly separated from the legislative branch.[21] To Jefferson he promptly posed the question of a declaration of rights, and after returning to America he observed that "Amendments to the Constitution, will be expected." [22] While Jefferson maintained that "a bill of rights is what the people are entitled to against every government on earth," [23] he was noncommittal on the Virginia General Assembly's resolution of November 20, 1788, calling for a second constitutional convention.[24]

As Abigail made preparations for the long anticipated return to Massachusetts, Jefferson wrote her, "I have considered you while in London as my neighbor." When he proposed that they continue their correspondence, she gratefully accepted,[25] but sixteen years were to elapse before it was resumed. The Adamses arrived in Boston aboard the *Lucretia* on June 17, 1788. The following autumn Jefferson requested leave of absence to take his daughters home and to attend to

17. TJ to JA, Nov. 13, 1787, below, 212.
18. TJ to David Humphreys, March 18, 1789, Boyd, XIV, 678.
19. James D. Richardson, ed., *Messages and Papers of the Presidents, 1789-1902* ([Washington?], 1903), I, 229.
20. See above, Chap. 5.
21. JA to TJ, Dec. 6, 1787, March 1, 1789, below, 213-14, 236.
22. JA to TJ, Nov. 10, 1787, March 1, 1789, below, 210, 236.
23. TJ to James Madison, Dec. 20, 1787, Boyd, XII, 440.
24. *Ibid.*, XIV, xxxviii-xxxix, and facing p. 329.
25. TJ to AA, Feb. 2, 1788, and AA to TJ, Feb. 21, 1788, below, 222, 226.

his affairs at Monticello.[26] His departure was to be delayed a year during which he watched with intense interest the first critical events of the French Revolution—the convening of the Estates General, the fall of the Bastille. In the autumn of 1789 he would return permanently to enter the service of the new government as secretary of state, again a colleague of John Adams, first vice-president of the United States.

Adams to Jefferson

London. Nov. 10. 1787

MY DEAR SIR

Mr. Boylston is going to Paris, with a Cargo of Sperma Cæti oil, and will be obliged to you for any assistance or advice you can give him.

I forwarded a few days ago, from Mr. Gerry, a Copy as I suppose of the Result of Convention.—It seems to be admirably calculated to preserve the Union, to increase Affection, and to bring us all to the same mode of thinking. They have adopted the Idea of the Congress at Albany in 1754 of a President to nominate officers and a Council to Consent: [27] but thank heaven they have adopted a third Branch, which that Congress did not. I think that Senates and Assemblies should have nothing to do with executive Power. But still I hope the Constitution will be adopted, and Amendments be made at a more convenient opportunity.

What think you of a Declaration of Rights? [28] Should not such a Thing have preceeded the Model?

People here are Solacing themselves in the Prospect of the Continuance of Peace: and the tryumphant Party in Holland carry a high hand.—I suspect that both are rather too sanguine.—They have very insufficient Grounds for so much Exultation. My worthy old Friends the Patriots in Holland are extreamly to be pittied: and so are their deluded Persecutors. That Country I fear is to be ruined, past all Remedy. I wish that all the good Men had Sense and Spirit enough to go to America. With the usual Sentiments Yours,

JOHN ADAMS

26. TJ to John Jay, Nov. 19, 1788, Boyd, XIV, 214-16.
27. Under Article 23 of the Albany Plan of Union all civil officers were to be nominated by the Grand Council and approved by the President-General. Albert Henry Smyth, ed., *The Writings of Benjamin Franklin* (N. Y., 1907), III, 224-25.
28. The Massachusetts Constitution of 1780, drafted chiefly by JA, was prefaced by a declaration of rights. F. N. Thorpe, ed., *Federal and State Constitutions, Colonial Charters, and Other Organic Laws* (Washington, 1909), III, 1880-1923.

Jefferson to Adams

Paris Nov. 13. 1787.

DEAR SIR

This will be delivered you by young Mr. Rutledge. Your knowledge of his father will introduce him to your notice. He merits it moreover on his own account.

I am now to acknolege your favors of Oct. 8 and 26. That of August 25. was duly received, nor can I recollect by what accident I was prevented from acknoleging it in mine of Sep. 28. It has been the source of my subsistence hitherto, and must continue to be so till I receive letters on the affairs of money from America. Van Staphorsts & Willinks have answered my draughts.—Your books for M. de la Fayette are received here. I will notify it to him, who is at present with his provincial assembly in Auvergne.

Little is said lately of the progress of the negociations between the courts of Petersburg, Vienna, and Versailles. The distance of the former and the cautious, unassuming character of it's minister here is one cause of delays: a greater one is the greediness and instable character of the emperor. Nor do I think that the Principal here [Brienne] will be easily induced to lend himself to any connection which shall threaten a war within a considerable number of years. His own reign will be that of peace only, in all probability; and were any accident to tumble him down, this country would immediately gird on it's sword and buckler, and trust to occurrences for supplies of money. The wound their honour has sustained festers in their hearts, and it may be said with truth that the Archbishop and a few priests, determined to support his measures because proud to see their order come again into power, are the only advocates for the line of conduct which has been pursued. It is said and believed thro' Paris literally that the Count de Monmorin 'pleuroit comme un enfant ["wept like a child"]' when obliged to sign the counter declaration.[29] Considering the phrase as figurative, I believe it expresses the distress of his heart. Indeed he has made no secret of his individual opinion. In the mean time the Principal goes on with a firm and patriotic spirit, in reforming the cruel abuses of the government and preparing a new constitu-

29. At Versailles on Oct. 27, 1787, British representatives signed a declaration that Britain would disarm if France gave satisfactory explanation on the Dutch question; Montmorin signed a counter declaration that France had never intended to interfere in the affairs of the Dutch Republic and retained no hostility. This concession further weakened the declining prestige of the kingdom of France. *Annual Register, 1787,* 282-83.

tion which will give to this people as much liberty as they are capable of managing. This I think will be the glory of his administration, because, tho' a good theorist in finance, he is thought to execute badly. They are about to open a loan of 100. millions to supply present wants, and it is said the preface of the Arret will contain a promise of the Convocation of the States general during the ensuing year. 12. or 15. provincial assemblies are already in action, and are going on well; and I think that tho' the nation suffers in reputation, it will gain infinitely in happiness under the present administration. I inclose to Mr. Jay a pamphlet which I will beg of you to forward. I leave it open for your perusal. When you shall have read it, be so good as to stick a wafer in it. It is not yet published, nor will be for some days. This copy has been ceded to me as a favor.

How do you like our new constitution? I confess there are things in it which stagger all my dispositions to subscribe to what such an assembly has proposed. The house of federal representatives will not be adequate to the management of affairs either foreign or federal. Their President seems a bad edition of a Polish king. He may be reelected from 4. years to 4. years for life. Reason and experience prove to us that a chief magistrate, so continuable, is an officer for life. When one or two generations shall have proved that this is an office for life, it becomes on every succession worthy of intrigue, of bribery, of force, and even of foreign interference. It will be of great consequence to France and England to have America governed by a Galloman or Angloman. Once in office, and possessing the military force of the union, without either the aid or check of a council, he would not be easily dethroned, even if the people could be induced to withdraw their votes from him. I wish that at the end of the 4. years they had made him for ever ineligible a second time. Indeed I think all the good of this new constitution might have been couched in three or four new articles to be added to the good, old, and venerable fabrick, which should have been preserved even as a religious relique.— Present me and my daughters affectionately to Mrs. Adams. The younger one continues to speak of her warmly. Accept yourself assurances of the sincere esteem and respect with which I have the honour to be, Dear Sir, your friend and servant,

TH: JEFFERSON

P.S. I am in negociation with de la Blancherie. You shall hear from me when arranged.

Abigail Adams to Jefferson

London Grosvenour Square December 5th 1787.

Mrs. Adams presents her respectfull compliments to Mr. Jefferson and asks the favour of him to permit petit to purchase for her ten Ells of double Florence of any fashionable coulour, orange excepted which is in high vogue here. Mrs. A. excepts green also of which she has enough. Mr. Muchier if in paris will be so kind as to take charge of it, and Mrs. Adams will send the money by Mr. Trumble who will be in paris some time next week.

By Letters this day received from Boston it appears that a convention [30] was agred too by both Houses, and that it is to meet, the second wednesday in Jan'ry.

Mr. King writes that Mr. Jeffersons commission is renewed at the court of France, and Mr. Adams's resignation accepted, so that we shall quit this country as soon in the spring as we can go with safety. Love to the Young Ladies and thank my dear polly for her pretty Letter.

Adams to Jefferson

London Decr. 6. 1787

DEAR SIR

The Project of a new Constitution, has Objections against it, to which I find it difficult to reconcile my self, but I am so unfortunate as to differ somewhat from you in the Articles, according to your last kind Letter.

You are afraid of the one—I, of the few. We agree perfectly that the many should have a full fair and perfect Representation.—You are Apprehensive of Monarchy; I, of Aristocracy. I would therefore have given more Power to the President and less to the Senate. The Nomination and Appointment to all offices I would have given to the President, assisted only by a Privy Council of his own Creation, but not a Vote or Voice would I have given to the Senate or any Senator, unless he were of the Privy Council. Faction and Distraction are the sure and certain Consequence of giving to a Senate a vote in the distribution of offices.

You are apprehensive the President when once chosen, will be chosen again and again as long as he lives. So much the better as it appears to me.

30. The Massachusetts convention to consider ratification of the United States Constitution.

—You are apprehensive of foreign Interference, Intrigue, Influence. So am I.—But, as often as Elections happen, the danger of foreign Influence recurs. The less frequently they happen the less danger.—And if the Same Man may be chosen again, it is probable he will be, and the danger of foreign Influence will be less. Foreigners, seeing little Prospect will have less Courage for Enterprize.

Elections, my dear sir, Elections to offices which are great objects of Ambition, I look at with terror. Experiments of this kind have been so often tryed, and so universally found productive of Horrors, that there is great Reason to dread them.

Mr. Littlepage who will have the Honour to deliver this will tell you all the News. I am, my dear Sir, with great Regard,

JOHN ADAMS

Adams to Jefferson

Grosvenor Square Decr 10. 1787

DEAR SIR

I last night received, the Ratification of my last Loan and the inclosed Resolution of Congress of 18 July last, for the Redemption of Prisoners of Algiers. It is probable You have received it before, but as it is, in your Department to execute it, and possible that you may not have received it, I thought it Safest to transmit it to you, as I have now the honour to do, here inclosed. Mr. Vanberckel, Son of the Minister, is arrived at Falmouth by the Packet, but not yet in London. By him, I expect my Dismission. The American Newspapers, already arrived both from New York and Boston, announce it to have passed in Congress, the 5. of October, and now as we say at Sea, huzza for the new world and farewell to the Old One.

All Europe resounds with Projects for reviving, States and Assemblies, I think: and France is taking the lead.—How such assemblies will mix, with Simple Monarchies, is the question. The Fermentation must terminate in Improvements of various kinds. Superstition, Bigotry, Ignorance, Imposture, Tyranny and Misery must be lessened somewhat.—But I fancy it will be found somewhat difficult, to conduct and regulate these debates. Ex quovis ligno non fit Mercurius.[31] The world will be entertained with noble sentiments and enchanting Eloquence, but will not essential Ideas be sometimes forgotten, in the anxious study of brilliant Phrases? Will

31. "An image of Mercury is not made out of any block of wood."

the Duke of orleans make a Sterling Patriot and a determined son of Liberty? [32] Will he rank with Posterity among the Brutus's and Catos?— Corrections and Reformations and Improvements are much wanted in all the Institutions of Europe Ecclesiastical and civil: but how or when they will be made is not easy to guess.—It would be folly I think to do no more than try over again Experiments, that have been already a million times tryed. Attempts to reconcile Contradictions will not succeed, and to think of Reinstituting Republicks, as absurdly constituted as were the most which the world has seen, would be to revive Confusion and Carnage, which must again End in despotism.—I shall soon be out of the Noise of all these Speculations in Europe leaving behind me however the most fervent good Wishes for the Safety and Prosperity of all who have the Cause of Humanity, Equity, Equality and Liberty at heart. With the tenderest Affection of Friendship, I am and ever shall be my dear Sir Yours,

JOHN ADAMS

Abigail Adams to Jefferson

Grosvenour Square december 12th 1787

Mrs. Adams's compliments to Mr. Jefferson and in addition to her former memorandum she requests half a dozen pr. of mens silk stockings. Mr. Trumble will deliver to Mr. Jefferson four Louis and one Guiney. Mr. parker will be so good as to take charge of them, if no opportunity offers before his return.

Jefferson to Adams

Paris Dec. 12. 1787.

DEAR SIR

In the month of July I received from Fiseaux & co. of Amsterdam a letter notifying me that the principal of their loan to the United states would become due the first day of January. I answered them that I had neither powers nor information on the subject, but would transmit their letter to the Board of treasury. I did so by the packet which sailed from

---

32. The Duke of Orleans was elected to the French Constitutional Convention and changed his name to Philippe Egalité; and, although he voted for the execution of his cousin Louis XVI in 1792, he himself was guillotined the following year. Leo Gershoy, *The French Revolution and Napoleon* (N. Y., 1933), 230, 276.

Havre Aug. 10. The earliest answer possible would have been by the packet which arrived at Havre three or four days ago. But by her I do not receive the scrip of a pen from any body. This makes me suppose that my letters are committed to Paul Jones who was to sail a week after the departure of the packet: and that possibly he may be the bearer of orders from the treasury to repay Fiseaux' loan with the money you borrowed. But it is also possible he may bring no order on the subject. The slowness with which measures are adopted on our side the water does not permit us to count on punctual answers: but on the contrary renders it necessary for us to suppose in the present case that no orders will arrive in time, and to consider whether any thing, and what should be done? As it may be found expedient to transfer all our foreign debts to Holland by borrowing there, and as it may always be prudent to preserve a good credit in that country because we may [be] forced into wars whether we will or no, I should suppose it very imprudent to suffer our credit to be annihilated by so small a sum as 51,000 guelders. The injury will be greater too in proportion to the smallness of the sum: for they will ask 'How can a people be trusted for large sums who break their faith for such small ones?' You know best what effect it will have on the minds of the money lenders of that country should we fail in this payment. You know best also whether it is practicable and prudent for us to have this debt paid without orders. I refer the matter therefore wholly to your consideration, willing to participate with you in any risk, and any responsability which may arise. I think it one of those cases where it is a duty to risk one's self. You will perceive, by the inclosed, the necessity of an immediate answer, and that if you think any thing can and should be done all the necessary authorities from you should accompany your letter. In the mean time should I receive any orders from the Treasury by P. Jones, I will pursue them, and consider whatever you shall have proposed or done, as *non avenue*. I am with much affection Dear Sir Your most obedient and most humble servt.,

TH: JEFFERSON

Jefferson to Adams

Paris Dec. 16. 1787.

DEAR SIR

I wrote you on the 12th instant, that is to say, by the last post. But as that channel of conveiance is sometimes unfaithful I now inclose you a copy of my letter of that date, and of the one of Fiseaux & co. inclosed in that. I have since received my letters by the packet, but, among them, nothing from the Board of Treasury. Still their orders may be among the dispatches with which Paul Jones is charged for me, who was to sail a week after the packet. If he brings any orders, what you shall have done as I observed in my former letter shall be considered as if not done. On further consideration and consultation the object of my letter seems to increase in importance and to render it indispensible in us to do what we can, even without orders, to save the credit of the U.S. I have conferred with Mr. Jacob Van Staphorst, who is here, on this subject. He thinks the failure would have so ill an effect that it should certainly be prevented, he supposes the progress of your late loan may by this time furnish money in the hands of Willincks and Van Staphorsts to face this demand, and at any rate that these gentlemen will exert themselves to do it. By his advice I wrote to ask of them if I might count on their doing it, provided I forwarded your orders, and I wrote to Fizeaux & Co. what steps I was taking, desired them to confer with Willincks and Van Staphorsts, and to regulate the expectations of our creditors accordingly. The answer of Willincks and Van Staphorsts which I shall receive the 22d. inst. and yours which I hope to receive about the same time will decide what is to be done. Still it will be about the 28th. before Fizeaux can receive it through me, and he sais notice should have been given by the middle of the month.

I see by the American papers that your commission to the United Netherlands continues till the spring. Will you have to go there to take leave? If you do, and will give me notice in time, I will meet you there. In so doing I shall gratify my wish to see you before you leave Europe, to confer with you on some subjects, and become acquainted with our money affairs at Amsterdam, and that ground in general on which it may be rendered necessary, by our various debts, for me sometimes to undertake to act. I am very ignorant of it at present. I am with great and sincere esteem Dr. Sir Your most obedient and mo. humble servt.,

TH: JEFFERSON

Adams to Jefferson

London Decr. 18 1787

DEAR SIR

Last night I received your Letter of the 12. Mr. Jarvis and Commodore Jones are arrived here from New york both charged with large Dispatches for you. Mr. Jarvis Sent his Packet on by Col. Trumbul who departed from hence for Paris last Thursday. Comr. Jones went off a day or two ago, but both will arrive to you before this Letter. The Papers they carry, with a Renovation of your Commission at the Court of Versailles contain I presume orders and Instructions about every Thing in Holland.

As my Dismission from the Service arrived at the Same time, not a word has been said to me. Nevertheless Nil Americanum Alienum,[33] and I have the honour to agree with you in Your opinion of the Propriety of keeping good our Credit in Holland. I should advise therefore that the Interest on Mr. Fizeaux's Loan at least should be paid, and the Creditors requested to wait for their Capitals till further orders can be obtained from Congress. If they will not consent to that, I would pay them Principal and Interest provided there is Money enough in the hands of our Bankers and neither you nor they have received contrary orders. No Authorities from me will be necessary. Your own Letter to Messrs. Willinks and Vanstapherst will be sufficient. But if they make any difficulty, which I cannot conceive for want of any orders from me, I will send them.

You have received Authority to negotiate the Redemption of our unfortunate Countrymen in Algiers. To you therefore I send a Petition which I received from them a few days ago. With the highest Regard, I am Dear Sir your most obedient and most humble Servant,

JOHN ADAMS

N.B.[34] The Letter which Colo. Trumbull will deliver addressed to Count Sarsfield, may be sent to his hotel as the Count is on the point of departure for Paris. On referring to a resolve of Congress of the 11th. of october 1787. I find the interest of the foreign debt and that part of the principal due in 1788. has commanded their attention and I suppose put in proper train for operation. Yours,

J. ADAMS

Adams to Jefferson

London Decr. 25. 1787

DEAR SIR

By the last Post I answered your Letter of the 12, and Yesterday received yours of the 16. Com. Jones has before now delivered you dis-

---

33. "Nothing proper to an American is foreign to me"; a condensed adaptation of Terence: *Homo sum; humani nihil a me alienum puto*—"I am a man, and I regard nothing proper to mankind as foreign to me."
34. Postscript in William Stephens Smith's hand but signed by JA.

patches that will serve no doubt for your direction. Mr. Van staphorst, will have no Objection to an handsome Commission, for paying off, the Debt Mr. Fizeaux mentions: and Mr. Fizeau, will be glad to have it paid off, that the Money Lenders not knowing what to do with their Money may be tempted to put it into his French loan. But I am persuaded the Money Lenders on receiving their Interest would very willingly let the Principal remain, till the arrangements of Congress can discharge it. It will cost the United States Eight Per Cent, to transfer this debt, and four or five thousand Guilders are worth saving.

It would rejoice me in my soul to meet you, before I embark for America. But I am so ill, of an uncommon Cold, the present weather is so formidable and a Journey to Holland in the winter is so cruel, that I am obliged to excuse myself from taking leave in Person of the States general, and shall send a Memorial. The Time for me is short and there are many Things to do, so that I must confine my self to London, but if you could venture over here and see the August Spectacle of Mr. Hastings's Impeachment,[35] you would make us all very happy.

I should advise you, by all means to make a Journey to Holland; but not before the Month of May. A Letter to some of the Corps Diplomatique, will introduce You to them and to Court, and Messrs. Willinks and Vanstaphorsts will shew you Amsterdam, and explain to you Money matters. With Sincere Esteem and affection, I am Dear Sir your most obedient and most humble Servant,

JOHN ADAMS

Jefferson to Adams

Paris Dec. 31. 1787.

DEAR SIR

Mr. Parker furnishes me an opportunity of acknoleging the receipt of your favors of Nov. 10. Dec. 6.[36] 10. 18. and 25. which I avoid doing thro post. The orders on the subject of our captives at Algiers have come to

35. Charged with financial extortions from the natives of India, the late governor-general had been impeached by the House of Commons on April 3, 1787; his trial began the following Feb. and he was finally acquitted in 1795. H. G. Keene, "Hastings, Warren," *Dictionary of National Biography*, XXV, 145.

36. This letter, recorded in Jefferson's Summary Journal of Letters as received on Dec. 17, 1787, has not been found. His summary indicates that Adams was recommending Antoine-Marie Cerisier, French historian and diplomat, who was attached to the French embassy in Holland, where Adams met him in 1780. C. F. Adams, "Life of John Adams," *Works*, I, 330; JA to John Luzac, Dec. 13, 1781, *ibid.*, VII, 492. See also Boyd, XII, 397.

me by the last packet. They are to be kept secret even from the captives themselves, lest a knolege of the interference of government should excite too extravagant demands. The settlement of the prices, in the first instance, is important as a precedent.—Willincks & Van Staphorsts answered that they had money enough to pay the February interest, and our draughts for salary for some time, but that the paiment of Fiseaux' capital would oblige them to advance of their own money: they observed too that the paiment of such a sum without the orders of the treasury would lay them under an unnecessary responsibility. I therefore concluded the business by desiring them to pay the year's interest becoming due tomorrow, and praying Mr. Fiseaux to quiet the lenders with that till I could procure the orders of the Treasury to whom I wrote immediately an account of the whole transaction. I was the better satisfied with this on receiving your letter of the 25th. by which I find it your opinion that our credit may not suffer so materially. The declining the paiment came from the Willincks, the Van Staphorsts having offered to advance their moiety. I inclose you a letter I have received from the Comptroller general and an arret on the subject of our commerce.[37] They are the proof sheets, as, at the moment of writing my letter, I have not yet received the fair ones. But the French column is correct enough to be understood. I would wish them not to be public till they are made so on the other side of the water. —I think the alliance of this court with the two imperial ones is going on well. You will have heard of the Emperor's having attempted to surprise Belgrade and failed in the attempt. This necessarily engages him in the war, and so tends to continue it. I think it settled that this country abandons the Turks.

Mr. Parker takes charge of the 10. aunes of double Florence for Mrs. Adams. The silk stockings are not yet ready. I had ordered them to be made by the hermits of Mont Calvaire [38] who are famous for the excellence and honesty of their work, and prices. They will come by the first good opportunity. Be so good as to present my respects to her, and to be assured of the sincere attachment and respect of Dear Sir your most obedient and most humble servant,

TH: JEFFERSON

37. Wroth and Annan, eds., *Acts of French Royal Administration*, no. 2060.
38. Carthusian monastery where silence was enjoined. TJ rented rooms there beginning in Sept. 1787. Malone, *Jefferson*, II, 137-38.

Jefferson to Adams

Paris Jan. 13. 1788.

DEAR SIR

I informed you in my letter of the 31st. of December of the measures I had taken relative to the reimbursement of the 51,000 gelders to Fizeaux & co. to wit, that I had asked the Willincks and Van Staphorsts to pay the interest, and written to the board of treasury for their orders as to the principal. I inclose you a letter just received from Fizeaux & Co. now Hugguer, Grand & Co. by which you will perceive that they have recieved the interest, but that the creditors will not consent to delay the reimbursement of their capital. I inclose you a copy also of what I now write to the Willincks & Van Staphorsts, and will beg of you to give or refuse your sanction, as you think best, but in a letter sent directly to them, because I find by their letters to Mr. Jac. Van Staphorst, they will not be contented with the indirect authorisation of your former letter to me. Perhaps in any other case, the creditors would have been quieted. But Fizeaux is retired from business and chuses to wind up all his affairs. Probably therefore he has not endeavoured to quiet the creditors; perhaps he may consider their clamours as an useful engine to hasten his extrication from this business. Be that as it may, their clamours, should they be raised, may do us great injury. But of this you are the best judge. I am with great and sincere esteem, Dear Sir, your most obedient and most humble servant,

TH: JEFFERSON

Adams to Jefferson

Grosvenor Square Jan. 31. 1788

DEAR SIR

Permit me to introduce to you my young Friend Mr. Alexander Edwards of South Carolina, a modest and amiable young Gentleman who came particularly recommended to me, and whom I have found by Several Months Acquaintance to merit every Attention and Encouragement. I am, my dear Sir yours most affectionately,

JOHN ADAMS

Jefferson to Abigail Adams, with Enclosure

Paris Feb. 2. 1788

DEAR MADAM

The silk you desired was delivered to Mr. Parker a month ago, on the eve of his departure for England, as he supposed. He went however to Holland. Mr. Valnay is so kind as to take charge of that now, as also of the silk stockings. I doubt whether you may like the stockings on first appearance: but I will answer for their goodness, being woven expressly for me by the Hermits of Mont Calvaire with whom I go and stay sometimes, and am favoured by them. They have the reputation of doing the best work which comes to the Paris market. I inclose you their little note of the weight and price, for they sell by weight. I inclose also a state of our accounts subsequent to the paiment of the small sum by Colo. Smith which balanced our former transactions. You will make such additions and amendments to it as you shall find right. I have not yet been able to find M. de la Blancherie at home, so as to settle Mr. Adams's affair with him; but I will do it in time, and render you an account. There being no news here to communicate to you, be pleased to accept my thanks for the many kind services you have been so good as to render me and your friendly attentions on every occasion. I have considered you while in London as my neighbor, and look forward to the moment of your departure from thence as to an epoch of much regret and concern for me. Insulated and friendless on this side the globe, with such an ocean between me and every thing to which I am attached the days will seem long which are to be counted over before I too am to rejoin my native country. Young poets complain often that life is fleeting and transient. We find in it seasons and situations however which move heavily enough. It will lighten them to me if you will continue to honour me with your correspondence. You will have much to communicate to me, I little which can interest you. Perhaps you can make me useful in the execution of your European commissions. Be assured they will afford me sincere pleasure in the execution. My daughters join me in affectionate Adieus to you. Polly does not cease to speak of you with warmth and gratitude. Heaven send you, madam, a pleasant and safe passage, and a happy meeting with all your friends. But do not let them so entirely engross you as to forget that you have one here who is with the most sincere esteem and attachment Dear Madam your most obedient and most humble servant,

TH: JEFFERSON

ENCLOSURE

Mrs. Adams in acct. with Th: J

	Dr.	Cr.
	£	£ s
1787. Oct. 3. To paid for 5. aunes cambrick sent by Dr. Cutting 60^{tt}	2-10	
By cash to Colo. Smith		2-10
Dec. 19. By cash by Mr. Trumbull 120^{tt}		5
1788. Jan. 9. To pd. Hermits of M. Calvaire 12 pr. silk stockings 168^{tt}		
To pd. for 10. aunes double Florence @ 4^{tt}-15 47-10		
23. To pd. Ct. Sarsfeld for books for Mr. Adams 79		
	294-10 12- 5-5	
Balance in favor of Th: J		7- 5-5
	14-15-5	14-15-5

[Endorsed:] Sent this Balance due to Mr Jefferson by Mr Parker Febry 22 1788 Abigail Adams.

Jefferson to Adams

Paris Feb. 6. 1788.

DEAR SIR

The Commissioners of the treasury have given notice to Willincks and Van Staphorsts that they shall not be able to remit them one shilling till the new government gets into action; and that therefore the sole resource for the paiment of the Dutch interest till that period is in the progress of the last loan. Willincks & V.S. reply that there is not the least probability of raising as much on that loan as will pay the next June interest, and that if that paiment fails one day, it will do an injury to our credit which a very long time will not wipe off. A Mr. Stanitski, one of our brokers, who holds 1,340,000 dollars of our domestic debt offers, if we will pay him one year's interest of that debt, he will have the whole of the loan immediately filled up, that is to say he will procure the sum of 622,840 florins still unsubscribed. His year's interest (deducting from it 10 percent which he will allow for paiment in Europe instead of America) will require 180,000 florins of this money. Messrs. W. & V. S. say that, by this means, they can pay Fiseaux debt, and all the Dutch interest and our current expences here, till June 1789. by which time the new government may be in action. They have proposed this to the commissioners of the treasury, but it is possible that the delay of letters going and coming, with the time necessary between their receiving the answer and procuring the money, may force the decision of this proposition on me at the eleventh hour. I wish therefore to avail myself of your counsel before your departure on this proposition. Your knowlege of the subject enables you to give the best opinion, and your zeal for the public interest, and, I trust, your friendly dispositions towards me will prompt you to assist me with your advice on this question, to wit, if the answer of the Commissioners does not come in time, and there shall appear no other means of raising the June interest, will it be worst to fail in that paiment, or to accept of about 700,000 florins, on the condition of letting 180,000 be applied to the paiment of a year's interest of a part of our domestic debt? Do me the friendship to give me an answer to this as soon as possible and be assured of the sentiments of esteem and respect with which I have the honour to be Dear Sir Your most obedient and most humble servt.,

TH: JEFFERSON

Adams to Jefferson

London Feb. 12. 1788

DEAR SIR

I have received your Letter of the 6th. and had before received the same Information from Amsterdam.

I know not how to express to you, the sense I have of the disingenuity of this Plott. The Difficulty of selling the obligations I believe to be mere Pretence, and indeed the whole appears to me to be a concerted Fiction, in consequence of some Contrivance or Suggestion of Mr. Parker, the great Speculator in American Paper, who, though I love him very well, is too ingenious for me. I feel myself obliged to write this in Confidence to you, and to put you on your Guard against the immeasurable avarice of Amsterdam as well as the ungovernable Rage of Speculation. I feel no Vanity in saying that this Project never would have been suggested, if it had not been known, that I was recalled. If I was to continue in Europe and in office I would go to Amsterdam and open a new Loan with John Hodshon before I would submit to it. The Undertakers are bound in Honour, as I understood it, to furnish the Money on the new Loan. They agreed to this upon Condition that I would go to Amsterdam to sign the Obligations. The Truth is that Messrs. Willinks and Vanstaphorst have been purchasing immense Quantities of American Paper, and they now want to have it acknowledged and paid in Europe. It appears to me totally impossible that you or I should ever agree to it, or approve it, and as far as I can comprehend it is equally impossible for the Board of Treasury or Congress to consent to it. You and I however cannot answer for them: but I think We cannot countenance any hopes that they will ever comply with it. The Continental Certificates and their Interest are to be paid in America at the Treasury of the United States. If a Precedent is set of paying them in Europe, I pretend not to Sufficient foresight to predict the Consequences. They appear however to me to be horrid. If the Interest of one Million Dollars is paid this Year in Europe, you will find the Interest of Ten Millions demanded next year. I am very sorry to be obliged at the moment of my Retirement to give opinions which may be misrepresented and imputed to Motives that my soul despizes: but I cannot advise you by any means to countenance this Project: but it is my Serious Opinion that the Judgment of Congress, or the Board of Treasury, ought to be waited for, at all hazards. If the Brokers, Undertakers and Money lenders will take such Advantages of Us, it is high time to have done with them; pay what is due as fast as we can, but never contract another farthing of Debt with them. If a little Firmness is shewn in adhering to the Resolution of waiting the orders of Congress, it is my opinion, Care will be taken in Amsterdam that our Credit shall not suffer. The Interest of our Commissioners, of the Brokers, Undertakers and Money Lenders, all conspire to induce them to prevent a failure. But in my Judgment a failure had better take Place than this Project. I shall not write with the same frankness to Willinks, but I shall give them my opinion that the Judgment of Congress must be waited for.

My dear Friend farewell. I pity you, in your Situation, dunned and teazed as you will be, all your Philosophy will be wanting to support you. But be not discouraged, I have been constantly vexed with such terrible Complaints and frightened with such long Faces these ten years. Depend upon it, the Amsterdammers love Money too well, to execute their Threats. They expect to gain too much by American Credit to destroy it. I am with Sincere Affection and great Esteem, your Friend and Servant,

JOHN ADAMS

Jefferson to Adams

Paris Feb. 20. 1788

DEAR SIR

I am in hopes daily of receiving a letter from you in answer to my last. The delay of the letters which contained the proposition to the board of treasury takes away all probability of their answering in time, and I foresee that I shall be closely pressed by circumstances on that point. I have settled your matter with de la Blancherie, at the sum you fixed (8 Louis). He demanded 12. but without a shadow of reason I think.

This letter will probably find you near your departure. I am in hopes it will be only a change of service, from helping us here, to help us there. We have so few in our councils acquainted with foreign affairs, that your aid in that department, as well as others will be invaluable. The season of the year makes me fear a very disagreeable passage for Mrs. Adams and yourself, tho we have sometimes fine weather in these months. Nobody will pray more sincerely than myself for your passage, that it may be short, safe and agreeable, that you may have a happy meeting with all your friends, be received by them with the gratitude you have merited at their hands, and placed in such a station as may be honourable to you and useful to them. Adieu, my dear Sir, and accept assurances of the unchangeable esteem and respect with which I am Your friend and servant,

TH: JEFFERSON

Abigail Adams to Jefferson

London Febry. 21 1788.

MY DEAR SIR

In the midst of the Bustle and fatigue of packing, the parade and ceremony of taking leave at Court, and else where, I am informed that Mr. Appleton and Mrs. Parker are to set out for Paris tomorrow morning. I Cannot permit them to go without a few lines to my much Esteemed Friend, to thank him for all his kindness and Friendship towards myself and Family, from the commencement of our acquaintance, and to assure him that the offer he has made of his correspondence, is much too flattering, not to be gratefully accepted.

The florence and stockings were perfectly to my mind, and I am greatly obliged to you sir, for your care and attention about them. I have sent by Mrs. Parker the balance due to you, agreable to your statement, which I believe quite right.

Be so good as to present my regards to the Marquiss de la Fayette and his Lady, and to the Abbés. Assure them that I entertain a gratefull remembrance of all their civilities and politeness during my residence in Paris. To Mr. Short and the young Ladies your daughters say every thing that is affectionate for me, and be assured my dear sir, that I am With the Greatest respect Esteem and regard Your Friend and Humble Servant,

ABIGAIL ADAMS

Abigail Adams to Jefferson

London Febry. 26. 1788

DEAR SIR

Mr. Adams being absent I replie to your Letter this day received, that Mr. Adams has written to you upon the subject you refer to. Our time here is short and pressing. Yet short as it is Mr. Adams is obliged to Set out on fryday for the Hague in order to take leave there. Owing wholy to the neglect of Congress in omitting to send him a Letter of recall, tho he particularly requested it of them, when he desired permission to return, and has several times since repeated the same request. A memorial would then have answerd, but now it cannot be received, and he finds at this late hour that he must cross that most horrid passage twice, and make a rapid journey there and back again as it would be greatly injurious to our credit and affairs to give any reasonable cause of offence. He would be delighted to meet you there. But time is so pressing that he cannot flatter himself with that hope, nor be able to stay a day after he has compleated his buisness. Yet as this Letter may reach you about the day he will leave London you will consider whether there is a possibility of seeing each other at the Hague.

I had sent my arrears to you before Mr. Trumble thought of informing me that it was to be paid to him. The Eight Louis you have since been so kind as to pay for Mr. Adams shall be paid Mr. Trumble.

I thank you my dear sir for all your kind wishes and prayers. Heaven only knows how we are to be disposed of. You have resided long enough abroad to feel and experience how inadequate our allowance is to our decent expences, and that it is wholy impossible for any thing to be saved from it. This our countrymen in general will neither know or feel. I have lived long enough, and seen enough of the world, to check expectations, and to bring my mind to my circumstances, and retiring to our own little farm feeding my poultry and improveing my garden has more charms for my fancy, than residing at the court of Saint James's where I seldom meet with characters so innofensive as my Hens and chickings, or minds so well improved as my garden. Heaven forgive me if I think too hardly of them. I wish they had deserved better at my Hands. Adieu my dear sir and believe me at all times and in all situations your Friend and Humble Servant,

A A

Jefferson to Adams

Paris Mar. 2. 1788. Sunday

Dear Sir

I received this day a letter from Mrs. Adams of the 26th. ult. informing me you would set out on the 29th. for the Hague. Our affairs at Amsterdam press on my mind like a mountain. I have no information to go on but that of the Willincks and Van Staphorsts, and according to that something seems necessary to be done. I am so anxious to confer with you on this, and to see you and them together, and get some effectual arrangement made in time that I determine to meet you at the Hague. I will set out the moment some repairs are made to my carriage. It is promised me at 3. oclock tomorrow; but probably they will make it night, and that I may not set out till Tuesday morning. In that case I shall be at the Hague Friday night. In the mean time you will perhaps have made all your bows there. I am sensible how irksome this must be to you in the moment of your departure, but it is a great interest of the U.S. which is at stake and I am sure you will sacrifice to that your feelings and your interest. I hope to shake you by the hand within 24. hours after you receive this, and in the mean time am with much esteem and respect Dear Sir Your affectionate friend and humble servt,

Th: Jefferson

Adams to Jefferson

The Hague March 17. 1788

His Excellency Mr. Jefferson is requested to pay the within Account.

John Adams

[Endorsed by TJ on face:] Mr. Adams's bill of coachire [39]

Jefferson to Adams

Paris Aug. 2. 1788.

Dear Sir

I have received with a great deal of pleasure the account of your safe arrival and joyful reception at Boston. Mr. Cutting was so kind as to send me a copy of the address of the assembly to you and your answer, which with the other circumstances I have sent to have published in the gazette of Leyden, and in a gazette here. It will serve to shew the people of Europe that those of America are content with their servants, and particularly content with you.

The war with the Turks, Russians, and Austrians goes on. A great victory obtained on the black sea over the Turks as commanded by the Captain Pacha, by the Russians commanded by Admiral Paul Jones will serve to raise the spirits of the two empires. He burnt six ships, among which was the admiral's and vice admiral's, took two, and made between three and four thousand prisoners. The Swedes having hastily armed a fleet of about 16. sail of the line, and marched an army into Finland, the king at the head of it, made us believe they were going to attack the Russians. But when their fleet met with three Russian ships of 100 guns each they saluted and passed them. It is pretty well understood that the expences of this armament are paid by the Turks through the negociations of England. And it would seem as if the king had hired himself to strut only, but not to fight, expecting probably that the former would suffice to divert the Russians from sending their fleet round to the Mediterranean. There are some late symptoms which would indicate that Denmark would

39. TJ was in Amsterdam March 10-30. In TJ's account book under March 21, 1788: "pd Mr. Adams's expences here 83/18 his coach hire to Hague 33/." Jefferson Papers, Lib. Cong.

still be opposed to Sweden though she should shift herself into the opposite scale. The alliance between England, Holland and Prussia is now settled. In the mean time this country is losing all it's allies one by one, without assuring to herself new ones. Prussia, Holland, Turkey, Sweden are pretty certainly got or getting into the English interest, and the alliance of France with the two empires is not yet secured. I am in hopes her internal affairs will be arranged without blood. None has been shed as yet. The nation presses on sufficiently upon the government to force reformations, without forcing them to draw the sword. If they can keep the opposition always exactly at this point, all will end well. Peace or war, they cannot fail now to have the States general, and I think in the course of the following year. They have already obtained the Provincial assemblies as you know, the king has solemnly confessed he cannot lay a new tax without the consent of the States general, and when these assemble they will try to have themselves moulded into a periodical assembly, to form a declaration of rights, and a civil list for the government. The Baron de Breteuil has lately retired from the ministry and been succeeded by M. de Villedeuil. Monsieur de Malesherbes will probably retire. The Marquis de la Fayette with several others have lately received a fillup for having assembled to sign a memorial to the king which had been sent up from Brittany. They took from the Marquis a particular command which he was to have ex[ercised du]ring the months of August and September this year [in the] South of France.[40] Your friends the Abbés are well and always enquire after you. I shall be happy to hear from you from time to time, to learn state news and state politics, for which I will give you in return those of this quarter of the earth. I hope Mrs. Adams is well; I am sure she is happier in her own country than any other. Assure her of my constant friendship and accept assurances of the same from Dear Sir Your most obedt. and most humble servt.

TH: JEFFERSON

P.S. Make freely any use of me here which may be convenient either for yourself or Mrs. Adams.

P.S. Aug. 6.   Later accounts inform us there have been two actions between the Russians and Turks. The first was of the gallies etc. on both sides. In this P. Jones, being accidentally present, commanded the right wing. The Russians repulsed the Turks. The second action was of the Russian gallies against the Turkish ships of war. The effect was what is stated in the preceding letter. But the command was solely in the prince

40. On July 12, 1788, Lafayette joined the Breton nobles in Paris in protesting against the decree abolishing the parlements. Shortly afterward he was deprived of his military command under the Duc d'Ayen in Languedoc and Roussillon. Gottschalk, *Lafayette*, 387-91.

of Nassau, P. Jones with his fleet of ships of war being absent. Prince Potemkin immediately got under march for Oczakow, to take advantage of the consternation it was thrown into. The Swedes have commenced hostilities against the Russians, and war against them is consequently declared by the empress.

Jefferson to Adams

Paris Nov. [i.e., Dec.] 5. 1788.

DEAR SIR

I had the pleasure of writing to you on the 2d. of Aug. and of adding a P.S. of Aug. 6. You will have known since that that the interposition of Denmark, as auxilliary to Russia against Sweden, has been suppressed magisterially by England and Prussia. This seemed to prove that these two powers did not mean to enter into the war; that on the contrary they wished seriously to quiet things on the Western side of Europe and let the war of the East go on. A new incident now arises which may still endanger the peace of the West. The Prussian party in Poland having obtained a majority in their confederated diet, have voted the establishment of a council of war independant of the king, and propose to hold a perpetual diet, during which you know the king is as nothing. Russia has formally declared she will consider this as a breach of the constitution settled in 1775. under the guaranty of the three powers; and Prussia has put an army into readiness to march at a moment's warning on the frontiers of Poland. The emperor after a disadvantageous campaign, is secretly trying to obtain peace of the Turks, in which he is sincerely aided by this court, and opposed we may be sure by that of London. We do not know how far the Emperor's plan includes Russia. If these powers obtain their peace of the Turks, they will probably give a rap of the knuckles at least to the K. of Prussia. The lunacy of the king of England will probably place the affairs of that country under a regency; and as regencies are generally pacific, we may expect they will concur with this country in an unwillingness to enter into war. The internal tranquillity of this country, which had never been so far compromitted as to produce bloodshed, was entirely reestablished by the announcing of the States general early in the next year, the reestablishment of the parliament and substitution of Mr. Neckar in the department of finance instead of the Archbishop of Sens. The parliament which had called for the States general only thro' fear that they could not obtain otherwise their own restoration, being once restored, began to fear those very States general and to prepare cavils at the forms of calling and organising them. The court to debarrass itself of the dispute, referred these to the same Notables who had acted, on a former occasion, with approbation. These Notables, being composed of Clergy, Nobility, members of parliament and some privileged persons of the tiers etat, have shamelessly combined against the rights of the people. The court wished the tiers etat should equal the two other orders by the number of their deputies in the States general, and that they should form one house only. 5 bureaux out of 6. of the Notables have voted that the people shall have only as many members as each of the other orders singly, and that they shall vote by orders: so that the votes of the two houses of clergy and nobles concurring, that of the tiers etat will be over-ruled. For it is not here as in England where each branch has a negative on the other two. The votes of the bureaux are not yet consolidated, but I see no reason to suppose that the separate votes will be changed in the consolidation. But in whatever manner the states shall be formed, they will meet in March probably, or April at furthest, and will obtain without much opposition from the court, or perhaps with none 1. their own periodical convocation: 2. their exclusive right to tax: 3. a transfer of the right, now exercised by usurpation by the parliaments, to register laws and propose previous amendments to them. Thus a change in their constitution is, I think, certain: and the life of the present king or the minority of his heir will give time to confirm it.

You recollect well the Arret of Dec. 29. 1787. in favor of our commerce, and which among other things gave free admission to our whale oils under a duty of about two Louis a ton. In consequence of the English treaty their oils flowed in and overstocked the market. The light duty they were liable to under the treaty, still lessened by false estimates, and aided by the high premiums of the British government enabled them to undersell the French and American oils. This produced an outcry of the Dunkirk fishery. It was proposed to exclude all European oils, which would not infringe the British treaty. I could not but encourage this idea, because it woud give to the French and American fisheries a monopoly of the French market. The Arret was so drawn up. But in the very moment of passing it they struck out the word *European* so that our oils became involved. This I believe was the effect of a single person in the ministry. As soon as it was known to me I wrote to M. de Montmorin and had conferences with him and the other ministers. I found it necessary to give them full information on the subject of the whale fishery, of which they knew little but from the partial information of their Dunkirk adventurers. I therefore wrote the Observations [41] (of which I enclose you a printed

41. *Observations on the Whale-Fishery*, Boyd, XIV, 242-54. See TJ to John Jay, Nov. 19, 1788, *ibid.*, 211-16; and editorial note to "Documents Concerning the Whale Fishery," *ibid.*, 217-25.

copy) had them printed to entice them to read them, and particularly developed the expence at which they are carrying on that fishery and at which they must continue it, if they do continue it. This part was more particularly intended for Mr. Neckar, who was quite a stranger to the subject, who has principles of oeconomy, and will enter into calculations. Other subjects are incidentally introduced, tho' little connected with the main question. They had been called for by other circumstances. An immediate order was given for the present admission of our oils, till they could form an arret: and at a conference, the draught of an Arret was communicated to me, which re-established that of Dec. 29.[42] They expressed fears that under cover of our name the Nova Scotia oils would be introduced, and a blank was left in the draught for the means of preventing that. They have since proposed that the certificate of their consul shall accompany the oils to authorize their admission, and this is what they will probably adopt. It was observed that if our states would prohibit all foreign oils from being imported into them, it would be a great safeguard, and an encouragement to them to continue the admission. Still there remains an expression in the Arret that it is provisory only. However we must be contented with it as it is; my hope being that the legislation will be transferred to the national assembly in whose hands it will be more stable, and with whom it will be more difficult to obtain a repeal, should the ministry hereafter desire it. If they could succeed in drawing over as many of our Nantucket men as would supply their demands of oil, we might then fear an exclusion. But the present arret, as soon as it shall be passed, will, I hope, place us in safety till that event, and that event may never happen. I have entered into all these details that you may be enabled to quiet the alarm which must have been raised by the arret of Sep. 28. and assure the adventurers that they may pursue their enterprises as safely as if that had never been passed, and more profitably, because we participate now of a monopolized instead of an open market. The inclosed Observations, tho' printed, have only been given to the ministers, and one or two other confidential persons. You will see that they contain matter which should be kept from the English, and will therefore trust them to the perusal only of such persons as you can confide in. We are greatly indebted to the Marquis de la Fayette for his aid on this as on every other occasion. He has paid the closest attention to it and combated for us with the zeal of a native.

The necessity of reconducting my family to America, and of placing my affairs there under permanent arrangements, has obliged me to ask of Congress a six months absence, to wit from April to November next. I hope therefore to have the pleasure of seeing you there, and particularly

42. "Arret Concerning Whale Oil, 7 December 1788," *ibid.*, 268-69.

that it will be at New York that I shall find you. Be so good as to present my sincere esteem to Mrs. Adams, and beleive me to be with very affectionate attachment Dear Sir Your friend and servt,

TH: JEFFERSON

Adams to Jefferson

Braintree near Boston Jany. 2 1789

MY DEAR FRIEND

Give me leave to introduce to you John Coffin Jones Esqr, an eminent Merchant of Boston and a late Member of the Legislature from that Town. His Character both in public and private Life is much respected, and his Intelligence will enable him to give you a much better account of the general and particular Politicks of this Country than I can. Our Fellow Citizens are in the midst of their Elections for the new Government, which have hitherto in general run very well. For my own Part, I have enjoyed a Luxury for the last Six Months which I have never before tasted for, at least eight and twenty Years, and have looked down upon all you Statesmen, with Sovereign Compassion. The new Government has my best Wishes and most fervent Prayers, for its Success and Prosperity: but whether I shall have any Thing more to do with it, besides praying for it, depends on the future suffrages of Freemen. I am with an affection that can never die, your Friend and Servant,

JOHN ADAMS

Jefferson to Adams

Paris Jan. 14. 1789.

DEAR SIR

I now do myself the pleasure to inclose to you a copy of the Arret explanatory of that of Sep. 28. on the subject of our whale oils. Mr. Necker in a letter to me has renewed the promise of taking off the 10. sous per livre at the end of the next year. But at the same time he observes that whenever the national fishery shall be able to supply their demand for whale oil we must expect a repeal of this Arret, which therefore expresses itself to be *provisory*. However, their navigation being the most expensive in Europe, they are the least likely to succeed in a whale fishery, without encouragements more extravagant than even those they now give: and it remains to be seen whether Mr. Necker will continue to give even the present. I am informed there will be fewer French adventurers the next year than there has been this: so that if there be an apparent increase of their fishery, it will be by drawing over more of our fishermen. It is probable the States-general will obtain a participation in the legislation, which will render their laws more stable, and more to be relied on. Mr. Necker has also promised that if the present Arret should at any time be repealed, there shall be a sufficient space of time allowed for the reception of the oils which shall have been previously embarked. But our principal, if not our only danger of a repeal being brought on, will come from the endeavors of the English to introduce their oils under colour of ours, perhaps even with the assistance of our own merchants. Some effectual means must be adopted to prevent them from getting our real ship papers, and our Consuls in the ports of France must be enabled to detect forged papers: and we must moreover convince this government that we use our utmost endeavors, and with good faith, to prevent the entry of English oils under the license given to us. I would advise our shippers of oil always to get the Certificate of the French consul in their state if it be practicable, because those will admit of the least doubt here. When this cannot be had, they may have recourse to the magistrates of the country, and in this case there should be a certificate under the seal of the state that the magistrate who has certified their oil to be the produce of the American fishery is a magistrate duly appointed and qualified by law, and that his signature is genuine. I presume it is the usage in all the states for the Governor's signature to accompany the great seal.

Oczakow is at length taken. The Russians say they gave the assault with 14,000 men, against 12,000 within the walls, that 7000 of these suffered themselves to be cut to peices before they surrendered, and that themselves lost 3000. The only circumstance to be believed in all this is that Oczakow is taken. Every thing else in Europe is quiet, except the internal affairs of Poland. The Prussian party there gains greater superiority daily. The K. of Prussia however will feel less bold on the probability that England will remain inactive in all things external. This secures to this country leizure for their internal improvements. These go on well. The report of Mr. Necker to the king, which has been published, renews the renunciation of the power of laying a new tax or continuing an old one without consent of the states general, admits they are to appropriate the public monies (and of course how much of it the king may spend), that ministers must be responsible, that the king will concur in fixing the periodical meeting of the states, that he will be ready to consider with them what modifications letters de cachet should be put under, and of the degree of liberty which may be given to the press; and further that all this shall be fixed by a convention so solemn as that his successors shall not be free to infringe it, that is to say that he will concur in a Declaration of rights. Nothing is said however of the States sharing in the legislation, but this will surely be pressed. They have given to the tiers etat a representation in the States equal to both the other orders, and it is probable they will form but one house and vote by persons: but that is not decided. Be so good as to present me affectionately to Mrs. Adams and to be assured yourself of the sincere esteem of dear Sir Your friend and servt.,

TH: JEFFERSON

Adams to Jefferson

Braintree March 1. 1789

DEAR SIR

The inclosed Letter from The Hon. Stephen Higginson Esqr. is upon a Subject of so much Importance, and contains so much Information that I cannot withold it from you. The little Jealousy, Envy or Caprice, that shall deprive our Merchants of the Benefit of Trading to the Isles of France and Bourbon, will only compell them to seek the Ultimate Markets upon the Continent, directly.[43]

In four days, the new Government is to be erected.[44] Washington appears to have an unanimous vote: and there is probably a Plurality if not a Majority in favour of your Friend.—It may be found easier to give Authority, than to yeild Obedience.

Amendments to the Constitution, will be expected, and no doubt discussed. Will you be so good as to look over the Code and write me your Sentiments of Amendments which you think necessary or usefull? That greatest and most necessary of all Amendments, the Seperation of the Executive Power, from the Legislative Seems to be better understood than it once was. Without this our Government is in danger of being a continual struggle between a Junto of Grandees, for the first Chair.

43. Higginson to JA, Boston, Jan. 17, 1789, Boyd, XIV, 599-602. The Isle de France was renamed Mauritius by the British after they got possession in 1815; Bourbon was renamed Réunion by the French in 1848.

44. The new House of Representatives did not secure a quorum until April 1, nor the Senate until April 6; Washington and Adams were inaugurated on April 30. Edward Channing, A History of the United States (N. Y., 1905-25), IV, 30, 32.

The Success of the new Plan will depend in the first Place upon a Revenue, to defray the Interest of the foreign and domestic debt. But how to get a Revenue? how to render Smuggling and Evasion Shameful?

You must expect the first Operations will be very Slow.—Mrs. A. and your old Admirer, my Son, desire their respects to you. With unabated respect, Esteem and Affection I am, dear Sir, your Friend and humble sert.,

JOHN ADAMS

Jefferson to Adams

Paris May 10. 1789.

DEAR SIR

Since mine of January 14. yours of Jan. 2. and Mar. 1. have been handed to me; the former by Mr. Jones, whom I am glad to know on your recommendation and to make him the channel of evidencing to you how much I esteem whatever comes from you.

The internal agitations of this country and the inactivity to which England is reduced by the state of imbecillity in which the madness of the King has terminated, will leave the Southwestern parts of Europe in peace for the present year. Denmark will probably continue to furnish only it's stipulated succours to Russia, without engaging in the war as a principal. Perhaps a pacification may be effected between Sweden and Russia: tho at present there is little appearance of it: so that we may expect that the war will go on this year between the two empires, the Turks and Swedes, without extending any further. Even the death of the emperor, should it take place, would hardly withdraw his dominions from the war this summer.

The revolution in this country has gone on hitherto with a quietness, a steadiness, and a progress unexampled. But there is danger of a balk now. The three orders which compose the states general seem likely to stumble at the threshold on the great preliminary question How shall they vote, by orders or persons? If they get well over this question, there will be no difficulty afterwards, there is so general a concurrence in the great points of constitutional reformation. If they do not get over this question (and this seems possible) it cannot be foreseen what issue this matter will take.[45]

45. The first revolutionary acts came on June 17, when the Third Estate declared itself to be the National Assembly; three days later it took the Oath of the Tennis Court and thereby defied Louis XVI.

As yet however, no business being begun, no votes taken, we cannot pronounce with certainty the exact state of parties. This is a summary view of European affairs.

Tho I have not official information of your election to the Presidency of the Senate; yet I have such information as renders it certain. Accept I pray you my sincere congratulations. No man on earth pays more cordial homage to your worth nor wishes more fervently your happiness. Tho' I detest the appearance even of flattery, I cannot always suppress the effusions of my heart.

Present me affectionately to Mrs. Adams, Colo. and Mrs. Smith. I hope to see you all this summer, and to return this fall to my prison; for all Europe would be a prison to me, were it ten times as big. Adieu my dear friend Your affectionate humble servt.,

TH: JEFFERSON

7

"The Age of Experiments in Government"

THE CORRESPONDENCE between Adams and Jefferson during the 1790's provides something less than even a bare outline of their participation in the political events which profoundly affected the development of the United States. The paucity of correspondence may be accounted for during the early years of the decade by their close personal contact in public affairs which made letters unnecessary, during the later years by their political differences.

When Jefferson learned that Adams had been elected vice-president of the United States, he wrote from France in May 1789 to congratulate him and pay "cordial homage." [1] Six months later he returned to Virginia on leave from his diplomatic post to learn that President Washington had appointed him secretary of state. [2] Reunited in New York, the first national capital, the old friends could engage in private conversation rather than letter writing. Although Jefferson was secretary of state for four years, he wrote only two letters to Adams about American foreign policy. The first recalled the disputes of long standing with Great Britain over the northeast boundary of the United States, [3] supposedly settled by the Treaty of 1783. It had been a vexation to Adams in London and remained an issue for more than a half-century. The other letter discussed the Consular Convention of 1788 with France, which the new Senate ratified in 1789. It must have given the secretary of state special satis-

1. TJ to JA, May 10, 1789, above, 238.
2. Malone, *Jefferson*, II, Chap. XIII.
3. TJ to JA, April 20, 1790, below, 244.

faction for he had drafted it as minister to France to replace an earlier text which Secretary John Jay had viewed with suspicion as being pro-French and which the old Congress had finally rejected.[4]

One of the first wedges separating Adams and Jefferson grew out of the inadvertent publication of Jefferson's views about Thomas Paine's *Rights of Man* (1791) as an antidote "against the political heresies which have sprung up among us."[5] Paine's work, a reply to Edmund Burke's hostile *Reflections on the French Revolution*, emphasized in its first installment the relationship between the contemporary insurgency in France and the American Revolution. In the second installment Paine criticized the English constitution as the bulwark of a reactionary government opposing the great revolutionary movements of the era. When Paine fled to France in 1792 to escape trial for sedition in England, he became a storm center of political controversy that raged throughout the decade. His writings had met a cordial response privately from Jefferson, who read a borrowed copy of the *Rights of Man* and returned it with a covering note expressing pleasure that it was to be reprinted. But the printer, without Jefferson's permission, published the note with its comment on "political heresies" (Jefferson confessed to Madison that he had in mind Adams's pro-British newspaper articles, "Discourses on Davila,"[6] in support of the British system of government), and thus Jefferson's name was coupled with Paine's in the reprint, which appeared early in May 1791.[7]

A month later, in a series of letters to the Boston *Columbian Centinel*, Publicola attacked the *Rights of Man* and its reputed sponsor. From the style of the letters most readers assumed that Adams was the author.[8] But everyone who "knew" Publicola's identity guessed wrong. He turned out to be twenty-four-year-old John Quincy Adams. Nevertheless, Jefferson's belated explanation of his own position could hardly satisfy the elder Adams.[9] He had already assured Jefferson, however, that "your motives for writing to me, I have not a doubt were the most pure and the most friendly; and I

4. TJ to JA, Nov. 25, 1791, below, 252.
5. TJ to JA, July 17, 1791, below, 246.
6. May 9, 1791, Ford, V, 332.
7. Malone, *Jefferson*, II, Chap. XXI.
8. Samuel F. Bemis, *John Quincy Adams and the Foundations of American Foreign Policy* (N. Y., 1950), 26-28. Hereafter cited as Bemis, *John Quincy Adams*.
9. TJ to JA, Aug. 30, 1791, below, 250-51.

have no suspicion that you will not receive this explanation from me in the same candid Light." [10] Adams had replied out of the kindliness of his heart and the friendship he cherished. Jefferson might better have left further comment on the incident unexpressed, along with the hope "that our friendship will never be suffered to be committed." [11]

When Adams published the first volume of his *Defence of the Constitutions*, he had predicted that it "will be an unpopular Work in America for a long time," [12] and the same could have been said of the "Discourses on Davila." Few works on political theory have ever been popular. It is not a favorite subject for politicians because they are practical men who have already made up their minds. Adams was realistic enough in basing his concept of balanced government upon the dominant self-interest of men which must be controlled for the benefit of society; and he found the best example of its attainment in the structure of the British government. But the "Discourses," like the *Defence*, were hard reading, easily misunderstood, and frequently misinterpreted, whether willfully or innocently. It might almost be said that Adams wrote too much; that he was too intellectual for most of his associates, whether "aristocrats" or "republicans." He protested Jefferson's statement that their differences as to the best form of government were well known to them both: "I do not know what your Idea is of the best form of government." As for himself, he denied ever having had a design "of attempting to introduce a Government of King, Lords and Commons . . . into the United States or . . . any Individual State." [13] Jefferson had not set forth his own ideas in writing for all to read, but privately he had referred to Adams's "apostacy to hereditary monarchy and nobility." [14] He, too, it would seem, had not read Adams's writings carefully.

After Jefferson resigned as secretary of state on December 31, 1793, he lived in uninterrupted retirement at Monticello for three years. Despite their political differences, he and Adams carried on a sporadic exchange, discussing the French Revolution, the surge of European refugees to America in its wake, and the unreadiness of Americans to accept foreign culture transplanted in their own soil. Vice-President

10. JA to TJ, July 29, 1791, below, 250.
11. TJ to JA, Aug. 30, 1791, below, 251.
12. JA to TJ, March 1, 1787, above, 176.
13. JA to TJ, July 29, 1791, below, 249.
14. TJ to Washington, May 8, 1791, Ford, V, 329.

Adams envied Jefferson's rural retirement "out of the hearing of the Din of Politicks and the Rumours of War." [15] In fact, throughout the eleven years, 1790-1800, during eight of which Jefferson held high public office, he spent fully one half of the time at Monticello. The Adamses' periods of relaxation at their home in Quincy could not be so prolonged.

Adams and Jefferson agreed that the United States should avoid embroilment in the European war which had erupted in 1793 between France and England. When war fever in the United States burned intensely against Great Britain the following year, Adams declared that "those who dread Monarchy and Aristocracy and at the same time Advocate War are the most inconsistent of all Men." [16] From his mountain top in Albemarle County, Jefferson expressed the hope that "this ... will be an age of experiments in government ... founded on principles of honesty, not of mere force." His countrymen should continue to engage "in agriculture or the pursuits of honest industry, independant in their circumstances, enlightened as to their rights, and firm in their habits of order and obedience to the laws." "Never," he wrote Adams, "was a finer canvas presented to work on than our countrymen." [17]

But the "Din of Politicks" echoed increasingly through their letters. By 1796 the Republican party, molded by Madison and headed by Jefferson, had emerged as a serious challenge to Federalist supremacy.[18] Jefferson hoped that party strife would not lead to personal estrangement, although he and Adams were rival candidates for the presidency in the election of 1796. Lacking the talents of the politician, Adams possessed the virtues which thoughtful men associated with the ideal of virtuous government and which provided him a substantial political following. It had been more than enough to re-elect him vice-president in 1792 by a comfortable majority over the astute anti-federalist Governor George Clinton of New York. It was still enough in 1796 to elect him president by three electoral votes, even though Hamilton shifted his support to Thomas Pinckney with the hope of defeating Adams.[19]

15. JA to TJ, April 4, 1794, below, 253.
16. JA to TJ, May 11, 1794, below, 255.
17. TJ to JA, Feb. 28, 1796, below, 260.
18. Noble E. Cunningham, *The Jeffersonian Republicans: The Formation of Party Organization* (Chapel Hill, 1957), Chap. V.
19. Edward Stanwood, *A History of the Presidency from 1788 to 1897* (Boston, 1898), Chaps. III-IV.

After this close contest was over but before the results were known, Jefferson wrote a letter, dated December 28, to Adams, deploring the efforts of the politicians and the press to set them at odds and congratulating him on the victory. Jefferson's supposition of Adams's election was correct, his desire sincere. Although he valued highly "the share . . . I may have had in the late vote," Jefferson disclaimed any "ambition to govern men." But suppose he had been elected instead of Adams. Had he said too much? Jefferson forwarded the letter unsealed to Congressman Madison for advice. Having received the letter after the news of Adams's election, Madison, exercising the discretion Jefferson had allowed him, decided not to send it.[20] Adams was therefore denied the sincere wishes of Jefferson and the testimony that he "retains still for you the solid esteem of the moments when we were working for our independance"[21]—testimony that might have eased their strained relations during Adams's presidency.

From the spring of 1796 until February 20, 1801, when President Adams advised President-elect Jefferson of horses and carriages available "in the stables of the United States," no letter passed between them. Nor, except on a few occasions, did they confer at the seat of government. As the crisis with France worsened and the insulting XYZ Affair provoked demands for a war of retaliation, Francophobe Federalists and Francophile Republicans indulged in another campaign of invective and scurrility through the newspaper columns. In 1798, amid the hysteria of quasi-war and unreasoning fear of foreigners in the United States, Congress passed the Alien and Sedition Acts, Adams signed them, and Jefferson, in protest and warning, drafted the Kentucky Resolutions and revised Madison's Virginia Resolutions. Both documents were as significant for their protest on behalf of civil liberties as for their defense of state rights;[22] yet, at the same time, Jefferson the politician occasionally aided the hack writer James Thomson Callender in his published abuse of Federalist leaders.[23]

20. TJ to Madison, Jan. 1 and 30, 1797, Ford, VII, 99, 115; Madison to TJ, Jan. 15, 1797, Gaillard Hunt, ed., *The Writings of James Madison* (N. Y., 1900-10), VI, 302-5.
21. TJ to JA, Dec. 28, 1796, below, 263.
22. Adrienne Koch and Harry Ammon, "The Virginia and Kentucky Resolutions: An Episode in Jefferson's and Madison's Defense of Civil Liberties," *Wm. and Mary Quart.*, 3d ser., 5 (1948), 174.
23. Cunningham, *Jeffersonian Republicans*, 169-72. For an adverse account of Jefferson's relations with Callender, see Worthington C. Ford, ed., *Thomas Jefferson and James Thomson Callender, 1798-1802* (Brooklyn, 1897); a more sympathetic appraisal is given in Frank L. Mott, *Jefferson and the Press* (Baton Rouge, 1943), 32-37.

Adams, with magnificent courage, sacrificed his political career by sending a new peace mission to France, thereby frustrating the demand of the High Federalists for all-out war.[24] But he succumbed to his feeling of fear and misgiving concerning the victory of the Jeffersonians in the election of 1800-1 and made innumerable "midnight appointments" of Federalists to office on the eve of Jefferson's accession to the presidency.[25]

Thus ended the first era of American national politics. Thus was suspended the friendship of two of its finest statesmen.

Jefferson to Adams

New York 20th. April 1790.

SIR

Encroachments being made on the Eastern limits of the United States by Settlers under the British Government, pretending that it is the Western and not the Eastern river of the Bay of Passamaquoddy which was designated by the name of St. Croix in the Treaty of Peace with that Nation, I have to beg the favour of you to communicate any facts which your memory or papers may enable you to recollect, and which may indicate the true River the Commissioners on both sides had in their view to establish as the boundary between the two Nations.[26] It will be of some consequence to be informed by what Map they traced the boundary. I have the honor to be with the greatest respect Sir Your most obt. and most hble. Servt.

TH: JEFFERSON

24. Joseph Charles, *The Origins of the American Party System: Three Essays* (Williamsburg, Va., 1956), 62-64.

25. See below, Chap. 8, *passim*.

26. The Treaty of Paris of 1783, of which JA had been one of the American negotiators, placed the northeastern boundary of the United States at the St. Croix River, but opinion differed as to which river the French name referred. For lack of diplomatic relations between the United States and Great Britain, no settlement could be made. In 1798 a joint commission on the boundary concluded that the Schoodic River was the dividing line. A. L. Burt, *The United States, Great Britain, and British North America, 1775-1815* (New Haven, 1940), Chap. V, 163-65. The northeastern boundary was settled by the Webster-Ashburton Treaty of 1842. Samuel F. Bemis, *A Diplomatic History of the United States* (N. Y., 1936), 262-64.

Jefferson to Adams

Philadelphia Nov. 26. 1790.

DEAR SIR

From a letter received from the President Mr. Lear is satisfied he cannot be here to-day and doubts even the possibility of his arrival tomorrow. Of course our expedition of to-day would be certainly fruitless,[27] and is therefore laid aside agreeably to a message I have received from Genl Knox and the attorney Genl [Edmund Randolph]. Yours affectionately and respectfully

TH: JEFFERSON

Jefferson to Adams

TH: JEFFERSON presents his respects to the Vice-president of the U. S. and has the honor to inclose him the copy of a letter from the President,[28] just now received.

Apr. 8. 1791.

Jefferson to Adams

P[h]iladelphia July 17. 1791.

DEAR SIR

I have a dozen times taken up my pen to write to you and as often laid it down again, suspended between opposing considerations. I determine

27. Members of President Washington's cabinet had planned to meet him on his way from Mount Vernon to Philadelphia, somewhere south of the city; but on Nov. 23 he wrote Lear from below Baltimore that the roads were "the most infamous . . . that ever were seen. . . . [We] have no expectation of reaching Baltimore to Night." John C. Fitzpatrick, ed., *The Writings of George Washington* (Washington, 1931-44), XXXI, 159. The President and Mrs. Washington arrived in Philadelphia on Nov. 27. Douglas S. Freeman, *George Washington: A Biography* (N. Y., 1948-57), VI, 286.

28. On April 4 Washington informed his secretaries of state, treasury, and war of his itinerary through the southern states and outlined the conditions on which they should conduct the government during his absence. Fitzpatrick, ed., *Writings of Washington*, XXXI, 272-73.

however to write from a conviction that truth, between candid minds, can never do harm.

The first of Paine's pamphlets on the Rights of man, which came to hand here, belonged to Mr. Beckley. He lent it to Mr. Madison who lent it to me; and while I was reading it Mr. Beckley called on me for it, and, as I had not finished it, he desired me, as soon as I should have done so, to send it to Mr. Jonathan B. Smith, whose brother meant to reprint it. I finished reading it, and, as I had no acquaintance with Mr. Jonathan B. Smith, propriety required that I should explain to him why I, a stranger to him, sent him the pamphlet. I accordingly wrote a note of compliment informing him that I did it at the desire of Mr. Beckley, and, to take off a little of the dryness of the note, I added that I was glad it was to be reprinted here and that something was to be publicly said against the political heresies which had sprung up among us etc.[29] I thought so little of this note that I did not even keep a copy of it: nor ever heard a tittle more of it till, the week following, I was thunderstruck with seeing it come out at the head of the pamphlet. I hoped however it would not attract notice. But I found on my return from a journey of a month that a writer came forward under the signature of Publicola,[30] attacking not only the author and principles of the pamphlet, but myself as it's sponsor, by name. Soon after came hosts of other writers defending the pamphlet and attacking you by name as the writer of Publicola. Thus were our names thrown on the public stage as public antagonists. That you and I differ in our ideas of the best form of government is well known to us both: but we have differed as friends should do, respecting the purity of each other's motives, and confining our difference of opinion to private conversation. And I can declare with truth in the presence of the almighty that nothing was further from my intention or expectation than to have had either my own or your name brought before the public on this occasion. The friendship and confidence which has so long existed between us required this explanation from me, and I know you too well to fear any misconstruction of the motives of it. Some people here who would wish me to be, or to be thought, guilty of improprieties, have suggested that I was Agricola, that I was Brutus etc. etc.[31] I never did in my life, either by myself or by any other, have a sentence of mine inserted in a newspaper without putting my name to it; and I believe I never shall.

While the empress is refusing peace under a mediation unless Oczakow

29. TJ's note to the printer, J. B. Smith, continued as follows: "I have no doubt our citizens will rally a second time round the standard of Common Sense." Ford, V, 354n.

30. John Quincy Adams, in the *Columbian Centinel*, Boston, June 1791.

31. Agricola rebutted Publicola in the Boston *Independent Chronicle*, Brutus in the *Columbian Centinel*.

and it's territory be ceded to her, she is offering peace on the perfect statu quo to the Porte, if they will conclude it without a mediation. France has struck a severe blow at our navigation by a difference of duty on tob[acc]o carried in our and their ships, and by taking from foreign built ships the capability of naturalization. She has placed our whale oil on rather a better footing than ever by consolidating the duties into a single one of 6. livres. They amounted before to some sous over that sum. I am told (I know not how truly) that England has prohibited our spermaceti oil altogether, and will prohibit our wheat till the price there is 52/ the quarter, which it is almost never is. We expect hourly to hear the true event of Genl. Scott's expedition.[32] Reports give favorable hopes of it. Be so good as to present my respectful compliments to Mrs. Adams and to accept assurances of the sentiments of sincere esteem and respect with which I am Dear Sir Your friend and servant.

TH: JEFFERSON

Adams to Jefferson

Braintree July 29. 1791.

DEAR SIR

Yesterday, at Boston, I received your friendly Letter of July 17th. with great pleasure. I give full credit to your relation of the manner in which your note was written and prefixed to the Philadelphia edition of Mr. Paines pamphlet on the rights of Man: but the misconduct of the person, who committed this breach of your confidence, by making it publick, whatever were his intentions, has sown the Seeds of more evils, than he can ever attone for. The Pamphlet, with your name, to so striking a recommendation to it, was not only industriously propogated in New York and Boston; but, that the recommendation might be known to every one, was reprinted with great care in the Newspapers, and was generally considered as a direct and open personal attack upon me, by countenancing the false interpretation of my Writings as favouring the Introduction of hereditary Monarchy and Aristocracy into this Country. The Question every where was, What Heresies are intended by the Secre-

---

32. Brigadier General Charles Scott's expedition against the Indian towns on the Wabash, May-June 1791, accomplished little except to arouse the Indians to greater efforts against General Arthur St. Clair later that year. Beverley W. Bond, Jr., *The Foundations of Ohio*, in Carl Wittke, ed., *The History of the State of Ohio* (Columbus, 1941-44), I, 323-24.

tary of State? The answer in the Newspapers was, The Vice Presidents notions of a Limited Monarchy, an hereditary Government of King and Lords, with only elective commons. Emboldened by these murmurs, soon after appeared the Paragraphs of an unprincipled Libeller in the New Haven Gazette, carefully reprinted in the Papers of New York, Boston and Philadelphia, holding up the Vice President to the ridicule of the World for his meanness, and to their detestation for wishing to subjugate the People to a few Nobles. These were soon followed by a formal Speech of the Lieutenant Governor of Massacuhsetts [Samuel Adams] very solemnly holding up the Idea of hereditary Powers, and cautioning the Publick against them, as if they were at that moment in the most imminent danger of them.[33] These Things were all accompanied with the most marked neglect both of the Governor [John Hancock] and Lieutenant Governor of this State towards me; and alltogether opperated as an Hue and Cry to all my Ennemies and Rivals, to the old constitutional faction of Pensilvania in concert with the late Insurgents of Massachusetts, both of whom consider my Writings as the Cause of their overthrow,[34] to hunt me down like a hare, if they could. In this State of Things, Publicola, who, I suppose, thought that Mr. Paines Pamphlet was made Use of as an Instrument to destroy a Man, for whom he had a regard, [whom] he thought innocent, and in the present moment [o]f some importance to the Publick, came forward.

You declare very explicitly that you never did, by yourself or by any other, have a Sentence of yours, inserted in a Newspaper without your name to it. And I, with equal frankness declare that I never did, either by my self or by any other, have a Sentence of mine inserted in any Newspaper since I left Philadelphia. I neither wrote nor corrected Publicola. The Writer in the Composition of his Pieces followed his own Judgment, Information and discretion, without any assistance from me.

You observe "That You and I differ in our Ideas of the best form of Government is well known to us both." But, my dear Sir, you will give me leave to say, that I do not know this. I know not what your Idea is of the best form of Government. You and I have never had a serious conversation together that I can recollect concerning the nature of Government. The very transient hints that have ever passed between Us have been

33. Samuel Adams's speech to the two houses of the Massachusetts legislature had been preceded by correspondence with JA, Sept.-Nov. 1790, in which they argued about the nature of republican government and popular sovereignty versus a mixed government "of three powers, forming a mutual balance." *Works*, VI, 411-26.

34. JA had condemned the Pennsylvania Constitution of 1776, which was replaced by a new one in 1790, providing for more balanced government; and he had strenuously opposed Shays's Rebellion in Massachusetts. See above, Chap. 5.

jocular and superficial, without ever coming to any explanation. If You suppose that I have or ever had a design or desire, of attempting to introduce a Government of King, Lords and Commons, or in other Words an hereditary Executive, or an hereditary Senate, either into the Government of the United States or that of any Individual State, in this Country, you are wholly mistaken. There is not such a Thought expressed or intimated in any public writing or private Letter of mine, and I may safely challenge all Mankind to produce such a passage and quote the Chapter and Verse. If you have ever put such a Construction on any Thing of mine, I beg you would mention it to me, and I will undertake to convince you, that it has no such meaning. Upon this occasion I will venture to say that my unpolished Writings, although they have been read by a sufficient Number of Persons to have assisted in crushing the Insurrection of the Massachusetts, in the formation of the new Constitutions of Pennsylvania, Georgia and South Carolina, and in procuring the Assent of all the States to the new national Constitution, yet they have not been read by great Numbers. Of the few who have taken the pains to read them, some have misunderstood them and others have willfully misrepresented them, and these misunderstandings and misrepresentations have been made the pretence for overwhelming me with floods and Whirlwinds of tempestuous Abuse, unexampled in the History of this Country.

It is thought by some, that Mr. Hancock's friends are preparing the Way, by my destruction, for his Election to the Place of Vice President, and that of Mr. Samuel Adams to be Governor of this Commonwealth, and then the Stone House Faction [35] will be sure of all the Loaves and Fishes, in the national Government and the State Government as they hope. The Opposers of the present Constitution of Pensilvania, the promoters of Shases Rebellion and County Resolves, and many of the Detesters of the present national Government, will undoubtedly aid them. Many People think too that no small Share of a foreign Influence, in revenge for certain untractable conduct at the Treaty of Peace, is and will be intermingled. The Janizaries of this goodly Combination, among whom are three or four, who hesitate at no falshood, have written all the Impudence and Impertinence which have appeared in the Boston Papers upon this memorable Occasion.

I must own to you that the daring Traits of Ambition and Intrigue, and those unbridled Rivalries which have already appeared, are the most melancholly and alarming Symptoms that I have ever seen in this Country:

35. Hancock's mansion on Beacon Hill was a two-story granite structure. Justin Winsor, ed., *The Memorial History of Boston* ... (Boston, 1881-86), III, 201-3; Anson E. Morse, *The Federalist Party in Massachusetts to the Year 1800* (Princeton, 1909), 62-66, 140.

and if they are to be encouraged to proceed in their Course, the sooner I am relieved from the Competition the happier I shall be.

I thank you, Sir very sincerely for writing to me upon this Occasion. It was high time that you and I should come to an explanation with each other. The friendship that has subsisted for fifteen Years between Us without the smallest interruption, and untill this occasion without the slightest Suspicion, ever has been and still is, very dear to my heart. There is no office which I would not resign, rather than give a just occasion to one friend to forsake me. Your motives for writing to me, I have not a doubt were the most pure and the most friendly; and I have no suspicion that you will not receive this explanation from me in the same candid Light.

I thank You Sir for the foreign Intelligence and beg leave to present You with the friendly compliments of Mrs. Adams, as well as the repeated Assurances of the friendship, Esteem and respect of Dear Sir Your most obedient and most humble Servant

John Adams

Jefferson to Adams

Philadelphia Aug. 30. 1791.

My dear Sir

I recieved some time ago your favor of July 29. and was happy to find that you saw in it's true point of view the way in which I had been drawn into the scene which must have been so disagreeable to you. The importance which you still seem to allow to my note, and the effect you suppose it to have had tho unintentional in me, induce me to shew you that it really had no effect. Paine's pamphlet, with my note, was published here about the 2d. week in May. Not a word ever appeared in the public papers here on the subject for more than a month; and I am certain not a word on the subject would ever have been said had not a writer, under the name of Publicola, at length undertaken to attack Mr. Paine's principles, which were the principles of the citizens of the U. S. Instantly a host of writers attacked Publicola in support of those principles. He had thought proper to misconstrue a figurative expression in my note; and these writers so far noticed me as to place the expression in it's true light. But this was only an incidental skirmish preliminary to the general engagement, and they would not have thought me worth naming, had not he thought proper to bring me on the scene. His antagonists, very criminally in my opinion presumed you to be Publicola, and on that presumption hazarded a personal attack on you. No person saw with more uneasiness than I did, this unjustifiable assault, and the more so, when I saw it continued after the printer had declared you were not the author. But you will perceive from all this, my dear Sir, that my note contributed nothing to the production of these disagreeable peices. As long as Paine's pamphlet stood on it's own feet, and on my note, it was unnoticed. As soon as Publicola attacked Paine, swarms appeared in his defence. To Publicola then and not in the least degree to my note, this whole contest is to be ascribed and all it's consequences.

You speak of the execrable paragraph in the Connecticut paper. This it is true appeared before Publicola. But it had no more relation to Paine's pamphlet and my note, than to the Alcoran. I am satisfied the writer of it had never seen either; for when I past through Connecticut about the middle of June,[36] not a copy had ever been seen by anybody either in Har[t]ford or New Haven, nor probably in that whole State: and that paragraph was so notoriously the reverse of the disinterestedness of character which you are known to possess by every body who knows your name, that I never heard a person speak of the paragraph but with an indignation in your behalf, which did you entire justice. This paragraph then certainly did not flow from my note, any more than the publications which Publicola produced. Indeed it was impossible that my note should occasion your name to be brought into question; for so far from naming you, I had not even in view any writing which I might suppose to be yours, and the opinions I alluded to were principally those I had heard in common conversation from a sect aiming at the subversion of the present government to bring in their favorite form of a king, lords, and commons.

Thus I hope, my dear Sir, that you will see me to have been as innocent *in effect* as I was in intention. I was brought before the public without my own consent, and from the first moment of seeing the effort of the real aggressor in this business to keep me before the public, I determined that nothing should induce me to put pen to paper in the controversy. The business is now over, and I hope it's effects are over, and that our friendship will never be suffered to be committed, whatever use others may think proper to make of our names.

The event of the King's flight from Paris and his recapture will have struck you with it's importance. It appears I think that the nation is firm within, and it only remains to see whether there will be any movement from without. I confess I have not changed my confidence in the favourable issue of that revolution, because it has always rested on my own

36. During May 17-June 19, 1791, TJ and Madison were on a tour from Philadelphia to New York and Albany, through Vermont and down the Connecticut River, to Hartford (June 8), and back to Philadelphia. Malone, *Jefferson*, II, 359-63.

ocular evidence of the unanimity of the nation, and wisdom of the Patriotic party in the national assembly. The last advices render it probable that the emperor will recommence hostilities against the Porte. It remains to see whether England and Prussia will take a part.

Present me to Mrs. Adams with all the affections I feel for her and be assured of those devoted to yourself by, my dear Sir, your sincere friend and servt.

TH: JEFFERSON

Jefferson to Adams

Philadelphia Nov. 25. 1791.

SIR

Supposing that the first Consular convention agreed on with France, and not ratified by Congress, may explain as well as account for some articles in that which was last agreed on and ratified, I take the liberty of inclosing, for the members of the Senate, copies of the two conventions as they were printed side by side, to shew where they differed.[37] These differences are not as great as were to be wished, but they were all which could be obtained. I have the honour to be with the most profound respect and esteem, Sir, Your most obedient and most humble servt.

TH: JEFFERSON

Jefferson to Adams

Philadelphia Mar. 1. 1793.

SIR

In consequence of the information I received from you on the first Wednesday in January that the lists of votes for President and Vice President were received at the seat of government from all the states except that of Kentucky, I sent a special messenger to the District judge of Kentucky for the list of the votes of that state lodged in his custody, and by the return of the messenger received yesterday the inclosed letter for you,

37. This was the ten-page circular which TJ had printed in Paris in 1788, presenting in parallel columns the texts of the Consular Convention of 1784 (viewed adversely by Secretary Jay in his report of 1785 and not ratified by Congress) and of 1788 (prepared by TJ and Montmorin, the French secretary of foreign affairs). The latter became the first treaty ratified by the Senate of the United States, in 1789. The bill for carrying the convention into effect was enacted into law April 24, 1792. "The Consular Convention of 1788," editorial note, Boyd, XIV, 67-92; the official English text as ratified, *ibid.*, 171-77; Hunter Miller, ed., *Treaties and Other International Acts of the United States* (Washington, 1931), II, 228-41.

which he informs me contains the list.[38] I have only to observe that tho' the term between the first Wednesday of January, and the second Wednesday in February was obviously insufficient at this season for the performance of the journey yet the law made it my indispensable duty to send the messenger. I have the honour to be with the most perfect esteem and respect Sir Your most obedt. and most humble servt.

TH: JEFFERSON

Adams to Jefferson

Philadelphia April 4. 1794

DEAR SIR

The inclosed Volume [39] was lately sent in to me by a Servant. I have since heard that the Author of it is in New York. The Book exhibits a curious Picture of the Government of Berne and is well worth reading.

I congratulate you on the charming Opening of the Spring, and heartily wish I was enjoying of it as you are upon a Plantation,[40] out of the hearing of the Din of Politicks and the Rumours of War. This felicity will not fall to my Share, I fear, before June. I am Sir with great Regard your humble Servant

JOHN ADAMS

Jefferson to Adams

Monticello Apr. 25. 1794.

DEAR SIR

I am to thank you for the book you were so good as to transmit me, as well as the letter covering it, and your felicitations on my present quiet. The difference of my present and past situation is such as to leave me nothing to regret but that my retirement has been postponed four years too long. The principles on which I calculate the value of life are entirely

38. Electoral votes cast for vice-president: JA 77; George Clinton 50; TJ 4; Aaron Burr 1. Washington had been re-elected president unanimously.

39. *Lettres de Jean Jacques Cart à Bernard Demuralt, trésorier du pays de Vaud, sur le droit public de ce pays, et sur les événements actuels* (Paris, 1793), protesting against the oppressive rule of Berne over Vaud and its principal city, Lausanne. French "liberation" in 1798 became a dubious improvement in political status. In 1814 Vaud became a canton in the Swiss Confederation.

40. TJ resigned from the secretaryship of state on Dec. 31, 1793.

in favor of my present course. I return to farming with an ardour which I scarcely knew in my youth, and which has got the better entirely of my love of study. Instead of writing 10. or 12. letters a day, which I have been in the habit of doing as a thing of course, I put off answering my letters now, farmerlike, till a rainy day, and then find it sometimes postponed by other necessary occupations.

The case of the Pays de Vaud is new to me. The claims of both parties are on grounds which I fancy we have taught the world to set little store by. The rights of one generation will scarcely be considered hereafter as depending on the paper transactions of another.[41]

My countrymen are groaning under the insults of Gr. Britain. I hope some means will turn up of reconciling our faith and honour with peace: for I confess to you I have seen enough of one war never to wish to see another. With wishes of every degree of happiness to you both public and private, and with my best respects to Mrs. Adams, I am, Dear Sir your affectionate and humble servt.

TH: JEFFERSON

Adams to Jefferson

Philadelphia May 11. 1794

DEAR SIR

Your favour of the 25th of last month came to my hands Yesterday and I am glad to find you so well pleased with your Retirement. I felt the same delightful Satisfaction after my Return from Europe, and I feel still every Summer upon my little farm all the Ardour, and more than all the Ardor of youth: to such a Degree that I cannot bear the thought of writing or reading, unless it be some trifle to fill up a vacant half hour.

The Case of the Pays de Vaud is curious enough. Dr. Cart the Writer of the Book I sent you is arrived at New York and Mr. Rosset whose Tryal and Sentence for high Treason, for dining at a civic feast and drinking two or three Patriotic Toasts, is mentioned in it, is here at Philadelphia. He has lent me in Manuscript a full account of his Tryal. As much as I have ever detested an Aristocratical Government, I did not believe that the Canton of Berne could have been so tyrannical, till I read his Manuscript.

41. This is a paraphrase of TJ's statement of principle to Madison, "which I suppose to be self evident, *that the earth belongs in usufruct to the living*': that the dead have neither power or rights over it." TJ to Madison, Sept. 6, 1789, Boyd, XV, 392-97.

I think nevertheless that "the Rights of one Generation of Men must Still depend, in some degree, on the Paper Transactions of another." The Social Compact and the Laws must be reduced to Writing. Obedience to them becomes a national Habit and they cannot be changed but by Revolutions which are costly Things. Men will be too Œconomical of their Blood and Property to have Recourse to them very frequently. This Country is becoming the Asylum of all the ardent Spirits in Europe. The Bishop of Autun and Mr. Beaumez are arrived and Dr. Priestley is expected.

The President has sent Mr. Jay to try if he can find any Way to reconcile our honour with Peace.[42] I have no great Faith in any very brill[i]ant Success: but hope he may have enough to keep Us out of a War. Another War would add two or three hundred Millions of Dollars to our Debt, raise up a many headed and many bellied Monster of an Army to tyrannize over Us, totally dissadjust our present Government, and accellerate the Advent of Monarchy and Aristocracy by at least fifty Years.

Those who dread Monarchy and Aristocracy and at the same time Advocate War are the most inconsistent of all Men.

If I had Your Plantation and your Labourers I should be tempted to follow your Example and get out of the Fumum ct Opes Strepitumque Romae ["the smoke, the wealth, the din of Rome"] which I abominate. I am Sir with much Esteem your Friend and Sert

JOHN ADAMS

Adams to Jefferson

Philadelphia Nov. 21. 1794

DEAR SIR

I am desired by our old Acquaintance Mr. D'Ivernois to transmit you the inclosed Papers for your inspection Opinion and Advice. The poor Fellow has been obliged to fly a second time into Banishment. The first time, he was driven out as a Democrat: but it is now, Day about, as they say, in Geneva, and he is compelled to run as an Aristocrat.

Shall We print his History? What shall We do with his Academy?

I have spent my Summer so deliciously in farming that I return to the old Story of Politicks with great Reluctance. The Earth is grateful. You find it so, I dare say. I wish We could both say the Same of its Inhabitants.

42. Chief Justice Jay was commissioned envoy extraordinary to Great Britain on April 19. From his mission resulted the unpopular, pro-British Jay's Treaty of 1794, ratified by the Senate, June 24, 1795. Bemis, *Jay's Treaty*, 197, Chap. XIII.

When will the Crisis of this fever in human Nature be over, and in what State of Health will it be left? Solitudinem faciunt, Libertatem appellant.[43]

Virginia I hope will send Us some good Senators. We grow very thin.[44] I begin to think the Senate scarcely numerous enough for so large a People. But this is not a time for Changes: We must go on as well as we can. Make my Compliments, if you please to your Daughters, whom I had once the Pleasure to see, and for whom I retain much Esteem. I am, Sir, with great Regard, your most obedient

JOHN ADAMS

Adams to Jefferson

Philadelphia Feb. 5. 1795

DEAR SIR

The inclosed Pamphlet and Papers I have received this Week from the Author, with his request to transmit them to you. I have before transmitted in the Course of this Winter, another Packet from the same Writer; [45] but have as yet no answer from you: so that I am uncertain whether you have received it.

Mr. Jays Treaty with Britain is not yet arrived at the Secretary of States Office, though there is some reason to suppose it is arrived at New York.

You will see by the Changes in the Executive Department [46] that the Feelings of Officers are in a Way to introduce Rotations enough, which are not contemplated by the Constitution. Those Republicans who delight in Rotations will be gratified in all Probability, till all the Ablest Men in the Nation are roted out. To me these Things indicate something to be amiss somewhere. If Public Offices are to be made Punishments, will a People be well served? Not long I trow. I am Sir with great Regard your most obedient

JOHN ADAMS

43. An adaptation of Tacitus: "They make a solitude and call it peace." JA substitutes "liberty" for "peace," comparing the mass extermination by French revolutionaries of their allies, on behalf of "liberty, equality, fraternity," with mass extermination by Roman imperialism on behalf of the *pax Romana.*

44. Senators from Virginia were lacking, John Taylor having resigned and James Monroe having accepted the mission to France. Their successors were both Jeffersonians: Henry Tazewell and Stevens Thomson Mason.

45. Probably from François D'Ivernois; see TJ to JA, Feb. 6, 1795, below, 257.

46. Secretary of War Henry Knox was succeeded by Timothy Pickering on Jan. 2, 1795; Secretary of the Treasury Alexander Hamilton by Oliver Wolcott on Feb. 2; Edmund Randolph was secretary of state and William Bradford attorney general. George Gibbs, *Memoirs of the Administrations of Washington and John Adams...* (N. Y., 1846), I, 167, 177.

Jefferson to Adams

Monticello Feb. 6. 1795.

DEAR SIR

The time which has intervened between the receipt of your favor, covering D'Ivernois' letter, and this answer, needs appology. But this will be found in the state of the case. I had received from him a letter similar to that you inclosed. As the adoption of his plan depended on our legislature, and it was then in session, I immediately inclosed it to a member [Wilson Cary Nicholas] with a request that he would sound well the opinions of the leading members, and if he found them disposed to enter into D'Ivernois' views, to make the proposition; but otherwise not to hazard it.[47] It is only three days since I have received from him information of his proceedings. He found it could not prevail. The unprepared state of our youths to receive instruction thro' a foreign language, the expence of the institution, and it's disproportion to the moderate state of our population, were insuperable objections. I delayed myself the honor of acknoleging the receipt of your letter, till I might be able to give you at the same time the result of the proposition it forwarded. I have explained this to M. D'Ivernois in the inclosed letter,[48] which my distance from any sea-port, and the convenience of your position will I hope excuse my committing to your care.

I have found so much tranquility of mind in a total abstraction from every thing political, that it was with some difficulty I could resolve to meddle even in the splendid project of transplanting the academy of Geneva, en masse, to Virginia; and I did it under the usual reserve of *sans tirer en consequence*. In truth I have so much occupation otherwise that I have not time for taking a part in any thing of a public kind, and I therefore leave such with pleasure to those who are to live longer and enjoy their benefits. Tranquility becomes daily more and more the object of my life, and of this I certainly find more in my present pursuits than in those of any other part of my life. I recall however with pleasure the memory of some of the acquaintances I have made in my progress through it, and retain strong wishes for their happiness. I pray you to accept with kindness those which I sincerely entertain for you, and to be assured of the high respect and esteem with which I am Dear Sir Your most obedt. and most humble servt.

TH: JEFFERSON

47. TJ to W. C. Nicholas, Nov. 22, 1794, Ford, VI, 513-15.
48. TJ to D'Ivernois, Feb. 6, 1795, *ibid.*, VII, 2-6.

Jefferson to Adams

Monticello May 27. 95.

DEAR SIR

I inclose you a letter from our friend D'Ivernois according to his request expressed in it. Our geographical distance is insensible still to foreigners. They consider America of the size of a [garden] of which Massachusetts is one square and Virginia another. I know not what may have been your sentiments or measures respecting the transplantation of the science of Geneva to this country. If not more [successful] than mine, the mission of their commissaries will make a bad matter worse. In our state we are already too wise to want instruction either foreign or domestic, and the worst circumstance is that the more ignorant we become the less value we set on science, and the less inclination we shall have to seek it.

We have had a hard winter and backward spring. This injured our wheat so much that it cannot be made a good crop by all the showers of heaven which are now falling down on us exactly as we want them. Our first cutting of clover is not yet begun. Strawberries not ripe till within this fortnight, and every thing backward in proportion. What with my farming and my nail manufactory I have my hands full. I am on horseback half the day, and counting and measuring nails the other half. I am trying potatoes on a large scale as a substitute for Indian corn for feeding animals. This is new in this country, but in this culture we cannot rival you. Present my sincere respects to Mrs. Adams and accept assurances of the respect and attachment of Dear Sir Your most obedt. and most humble servt.

TH: JEFFERSON

Adams to Jefferson

Philadelphia January 31. 1796

DEAR SIR

I have received from our old Acquaintance D'Ivernois the inclosed Volume for you in the Course of the last Week.[49]

49. Francois D'Ivernois, Des révolutions de France et de Genève (London, 1795). His plans for transplanting the Geneva Academy to the United States did not materialize.

I consider all Reasoning upon French Affairs of little moment. The Fates must determine hereafter as they have done heretofore. Reasoning has been all lost. Passion, Prejudice, Interest, Necessity has governed and will govern; and a Century must roll away before any permanent and quiet System will be established. An Amelioration of human affairs I hope and believe will be the result, but You and I must look down from the Battlements of Heaven if We ever have the Pleasure of Seeing it.

The Treaty is not arrived [50] and Congress seems averse to engage in Business with Spirit till that is considered.

I envy you the Society of your Farm but another Year and one Month may make me the Object of Envy. Mean time I am, with Esteem and Affection your

JOHN ADAMS

Jefferson to Adams

Monticello Feb. 28. 96.

I am to thank you, my dear Sir, for forwarding Mr. D'Ivernois' book on the French revolution. I recieve every thing with respect which comes from him. But it is on politics, a subject I never loved, and now hate. I will not promise therefore to read it thoroughly. I fear the oligarchical executive of the French will not do. We have always seen a small council get into cabals and quarrels, the more bitter and relentless the fewer they are. We saw this in our committee of the states; [51] and that they were, from their bad passions, incapable of doing the business of their country. I think that for the prompt, clear and consistent action so necessary in an Executive, unity of person is necessary as with us. I am aware of the objection to this, that the office becoming more important may bring on serious discord in elections. In our country I think it will be long first; not within our day; and we may safely trust to the wisdom of our successors the remedies of the evil to arise in theirs. Both experiments however

50. Jay's Treaty. See above, 255, n. 42.
51. Under the Articles of Confederation the only executive authority was granted in Article IX to a "Committee of the States," consisting of one delegate from each state, to function only during recesses of Congress. It lacked sufficient authority to be effective and in Jan. 1784 TJ, who had proposed such a committee as early as 1775, prepared a report to Congress outlining enlarged powers for this peculiar executive body. "Report on the Powers of the Committee of the States," editorial note, Boyd, VI, 516-22.

are now fairly committed, and the result will be seen. Never was a finer canvas presented to work on than our countrymen. All of them engaged in agriculture or the pursuits of honest industry, independant in their circumstances, enlightened as to their rights, and firm in their habits of order and obedience to the laws. This I hope will be the age of experiments in government, and that their basis will be founded on principles of honesty, not of mere force. We have seen no instance of this since the days of the Roman republic, nor do we read of any before that. Either force or corruption has been the principle of every modern government, unless the Dutch perhaps be excepted, and I am not well enough informed to except them absolutely. If ever the morals of a people could be made the basis of their own government, it is our case; and he who could propose to govern such a people by the corruption of their legislature, before he could have one night of quiet sleep, must convince himself that the human soul as well as body is mortal. I am glad to see that whatever grounds of apprehension may have appeared of a wish to govern us otherwise than on principles of reason and honesty, we are getting the better of them. I am sure, from the honesty of your heart, you join me in detestation of the corruption of the English government, and that no man on earth is more incapable than yourself of seeing that copied among us, willingly. I have been among those who have feared the design to introduce it here, and it has been a strong reason with me for wishing there was an ocean of fire between that island and us. But away politics.

I owe a letter to the Auditor [Richard Harrison] on the subject of my accounts while a foreign minister, and he informs me yours hang on the same difficulties with mine. Before the present government there was a usage either practised on or understood which regulated our charges. This government has directed the future by a law. But this is not retrospective, and I cannot conceive why the treasury cannot settle accounts under the old Congress on the principles that body acted on. I shall very shortly write to Mr. Harrison on this subject, and if we cannot have it settled otherwise I suppose we must apply to the legislature. In this I will act in concert with you if you approve of it. Present my very affectionate respects to Mrs. Adams, and be assured that no one more cordially esteems your virtues than Dear Sir Your sincere friend and servt.

TH: JEFFERSON

Adams to Jefferson

Philadelphia April 6. 1796

Dear Sir

Since my Receipt of your favour of the 28 of February I have call'd on the Auditor and had some Conversation with him and with The Secretary of The Treasury and with The Secretary of State upon the Subject of Accounts and they think that some Regulation may be made by Congress which will reach the Cases without any formal Memorial on our Part and indeed without mentioning Names. The Secretary of The Treasury has it under Consideration: But if they finally determine that they cannot accomplish the object without our Interposition I will join you with all my Heart in an Application to Congress.

D'Ivernois is industrious and clever, but he is in Pay, Pension or Employment of some kind or other under Mr. Pitt, and some of his late Publications have a tang of the Cask from whence he draws his Wine. It is good to read all those Party Pamphlets and believe in none of them.

This is indeed as you say the Age of Experiments in Government. One Tryal has been fairly made in America and France of Nedhams perfect Commonwealth,[52] and at length given up. Holland is trying it again and if Britain should have a Revolution she will try it too. An hundred thousand Dutchmen guillotined or beknifed will convince Holland as soon as five hundred thousand Frenchmen and Women have convinced France. How many Hecatombs must be slaughtered to convince John Bull I cannot calculate.

The Plural Executive in France is a new Attempt borrowed from a conceit of De Mably in his posthumous Dialogue with Lord Stanhope.[53] The Danger of Corruption and Intrigue in Elections is rather multiplied five fold, than diminished by this. And Jealousy, Emulation and Division among them are inevitable.

Corruption in Elections has heretofore destroyed all Elective Governments. What Regulations or Precautions may be devised to prevent it in future, I am content with you to leave to Posterity to consider. You and

52. Marchamont Nedham, *The Excellency of a Free State, or the Right Constitution of a Commonwealth* (London, 1656), reprinted, 1767, ed. by Richard Barron under the auspices of Thomas Hollis. JA used Nedham to exemplify the argument on behalf of a sovereign unicameral democratic legislature in his *Defence of the Constitutions of the United States*, III, Chap. IX.

53. Abbé de Mably, *Des droits et des devoirs du citoyen* (1789), in the form of letters dated in Aug. 1758.

I shall go to the Kingdom of the just or at least shall be released from the Republick of the Unjust, with Hearts pure and hands clean of all Corruption in Elections: so much I firmly believe. Those who shall introduce the foul Fiend on the Stage, after We are gone must exorcise him as they can. With great Esteem and regard I am, Sir your most obedient

JOHN ADAMS

Jefferson to Adams

Monticello Dec. 28. 1796 [54]

DEAR SIR

The public and the public papers have been much occupied lately in placing us in a point of opposition to each other. I trust with confidence that less of it has been felt by ourselves personally. In the retired canton where I am, I learn little of what is passing: pamphlets I see never; papers but a few; and the fewer the happier. Our latest intelligence from Philadelphia at present is of the 16th. inst. but tho' at that date your election to the first magistracy seems not to have been known as a fact, yet with me it has never been doubted. I knew it impossible you should lose a vote North of the Delaware, and even if that of Pensylvania should be against you in the mass, yet that you would get enough South of that to place your succession out of danger.[55] I have never one single moment expected a different issue: and tho' I know I shall not be believed, yet it is not the less true that I have never wished it. My neighbors, as my com-

54. This letter was never received by JA. It was enclosed, unsealed, by TJ in his letter to Madison dated Jan. 1, 1797, with this request: "The papers by the last post [which included Madison's letter of Dec. 19, 1796, to TJ] not rendering it necessary to change anything in the letter I enclose it open for your perusal, not only that you may possess the actual state of dispositions between us, but that if anything should render the delivery of it ineligible in your opinion, you may return it to me." Ford, VII, 99. In his reply of Jan. 15, 1797, Madison said he had decided to suspend delivery of the letter addressed to JA for several cogent reasons; if, after considering them, TJ still felt it was expedient to deliver the letter, it would be done. By this time Madison knew that JA had been elected president. "As you have, no doubt retained a copy of the letter [of Dec. 28] I do not send it back as you request." Hunt, ed., *Writings of Madison*, VI, 302-5. TJ had not retained a copy, but he had prepared a "Statement by memory of a letter written to J. Adams. copy omitted to be retained." Ford, VII, 97-98n.

55. JA received 71 electoral votes, TJ 68, Thomas Pinckney 59. TJ's judgment was correct: JA received the unanimous vote of the 7 states northeast of the Delaware, 1 of Pennsylvania's 15 votes, 3 from Delaware, 7 from Maryland, 1 from Virginia, and 1 from North Carolina.

purgators, could aver that fact, because they see my occupations and my attachment to them. Indeed it is possible that you may be cheated of your succession by a trick worthy the subtlety of your arch-friend [Alexander Hamilton] of New York, who has been able to make of your real friends tools to defeat their and your just wishes. Most probably he will be disappointed as to you; and my inclinations place me out of his reach. I leave to others the sublime delights of riding in the storm, better pleased with sound sleep and a warm birth below, with the society of neighbors, friends and fellow laborers of the earth, than of spies and sycophants. No one then will congratulate you with purer disinterestedness than myself. The share indeed which I may have had in the late vote, I shall still value highly, as an evidence of the share I have in the esteem of my fellow citizens. But while, in this point of view, a few votes less would be little sensible, the difference in the effect of a few more would be very sensible and oppressive to me. I have no ambition to govern men. It is a painful and thankless office. Since the day too on which you signed the treaty of Paris our horizon was never so overcast. I devoutly wish you may be able to shun for us this war by which our agriculture, commerce and credit will be destroyed. If you are, the glory will be all your own; and that your administration may be filled with glory and happiness to yourself and advantage to us is the sincere wish of one who tho', in the course of our voyage thro' life, various little incidents have happened or been contrived to separate us, retains still for you the solid esteem of the moments when we were working for our independance, and sentiments of respect and affectionate attachment.

TH: JEFFERSON

Adams to Jefferson

Washington Feb. 20. 1801

SIR

In order to save you the trouble and Expence of purchasing Horses and Carriages, which will not be necessary, I have to inform you that I shall leave in the stables of the United States seven Horses and two Carriages with Harness and Property of the United States. These may not be suitable for you: but they will certainly save you a considerable Expence as they belong to the studd of the President's Household. I have the honor to be with great respect Sir your most obedient and humble servant,

JOHN ADAMS

Jefferson to Adams

TH: JEFFERSON presents his respects to Mr. Adams and incloses him a letter which came to his hands last night; on reading what is written within the cover, he concluded it to be a private letter, and without opening a single paper within it he folded it up and now has the honor to inclose it to Mr. Adams, with the homage of his high consideration and respect.

Washington Mar. 8. 1801.

Adams to Jefferson

Stony Field,[56] Quincy March 24. 1801.

SIR

I have recd. your favour of March 8 with the Letter inclosed, for which I thank you. Inclosed is a letter to one of your Domesticks Joseph Doughtery.

Had you read the Papers inclosed they might have given you a moment of Melancholly or at least of Sympathy with a mourning Father. They relate wholly to the Funeral of a Son [57] who was once the delight of my Eyes and a darling of my heart, cutt off in the flower of his days, amidst very flattering Prospects by causes which have been the greatest Grief of my heart and the deepest affliction of my Life. It is not possible that any thing of the kind should hapen to you, and I sincerely wish you may never experience any thing in any degree resembling it.

This part of the Union is in a state of perfect Tranquility and I See nothing to obscure your prospect of a quiet and prosperous Administration, which I heartily wish you. With great respect I have the honor to be Sir your most obedient and very humble Servant.

JOHN ADAMS

56. This was the "Old House," acquired by JA in 1787 before his return from Great Britain and first named "Peacefield" by him. Later he referred to it as "Mount Wollaston" and eventually as "Montezillo." [National Park Service], *Adams National Historic Site, Massachusetts* (Washington, 1954); JA's letters, 1812-26, below, Vol. II.

57. Charles Adams (1770-1800), who had married Sarah, one of Colonel William Stephens Smith's sisters. Stewart Mitchell, ed., *New Letters of Abigail Adams, 1788-1801* (Boston, 1947), 261-62.

8

"Faithfull are the wounds of a Friend"

O<small>N</small> A<small>PRIL</small> 17, 1804, Mary Jefferson Eppes died at Monticello at the age of twenty-five. Pressing presidential duties, made heavier by the session of Congress extending through March, required Jefferson's presence in Washington, but he arrived home before his daughter's death.[1] With unaccustomed lack of restraint, he poured forth his grief to the friend of his boyhood, John Page. "Having lost even the half of all I had, my evening prospects now hang on the slender thread of a single life [his daughter Martha Randolph]. Perhaps I may be destined to see even this last chord of parental affection broken!"[2]

It was in this depressed state of mind that he received Mrs. Adams's letter of May 20. Nearly three and a half years of silence between them had elapsed since they last conversed in Washington. In making this friendly gesture, she could not overlook the fact that he was president of the United States and not merely "the private inhabitant of Monticello." Various reasons had withheld her pen "untill the powerfull feelings of my heart, have burst through the restraint" and given expression to her condolence. Mrs. Adams's love for Polly during her girlhood in England and France had, of course, never been forgotten. It had strengthened the bond of friendship, as Mrs. Adams's letters from London testified. And this had made irresistible the urge

---

1. TJ to Mary Jefferson Eppes, Feb. 26, 1804; TJ to John W. Eppes, March 15, 1804, Henry S. Randall, *The Life of Thomas Jefferson* (N. Y., 1858), III, 98-99; TJ to Madison, April 23, 1804, Ford, VIII, 300.
2. TJ to Governor John Page, June 25, 1804, Randall, *Jefferson*, III, 103.

to transmit a letter from "her who once took pleasure in subscribing Herself your Friend." [3]

Jefferson, not overlooking this final clause couched in the past tense, welcomed the opportunity to renew correspondence with Mrs. Adams, but before he replied, he wrote to his bereaved son-in-law, John Wayles Eppes and, with mixed feelings, forwarded her letter. That "the sentiments expressed in it are sincere," Jefferson had no doubt. "Her attachment was constant. Although all of them point to another object directly, yet the expressing them to me is a proof that our friendship is unbroken on her part." [4] The real proof, however, remained to be demonstrated in their ensuing correspondence.

Jefferson explained to Eppes that only one act of John Adams had given him personal displeasure during their long friendship, the "midnight appointments" of Federalists to office by President Adams just before the expiration of his term of office. Now Jefferson made the same point to Mrs. Adams, after expressing regret that circumstances of any kind should have caused estrangement. Having "opened myself to you without reserve," he could only entreat her forgiveness for thus taking advantage of her letter of condolence.[5] In this letter and those that followed, the former friends aired their grievances, dispelled some misunderstanding, and found relief through their frank discussion; but they failed to reach any common ground on which incidents might have been minimized or dismissed in favor of mutual interests of deeper significance, as Jefferson and John Adams might more surely have arrived at under similar circumstances. She could not allow their friendship an unfettered renewal.

The grievances of Mrs. Adams over Jefferson's leniency toward James Callender were answered only partially to her satisfaction. Callender had defamed Adams and his administration with at least the tacit support of Jefferson; after Callender was found guilty under the Sedition Act, President Jefferson released him and remitted his fine. That this was within the executive power could not be denied, and the President also justified the release of Callender—a despicable character who turned against his defender—by a damning of the act under which the journalist had been convicted.

Mrs. Adams's complaint about Jefferson's removal of John Quincy

3. AA to TJ, May 20, 1804, below, 269.
4. TJ to John W. Eppes, June 4, 1804, Randall, *Jefferson*, III, 99-100.
5. TJ to AA, June 13, 1804, below, 271.

Adams as commissioner of bankruptcy involved a mother's pride. When the President explained that Congressional action had terminated the appointment, she accepted his explanation and absolved him of personal unkindness.[6] As for Jefferson's initial objection to the "midnight appointment" of Federalist judges, he omitted further discussion of what he must have regarded as an inadequate explanation by Mrs. Adams.

At the bottom of their disagreements, still irreconcilable, were the political differences of the 1790's, which had produced rival parties and led to the "revolution of 1800." Mrs. Adams had attributed the dissension during President Adams's administration to the opposition party, and Jefferson was the leader of the Republicans whose talk of popular rule made her anxious for the fate of the country. "I feel perhaps too keenly the abuse of party," she wrote to her son Thomas in November 1796.[7] Washington's successor would not enjoy the public confidence and overwhelming support which had never failed the general. In 1798 Mrs. Adams deplored the support by French agents of "*the Man of the People*" and she warned that if a heedless Congress did not "give the President a respit, they will have Jefferson sooner than they wish."[8] During this period of political transition, Jefferson was in the anomalous position of being a Republican vice-president in a Federalist administration. In March 1797 after the Republicans refused to co-operate with Adams in organizing a mission to France, Jefferson stated that the President never "consulted me as to any measures of the government."[9] Given all these conflicting conditions, even friendships of long standing were severely tested. And now in 1804 Mrs. Adams reminded Jefferson that when he last visited her in Washington, "you assured me, that if it should lay in your power to serve me or my family, nothing would give you more pleasure."[10] If Jefferson meant what he said, did subsequent acts of his belie his sincerity? The impasse could not be dissolved as long as they viewed it exclusively in political terms. The political wounds of 1800-1 were still sensitive and unhealed.

6. AA to TJ, Oct. 25, 1804, below, 281.
7. AA to Thomas B. Adams, Nov. 8, 1796, *Letters of Mrs. Adams*, II, 231-32; Whitney, *Abigail Adams*, 277.
8. AA to Mrs. Mary Cranch, March 20 and May 20-21, 1798, Mitchell, ed., *New Letters of Abigail Adams*, 147, 178.
9. TJ's "Anas," Ford, I, 273.
10. AA to TJ, Oct. 25, 1804, below, 281.

In his exaltation of freedom of opinion, Jefferson was more earnest than tactful, more virtuous than charitable; and his generalizations to Mrs. Adams on that score were a bit gratuitous. "Both of our political parties, at least the honest portion of them," he declared, "agree conscientiously in the same object, the public good: but they differ essentially in what they deem the means of promoting that good. One side believes it best done by one composition of the governing powers, the other by a different one. One fears most the ignorance of the people: the other the selfishness of rulers independant of them. Which is right, time and experience will prove." [11] And time, in 1804, seemed to run in favor of the Republicans, if Jefferson thought about it in that light. Mrs. Adams, who was never wanting a pointed reply, begged to "be permitted to pause, and ask you whether in your ardent zeal, and desire to rectify the mistakes and abuses as you may consider them, of the former administrations, you are not led into measures still more fatal to the constitution, and more derogatory to your honour, and independence of Character? Pardon me Sir if I say, that I fear you are." [12]

Offering her sincere wishes for his administration, Mrs. Adams proceeded to "close this correspondence." [13] Six years later, when Jefferson sent this correspondence to Dr. Benjamin Rush as evidence of an unsuccessful rapprochement, he regretted the prolonged misunderstanding with Mrs. Adams; but "yielding to an intimation in her last letter, I ceased from further explanation." [14] The lady had had the last word.

Abigail Adams to Jefferson

Quincy May 20th 1804

SIR

Had you been no other than the private inhabitant of Monticello, I should e'er this time have addrest you, with that sympathy, which a recent event has awakend in my Bosom. But reasons of various kinds withheld my pen, untill the powerfull feelings of my heart, have burst through the

11. TJ to AA, Sept. 11, 1804, below, 280.
12. AA to TJ, Oct. 25, 1804, below, 281.
13. *Ibid.*
14. TJ to Rush, Jan. 16, 1811, Ford, IX, 298.

restraint, and called upon me to shed the tear of sorrow over the departed remains, of your beloved and deserving daughter,[15] an event which I most sincerely mourn.

The attachment which I formed for her, when you committed her to my care: upon her arrival in a foreign Land: has remained with me to this hour, and the recent account of her death, which I read in a late paper, brought fresh to my remembrance the strong sensibility she discoverd, tho but a child of nine years of age at having been seperated from her Friends, and country, and brought, as she expressed it, "to a strange land amongst strangers." The tender scene of her seperation from me, rose to my recollection, when she clung around my neck and wet my Bosom with her tears, saying, "O! now I have learnt to Love you, why will they tear me from you" [16]

It has been some time since that I conceived of any event in this Life, which could call forth, feelings of mutual sympathy. But I know how closely entwined around a parents heart, are those chords which bind the filial to the parental Bosom, and when snaped assunder, how agonizing the pangs of seperation.[17]

I have tasted the bitter cup, and bow with reverence, and humility before the great dispenser of it, without whose permission, and over ruling providence, not a sparrow falls to the ground. That you may derive comfort and consolation in this day of your sorrow and affliction, from that only source calculated to heal the wounded heart—a firm belief in the Being: perfections and attributes of God, is the sincere and ardent wish of her, who once took pleasure in subscribing Herself your Friend

ABIGAIL ADAMS

Jefferson to Abigail Adams

Washington June 13.04.

DEAR MADAM

The affectionate sentiments which you have had the goodness to express in your letter of May 20. towards my dear departed daughter, have awakened in me sensibilities natural to the occasion, and recalled your kindnesses to her which I shall ever remember with gratitude and friend-

15. Mary Jefferson Eppes (Mrs. John Wayles Eppes, d. April 17, 1804). Malone, *Jefferson*, I, 434.
16. See AA to TJ, July 6 and 10, 1787, above, 183-84, 185.
17. Her son, Charles Adams, had died on Nov. 30, 1800.

ship. I can assure you with truth they had made an indelible impression on her mind, and that, to the last, on our meetings after long separations, whether I had heard lately of you, and how you did, were among the earliest of her enquiries. In giving you this assurance I perform a sacred duty for her, and at the same time am thankful for the occasion furnished me of expressing my regret that circumstances should have arisen which have seemed to draw a line of separation between us. The friendship with which you honoured me has ever been valued, and fully reciprocated; and altho' events have been passing which might be trying to some minds, I never believed yours to be of that kind, nor felt that my own was. Neither my estimate of your character, nor the esteem founded in that, have ever been lessened for a single moment, although doubts whether it would be acceptable may have forbidden manifestations of it. Mr. Adams's friendship and mine began at an earlier date. It accompanied us thro' long and important scenes. The different conclusions we had drawn from our political reading and reflections were not permitted to lessen mutual esteem, each party being conscious they were the result of an honest conviction in the other. Like differences of opinion existing among our fellow citizens attached them to the one or the other of us, and produced a rivalship in their minds which did not exist in ours. We never stood in one another's way: for if either had been withdrawn at any time, his favorers would not have gone over to the other, but would have sought for some one of homogeneous opinions. This consideration was sufficient to keep down all jealousy between us, and to guard our friendship from any disturbance by sentiments of rivalship: and I can say with truth that one act of Mr. Adams's life, and one only, ever gave me a moment's personal displeasure. I did consider his last appointments to office as personally unkind.[18] They were from among my most ardent political enemies, from whom no faithful cooperation could ever be expected, and laid me under the embarrasment of acting thro' men whose views were to defeat mine; or to encounter the odium of putting others in their places. It seemed but common justice to leave a successor free to act by instruments of his own choice. If my respect for him did not permit me to ascribe the whole blame to the influence of others, it left something for friendship to forgive, and after brooding over it for some little time, and not always resisting the expression of it, I forgave it cordially, and re-

18. The Judiciary Act, passed Feb. 13, 1801, reduced the membership of the Supreme Court to five, increased the number of district judges, and relieved the Supreme Court justices from traveling the circuit. President Adams appointed Federalists to these new positions, to the discomfiture of his successor. The act was repealed by the Republican Congress of 1802. If the act was partisan in origin, it did provide some needed reforms. Max Farrand, "The Judiciary Act of 1801," *Amer. Hist. Rev.*, 5 (1899-1900), 682-86.

turned to the same state of esteem and respect for him which had so long subsisted. Having come into life a little later than Mr. Adams, his career has preceded mine, as mine is followed by some other, and it will probably be closed at the same distance after him which time originally placed between us. I maintain for him, and shall carry into private life an uniform and high measure of respect and good will, and for yourself a sincere attachment. I have thus, my dear Madam, opened myself to you without reserve, which I have long wished an opportunity of doing; and, without knowing how it will be recieved, I feel relief from being unbosomed. And I have now only to entreat your forgiveness for this transition from a subject of domestic affliction to one which seems of a different aspect. But tho connected with political events, it has been viewed by me most strongly in it's unfortunate bearings on my private friendships. The injury these have sustained has been a heavy price for what has never given me equal pleasure. That you may both be favored with health, tranquility and long life, is the prayer of one who tenders you the assurances of his highest consideration and esteem.

TH: JEFFERSON

Abigail Adams to Jefferson

Quincy July 1st 1804

SIR

Your Letter of June 13th came duly to hand; if it had contained no other sentiments and opinions than those which my Letter of condolence could have excited, and which are expressed in the first page of your reply, our correspondence would have terminated here: but you have been pleased to enter upon some subjects which call for a reply: and as you observe that you have wished for an opportunity to express your sentiments, I have given to them every weight they claim.

"One act of Mr. Adams's Life, and *one* only, you repeat, ever gave me a moments personal displeasure. I did think his last appointments to office personally unkind. They were from among my most ardent political enemies."

As this act I am certain was not intended to give any personal pain or offence, I think it a duty to explain it so far as I then knew his views and designs. The constitution empowers the president to fill up offices as they become vacant. It was in the exercise of this power that appointments were made, and Characters selected whom Mr. Adams considerd, as men faithfull to the constitution and where he personally knew them, such as were capable of fullfilling their duty to their country. This was done by president Washington equally, in the last days of his administration so that not an office remaind vacant for his successor to fill upon his comeing into the office. No offence was given by it, and no personal unkindness thought of. But the different political opinions which have so unhappily divided our Country, must have given rise to the Idea, that personal unkindness was intended. You will please to recollect Sir, that at the time these appointments were made, there was not any certainty that the presidency would devolve upon you,[19] which is an other circumstance to prove that personal unkindness was not meant. No person was ever selected by him from such a motive—and so far was Mr. Adams from indulging such a sentiment, that he had no Idea of the intollerance of party spirit at that time, and I know it was his opinion that if the presidency devolved upon you, except in the appointment of Secretaries, no material Changes would be made. I perfectly agree with you in opinion that those should be Gentlemen in whom the president can repose confidence, possessing opinions, and sentiments corresponding with his own, or if differing from him, that they ought rather to resign their office, than cabal against measures which he may think essential to the honour safety and peace of the Country. Much less should they unite, with any bold, and dareingly ambitious Character, to over rule the Cabinet, or betray the Secrets of it to Friends or foes. The two Gentlemen who held the offices of secretaries,[20] when you became president were not of this Character. They were appointed by your predecessor nearly two years previous to his retirement. They were Gentlemen who had cordially co-opperated with him, and enjoyed the public confidence. Possessing however different political sentiments from those which you were known to have embraced, it was expected that they would, as they did, resign.

I have never felt any enmity towards you Sir for being elected president of the United States. But the instruments made use of, and the means which were practised to effect a change, have my utter abhorrence and detestation, for they were the blackest calumny, and foulest falshoods. I had witnessed enough of the anxiety, and solicitude, the envy jealousy and reproach attendant upon the office as well as the high responsibility of the Station, to be perfectly willing to see a transfer of it. And I can truly say, that at the time of Election, I considerd your pretentions much

19. Since the electoral vote in 1800 was a tie, 73-73, between TJ and Aaron Burr, the election was thrown into the House of Representatives, where on Feb. 17, 1801, on the thirty-sixth ballot TJ was elected president. Cunningham, *Jeffersonian Republicans*, 239, 244. Since JA's appointments were not made until the beginning of March, AA's chronology is in error; therefore her defense of JA fails in part.

20. Benjamin Stoddert, secretary of the navy, 1798-1801; Samuel Dexter, secretary of war, 1800, secretary of the treasury, 1801-2.

superior to his [Mr. Burr's], to whom an equal vote was given. Your experience I venture to affirm has convinced you that it is not a station to be envy'd. If you feel yourself a free man, and can act in all cases, according to your own sentiments, opinions and judgment, you can do more than either of your predecessors could, and are awfully responsible to God and your Country for the measures of your Administration. I rely upon the Friendship you still profess for me, and (I am conscious I have done nothing to forfeit it), to excuse the freedom of this discussion to which you have led with an unreserve, which has taken off the Shackles I should otherways have found myself embarrassed with.–And now Sir I will freely disclose to you what has severed the bonds of former Friendship, and placed you in a light very different from what I once viewd you in.

One of the first acts of your administration was to liberate a wretch [21] who was suffering the just punishment of the Law due to his crimes for writing and publishing the basest libel, the lowest and vilest Slander, which malice could invent, or calumny exhibit against the Character and reputation of your predecessor, of him for whom you profest the highest esteem and Friendship, and whom you certainly knew incapable of such complicated baseness. The remission of Callenders fine was a public approbation of his conduct. Is not the last restraint of vice, a sense of shame, renderd abortive, if abandoned Characters do not excite abhorrence.[22] If the chief Majestrate of a Nation, whose elevated Station places him in a conspicuous light, and renders his every action a concern of general importance, permits his public conduct to be influenced by private resentment, and so far forgets what is due to his Character as to give countanance to a base Calumniater, is he not answerable for the influence which his example has upon the manners and morals of the community?

Untill I read Callenders seventh Letter containing your compliment to him as a writer and your reward of 50 dollars, I could not be made to believe, that such measures could have been resorted to: to stab the fair fame and upright intentions of one, who to use your own Language "was acting from an honest conviction in his own mind that he was right."

21. James Thomson Callender, Scottish immigrant and pamphleteer, began his rabid attacks on the Federalist administration in 1797. After a stint in Philadelphia he moved to Virginia and wrote for the Richmond *Examiner,* a Republican paper. In 1800 Callender published *The Prospect before Us,* attacking the Federalist leaders. For his remarks about JA he was tried under the Sedition Law, fined $200, and sentenced to nine months' imprisonment by Justice Samuel Chase in June 1800. President Jefferson pardoned him in 1801 and remitted his fine. James Morton Smith, *Freedom's Fetters: The Alien and Sedition Laws and American Civil Liberties* (Ithaca, 1956), Chap. XV; Dumas Malone, "Callender, James Thomson," *DAB,* III, 425-26.

22. The most recent article on Callender and TJ is Charles A. Jellison, "That Scoundrel Callender," *Va. Mag. of Hist. and Biog.,* 67 (1959), 295-306.

This Sir I considerd as a personal injury. This was the Sword that cut assunder the Gordian knot, which could not be untied by all the efforts of party Spirit, by rivalship by Jealousy or any other malignant fiend.

The serpent you cherished and warmed, bit the hand that nourished him,[23] and gave you sufficient Specimens of his talents, his gratitude his justice, and his truth. When such vipers are let lose upon Society, all distinction between virtue and vice are levelled, all respect for Character is lost in the overwhelming deluge of calumny—that respect which is a necessary bond in the social union, which gives efficacy to laws, and teaches the subject to obey the Majestrate, and the child to submit to the parent.

There is one other act of your administration which I considerd as personally unkind, and which your own mind will readily suggest to you, but as it neither affected character, or reputation, I forbear to state it.

This Letter is written in confidence—no eye but my own has seen what has passed. Faithfull are the wounds of a Friend. Often have I wished to have seen a different course pursued by you. I bear no malice I cherish no enmity. I would not retaliate if I could—nay more in the true spirit of christian Charity, I would forgive, as I hope to be forgiven. And with that disposition of mind and heart, I subscribe the Name of

ABIGAIL ADAMS

Jefferson to Abigail Adams

Washington July 22.04.

DEAR MADAM

Your favor of the 1st inst. was duly recieved, and I would not again have intruded on you but to rectify certain facts which seem not to have been presented to you under their true aspect. My charities to Callendar are considered as rewards for his calumnies. As early, I think, as 1796, I was told in Philadelphia that Callendar, the author of the Political progress of Britain, was in that city, a fugitive from persecution for having written that book, and in distress.[24] I had read and approved the book: I con-

---

23. Callender soon turned against TJ, attacked the Republican administration with his vitriolic pen, and propagated scandal concerning TJ's private life. He died in 1803. *DAB,* III, 425-26.

24. Callender's pamphlet, criticizing the British government, had led to his indictment for sedition in Jan. 1793. He did not answer the court summons and so became a fugitive from justice and fled to the United States. *Ibid.*

sidered him as a man of genius, unjustly persecuted. I knew nothing of his private character, and immediately expressed my readiness to contribute to his relief, and to serve him. It was a considerable time after, that, on application from a person who thought of him as I did, I contributed to his relief, and afterwards repeated the contribution. Himself I did not see till long after, nor ever more than two or three times. When he first began to write he told some useful truths in his coarse way; but no body sooner disapproved of his writings than I did, or wished more that he would be silent. My charities to him were no more meant as encouragements to his scurrilities than those I give to the beggar at my door are meant as rewards for the vices of his life, and to make them chargeable to myself. In truth they would have been greater to him had he never written a word after the work for which he fled from Britain. With respect to the calumnies and falsehoods which writers and printers at large published against Mr. Adams, I was as far from stooping to any concern or approbation of them as Mr. Adams was respecting those of Porcupine,[25] Fenno, or Russell, who published volumes against me for every sentence vended by their opponents against Mr. Adams. But I never supposed Mr. Adams had any participation in the atrocities of these editors or their writers. I knew myself incapable of that base warfare, and believed him to be so. On the contrary, whatever I may have thought of the acts of the administration of that day, I have ever borne testimony to Mr. Adams's personal worth, nor was it ever impeached in my presence without a just vindication of it on my part. I never supposed that any person who knew either of us could believe that either meddled in that dirty work.

But another fact is that I 'liberated a wretch who was suffering for a libel against Mr. Adams.' I do not know who was the particular wretch alluded to: but I discharged every person under punishment or prosecution under the Sedition law, because I considered and now consider that law to be a nullity as absolute and as palpable as if Congress had ordered us to fall down and worship a golden image; and that it was as much my duty to arrest it's execution in every stage, as it would have been to have rescued from the fiery furnace those who should have been cast into it for refusing to worship their image. It was accordingly done in every instance, without asking what the offenders had done, or against whom they had offended, but whether the pains they were suffering were inflicted under the pretended Sedition law. It was certainly possible that my motives for contributing to the relief of Callender and liberating sufferers under the Sedition law, might have been to protect, encourage and reward

25. *Porcupine's Gazette* was a Federalist newspaper published in Philadelphia, 1797-99, by William Cobbett.

slander: but they may also have been those which inspire ordinary charities to objects of distress, meritorious or not, or the obligations of an oath to protect the constitution, violated by an unauthorized act of Congress. Which of these were my motives must be decided by a regard to the general tenor of my life. On this I am not afraid to appeal to the nation at large, to posterity, and still less to that being who sees himself our motives, who will judge us from his own knolege of them, and not on the testimony of a Porcupine or Fenno.

You observe there has been one other act of my administration personally unkind, and suppose it will readily suggest itself to me. I declare on my honor, Madam, I have not the least conception what act is alluded to. I never did a single one with an unkind intention.

My sole object in this letter being to place before your attention that the acts imputed to me are either such as are falsely imputed, or as might flow from good as well as bad motives, I shall make no other addition than the assurances of my continued wishes for the health and happiness of yourself and Mr. Adams.

TH: JEFFERSON

Abigail Adams to Jefferson

Quincy August 18th 1804

SIR

Your Letter of July 22d was by some mistake in the post office at Boston sent back as far as New York, so that it did not reach me untill the eleventh of this Month. Candour requires of me a reply. Your statement respecting Callender, (who was the wretch referd to) and your motives for liberating him, wear a different aspect as explaind by you, from the impression which they had made, not only upon my mind, but upon the minds of all those, whom I ever heard speak upon the subject. With regard to the act under which he was punished, different persons entertain different opinions respecting it. It lies not with me to decide upon its validity. That I presume devolved upon the supreem Judges of the Nation: but I have understood that the power which makes a Law, is alone competent to the repeal. If a Chief Majestrate can by his will annul a Law, where is the difference between a republican, and a despotic Government? That some restraint should be laid upon the asassin, who stabs reputation, all civilized Nations have assented to. In no Country has calumny falshood, and revileing stalked abroad more licentiously, than in this. No political

Character has been secure from its attacks, no reputation so fair, as not to be wounded by it, untill truth and falshood lie in one undistinguished heap. If there are no checks to be resorted to in the Laws of the Land, and no reperation to be made to the injured, will not Man become the judge and avenger of his own wrongs, and as in a late instance, the sword and pistol decide the contest? [26] All the Christian and social virtues will be banished the Land. All that makes Life desirable, and softens the ferocious passions of Man will assume a savage deportment, and like Cain of old, every Mans hand will be against his Neighbour. Party spirit is blind malevolent uncandid, ungenerous, unjust and unforgiving. It is equally so under federal as under democratic Banners, yet upon both sides are Characters, who possess honest views, and act from honorable motives, who disdain to be led blindfold, and who tho entertaining different opinions, have for their object the public welfare and happiness. These are the Characters, who abhor calumny and evil speaking, and who will never descend to News paper revileing. And you have done Mr. Adams justice in believing him, incapable of such conduct. He has never written a line in any News paper to which his Name has not been affixed, since he was first elected president of the united States. The writers in the public papers, and their employers are alltogether unknown to him.

I have seen and known that much of the conduct of a public ruler, is liable to be misunderstood, and misrepresented. Party hatred by its deadly poison blinds the Eyes and envenoms the heart. It is fatal to the integrity of the moral Character. It sees not that wisdom dwells with moderation, and that firmness of conduct is seldom united with outrageous voilence [i.e., violence] of sentiment. Thus blame is too often liberally bestowed upon actions, which if fully understood, and candidly judged would merit praise instead of censure. It is only by the general issue of measures producing banefull or benificial effects that they ought to be tested.

You exculpate yourself from any intentional act of unkindness towards any one. I will freely state that which I referd to in my former Letter, and which I could not avoid considering as personal resentment. Soon after my eldest son's return from Europe, he was appointed by the district Judge to an office into which no political concerns enterd, personally known to you, and possessing all the qualifications, you yourself being Judge, which you had designated for office. As soon as congress gave the appointments to the president you removed him.[27] This looked so particularly pointed, that some of your best Friends in Boston, at that time

26. Referring, no doubt, to the duel between Hamilton and Burr, fought on July 11, 1804, in which Hamilton was killed.

27. In his letter of Sept. 11, 1804, to AA, TJ provided a correct and satisfying answer to her complaint. See Bemis, *John Quincy Adams*, 112.

exprest their regret that you had done so. I must do him the Justice to say, that I never heard an expression from him of censure or disrespect towards you in concequence of it. With pleasure I say that he is not a blind follower of any party.

I have written to you with the freedom and unreserve of former Friendship to which I would gladly return could all causes but mere difference of opinion be removed. I wish to lead a tranquil and retired Life under the administration of the Government, disposed to heal the wounds of contention, to cool the rageing fury of party animosity: to soften the Rugged Spirit of resentment, and desirious of seeing my Children and Grand Children, Heirs to that freedom and independance which you and your predesessor, united your efforts to obtain. With these sentiments I reciprocate my sincere wishes for your Health and happiness.

ABIGAIL ADAMS

Jefferson to Abigail Adams

Monticello. Sep 11.04.

Your letter, Madam, of the 18th. of Aug. has been some days recieved, but a press of business has prevented the acknolegement of it. Perhaps indeed I may have already trespassed too far on your attention. With those who wish to think amiss of me, I have learnt to be perfectly indifferent: but where I know a mind to be ingenuous, and to need only truth to set it to rights, I cannot be as passive.

The act of personal unkindness alluded to in your former letter is said in your last to have been the removal of your eldest son from some office to which the judges had appointed him. I conclude then he must have been a Commissioner of bankruptcy, but I declare to you on my honor that this is the first knolege I have ever had that he was so. It may be thought perhaps that I ought to have enquired who were such, before I appointed others, but it is to be observed that the former law permitted the judges to name Commissioners occasionally only for every case as it arose, and not to make them permanent officers. Nobody therefore being in office there could be no removal. The judges you well know have been considered as highly federal; and it was noted that they confined their nominations exclusively to federalists. The legislature, dissatisfied with this, transferred the nomination to the President, and made the offices permanent. The very object in passing the law was that he should correct, not confirm, what was deemed the partiality of the judges. I thought it therefore proper to enquire, not whom they had employed, but whom I ought to appoint to fulfil the intentions of the law. In making these appointments I put in a proportion of federalists equal I believe to the proportion they bear in numbers through the union generally. Had I known that your son had acted, it would have been a real pleasure to me to have preferred him to some who were named in Boston in what were deemed the same line of politics. To this I should have been led by my knolege of his integrity as well as my sincere dispositions towards yourself and Mr. Adams.

You seem to think it devolved on the judges to decide on the validity of the sedition law. But nothing in the constitution has given them a right to decide for the executive, more than to the Executive to decide for them. Both magistracies are equally independant in the sphere of action assigned to them. The judges, believing the law constitutional, had a right to pass a sentence of fine and imprisonment, because that power was placed in their hands by the constitution. But the Executive, believing the law to be unconstitutional, was bound to remit the execution of it; because that power has been confided to him by the constitution. That instrument meant that it's co-ordinate branches should be checks on each other. But the opinion which gives to the judges the right to decide what laws are constitutional, and what not, not only for themselves in their own sphere of action, but for the legislature and executive also in their spheres, would make the judiciary a despotic branch.

Nor does the opinion of the unconstitutionality and consequent nullity of that law remove all restraint from the overwhelming torrent of slander which is confounding all vice and virtue, all truth and falsehood in the US. The power to do that is fully possessed by the several state legislatures. It was reserved to them, and was denied to the general government, by the constitution according to our construction of it. While we deny that Congress have a right to controul the freedom of the press, we have ever asserted the right of the states, and their exclusive right, to do so. They have accordingly, all of them, made provisions for punishing slander, which those who have time and inclination resort to for the vindication of their characters. In general the state laws appear to have made the presses responsible for slander as far as is consistent with their useful freedom. In those states where they do not admit even the truth of allegations to protect the printer, they have gone too far.

The candour manifested in your letter, and which I ever believed you to possess, has alone inspired the desire of calling your attention once more to those circumstances of fact and motive by which I claim to be judged. I hope you will see these intrusions on your time to be, what they really are, proofs of my great respect for you. I tolerate with the utmost latitude the right of others to differ from me in opinion without imputing to them criminality. I know too well the weakness and uncertainty of human reason to wonder at it's different results. Both of our political parties, at least the honest portion of them, agree conscientiously in the same object, the public good: but they differ essentially in what they deem the means of promoting that good. One side believes it best done by one composition of the governing powers, the other by a different one. One fears most the ignorance of the people: the other the selfishness of rulers independant of them. Which is right, time and experience will prove. We think that one side of this experiment has been long enough tried, and proved not to promote the good of the many; and that the other has not been fairly and sufficiently tried. Our opponents think the reverse. With whichever opinion the body of the nation concurs, that must prevail. My anxieties on the subject will never carry me beyond the use of fair and honorable means, of truth and reason: nor have they ever lessened my esteem for moral worth; nor alienated my affections from a single friend who did not first withdraw himself. Wherever this has happened I confess I have not been insensible to it: yet have ever kept myself open to a return of their justice.

I conclude with sincere prayers for your health and happiness that yourself and Mr. Adams may long enjoy the tranquility you desire and merit, and see, in the prosperity of your family, what is the consummation of the last and warmest of human wishes.

TH: JEFFERSON

Abigail Adams to Jefferson

Quincy October 25 1804

SIR

Sickness for three weeks past, has prevented my acknowledging the receipt of your Letter of Sepbr the 11th. When I first addrest you, I little thought of entering into a correspondence with you upon political topicks. I will not however regret it, since it has led to some elucidations and brought on some explanations, which place in a more favourable light occurrences which had wounded me.

Having once entertained for you a respect and esteem, founded upon the Character of an affectionate parent, a kind Master, a candid and benevolent Friend, I could not suffer different political opinions to obliterate them from my mind, and I felt the truth of the observation, that the Heart is long, very long in receiving the conviction that is forced upon it by reason. Affection still lingers in the Bosom, even after esteem has taken its flight. It was not untill after circumstances concured to place you in the light of a rewarder and encourager of a Libeller whom you could not but detest and despise, that I withdrew the esteem I had long entertaind for you. Nor can you wonder Sir that I should consider as personal unkindnesses the instances I have mentiond. I am pleased to find that, which respected my son, all together unfounded. He was as you conjecture appointed a commissioner of Bankrupcy together with Judge Daws, and continued to serve in it, with perfect satisfaction to all parties. At least I never heard the contrary, untill superseded by a new appointment. The Idea sugested, that no one was in office, merely because it was not perminent, and concequently no removal could take place, I cannot consider in any other light, than what the Gentlemen of the Law would term a quible—as such I pass it. Judge Daws was continued, or reappointed which placed Mr. Adams, in a more conspicuous light, as the object of personal resentment. Nor could I upon this occasion refrain calling to mind the last visit you made me at Washington, when in the course of conversation you assured me, that if it should lay in your power to serve me or my family, nothing would give you more pleasure. I will do you the justice to say at this hour: that I believe what you then said, you then meant. With respect to the office it was a small object but the disposition of the remover was considerd by me as the barbed arrow. This however by your declaration, is withdrawn from my mind. With the public it will remain, and here Sir may I be permitted to pause, and ask you whether in your ardent zeal, and desire to rectify the mistakes and abuses as you may consider them, of the former administrations, you are not led into measures still more fatal to the constitution, and more derogatory to your honour, and independence of Character? Pardon me Sir if I say, that I fear you are.

I know from the observations which I have made that there is not a more difficult part devolves upon a chief Majestrate, nor one which subjects him to more reproach, and censure than the appointments to office, and all the patronage which this enviable power gives him, is but a poor compensation for the responsibility to which it subjects him. It would be well however to weigh and consider Characters as it respects their Moral worth and integrity. He who is not true to himself, nor just to others, seeks an office for the benifit of himself, unmindfull of that of his Country.

I cannot agree, in opinion, that the constitution ever meant to withhold from the National Government the power of self defence, or that it could be considerd an infringment of the Liberty of the press, to punish the licentiousness of it.[28]

Time Sir must determine, and posterity will judge with more candour, and impartiality, I hope than the conflicting parties of our day, what measures have best promoted the happiness of the people: what raised them from a state of depression and degradation to wealth, honor, and reputation; what has made them affluent at home, and respected abroad, and to whom ever the tribute is due to them may it be given.

I will not Sir any further intrude upon your time, but close this correspondence, by my sincere wishes, that you may be directed to that path which may terminate in the prosperity and happiness of the people over whom you are placed, by administring the Government with a just and impartial hand. Be assured Sir that no one will more rejoice in your success than

ABIGAIL ADAMS

Quincy Nov. 19. 1804. The whole of this Correspondence was begun and conducted without my Knowledge or Suspicion. Last Evening and this Morning at the desire of Mrs. Adams I read the whole. I have no remarks to make upon it at this time and in this place.

J. ADAMS [29]

28. AA expressed the Federalist argument that freedom of speech and of the press could be defined only by the English common law, and that the First Amendment had not deprived Congress of the power to pass a sedition law. The Republicans argued that the First Amendment "not only rejected the English common law concept of libels against the government but also prohibited Congress from adding any restraint, either by previous restrictions, by subsequent punishment, or by an alteration of jurisdiction or mode of trial." Smith, *Freedom's Fetters*, 136, 140.

29. This note, in JA's hand, appears at the end of the letter-book copy in the Adams Papers.